LINDA PORTER

Crown of Thistles

The Fatal Inheritance of Mary Queen of Scots

MACMILLAN

First published 2013 by Macmillan
an imprint of Pan Macmillan, a division of Macmillan Publishers Limited
Pan Macmillan, 20 New Wharf Road, London N1 9RR
Basingstoke and Oxford
Associated companies throughout the world
www.panmacmillan.com

ISBN 978-1-4472-4591-9

A CIP catalogue record for this book is available from the British Library.

Typeset by SetSystems Ltd, Saffron Walden, Essex
Printed and bound by CPI Group (UK) Ltd, Croydon, CR0 4YY

Visit **www.panmacmillan.com** to read more about all our books
and to buy them. You will also find features, author interviews and
news of any author events, and you can sign up for e-newsletters
so that you're always first to hear about our new releases.

For Isobel

Contents

⊰∻⊱

Author's Note

The idea for this book came to me when I realized that my knowledge of sixteenth-century history in the British Isles was heavily weighted towards England. This, I fear, is a product of the never-ending love affair that the English have with their Tudor monarchs, or, more accurately, Henry VIII and Elizabeth I. But there is a great deal more to the past of these islands than Henry's six wives and the mythical Golden Age of his younger daughter. Wales and Ireland have, of course, their own stories to tell, but it was Scotland, in particular, and the long-standing rivalry between the Tudors and the Stewarts, that intrigued me. For most English-speaking people, Mary Queen of Scots is the only Scottish ruler they have heard of, with the possible exception of Robert the Bruce. And Mary herself, the doomed, romantic queen of popular fiction and wildly inaccurate films, arrives somehow fully-formed on the English scene in Elizabeth's time, with only the sketchiest of backgrounds and considerable misapprehension about the extraordinary events that had brought about her desperate flight from her homeland. But what lay behind this? The rivalry between the Tudors and the Stewarts did not start with Mary and her cousin Elizabeth. In order to understand it, I needed to go further back and to look at the relationship between England and Scotland against a longer time-frame. That is how this book was born.

The reigns of the charismatic James IV and his capable son, James V (Mary's father), are not as well-known as they should be, even in Scotland, let alone south of the border. There are a number of reasons that might explain this, starting with the obvious explanation that James IV's death at the battle of Flodden in 1513 has obscured the achievements of one of the period's most interesting rulers and the long minority of James V is so confusing that it tends to overshadow his success as an adult king. Yet both men enhanced Scotland's role in Europe and neither was afraid of opposing the Tudors – indeed, James V spent his life successfully evading the clutches of his uncle, Henry VIII. For the Tudors, Scotland, a country with which they shared a border, was a constant source of aggravation, and one that they did not handle well. Its alliance with France posed serious diplomatic problems, exacerbated by the legitimate claim of the descendants of James IV and his wife, Margaret Tudor, to the English throne. Mary Queen of Scots was acutely aware of this and it was her overriding aim to be acknowledged as Elizabeth's heir. The tensions that underlay Anglo-Scottish relations were also played out against the backdrop of almost constant war in Europe and the growing dislocation caused by the Reformation.

The interwoven history of England and Scotland between 1485 and 1568 is one of high drama and its players are some of Britain's greatest kings and queens. This is also a tale of powerful families, ambitious politicians and churchmen, of battles and intrigue, murder, rape and betrayal, of splendid courts and sibling rivalries. And, despite the prevalence of women rulers in the sixteenth century, it shows how difficult it was to be queen, whether a consort or a ruler in one's own right.

Over the years, Scottish historians have been somewhat guilty, perhaps, of keeping their history to themselves. I hope they will not be too disgruntled by an Englishwoman's attempts to give the Stewart monarchs their due in sixteenth-century Britain. The outcome of the referendum on Scottish independence will decide whether Britain is once again divided. One wonders what Mary Queen of Scots would have thought. Her detractors would, of course, argue that she had her own dynastic interests at heart rather than those of Scotland itself.

Writing this book has been a long journey and I would like to thank all of those who have helped me along the way. Dr Sean Cunningham at the National Archives at Kew spent time with me going over key documents and Dr Julian Goodare at the University of Edinburgh was generous in discussing ideas, also saving me from a number of errors in the section on Mary's personal rule. Research in Scotland has been one of the great pleasures of this experience and I must acknowledge the friendliness and willingness to help of the staffs of the National Library of Scotland and the National Archives of Scotland as well as those in numerous fascinating buildings managed by Historic Scotland and the National Trust for Scotland. In England, the librarians of the London Library were always efficient and welcoming, as were their counterparts in the British Library and the staff of the National Archives. Georgina Morley, my editor at Macmillan, has been as enthusiastic as ever, ably assisted by Tania Wilde, who saw the book through its production stages. I should also like to thank Lorraine Green for her meticulous copy-editing. My agent, Andrew Lownie, continues to provide his unobtrusive but vital support. Above all, I should like, once more, to acknowledge the immense help given by my husband, George, in holding things together while I shut myself away and wrote.

LINDA PORTER
January 2013

Conventions and Conversions

Quotations used in this book are from both English and Scottish sources. Sixteenth-century Scots was a separate language, though it shared a number of English words. In most cases, spelling has been modernized but the quotations themselves have not, as I believe that we should let our ancestors speak for themselves.

Monetary equivalents are impossible to give accurately and are disliked by purists. I have used the Measuringworth.com website's 2010 RPI figures to give what is intended as an indication, to today's reader, of the larger sums of money involved. It should be remembered that the Scottish pound was worth about one-third of the English pound in the 1530s. According to Andrea Thomas in her book *The Princelie Majestie* (Edinburgh, 2005), the French crown was worth about one Scottish pound and there were approximately two and a quarter livres tournois to the Scottish pound.

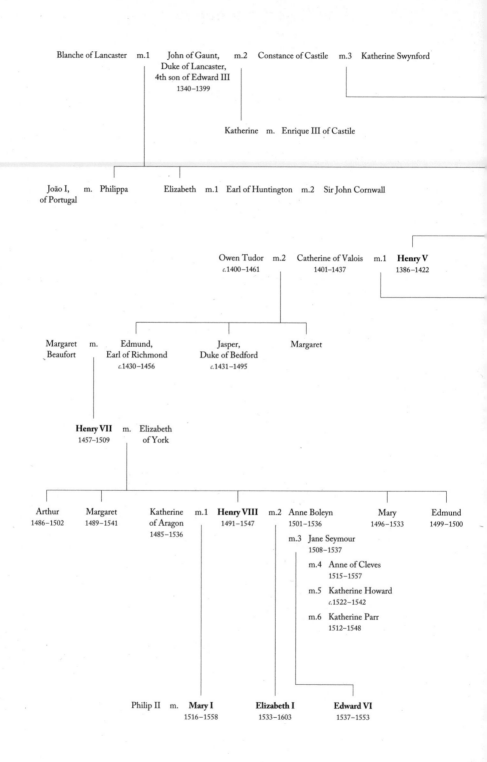

Blanche of Lancaster m.1 John of Gaunt, m.2 Constance of Castile m.3 Katherine Swynford
Duke of Lancaster,
4th son of Edward III
1340–1399

Katherine m. Enrique III of Castile

João I, m. Philippa Elizabeth m.1 Earl of Huntington m.2 Sir John Cornwall
of Portugal

Owen Tudor m.2 Catherine of Valois m.1 **Henry V**
c.1400–1461   1401–1437   1386–1422

Margaret m. Edmund, Jasper, Margaret
Beaufort   Earl of Richmond Duke of Bedford
           c.1430–1456 c.1431–1495

Henry VII m. Elizabeth
1457–1509   of York

Arthur   Margaret   Katherine m.1 **Henry VIII** m.2 Anne Boleyn   Mary   Edmund
1486–1502 1489–1541 of Aragon   1491–1547   1501–1536   1496–1533 1499–1500
                      1485–1536

                              m.3 Jane Seymour
                                  1508–1537

                              m.4 Anne of Cleves
                                  1515–1557

                              m.5 Katherine Howard
                                  c.1522–1542

                              m.6 Katherine Parr
                                  1512–1548

Philip II m. **Mary I**   **Elizabeth I**   **Edward VI**
            1516–1558   1533–1603   1537–1553

The Tudors and Lancastrians

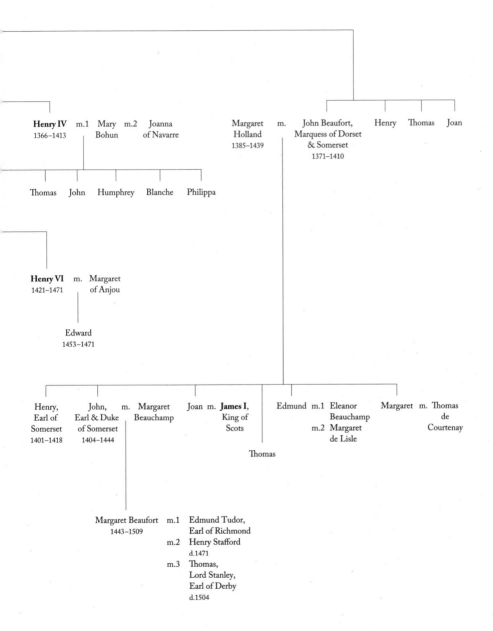

The Stewarts

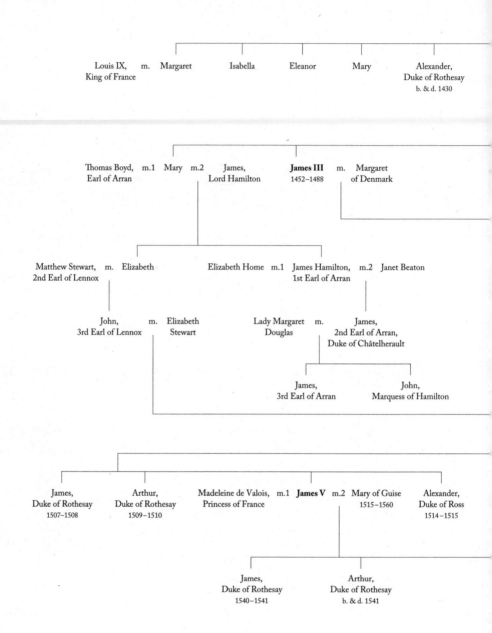

Louis IX,   m.   Margaret   Isabella   Eleanor   Mary   Alexander,
King of France   Duke of Rothesay
                                                            b. & d. 1430

Thomas Boyd,   m.1   Mary   m.2   James,   **James III**   m.   Margaret
Earl of Arran   Lord Hamilton   1452–1488   of Denmark

Matthew Stewart,   m.   Elizabeth   Elizabeth Home   m.1   James Hamilton,   m.2   Janet Beaton
2nd Earl of Lennox   1st Earl of Arran

John,   m.   Elizabeth   Lady Margaret   m.   James,
3rd Earl of Lennox   Stewart   Douglas   2nd Earl of Arran,
                                                    Duke of Châtelherault

James,   John,
3rd Earl of Arran   Marquess of Hamilton

James,   Arthur,   Madeleine de Valois,   m.1   **James V**   m.2   Mary of Guise   Alexander,
Duke of Rothesay   Duke of Rothesay   Princess of France   1515–1560   Duke of Ross
1507–1508   1509–1510   1514–1515

James,   Arthur,
Duke of Rothesay   Duke of Rothesay
1540–1541   b. & d. 1541

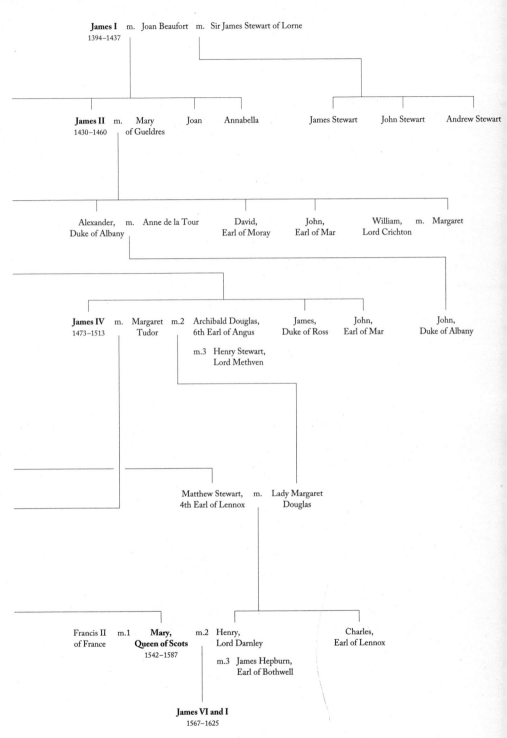

James I   m.   Joan Beaufort   m.   Sir James Stewart of Lorne
1394–1437

James II   m.   Mary   Joan   Annabella   James Stewart   John Stewart   Andrew Stewart
1430–1460   of Gueldres

Alexander,   m.   Anne de la Tour   David,   John,   William,   m.   Margaret
Duke of Albany   Earl of Moray Earl of Mar Lord Crichton

James IV   m.   Margaret   m.2   Archibald Douglas,   James,   John,   John,
1473–1513   Tudor   6th Earl of Angus   Duke of Ross Earl of Mar   Duke of Albany

                          m.3   Henry Stewart,
                                Lord Methven

Matthew Stewart,   m.   Lady Margaret
4th Earl of Lennox   Douglas

Francis II   m.1   Mary,   m.2   Henry,   Charles,
of France   Queen of Scots   Lord Darnley   Earl of Lennox
                   1542–1587

                                  m.3   James Hepburn,
                                        Earl of Bothwell

James VI and I
1567–1625

Prologue

~~~

The chilly summer morning brought only a muffled and impenetrable dawn. A sea mist, or *haar*, as it was known locally, enveloped the coastline, completely obscuring two galleys that had sailed unannounced into Edinburgh's port on the Firth of Forth. 'In the memory of man, that day of the year, was never seen a more dolorous face of the heaven . . . Besides the wet and corruption of the air, the mist was so thick and so dark that scarce might any man espy another the length of two pair of boots. The sun was not seen to shine two days before, nor two days after. That forewarning God gave unto us; but alas, the most part were blind.'¹

If such gloomy premonitions were still far from the thoughts of most of the passengers on the two vessels, one, at least, made no secret of the fact that she had undertaken the voyage with mixed emotions. On board, and very much the centre of attention, as she had been all her life, was Mary Stewart. An unusually tall young woman of eighteen, regal in bearing and acknowledged for her charm and warmth, she had been a queen since she was six days old. Accustomed to being fêted and adored, she was gentle by nature and had given orders that the lash was not to be used on the rowers during the crossing. But she remained convinced that monarchs were divinely appointed and was always supremely conscious of her royal status. In matters of faith she was conservative, though not obsessively so. Raised in the Catholic religion of her ancestors (and the majority of the population in France, her adopted country), Mary had never known her beliefs rejected or her right to command the devoted loyalty of those around her questioned. Neither education nor experience had in any way prepared this undoubtedly intelligent girl for the challenges that lay ahead.

Scotland, the country she had left behind at the age of five, whose language she still spoke but without the fluency of the French that had long since become natural to her, was engulfed by religious change and struggles for power between its unreliable nobility. Small and poor, harassed by England, its southern neighbour, Scotland may have been on the fringes of Europe, but its strategic importance in the never-ending machinations of European diplomacy was enhanced by Mary's father and grandfather, both of whom were dominating figures. After Mary left Scotland in 1548, the position of the monarchy had changed. Lacking the strong personality of a resident ruler, the realm became unstable. A centuries-old battle for influence in Scotland, exacerbated by the religious upheaval of the Reformation, was still being fought between the English and the French. Behind it lay the larger question of who would control the entire British Isles. This problem had not been solved by any of the young queen's immediate predecessors, in Scotland or England, and a deep-rooted tension remained between the occupants of the two thrones. The reality facing Mary Stewart on that dreary Scottish morning was one that would have given pause to even the wiliest and most experienced of monarchs. For Mary was very much alone. Her beloved mother and her young husband had died within six months of each other the previous year. She never knew her grandfather, the energetic, charismatic James IV, or her own father, his astute son, James V. Nor had she met any of her Tudor relatives. Henry VIII, her great-uncle, died the year prior to her departure for France and though as a baby she was the intended bride for his son, Edward VI, she had never seen him or either of his sisters. When the elder of these, Queen

Mary, died in 1558, the throne had passed to the Protestant Elizabeth. Now the rivalry between the English and the Scots rested in the persons of two women who could not ignore one another but were total strangers.

Mary knew no one well in her kingdom except for Lord James Stewart, a much older half-brother of dubious loyalty, on whose goodwill and support she was crucially dependent. She was exchanging a country where she was a widowed queen consort for a realm where she had long been an absent queen regnant. To her subjects she was unknown, a serious disadvantage in a land where the personal accessibility of the king had been a major element of Stewart success, and the land of her birth was equally unfamiliar to its own queen. But Mary had been frozen out of France, the country she loved, by her mother-in-law, Catherine de Medici, and by the realization that as a childless queen dowager she could play no further role there. The death of her husband, Francis II, in December 1560, left Mary with no choice but to return to Scotland. Whether she was genuinely welcome there was another matter.

Yet Mary possessed an optimistic nature and was accustomed to getting her way. She was well aware of the effect she had on others. So, as she waited for the fog to clear, the queen of Scots put the sorrow of parting from the France she loved behind her. She accepted, with deep regret, that her life had changed. She did not, however, leave everything from her past behind. She was accompanied by three of the four Marys, the daughters of leading Scottish families, who had sailed with her from Scotland thirteen years earlier, and by a retinue of loyal French servants. As much as she could, she had taken her French life back with her across the North Sea. A vast array of personal belongings – horses, furniture, beds, rugs, tapestries, jewels, plate and a wardrobe more magnificent than that of her cousin, Queen Elizabeth of England – would soon follow, carried on a dozen ships. Mary was not returning to Scotland without her creature comforts. Ever conscious of her image, she was the daughter of kings and determined to live like them in splendour. Her youth and

singular power to captivate were important weapons and she
meant to use them to the full. She was also ambitious and
dynastically aware, conscious of her legitimate descent from the
Scottish House of Stewart and from the Tudor king Henry VII
of England. Mary's distant cousin and 'sister queen', Elizabeth,
had only been on the throne in England three years and was of
questionable legitimacy. She was also a heretic, unmarried and
childless, though efforts were being pursued vigorously to find
the English queen a husband. For contemporaries, both Mary
and Elizabeth appeared equally vulnerable as unsupported female
monarchs in a male-dominated world. Mary, though, was constant in the belief that she was Elizabeth's rightful heir and,
quite possibly, if Elizabeth's position on England's throne should
become untenable, her replacement. The Scottish queen's goal
was nothing less than to unite the two kingdoms of England and
Scotland under one crown. It was just a matter of waiting, and
perhaps not even for too long.

By late morning, the sea fog lifted and Mary was able to go
ashore. Her arrival, after a voyage of just five days, took her
brother and the Scottish government by surprise. There was to
be no rapturous welcome but, as the weather improved, the
people came out to greet her. It was a much more muted
reception than she habitually received, but welcome nonetheless.
Mary Queen of Scots was home at last.

Part One

❧

Ill-Gotten Thrones

1485–1488

CHAPTER ONE

'This pretty lad'

*'We will unite the red rose and the white ... England
hath long been mad and scarred herself.'*

Henry VII in William Shakespeare's *Richard III*

ON ANOTHER DAY IN AUGUST, seventy-six years earlier, Mary
Stewart's great-grandfather was standing in a field in the heart
of England. This may sound idyllic but the reality was not that
of a pleasant pastoral scene. The noise of battle and the fear of
death were all around him. He had good reason to wonder how
much longer he might breathe the air of a country he had never
yet been able to call home. The life he knew best was that of a
wandering exile, often in flight, always penurious, harbouring
schemes and consorting with unreliable malcontents. But there
was one clear aim that underpinned his determination after all
the uncertain years of living in foreign courts, surviving on the
transitory goodwill of European rulers who reckoned his presence
might give them a political edge in the realization of their own
ambitions. He wanted the throne of England. His hopes were
based on a distant and dubious claim, but the prolonged upheavals of the fifteenth century had presented others with unforeseen
opportunities and he had gambled that such good fortune might
also be his, in the right circumstances. Most people in England
would probably never even have heard his name, such a rank
outsider was he. Living so long across the water, the Breton and

French tongues came more easily to him than English. But that scarcely mattered on 22 August 1485. As the fighting raged, his own safety seemed the first priority. There are signs that he was not entirely confident of success on the battlefield and with good reason. Supporters were fickle and uncommitted, his forces were outnumbered two to one and he had chosen survival over heroism by staying behind the vanguard of his troops and preparing an escape route if the day went against him. He could always try again.

But his enemy had seen a chance to put a decisive end to the fighting that rolled across the countryside of Leicestershire that summer's day. It was a battle in which the rebels were achieving a surprising degree of success, but although the larger force led by the king had been outmanoeuvred, it was by no means beaten. It was noted that the pretender was separated from his main force, with just his immediate bodyguard and a small number of horsemen and infantry to protect him. His vulnerability was obvious. In late medieval warfare, the death of a leader almost inevitably led to the capitulation of his forces. A direct onslaught, perhaps even hand-to-hand combat between the rivals, might settle things once and for all. As a tactic, it was not without risk, but the rewards – the removal of a continuing threat and the promise of stability in a strife-torn country – would be worth the gamble. Urged on by his advisers and doubtless following his own well-honed battle instincts, the king did not hesitate for long. A cavalry charge, led by the monarch himself, bore down on the small force of men gathered around the pretender's standard, a red dragon which proclaimed his Welsh ancestry. As the riders approached, the man in the field knew that his life hung in the balance. Henry Tudor, unlikely heir to the House of Lancaster, was about to come within a spear's length of Richard III, the Yorkist king he had pledged to overthrow. A matter of minutes would decide his fate.

✁

'HE WAS a comely personage, a little above just stature, well and straight-limbed, but slender. His countenance was revered, and a little like a churchman, and as it was not strange or dark so neither was it winning or pleasing, but as the face of one well disposed. But it was to the disadvantage of the painter, for it was best when he spoke.'[1] This description, although written more than a century after the death of Henry Tudor, captures what we know of him perfectly. A considered person, not given to great public displays of emotion, somewhat ascetic in appearance, not exactly handsome, but with an interesting and by no means unattractive face, the whole man only at his most appealing when he was animated. His portraits show that he did, indeed, have something of the churchman about him: a calm and also an inscrutability, a sense that you would never entirely know what he was thinking. It gave him an air of authority which must have been invaluable for a man who had never been part of any establishment, never so much as managed an estate or led men, in war or peace, and who had existed on the periphery of the English ruling class. He was of it but not part of it. His background and the dislocation of long years of civil strife had set him apart from those whom he might view as his peers. This distinctiveness marked him and would characterize his approach to the dangerous business of winning the throne. For Henry Tudor, nothing had been simple. His background was unusually complicated and the circumstances of his birth compellingly strange.

He was the grandson of Shakespeare's 'Fair Kate', Catherine de Valois, the wife of Henry V. This gave him royal French blood. On his father's side, however, the antecedents were much less illustrious, for Catherine, left a widow after her husband's early death in 1421, had, by the start of the next decade, married again. Her second marriage, to Owen Tudor, a Welshman in her household, was kept secret until she died in 1437. By that time, she had borne Owen four children and inadvertently complicated the politics of England during the long minority of Henry VI. The regency government for the young king was uneasy about the existence of half-brothers, especially ones linked to the French royal family at a time when England was in the process of losing its extensive empire in France. The two eldest sons of the unlikely alliance of a French queen and a Welsh squire, Edmund and Jasper Tudor, were removed from their father and brought up together at Barking Abbey in Essex. They did, though, find favour with King Henry VI, who seems to have been fond of his half-brothers, and as he began to make his own decisions, their fortunes rose. In 1452, shortly before England's descent into the beginnings of the Wars of the Roses, Edmund was made earl of Richmond and Jasper earl of Pembroke. The lands and prestige that went with these titles meant that the Tudors became persons of significance. Just one year later their position was further enhanced when they were granted joint wardship of the heiress of another great landed family with a doubtful past – Margaret Beaufort, the ten-year-old daughter of the late John, duke of Somerset, who had died in disgrace after a costly and disastrous expedition to France. But it was her surname, rather than her father's failure, that made Margaret important. Aside from her wealth, her desirability lay in the fact that she was the great-granddaughter of John of Gaunt and had a potential claim to the throne of England herself. Not that this claim was without impediment, since the Beauforts were the offspring of John of Gaunt's initially adulterous liaison with Katherine Swynford. Though eventually regularized, the relationship cast a long shadow over fifteenth-century England, since this 'bastard' branch of John of Gaunt's line was not considered to have a rightful claim to the throne and Henry IV had expressly excluded his half-kindred from the succession.

Henry VI, a king not otherwise noted for his decisiveness, took a keen interest in the fortunes of his little cousin. Just a year after her birth he gave her wardship and marriage to his chief minister, the duke of Suffolk. This was probably intended to bolster Suffolk's wealth and status but as the duke's political fortunes took a dramatic turn for the worse in 1450, he saw an opportunity to salvage the prospects of his heir, seven-year-old

John de la Pole, by marrying the boy to Margaret Beaufort, who was then six. Such marriages seem to us now to be both ludicrous and shocking, but they were common at the time and viewed as sensible business arrangements that could be, and indeed often were, revoked at a later date. This is exactly what happened to the first marriage of Lady Margaret. Summoned to court with her mother on Valentine's Day 1453, Margaret now faced the considerable ordeal of making public her decision, since the law required she must do so in front of witnesses, including a bishop. There was no lovers' romance for her.

The initiative for this public dissolution of her marriage contract with Suffolk's son was not, however, Margaret's. At nine years old, she was directed by others. The king was bringing pressure on her to choose his half-brother, Edmund Tudor, over John de la Pole. She later remembered that Henry 'did make means for Edmund, his brother, then the earl of Richmond'. Uncertain what to do, but no doubt mindful of the king's own preferences, Margaret agonized over her decision. It was then suggested that she pray overnight to St Nicholas, who would guide her choice. By the morning her mind was made up. She would put aside the boy she scarcely knew for a much older man who was also a stranger. Thus she had made her own choice (or so she thought) and also pleased the king. But there were much greater political and dynastic considerations involved, for Henry, though married for some years, had no children and was faced with growing discontent among his fractious nobility. It is possible that, without an heir himself, Henry intended to nominate his brother Edmund in Margaret Beaufort's right.

He did not, however, do so and in fact his wife, Margaret of Anjou, was already pregnant, though at too early a stage for it to have been known at the time Margaret Beaufort and her mother came to court. The visit made a great impression on the child, who was enchanted by the magnificence of the spectacle, the opulent jewels and dresses of the queen and her ladies, and the warmth of the welcome from the king, whom she seems to have genuinely revered and liked. He also brought home to her the importance of her position and instilled in her a sense of who she was. There was no resentment of the role he had played in severing her from her child-husband. Perhaps she remembered him afterwards with fondness because of his attention to her and the contrast with the dark times that followed for England. Only a few months later, Henry suffered a severe mental collapse and the country slid towards civil war.

Despite her proximity to the throne and the attractions of her wealth, Margaret grew up in a happy environment, among the children of her mother's first marriage, the St John family, to whom she would remain close. But her childhood ended prematurely when Edmund Tudor married her as soon as she was twelve years old, in May 1455. This was the legal age of marriage for females and Edmund clearly saw no reason for delay, though another year was to elapse before Margaret conceived. This may have had more to do with the point at which his very young bride reached puberty than any early abstention on Edmund's part from marital relations. He was clearly keen to make his wife pregnant as soon as possible, so that he could secure a permanent interest in her estates through their offspring. It was not uncommon for girls of noble birth to be married at a very young age and to go to live with their frequently much older husbands (Edmund, then in his mid-twenties, was actually a younger spouse than was often the case in such marriages) but it was very unusual for such wives to bear children before their mid-teens.

Margaret had moved with Edmund Tudor to south Wales a few months after their wedding, where he was essentially acting as the king's lieutenant. It was a traditionally restless area, resistant to rule from London even before the outbreak of more widespread strife in Henry VI's realm in the 1450s. Local grievances and the fact that the Tudor brothers had briefly flirted with the Yorkists before reverting to full support of their half-brother made Edmund a target for the disaffected. Margaret was not with him at Carmarthen Castle in the summer of 1456 when he was attacked by two thousand troops under the leadership of the duke of York's men, Sir William Herbert and Sir Walter Devereux, and captured. Briefly imprisoned in the castle, Edmund was released but fell ill, probably with the plague, and never recovered. By the beginning of November he was dead, leaving Margaret, who was six months pregnant, a widow at the age of thirteen. His insensitivity and callousness in impregnating her at such a tender age have often been criticized but we know nothing of their relationship. It is unlikely that affection played much part in it and Edmund clearly felt that the risks to his wife's health, and that of any child she might bear, made it worthwhile ignoring convention. He obviously had not calculated on dying himself.

This may seem like a sort of rough justice but it left Margaret in danger. With winter setting in and the political situation in Wales so uncertain, she could not return to her mother in England. Her own safety and that of her unborn child were at stake. She needed to be somewhere secure and as free as possible from the threat of disease. It was now that Jasper Tudor, her brother-in-law, a man who would play a vital role in her future, came to the rescue. Margaret took refuge with him in Pembroke Castle and it was there, on 28 January 1457, that her child was born. He was named Henry, presumably as a sign of his Lancastrian birthright. His mother was still four months short of her fourteenth birthday.

It had been an extremely difficult birth which imperilled the lives of both mother and child. Margaret was small for her age and should never have conceived so early. The price she paid was that she was subsequently unable to have children. Yet the bond with the son born when she was scarcely more than a child herself was strong and unshakeable. She was committed to supporting him from the moment of his birth. Margaret Beaufort would grow into a clever and ambitious woman, able to manipulate, to adapt and, above all, to bide her time. Henry VI had made her conscious of who she was. It was an awareness that she was determined to inculcate in her son, no matter what vicissitudes might befall them both.

❧

IF SHE HAD been unlucky in her husband, Margaret Beaufort was fortunate in his brother. Jasper Tudor, by now completely committed to the Lancastrian cause, took an active interest in the well-being of Edmund's widow and her child. Later, he would share exile, hardship and uncertainty with his nephew, acting as mentor at a crucial stage in Henry Tudor's life. The ties that bound them were strong. But his immediate concern, once it was clear that Margaret had survived her ordeal, was to help her find a new husband. Single himself, he could offer her neither the domestic peace nor personal security that could be hoped for in a new marriage. And they both knew that Pembroke Castle, despite Jasper's attempts to increase its comforts, was still more of a fortress than a home. It was not an appropriate place for Margaret and her baby to remain permanently. By March 1457, Margaret was with Jasper in eastern Wales, at a manor belonging to the duke of Buckingham, one of the few nobles in the realm who could rival the duke of York in power. There, apparently with her full support, a marriage was arranged with Buckingham's second son, Henry Stafford. The precise timing of this, the third marriage in Margaret's young life, is not known, but it was probably at the beginning of 1458.

Relieved that she was now able to influence her affairs with some dignity, Margaret approached her life with Henry Stafford with renewed confidence. Theirs appears to have been a happy relationship, made easier by a financial settlement from Stafford's father when he died in 1460 and by Margaret's sizeable income from her own estates. The couple were wealthy enough to live in considerable style, though there is little information on their whereabouts in the years immediately after their marriage, or whether the infant Henry Tudor always stayed with them. Given the concern of both his mother and new stepfather to protect his interests, it is probable that Margaret did not want him too far distant, though his day-to-day routine would have been the responsibility of his nursery staff. The stability of Henry's early childhood was not, however, to last long. By the time he was four years old, he had been removed from his mother's care.

The year 1461 saw the fortunes and allegiances of Henry's uncle and stepfather diverge, in ways that had a direct impact on the child himself. Both Jasper Tudor and Henry Stafford had maintained their support for Henry VI but they had picked the losing side. In February 1461, Jasper and his father, Owen Tudor, widower of Catherine of Valois, confronted a Yorkist force at Mortimer's Cross in Herefordshire. They were vanquished and Owen summarily executed. Jasper, his hatred of the Yorkists even stronger now, escaped back into south Wales, where he vowed to avenge his father 'with the might of Our Lord and the assistance of . . . our kinsmen and friends, within short time'.[2] The threat, though heartfelt, could not be realized. Yorkist power was firmly established within months. Jasper, skilled in the arts of disguise and evading capture, fled into exile, first in Scotland and then in France. So began his long life as a fugitive in the courts of France (where he was well received as a blood relative by Louis XI) and Brittany, constantly striving for the restoration of the House of Lancaster, for the recovery of his own lands in Wales and, as time went by, the rights of his nephew, Henry Tudor. Jasper's misfortune, his life as a 'diplomatic beggar', as it has been called, would not, ultimately, be in vain.[3] He could not have foreseen, in 1461, that all the Lancastrian hopes might one day rest on Margaret Beaufort's son.

Less than two months after his grandfather's death, young Henry's stepfather fought for the cause of King Henry VI at the battle of Towton, in Yorkshire. But unlike many who were massacred as they fled one of the bloodiest battles ever fought on English soil, Stafford survived. The victory at Towton was decisive for the Yorkists, bringing Edward IV to the throne and precipitating the flight of the Lancastrian royal family to Scotland. This might well have been enough in itself to cause the Staffords to rethink their allegiances, but events much closer to home gave them no alternative. In September 1461, Pembroke Castle fell to a Yorkist force led by Sir William Herbert, an old adversary of the Tudors and a diehard supporter of the new king. It is often said that Margaret, her son and second husband were in the castle when it capitulated but there does not seem to be any firm proof of their whereabouts. Whether personally humiliated or not, they were bound to acknowledge that Herbert was now the representative of royal authority in south Wales. Keen to protect their estates, the Staffords accepted that they could not oppose the new regime. A year later, Herbert, newly ennobled, acquired the wardship and marriage of Margaret's son. It cost him £1,000, the equivalent of half a million pounds today, an indication of Herbert's wealth and also of Henry Tudor's perceived worth. Henry was removed from his mother and taken to live at Raglan Castle. He saw her occasionally during the years that followed, though it would be more than two decades before they spent much time in each other's company again. He was a child with prospects but in 1461, with his uncle in exile and his mother treading cautiously in her reappraisal of the family fortunes, the most she and her husband felt they could do for him was to become loyal subjects of Edward IV and watch and wait.

∞

AT RAGLAN, Henry was brought up in what was probably the greatest fortress-palace of its day. Defended by a moat and its formidable 'Yellow Tower', the stronghold also boasted a luxurious palace, built in the latest French style with superb masonry work and a double courtyard. Even a child parted from his mother at such a tender age must have come to appreciate its grandeur. Henry seems also to have been grateful for the care and attention shown him by Herbert's wife, Anne Devereux, the daughter of another prominent Welsh family. There were two other boys, both slightly older than him, in the family circle: Herbert's heir (also called William) and Henry Percy, who became earl of Northumberland in 1470. Percy was, like Henry

Tudor, Herbert's ward. In addition, there were the daughters of the Herbert family, one of whom, Maud, was intended by Herbert as Henry's bride. So it was not an isolated childhood and though Henry's lands had been reassigned by Edward IV, he was still styled, even by his guardian, as the earl of Richmond. Little is known of his education except what was written years later by Bernard André, the Frenchman appointed by Henry as his official historian. There were two priests who acted as tutors: Edward Haseley and Andrew Scot. Haseley became dean of Warwick and was later given an annuity by Henry for his services; Scot was an Oxford man. Henry appears to have been an apt pupil and his attainments must have pleased his mother when she learned about them on her rare visits or, more frequently, by messages that passed between her household and that of the Herberts.

The education of fifteenth-century aristocrats encompassed more than scholarly learning (overemphasis on the schoolroom was viewed with disapproval) and Henry also learned the vital physical skills of a gentleman of his class: archery, swordsmanship, riding and hunting. By the time he was twelve, such attributes were well enough developed for Lord Herbert to introduce his ward to the reality of political strife in England. It was to be an unforgettable baptism. Henry Tudor had spent eight years in a Yorkist household and, whatever the allegiances of his kindred, was being raised as a loyal subject of Edward IV. But by the end of the 1460s, Edward was losing his grip on England. His marriage to Elizabeth Woodville had insulted the French king, whose sister-in-law, Bona of Savoy, was spurned as a bride when the marriage negotiations were well-advanced. The Woodville match also divided Edward's supporters at home. Meanwhile, the Lancastrians were recovering their strength and Jasper Tudor, their main hope if they could gain back Wales, was raiding in the north of that country. His success was only temporary but the connection between uncle and nephew was not lost on Henry Tudor's guardian. In 1469, Herbert took the boy with him on campaign, perhaps thinking to ensure his loyalty to Edward IV as well as continue his practical training for warfare. If so, it was a disastrous miscalculation. At the battle of Edgecote, near Banbury, troops loyal to the turncoat earl of Warwick defeated Lord Herbert, who had quarrelled with his fellow commander, the earl of Devon, the night before and as a result had been deprived of his archers. As the day turned against Herbert and Welsh losses began to mount, Henry Tudor was led from the field by Sir Richard Corbet. He never saw his guardian again. Herbert was executed on the orders of Warwick and Henry was taken to Herbert's brother-in-law, Lord Ferrers, at Weobley in Herefordshire. He was joined by Herbert's widow, who assumed responsibility for his safety during the uncertain summer months of 1469. He remained with her for a year but his time in the Herberts' care was effectively over.

The balance of power in England was shifting and Margaret Beaufort, though anxious about her son's safety, saw an opportunity to recover his wardship. Hard bargaining ensued between the lawyers of the Staffords and the Herberts, but Margaret had set her sights on a more ambitious agenda and this required her to take a political gamble that would have a far-reaching impact on both her son and herself. She was determined to secure a title and lands for Henry, to ensure that he was no longer a pawn in the hands of others. Believing that the Richmond title was rightfully Henry's, she appealed directly to Edward IV's traitorous brother, the duke of Clarence, then owner of the 'honour of Richmond', as the power to grant its title and lands was known. She was not entirely successful, as Clarence, never a man to give up wealth easily, only agreed to return the title and estates on his death. It looked like Henry Tudor would have a long wait.

But who could be sure where the twists and turns of the struggle for domination of England might lead? Confusing as the events of 1469–71 seem to us now, for contemporaries it was impossible to predict the outcome of so much upheaval. Margaret and her husband had worked hard to be seen as loyal supporters of Edward IV, distancing themselves from her unpredictable Beaufort relatives and developing their contacts with the family of Elizabeth Woodville, Edward's wife, when Stafford's nephew, the young duke of Buckingham, married the queen's sister. But Margaret's appeal to Clarence on her son's behalf compromised all this. It looked like plotting with the king's enemies, even if Clarence and his brother were eventually reconciled. Despite Henry Stafford's attempts to demonstrate his loyalty, Margaret's actions could not be undone. In the early autumn of 1470, however, she had every reason to believe that her re-emergence on the political scene was thoroughly justified.

Faced with rebellion and treachery within his own family and deserted by the powerful earl of Warwick, who had styled himself the 'Kingmaker', Edward IV could not hold on to his kingdom. In September 1470 he fled to Holland. Within a month, Henry VI was brought out of confinement at the Tower of London and restored to the throne. Jasper Tudor returned to Wales and was reunited at Hereford with the nephew he had not seen for almost ten years. Henry Tudor was now able to spend time with both his uncle and mother, whose unwavering support for him seemed fully justified. One of his abiding memories of this period, however, was a brief meeting with the gentle and pious king. On 27 October he was rowed down the Thames in his stepfather's barge for a royal audience.

Henry VI had always been well disposed towards Margaret Beaufort and he seems to have greeted her son warmly. What passed between them is unknown but the story was later given out that he had prophesied that Henry Tudor would one day become king. There is every reason to assume that he had been gentle and welcoming to the boy, but the gloss put upon young Tudor's reception is probably Tudor propaganda that was picked up by Shakespeare: 'This pretty lad will prove our country's bliss' is likely to be sheer dramatic invention.

For young Henry Tudor, the promise of such bliss was soon to be a distant vision. Henry VI had been a weak and unpredictable king before; he was now simply unfit to rule at all. In reinstating him, the Lancastrians lost an opportunity for a painless abdication and the assumption of power by his seventeen-year-old son, Edward of Westminster, who remained in France while attempts were made to cobble together an administration that would help the mentally unstable monarch function. Henry VI never seems to have been enthusiastic about his restoration, preferring the quiet certainties of honourable captivity to the cut and thrust of power in a country where the struggle for dominance seemed never-ending. Taking advantage of the fluid situation and hoping to build on his solid support in London, Edward IV landed without opposition in Yorkshire in March 1471. He defeated and killed Warwick at the battle of Barnet in April and then moved west to meet the forces of Margaret of Anjou, who had landed with her son in Dorset. On 4 May, still waiting for the soldiers that Jasper Tudor and his nephew were bringing from Wales, the queen's commander, Edmund Beaufort, duke of Somerset, cousin of Margaret Beaufort, met Edward IV's army at Tewkesbury in Gloucestershire. The vicious fighting and subsequent bloodletting effectively destroyed the Lancastrian cause. Edward of Westminster was killed fleeing the field, while Somerset was inveigled out of Tewkesbury Abbey, where he had taken sanctuary, on a false promise of safety by Edward IV and executed two days later. To ensure an unequivocal Yorkist success, Henry VI was murdered in the Tower of London, almost certainly on Edward's orders, on the night of 21 May.

Jasper and Henry Tudor retreated to Pembroke Castle but it was doubtful that they could hold out there for long. Fearful for her son's safety and understandably mistrusting any offer of pardon from the king, Margaret Beaufort counselled her son to flee the country. He was now firmly connected in Edward IV's mind with the Lancastrian cause and his mother valued his life more than his company. She would entrust him to the brother-in-law who had been an unshakeable ally and pray to God that she would, one day, see him again. Jasper, that inveterate evader of the Yorkists, was able to spirit his nephew out of Pembroke Castle to the small port of Tenby, where his local contacts allowed them to make good their escape by sea. Even then, nothing was easy. They intended to make for the French coast, but storms blew them off course and they finally landed in Brittany at the end of September 1471. So began, at fourteen years old, Henry Tudor's long period of exile. He would be twice that age before he saw his mother or England again.

∽

BRITTANY GAVE Henry Tudor sanctuary but also something more – a hard schooling in the reality of power politics in Europe. This would add a dimension to his understanding that Edward IV lacked. It also taught him that trust must be awarded with extreme care, that security was a luxury scarcely to be expected, but that being an outsider provided a perspective that could be enlightening. We know little about most of his time in Brittany, since few records survive. Though honourably treated at the expense of Duke Francis II of Brittany, Henry and his uncle were essentially under house arrest. In addition, they would very soon have realized that they were caught up in a wider political struggle. Duke Francis was determined to maintain his independence from France and the Yorkists needed his support as their own relations with the French king Louis XI ebbed and flowed. The Tudors were separated in 1474 when a plot to assassinate them was feared. It came to nothing but two years later Henry's position was thrown into doubt when Duke Francis, apparently believing Edward IV's promises of finding an appropriate Yorkist bride and grants of land for his 'guest', agreed to the young man's return. But no matter how much his mother, now remarried after Stafford's death to the Yorkist Lord Thomas Stanley, might have wanted such an outcome, Henry himself was not convinced of the English monarch's good faith. As he was about to embark at St Malo, Henry pretended to be ill. His departure was delayed and, even as Duke Francis reconsidered his agreement with Edward, Henry took sanctuary in the cathedral. He was permitted to stay, and later brought together again with his uncle for a time.

But the danger and uncertainty over his future remained.

Despite it all, the glimpses of his lifestyle from remaining records show that he did not sit fretting inside the succession of Breton castles that became his temporary homes. He grew into an active young man, sometimes in the company of Duke Francis's own soldiers. His education was not overlooked and he was well prepared in the skills of warfare. Gradually, as his prowess developed, his expenses, particularly for horses, began to outstrip those of his uncle.[4] Duke Francis, despite frequent bouts of illness, was a generous host. Yet Henry was not free and his prospects, seen even in the most positive light, were indeterminate. He had been twelve years in exile when, in 1483, his situation changed dramatically. He was about to be transformed from being no more than a member of the diffused Lancastrian opposition to a claimant to the throne.

The catalyst was the unexpected death of Edward IV on 9 April. The handsome hedonist had turned into an overweight, self-indulgent man (a path closely paralleled by his grandson, Henry VIII) but no one was prepared for the stroke that ended his life after more than twenty years on the throne. He had a large family but the girls, renowned for their beauty, had come before the boys. His heir, now Edward V, was only twelve years old, too young to rule for himself. It soon became apparent that faction, rather than harmony, would characterize the transition towards a new government. Few, however, could have predicted the dramatic outcome of what at first seemed no more than a family squabble for control of the new monarch. Ranged against each other were the queen's family, the Woodvilles, and the supporters of the late king's youngest brother, Richard, duke of Gloucester.

The Woodvilles were certainly numerous. Edward IV had married into a fertile family and the extensive granting of favours to his wife's relatives, though only to be expected, did not sit well with some of the English aristocracy. Nor did the fact that the Woodvilles had, until Elizabeth's good fortune, been Lancastrian supporters. When Edward met her she was the widow of Sir John Grey, who had been killed at the second battle of St

Albans in 1461, and the mother of two young sons. This dubious past was now well behind her and she appeared to be on reasonable terms with the duke of Gloucester at the time that her husband died. As he was based in the north of England, distance may have made their relationship easier. When circumstances brought them closer together, things did not go well at all.

It speedily became obvious that the duke would not stay meekly on the sidelines while the reins of government were taken by others. The role of queens during the minority of their sons had never been formalized in England but there were precedents for the appointment of uncles as Protectors. Allied with the duke of Buckingham and Sir William Hastings, one of Edward IV's most loyal ministers, the duke ensured, within three weeks of his brother's death, that he would not be passed over. He knew that control of the person of the king was the key to the exercise of real power. In truth, the Woodvilles lost the initiative when they took too long to bring Edward V from his residence in Ludlow to London. On the last day of April 1483 the queen's brother and younger son by her first marriage, totally unsuspecting after an apparently pleasant dinner the night before with Gloucester, were arrested at Stony Stratford in Northamptonshire. The king himself, though dismayed by this sudden turn of events, was compelled to continue his journey towards his coronation under the control of his other uncle. On hearing the news, Elizabeth Woodville, with her younger son and daughters, fled into sanctuary in Westminster Abbey.

This was, however, only the first phase of Richard's coup d'état. It has been suggested that his subsequent actions were at least in part driven by a fear that he would lose his lands and power base in the north of England rather than the burning desire to become king. Perhaps he did not know himself when he took on the Woodvilles in April. Yet by 24 June he had destroyed Lord Hastings (summarily executed after a council meeting in which the Protector claimed there were plots against him), imprisoned Margaret Beaufort's husband Lord Stanley, the bishop of Ely and the archbishop of York, persuaded the queen to give up her younger son, and published a detailed statement that demonstrated the illegitimacy of the king and his brother because of an alleged pre-contract of marriage that Edward IV had undertaken before he wed Elizabeth Woodville. This left Richard as the sole legitimate heir of his brother but in case people were not persuaded of the legalities, he also brought his army down from Yorkshire in an unsubtle move intended to cow any opposition. On 6 July he was crowned King Richard III in Westminster Abbey. In less than three months he had moved from magnate in the north to monarch of all England. It may well be that, with hindsight, his actions look more carefully planned than they actually were. What cannot be denied, however, is that he ruthlessly removed his brother's heirs from their inheritance (a document of the time refers to 'Edward bastard late said king of England') and that they never emerged from their confinement in the Tower of London.

Richard III, who had come by the throne with the speed and organization of a professional soldier, remains the most controversial of English monarchs. Tudor propaganda and Shakespeare's colourful, if wildly inaccurate, portrait of one of the most consummate villains ever to walk the stage served to blacken his image for centuries. No contemporary portrait of him survives, but the nearest, and therefore probably the most accurate, dates from about 1510. If this is a reasonable likeness, it reveals a man who appears wary and tired. He does not look at ease with himself. Even today, when a more balanced view of his actions has been suggested by historians, the popular perception is still that of the hunchbacked monster who left a trail of murder on his way to the throne. Attempts to clear him of all the charges that could be brought against him have merely polarized opinion still further. Yet there is no doubt that the manner of his rise to power shocked contemporaries in an age that was inured to violence and double-dealing. It is not surprising that Richard seems to have known from the outset of his reign that he might have difficulties keeping his crown. But when he looked around, he would not have seen many serious contenders able to try their own hand at usurpation. He was also bolstered by a strong religious faith in the justifications of his actions. It seems unlikely that he was overly troubled, in the summer of 1483, at the thought of Henry Tudor as a serious opponent. By the autumn, he knew differently.

⚬

IT WAS NOT long before the new king discovered the challenges awaiting him. There were conspiracies everywhere, especially in the south of England, and it was soon brought home to Richard that commanding loyalty in the north was an insufficient guarantee of stability. He had also made implacable enemies in his struggle with the Woodvilles. The significance of this was not lost on one observer. Margaret Beaufort had hoped, before Edward IV's death, that her patient adherence to the Yorkist cause, coupled with Lord Stanley's rising power and political influence, might finally bring about her son's return and the restoration of his lands. Richard III's seizure of the throne, and the likelihood that the Princes in the Tower were dead, prompted her to rethink her strategy. A greater possibility than mere restitution now beckoned. So Margaret, who had carried the train of Richard's queen at the coronation on 6 July, was within two months entering into dangerous secret negotiations with Elizabeth Woodville. Her sights were now set much higher: on the arrangement of a marriage between Princess Elizabeth of York and Henry Tudor. Her son would claim the throne and make Elizabeth his queen. Using her personal physician, Margaret established contact with the queen dowager and proceeded to raise loans in the City of London to give financial underpinning to her quest. She sent a trusted servant to Brittany to apprise her son of what was afoot, urging that he prepare an invasion. By late September, she had a further important ally from amongst the English nobility. The duke of Buckingham, the man who had helped Richard III to the crown, regretted his actions sufficiently to rebel himself.

The conjunction of these two strands of revolt appeared to present a major crisis for Richard III so soon after he had been crowned. It was not the most obvious combination of interests and Buckingham's motives remain unclear. Although he wrote to Henry in late September 1483, giving Tudor the date he proposed for his own rising and other particulars that would allow them to coordinate their actions, he made no mention of Henry's claim to the throne. Perhaps this is hardly surprising, since, as a direct descendant of Edward III in a line of unimpeachable legitimacy, he knew very well that he had a realistic claim of his own. It may have occurred to Buckingham that his proximity to the throne might make him a target and that a preemptive strike would safeguard his own life. In any case, the original idea of a rebellion was probably not his but the product of the growing influence of John Morton, bishop of Ely, who seems to have used his time as a prisoner in Brecon, one of Buckingham's castles in Wales, to bend the ear of the duke about his prospects. Certainly, Buckingham was related to both the Woodvilles and the Beauforts. His wife Katherine was the dowager queen's sister and Margaret Beaufort was his mother's cousin. The duke was only three years older than Henry Tudor and appears to have been rather a changeable young man. Edward IV had excluded him from a role in government and though he had been instrumental in bringing Richard III to power, there seems to have been an underlying resentment that Morton sensed.

Though it was never clear how matters would move forward if the conspiracy succeeded in overthrowing Richard, the alliance of the duke and the exile was never put to the test. Despite risings across the south of England, Buckingham, who was an unpopular lord in Wales, was not able to raise his own tenants. The autumn weather turned wet and made roads impassable. As his support failed to materialize, Buckingham took refuge in the house of a servant who promptly betrayed him to the king. Richard had acted with his customary vigour in putting down the opposition and he was not disposed to show any mercy to a high-born traitor. Buckingham, 'the most untrue creature living', as the king furiously described him, was executed at Salisbury on 2 November. Henry Tudor, who tried hard to raise men and put together a fleet in a short space of time, did not even leave the port of Paimpol in Brittany until about the same date. His force of fifteen ships and five thousand men also fell victim to the weather and was scattered by the time Henry and just one other ship reached the Devon coast. He did not know of Buckingham's fate, but the decision to abandon the mission and return to Brittany was the only one he could have made. Blown off course, as he had been in 1471, he made landfall in Normandy and was soon back in Brittany. His cause, however, was far from lost.

A substantial group of exiles from England, men of influence and determination, now joined him. Among them were Elizabeth Woodville's brother and her surviving son from her first marriage. Their hopes rested on Henry Tudor, no longer a lonely exile with no prospects but suddenly, thanks to circumstances and his mother's initiative, a pretender to the Crown of England. This new relationship was sanctified before God in Rennes Cathedral, on Christmas Day 1483. Edward Hall wrote in his *Chronicle*:

> On which day all the English lords went with great solemnity to the chief church of the city and there each gave faith and promise to the other. The earl himself first took a corporal oath, and on his honour promising that incontinent [immediately] after he should return, he would be conjoined in matrimony with the lady Elizabeth, daughter to King Edward IV. Then all the company swore to him fealty, and did to him homage as though he had been that time the crowned king and anointed prince, promising faithfully and firmly assuring that they would not only lose their worldly substance, but also be privated [deprived] of their lives and worldly felicity, rather than to suffer king Richard, that tyrant, longer to rule and reign over them.[5]

Such a symbolic gesture, coming at the end of a year that had both raised and dashed his hopes, made him a king in waiting. But he was still some way from fulfilling his mother's dream.

The realization that the figurehead of the main opposition to the king's rule was the stepson of Lord Stanley brought Margaret Beaufort and her third husband into great peril. Margaret narrowly avoided attainder and Stanley's eloquence before Richard III, when he somehow managed to convince a very sceptical audience that he had nothing to do with his wife's actions, probably played a vital part in preventing imprisonment or worse. But Margaret lost her titles and estates, which were given over to her husband, and she was deprived of her liberty when Stanley undertook to keep her under strict supervision and control. The effect of this on their relationship can only be imagined, but neither came out of it as badly as might have been expected. Stanley's professed loyalty made him important to Richard III, especially in Wales, where support of Richard was scarce, and Margaret, 'albeit that in King Richard's days she was oft in jeopardy of her life, yet she bore patiently all troubles in such wise that it is wonder to think it',[6] had managed for much of the Yorkist years to balance pragmatic adherence to the regime with unflinching support for her fugitive son. In Margaret's case, piety and plotting were both important parts of her daily life. That there might be a moral contradiction between these extremes never occurred to her.

Yet while it was possible to limit the opposition caused by malcontents in England, Richard could not afford to ignore the growing band of influential exiles gathered around the unlikely figure of Henry Tudor in Brittany. His main aim in scotching Tudor's hopes was to persuade the duke of Brittany to give up the young man he had supported since 1471. Francis had resisted English offers before, but in the early summer of 1484 Richard III made a generous offer of support, through the Breton treasurer, Pierre Landais, that the Bretons accepted during one of Duke Francis's many bouts of illness. In return for archers and money, Brittany would hand over Henry Tudor. Fortunately for Henry, the clever and ubiquitous Morton, bishop of Ely, still had his own sources in Richard's government and got wind of the deal. Though Morton was himself in Flanders, his efficient courier network was able to inform Henry Tudor swiftly. With Brittany no longer a safe haven, negotiations were opened with the French government for Henry and his supporters to go into France. Following his uncle and other nobles, Henry slipped across the border from Brittany into Anjou, disguised as a servant. The story goes that he was only an hour away from being intercepted by a Breton force sent to arrest him. When Duke Francis found out about the change of policy implemented in his name he generously offered money for the remaining rank and file of Henry's stranded court-in-exile to join him in France. Henry's place of residence had changed but he would have known in the spring of 1484 that, though safe for the time being, he was now at the mercy of a larger, more powerful government, one that would not hesitate to manipulate him ruthlessly in the pursuit of its own ends in the wider European context.

FRANCE WAS NOT without its own problems. Charles VIII was only fourteen years old and his kingdom was ruled by a regency government led by his elder sister, Anne de Beaujeu. With her husband, Pierre, directing the council and the princess herself in charge of the person of her brother, the young king was not always grateful for their direction. Though understandable, Charles's chafing at the bit did not do his sister justice. At twenty-two years old, she was to prove an able stateswoman and a steadying influence in uncertain times. Her success suggests she would have made an excellent monarch in her own right, but Salic law, which allowed only males to occupy the throne in France, forbade such a possibility.

At first there were only hints of how the French might make use of Henry Tudor. Absorbed with trying to impose her own authority, Anne had to deal with domestic difficulties and the threat posed by the Orléans faction of her family. She was not in a position to give direct help yet. But her underlying aim, like that of her father, was to unite Brittany with France. While Richard III and his ally the Archduke Maximilian publicly supported the independence of Brittany, the French government was content at least to maintain Henry Tudor. Any more positive help seemed likely to be modest and its timing contingent on how seriously the French viewed the likelihood of Richard III intervening militarily on Brittany's behalf.

Henry's hopes rose and fell as the months went by. His situation was almost entirely dependent on events elsewhere. In England, Richard III had strengthened his hold on power by persuading Elizabeth Woodville to come out of sanctuary in Westminster Abbey and rejoin the court. There was talk of good marriages for her daughters, though the question of their legitimacy remained unresolved. And then the wheel of fortune turned again. Richard was dealt a heavy blow when his son, Prince Edward, died in April 1484, followed within the year by Richard's wife, Anne Neville. Suddenly, Richard's own dynastic hopes had evaporated. There were rumours that he intended to marry his niece, Elizabeth of York, a course of action that the king was forced to deny publicly. This news alarmed Henry Tudor but Richard, whatever his intentions might privately have been, did not go through with it. The passage of time was leaving both Richard and Henry with fewer options. There had also been notable additions to Henry's cause, such as the earl of Oxford, the most senior surviving Lancastrian commander, who effected a daring escape from a castle in the Pale of Calais, bringing with him two other experienced soldiers to bolster Henry's hopes. By the beginning of 1485 it was clear that the only serious rival to the widowed and childless English king was the little-known Welshman still living in exile across the sea.

Richard had suffered personal losses but in England the strong core of support among the new aristocracy created by the Yorkists was not ready to desert him for an unfamiliar rebel with a distant claim to the throne. Mindful of the advice that 'the king of France is young and the kingdom governed by a number of princes who agree ill, so that the king of England will never have so good an opportunity as he has at present',[7] he had already moved into a vigorous propaganda campaign to discredit the pretender to his crown. In a proclamation distributed throughout England, Henry's supporters were described as 'open murderers, adulterers and extortioners . . . and to abuse and blind the commons of this said realm [they] have chosen to be their captain . . . Henry, late calling himself earl of Richmond, which of his ambitious and insatiable covetousness . . . encroaches upon the name and title of royal estate of this realm of England. Whereunto he has no manner, interest, right or colour [quality] as every man well knows.' To achieve his aims, it was alleged, Henry had agreed to give up England's ancient claim to the throne of France, to the French lands that had belonged to the early Plantagenets and even to Calais itself, the last remaining outpost of a once substantial English empire in France. This traitor and his brutal henchmen would terrorize England once they arrived, perpetrating 'the most cruel murders, slaughters, robberies and disinheritances that ever were seen in any Christian realm'. The country's hope lay in Richard III, 'our sovereign lord', who 'as a well-willed, diligent and courageous prince will put his most royal person to all labour and pain necessary . . . for the resistance and subduing of his enemies.'[8]

Such vituperation suggests that Richard had accepted that armed confrontation was fast approaching. By the summer of 1485 Henry Tudor was running out of money, the loyalty of one of his key supporters, Elizabeth Woodville's son, the marquess of Dorset, was wavering, and the possibility of his marriage to the Yorkist heiress looked to be receding. Most serious of all, the French no longer needed him. The collapse of the Breton government removed the threat of English interference on behalf of the duchy and any diplomatic reason for sponsoring Tudor. This loss of what had always been uncertain support forced

Henry's hand. By mid-July he was seeking loans and putting together a military force to invade England. He had already written to potential supporters there but his tone, though positive, was still one more of hope than expectation:

> Being given to understand your good devoir and entreaty to advance me to the furtherance of my rightful claim, due and lineal inheritance of that crown, and for the just depriving of that homicide and unnatural tyrant, which now unjustly bears dominion over you, I give you to understand that no Christian heart can be more full of joy and gladness than the heart of your poor exiled friend, who will, upon the instant of your sure advertising what power you will make ready, and what captains and leaders you get to conduct, be prepared to pass over the sea with such force as my friends here are preparing for me. And if I have such good speed and success as I wish . . . I shall ever be most forward to remember and wholly to requite this your great and most loving kindness in my just quarrel.[9]

The force that he referred to was only about half the size of the one scattered by storms nearly two years earlier. It probably comprised about two thousand men and no more than seven ships. Most of the soldiers were mercenaries from different European countries: France, Switzerland, Brittany and Scotland. Only four to five hundred of them were English. But if their numbers were not impressive, Henry and his advisers had chosen experienced men, familiar with the latest military tactics and weaponry. On 1 August 1485 the little fleet left the mouth of the Seine at Honfleur in Normandy and passed without incident across the Channel and into the Irish Sea. Six days later it made landfall at Mill Bay near Haverfordwest on the Pembroke coast. His faithful uncle Jasper at his side, Henry Tudor had, at last, come home to Wales. If there was relief, there must also have been a great deal of apprehension as to what might follow.

HENRY'S PRIORITY was to gather men in his support. He needed a larger force behind him if there was to be any prospect of defeating Richard III in battle. But the underlying plan of his campaign had been carefully considered. As soon as he landed, he had sent out letters, signed as king, and riders had spread out across Wales bringing the news of his arrival and seeking commitment to his cause. Eloquent and carefully phrased, Henry's letters transformed him from 'your poor exiled friend' to a rightful king:

> Through the help of Almighty God, the assistance of our loving friends and true subjects and the great confidence that we have to the nobles and commons of this our principality of Wales, we be entered into the same, purposing by the help above rehearsed to descend into our realm of England not only for the adeption [recovery] of the crown unto us of right appertaining but also for the oppression of that odious tyrant Richard, late duke of Gloucester, usurper of our said right . . .[10]

These were sound tactics, for it was by no means inevitable that Wales would answer the call of an almost forgotten pretender, hoping that his Welsh ancestry and the locally strong affection for his Uncle Jasper would make a material difference to his prospects. Richard III had done his best to ensure that his own men were in charge of the key fortresses of the country and that Henry Tudor could not move unimpeded through Wales towards confrontation with the Yorkist king. Henry stayed in the west of Wales for some days, taking his force across the Pembroke peninsula and along the Cardiganshire coast before reaching Aberystwyth by about 12 August. Five days or so later, having traversed difficult terrain in mid-Wales, he reached the English border at Shrewsbury. He had encountered little resistance and his army was growing, thanks to locally influential Welsh leaders whose loyalty to Richard III was far less certain than the king had hoped. At Shrewsbury, though, Henry was firmly rebuffed by the local dignitaries: 'Master Mitton made and swore, being head bailiff and a stout wise gentleman that he knew him for no king but only King Richard to whom he was sworn'.[11] Tudor pleaded with Mitton but to no avail, until messengers from his stepfather's brother, Sir William Stanley, arrived and persuaded the townspeople to change their minds.

Henry had marched largely unimpeded through Wales but any hope he may have entertained of joining up with the Stanleys and marching down Watling Street to London without engaging Richard's forces was not to be realized. Richard could command a much larger army and was not likely to sit around waiting for Tudor to outwit him. The king was at Nottingham, where he had spent much of the summer expecting news of an invasion by his rival. But he did not learn of Henry's landing until 11 August, thus losing some time and giving Henry the opportunity to establish himself in Wales. In the space of a week the king summoned his main commanders, the duke of Norfolk and the earl of Northumberland, continued to recruit men and prepared himself for battle. He also held what he probably believed was a singular advantage, if not actually a trump card. Lord Stanley, Margaret Beaufort's husband, had been forced to leave his eldest son by an earlier marriage, Lord Strange, with the king. The young man was effectively a hostage for the Stanley family's loyalty, still seen as unreliable despite Stanley's best efforts to persuade Richard otherwise. This negation of the Stanley threat (or so Richard hoped) was expected to have a material impact on the outcome of a major confrontation between Tudor and Yorkist forces. Between them, the Stanley brothers could muster about six thousand men, more than enough to change the course of a battle. Richard could not force them to fight for him but he could ensure that they stayed on the sidelines. And that indeed is where they were as the two armies approached each other in the Midlands at the beginning of the third week of August 1485.

The Stanleys were equally important to Henry Tudor. On 19 August Henry met Sir William Stanley at Stafford, hoping for a firm commitment that the brothers would support him and, in so doing, put him on the throne. He may have received assurances of goodwill but the Stanleys were careful to avoid joining their forces with Henry's. Margaret Beaufort's husband no doubt did have concerns for the safety of his son but he was as much of a pragmatist now as he had always been. There may have been fair words but Henry's army, though swelled by recruits gathered in Shropshire, was a separate entity from the Stanleys. Lord Stanley passed through Lichfield consciously avoiding his stepson. The town opened its gates to Henry Tudor and he moved on, towards Tamworth. Though a number of men had already started to desert the king, the uncertainty over the Stanleys' intentions seems to have got the better of Henry on the night of 20–21 August, when he became detached from the main body of his troops and went missing until about dawn, to the consternation of his commanders.

Perhaps rather than a late loss of nerves he really had received messages from the Stanleys, as he subsequently explained. At any rate, he met both the brothers at Atherstone on 21 August. The outcome was by no means satisfactory. Lord Stanley offered four of his best knights and their troops but would not agree to put the greater Stanley force under the command of the earl of Oxford. Henry knew then that his stepfather would not commit wholly to his cause and that Stanley's troops would probably decide the battle. For half a lifetime he had had little reason to trust others or expect their unswerving commitment. Nothing had changed on that late summer eve. The man who would be king needed to rely on his own leaders, most of whom had not known him for more than eighteen months, and pray that God would uphold his cause.

❧

RICHARD III arrived in Leicester on the night of 20 August 1485. He was ready to fight and eager to be done with Henry Tudor, who, he wrote 'intending our utter destruction, the extreme subversion of this our realm and disinheriting of our true subjects of the same, towards whose recountering, God being our guide, we be utterly determined in our own person to remove in all haste goodly that we can or may.' From Leicester he moved about fourteen miles to the west, to engage the smaller force of his enemy in the gently undulating countryside close to the old Roman road of Watling Street. On 22 August, the confrontation itself took place.

History knows it as the battle of Bosworth but despite a fair amount of contemporary or near-contemporary comment, there is still a great deal that remains unclear about the battle. Many books have been written over hundreds of years on the subject, positing different ideas about its location and the movement of the opposing forces. Recent archaeological research has apparently proved them all wrong. The discovery of cannon shot, the badge of the White Boar and other military paraphernalia such as swords and armour now puts the site of the battle two miles to the south and west of the current battlefield centre, in terrain that would have been more open than it is now, dotted with low hills and criss-crossed with marshy areas. The nearest village, Stoke Golding, has long boasted that it is the birthplace of the Tudor dynasty and the discovery of so much evidence in the fields nearby adds weight to that claim.

The ground had been chosen by Richard III, whose forces outnumbered Henry's by about two to one. We cannot be certain where either he or Henry camped with their armies on the night of 21–2 August. Henry was probably to the west, at Merevale Abbey and the nearby village of Atherstone, and Richard was further east, at Sutton Cheney. The king's troops may actually have camped on Albion Hill, the highest piece of local ground, but the recent finds further south indicate that the main part of the battle was not fought there. It was Henry who had to march to engage Richard, breaking camp at sunrise (just before six) and proceeding along Watling Street to its junction with Fenn Lanes, where his troops made rendezvous and formed line of march. The Stanleys, as they had intimated, kept their distance and formed a separate battle array between the two other armies, on rising ground to the south that enabled them to have a good view of how the fighting was going.

As Henry's army advanced along the Roman road it came under artillery attack from Richard's forces. Such opening salvoes were common in late medieval battles and though they were intended to terrify as much as anything else, they also revealed where Richard and his forces actually were. Henry and his commanders would then have known that the king had an impressive array and could begin to understand how he might deploy it. The royal vanguard, with archers at front and cavalry protecting the infantry, was under the command of John Howard, duke of Norfolk. The rearguard, under the earl of Northumberland, was probably deployed in line with the vanguard to make a wide-sweeping array that was intended to envelop the smaller force of Henry Tudor. The king himself was behind the main battle line, surrounded by a lifeguard of no more than two hundred cavalry.

Henry, without the crucial support of the Stanleys, had to trust to the earl of Oxford and put most of his troops in a vanguard that, though less deep, could at least appear to match the frontage of Richard's battle array. Henry stayed with the main battle, behind Oxford, but it was a meagre force, probably no more than a troop of cavalry and a company of foot. It left him dangerously exposed once Oxford moved off. The earl, however, was a canny fighter. Richard's first artillery barrage had helped him form a plan that was, essentially, to outmanoeuvre the king and divide his forces. The battle-hardened Oxford knew his military text books. What had worked for Roman generals might also work for him. If he could drive a wedge through Richard's vanguard, he could diminish the impact of Norfolk's archers and give the infantrymen of Henry Tudor's army a chance of making an effective attack. The outcome of fierce hand-to-hand fighting was unpredictable – panic and confusion were powerful forces in themselves – and Henry's commanders knew that only decisive action would sway the Stanleys.

For some while (we do not know how long) the fighting was brutal yet without obvious advantage to either side. If Richard had hoped that sheer weight of numbers would bring about a quick victory, he now knew that Tudor's forces were not ready to break and run and that Norfolk was in difficulties. He needed to change the indeterminate nature of the conflict and it was pointed out to him that the isolated position of his rival, behind the main force of Oxford's troops, presented him with just such an opportunity. Victory did not have to be achieved through hours of killing. A cavalry charge directed at Henry and the small force guarding him would annihilate the pretender and trample his red dragon banner into the earth. Their leader dead, Henry's forces would almost certainly flee the field and Richard, in this one decisive moment, would be England's undisputed king. It was a bold idea, typical of the soldier that Richard had long been and the ruler he now was. The odds seemed to have been on his side. Yet it cost him his life.

Richard III got to within what was literally striking distance of Henry Tudor but it was not quite close enough. He was thwarted in the end by Henry's French pikemen, who had just enough time to close ranks around their leader. The eighteen-foot-long pikes they wielded could not be pushed aside by men on horseback. So the king was forced to dismount and try with his followers to hack his way through, evidently hoping to come face-to-face with Henry and slay him personally. Richard's determination and valour were acknowledged even by his enemies, but Henry and his guards fought vigorously as well and their response, coupled with Richard's increasingly desperate situation, since he was now cut off from his own troops, finally caused the watching Stanleys to abandon their neutrality. The intervention of Sir William Stanley's soldiers decided the outcome of the battle of Bosworth Field. Richard fought on, even as the Stanleys charged. He killed Henry's standard-bearer and was still making for Tudor himself, despite being urged to flee the field. Finally, he was surrounded and battered to death. Hearing the cheers from the Stanleys' forces, Norfolk's troops scattered and ran for their lives. Northumberland's, whether through treachery or too great a distance from the action, had played no part in the fighting. Henry Tudor, probably more dazed than triumphant, had emerged victorious. He would subsequently ascribe his success – and his claim to rule England – to the providence of God.

Legend has it that the gold circlet Richard wore on his head, over his armour, was knocked off and rolled under a hawthorn bush as his enemies cut him down. The crown was subsequently retrieved by Lord Stanley, who placed it on his stepson's head in a powerful gesture that marked the moment when the Tudor dynasty came into being. This is a good story but probably one that gained in the telling by the Tudor propaganda machine.

Richard's dead body was shamefully treated. Polydore Vergil wrote some thirty years later that it was:

> carried to the town of Leicester, as he gorgeously the day before with pomp and pride departed out of the same town. For his body was naked and despoiled to the skin and nothing left about him, not so much as a clout to cover his privy members, and was trussed behind a pursuivant of arms called blanche sanglier, or white boar, like a hog or a calf, the head and arms hanging on the one side of the horse and the legs on the other side, and all besprinkled with mire and blood.[12]

The body was displayed in the church of the Greyfriars for several days, lest there be any doubt that Richard had died. There was no respect for the loser of Bosworth. Richard was buried without a headstone and only some years later did Henry provide a small sum for a coffin to house the remains of the last Plantagenet king.

∽

AT TWENTY-EIGHT, Henry Tudor was no longer a 'pretty lad'. In looks he was still personable, but an itinerant and uncertain youth had shaped a cautious personality. He was not a man who took anything for granted. The immense challenge of ruling the larger of the two realms that formed the island of Britain lay ahead of him. He had come by his crown in blood and battle. Three years later, in the kingdom of Scotland, a much younger man, destined to be Henry's rival for the remaining years of the fifteenth century, won a throne the same way.

CHAPTER TWO

The Field of Stirling

'Nothing achieved by violence can endure.'

Queen Margaret of Denmark's dying words to her eldest son,
the future James IV of Scotland

THE ABBEY OF CAMBUSKENNETH stood among peaceful meadows on a bend on the northern bank of the river Forth, below the town of Stirling. Founded as an Augustinian religious house in 1147 by David I, one of Scotland's most pious kings, it was not a prosperous place in late medieval times. Many reports over the years spoke of its poverty, of the small number of brothers who lived there and the depredations suffered from warfare and the unwanted attentions of the various armies that periodically fought in the area, during and beyond the struggle for Scottish independence in the fourteenth century. Its once beautiful gardens had brought in enough income to endow the abbey with several altars, but this was insufficient compensation for the constant disputes with neighbouring landowners over cattle and sheep rustling and ownership of fisheries in the river. Cambuskenneth was still functioning but had seen better days.

Thus it was probably with resignation rather than enthusiasm that the monks watched as a party of horsemen approached the abbey's gates and requested entry on a day towards the end of June 1488. The visitors might have been pilgrims or travellers but in fact they were neither. It would soon have become apparent to anyone not forewarned that this was a cortège. Accompanying the coffin was a group of lords who kept a watchful, if respectful, eye on the youth who rode with them. The boy was their new king, the fifteen-year-old James Stewart, who had become the fourth monarch of that name two weeks earlier. His throne had been won in battle, on a field close to where the pivotal conflict at Bannockburn, which saw the English pushed back out of Scotland, was fought 150 years earlier.

But the victory, though clear in military terms, was clouded by doubt and suspicion. For James had rebelled against his own father and now came, or, perhaps more accurately, was being brought, to bury him within the walls of Cambuskenneth Abbey. Though James III would share the tomb of his wife, Margaret of Denmark, who had died two years earlier, the proceedings of that midsummer's day were not intended as a private family funeral. Rather, they were a reminder to the young king that he was complicit in his father's death and that the lords could, at that point, make or break him. The lesson was not lost on James IV. Yet even as his guilt mingled with grief, there was the inescapable fact that he was, indeed, king. The doubts about his future that had plagued him in recent times were finally laid to rest with the father whose love he had lost some years before.

⁂

JAMES ACQUIRED his crown almost as strangely as Henry Tudor did in England, though by a very different path. Scotland in the fifteenth century was not convulsed by periodic bouts of civil war, with rival claimants jockeying for the throne, as England had been. In fact, it proved a refuge for the Lancastrians during the 1460s, when the queen regent gave shelter to Henry VI and Margaret of Anjou after the defeat at Towton. The country had, though, known its share of troubles. Like James IV, his father and grandfather had come to the throne as minors, and in difficult circumstances, both after untimely deaths. Government continued to function, often quite successfully, yet there were inevitable clashes with overmighty nobles and a great deal of competition among the aristocracy for power and influence. Throughout the fifteenth century the great families – the Douglases, the Livingstons, the Humes, the Boyds, the Campbells, the Kennedys, the Hepburns and many others – vied for power and influence at court. The blood feud was a way of life, passed down from one generation to the next, and the Stewart kings themselves, who had occupied the throne for just over a century, were no strangers to violence. James I of Scotland was murdered by disaffected nobles and his bereaved English queen, Joan Beaufort, participated personally in the torture of his assassins. James II, a man with a temper to match the fiery red birthmark on his face, created over a century of ill feeling between the Crown and the Douglas family when he invited the recalcitrant earl William Douglas to a meeting at Stirling in 1452 and, piqued by his guest's refusal to toe the line, stabbed him to death. This king's subsequent demise when he stood too close to one of his own cannon and it exploded must have seemed like rough justice to the Douglases.

The throne passed once more to a child, the eight-year-old who became James III in 1460. But while there were tensions among the Scottish nobility, relations within the Stewart royal family itself were scarcely any better. James III seems to have disliked his own family intensely but not to have realized or cared that this might become a permanent disadvantage when trying to govern Scotland. Perhaps it was a product of his upbringing, personally supervised by his wealthy and sophisticated mother, Mary of Gueldres, the niece of the duke of Burgundy. Mary instilled in her son the importance of his position, a strong sense of his own superiority, and, in a departure from prevailing wisdom in Scotland, the notion that seeking peace with England might be a better policy than endless confrontation. She does not seem to have considered how such a change would be received by her son's subjects. Another aspect that the queen mother either overlooked, or could not adequately address, was how her son was to achieve harmonious, or at least cordial, dealings with his own family. James had three half-uncles, two younger brothers and two sisters, all of whom would play a part in his reign, and his relationships with every one of them would eventually break down.

Fully prepared to reign, but less well equipped for the human aspect of ruling, James III grew up a young man with a high opinion of himself. He did not like to be questioned. His self-confidence was shaken in the uncomfortable period between the death of his mother in 1463 and his own marriage six years later, when the Boyd family dominated court offices after humiliatingly kidnapping him as he hunted near Linlithgow in the summer of 1466. Such an experience, and the mistrust it bred, was not easily forgotten. But in 1469 he felt he could put it all behind him. At the age of seventeen, he married Princess Margaret of Denmark in Holyrood Abbey and took the reins of government into his own hands. Only in the most dramatic of circumstances would it prove possible to loosen his grip.

∽

THE NEW ROYAL COUPLE were pleasing in appearance. James was dark and rather severe, while his twelve-year-old bride was probably auburn-haired, with an oval face, slim figure, rather long nose and neat mouth. She is the first Scottish queen whose portrait survives. It may be somewhat stylized, but it gives an impression of a refined and interesting face. Since she was very young, time would be needed so that she could settle in to her new role and get to know Scotland, a country that now included domains previously ruled by her Danish father. Under the terms of the Treaty of Copenhagen of 1468, Margaret's dowry was set at 60,000 Rhenish florins, but the cash-strapped Christian I was obliged to pledge first Orkney and then Shetland as surety for down payments that were never actually realized, and so the Northern Isles passed to the control of Scotland. This extension of Scottish territory was a welcome boost for a king who later pursued grandiose, if rather vague, pretensions to developing a Scottish empire through invading Brittany and pursuing his claim to his mother's duchy of Gueldres. First and foremost, however, he needed heirs to bolster his own domestic position and after taking his young bride on a tour of northern Scotland twelve months after they were married, three more years were to pass before, in stark contrast with the unfortunate Margaret Beaufort in England, she was felt to have reached childbearing age. Then the Danish queen promptly did her duty and there was rejoicing when a son, Prince James, was born on 17 March 1473, at Stirling, one of the castles given to his mother on her marriage.

There are glimpses of the favour shown to Queen Margaret around this time in her wardrobe accounts. She lived well and dressed superbly, as befitted her role. A gown of crimson satin with a long train and a similar dress in damask were purchased, probably for the ceremonial opening of parliament in 1474. These garments would have been adorned by some of the queen's splendid collection of bejewelled gold belts. Round her neck and on the caps she wore on her head were the pearls that she seems to have loved; one string was made up of fifty-one pearls. Other jewellery included brooches and rings, often made out of gold, sapphires and rubies. The luxury extended to Margaret's outdoor pursuits. For riding and hunting, she had blue velvet saddles with gilded trimmings. And, in an age that had very different standards of personal hygiene from the modern world, Margaret ensured that when she did take baths in draughty Scottish palaces, the tub was well covered by broadcloth and that she herself could be wrapped in a large bath sheet. Nor had any expense been spared for the nursery of her firstborn son. The heir to the throne could look up at the silken canopy that covered his cradle and enjoy the comfort of linen shirts and lawn baby caps, with a white coat lined with miniver (squirrel fur) for colder days.[1]

Two more sons followed: a second James, known as the marquess of Ormonde, in 1476 and John, earl of Mar, in 1479. Margaret had proved an exemplary bearer of male heirs and a dutiful wife. In the first years of their marriage, little is known about the true feelings of the king and queen for each other but there are hints that the relationship became more remote as the years passed. The main evidence for this comes in a brief life of Margaret written after her death by the Italian Giovanni Sabadino and dedicated to the wife of the ruler of Bologna, whose son had been knighted by Christian of Denmark, Margaret's father. It is a curious document and, like many similar accounts of the period, is intended as much as hagiography as biography. In it we learn that Margaret 'was a woman of such lofty and wonderful virtue, chastity and prudence that she deserves to be ranked above all the women of that region in excellence of reputation; she brought to the world a beauty, a modesty and a prudence unequalled in their glory and splendour.' The writer goes on to praise the queen's religious devotion and generosity to the Church, her graciousness and her support to those in need. Open to all, she granted audiences freely and speedily and was a shrewd and scrupulous judge of what she heard. Yet while this may make Margaret sound almost too good to be true, and perhaps overemphasizes her success in the traditional intercessional role of queen consort, Sabadino soon reveals aspects of her relationship with her husband that must have caused tension. The veracity of at least some of his claims appears to be borne out by subsequent events. For it was the breakdown of his parents' marriage that played a major part in the development of Prince James.

Not only, it was claimed, was Margaret more popular than her husband with the Scottish people, 'since she possessed more aptitude than he for ruling the Kingdom', a circumstance that he, not unnaturally, resented, but she would only sleep with him in order to bear children: 'She was a woman of such chastity and modesty that it was understood she would have no relations with her husband except for the procreation of children.'[2] Yet though her Italian eulogist finds this an admirable, even holy restraint, it is quite possible that James III did not. We have no way of knowing the precise truth and this interest in the royal couple's sex life, though wrapped up in the language of holiness and virtue, seems strangely prurient, despite our own preoccupation with such things nowadays. What can, perhaps, be deduced from this picture of a competent and virtuous queen married to a man who was a poor leader and a grudging husband is that, as political problems in Scotland intensified, the king and queen drifted apart, she to bring up their children in Stirling Castle and he to deal with disaffection from his nobles and treason from within his own family, the Stewarts. By the year 1482, James III had more pressing concerns than the coldness that had crept into his marriage. A great crisis threatened to sweep him from the throne.

⚮

JAMES'S REMOTE STYLE of government and his Anglophile policy won him few friends. Reluctant to distribute patronage, reliant on parliament to raise money through extraordinary taxation and freely availing himself of money from forfeitures of land and casualty payments (revenues accruing to the Crown from the profits of justice), where remissions were being granted at a price and thus undermining the exercise of the law in Scotland, James ploughed on regardless. At home, he debased the coinage to help pay off debts and then hoarded bullion himself. Abroad, he abandoned the long-standing 'Auld Alliance' with France, Scotland's traditional ally against England, for a treaty of peace and a marriage alliance with England. The intention was for the infant Prince James, then only one year old, to marry Princess Cecily, the second daughter of Edward IV. By the late 1470s, at the time his own third son was born to his increasingly estranged queen, James III's unpopularity was deep-seated. He confined himself largely to Edinburgh, seldom travelling, careless of administering the law in the justice ayres, or travelling assizes, that were viewed as a key aspect of royal authority and visibility in Scotland. Perhaps he felt safe inside the massive walls of Edinburgh Castle, playing and listening to music with his group of favourites, most regarded with disdain as too low-born by his nobility. His distant style of government, his lack of interest in manly pursuits, even his indifferent horsemanship, were completely at odds with what most Scots, high or low, expected from their monarch. But at least his relations with his wife and sons still retained a semblance of normality. The same could hardly be said for his Stewart relatives. Here was animosity on a large scale that would breed the gravest of difficulties.

The story of James III's dealings with his half-uncles, his two brothers and two sisters (and, eventually, his eldest son) reads almost like a revenge tragedy by one of the Jacobean playwrights, though, of course, it took place much earlier. Determined to establish his authority in his own family as well as his kingdom, any affection that might, in previous years, have existed between the king and his sisters was long dead. Mary, his elder sister, had been tricked into returning to Scotland from the exile she had shared with the earl of Arran, her first husband, and forced to marry Lord Hamilton, a crony of James III. Margaret, the younger sister, was so appalled at the king's attempts to force her into marriage with Anthony Woodville, brother-in-law of the king of England, that she deliberately became pregnant by Lord Crichton. Meanwhile, the three half-uncles, the earls of Atholl and Buchan and the bishop-elect of Moray, were all discontented with James's policies and treatment and were by no means disposed to support him because he was of their blood. But James could live with the behaviour of his sisters, no matter how intensely they disliked him, and his uncles, though unreliable, did not present an immediate threat. The king's sights were set, instead, on his two brothers, Alexander, duke of Albany, and John, earl of Mar.

It was a signal disadvantage for a king like James III, utterly lacking in charisma, to have a younger brother who was amply possessed of all the qualities he so conspicuously lacked. His contemporaries saw the duke as a man of action and a true Scottish patriot. They drew the obvious conclusion that his energies and abilities made him a better prospect as king than the taciturn Anglophile currently occupying the throne in 1479. Five years earlier, he had not been on bad terms with James III, but the unpopular permanent alliance with England affected Albany and other Border lords directly, since it forbade their followers to raid into England. Such raiding was a way of life, encompassing family honour and affecting livelihoods, and its sudden cessation did not sit well with the duke of Albany and his neighbours. The Borders were a long-disputed area, full of romance and violence, and the passions that this beautiful country evoked could not be signed away in a treaty, no matter how beneficial peace might have been in the long run. There was much agreement with the anti-English sentiments expressed in the epic poem Blind Harry's *Wallace*, published in 1478, which told the tale of the Scottish patriot William Wallace. Wallace's hatred of the English struck a chord with the Scots:

> *Then Wallace said, 'O Southron! all man-sworn!*
> *For perfidy such rogues were never born;*
> *Their former treachery did we not feel?*
> *Eve'n when the truce was signed with their great seal'*[3]

From 1474 onwards, when the treaty with England was signed, Albany found that he had a cause and followers. He was plunged into conflict with his brother that grew worse over the next few years. It is no coincidence that Blind Harry's poem was written with the involvement of Albany's own steward, Sir James Liddale of Halkerston. Consistently favouring his own affinity, at odds with royal officials, one of whom he was accused of murdering, the final straw for Albany seems to have come early in 1478 when he was pressured into divorcing his first wife, probably to pave the way for an English marriage desired by the king. A year later, James III decided that only military might could bring the duke to heel. Albany was besieged in Dunbar Castle by the king's forces but managed to flee to France. James's failure to capture his brother was compounded by the refusal of a recalcitrant parliament to brand the duke a traitor and forfeit his estates.

Having achieved the worst of all possible outcomes and with his brother now a focus for discontent beyond his reach, with powerful backers, James turned his attention to his youngest brother, John, earl of Mar. The earl had spent most of the 1470s in the north, living in Aberdeen, where he defended the king's interests. In 1479 he came south to attend parliament but his attitude to the vicious dispute between his two elder brothers is not known. Evidently, it was not positive enough in its support of the king to assuage any fears James might have had about Mar's loyalty. At the beginning of 1480 he was under arrest and by the summer he was described as dead and forfeited. It seems unlikely that the death was a natural one and while lurid tales of his having been bled to death or drowned in a brewer's vat cannot be verified, contemporaries certainly believed that the king had ordered Mar's death. James paid for Masses to be said in St Andrews for his brother's soul, but this show of remorse did nothing for his reputation and the continued downward spiral of his popularity. Even the collapse of the English peace and renewal of Anglo–Scottish warfare could not salvage James III's position. Still, he managed to totter on for two more years, until, in the summer of 1482, the long-expected crisis broke. Its focus was the intractable rivalry between James and Albany but it would have the unanticipated outcome of irreparably damaging relations between the king, his wife and his eldest son.

∽

THOUGH HE HAD been welcomed in France and provided with a new, very rich wife (Anne de la Tour, daughter of the count of Auvergne), Alexander, duke of Albany, was aiming for the Crown of Scotland and he was prepared to forget his anti-English scruples if this helped him in his goal. It should be stressed that this was not just a flight of fancy on Albany's part; many Scots, including James III's unreliable half-uncles, preferred the duke. By June 1482 he had left France and gone to England, where he signed a treaty with Edward IV promising to do homage (an unwelcome reminder of the restraints so hated by William Wallace) and return Berwick and other lands in the

Borders in exchange for English support in his quest for the throne of Scotland. In July, accompanied by Richard, duke of Gloucester, and with twenty thousand men at his back, he entered Scotland to confront his brother. James himself, whatever his other deficiencies, was never one to give up meekly. Using the ancient Scottish feudal custom, he had summoned the Scottish host to meet him at Lauder in Berwickshire, there to confront the huge force coming up from England. But battle was never joined because, on 22 July 1482, the king was seized by a group of nobles led by his own half-uncle, the earl of Buchan, and the earl of Angus. Several of his closest favourites – men accused, as was traditional, of giving him bad counsel – were hanged over Lauder Bridge. James III himself was taken back to Edinburgh, where the great castle that had long been his chosen residence now became his prison. But his captors refused to give up their king while the English army remained on Scottish soil. By mid-August, Gloucester and his forces had left, allowing Albany himself to claim that he had helped avoid bloodshed and devastation. And while James III remained confined for his own good, Albany went to Stirling to discuss his brother's future, and that of the heir, Prince James, with Queen Margaret.

After the birth of her third son, the queen seems to have spent most of her time at Stirling, living in the impressively sited castle above the town. If she had not played a major role in Scottish politics before 1482, the events of that summer propelled her centre stage. Entrusted with the education and upbringing of Prince James (then known as the duke of Rothesay, the traditional title of the heir to the Scottish throne), in stark contrast to England, where queens consort played little part in the preparation of their sons for kingship, Margaret now found herself consulted by her brother-in-law and those who held her husband. How much she knew in advance of the plans to seize and hold James III cannot be stated with certainty but she was definitely involved from the moment the king returned, in captivity, to Edinburgh. For the preceding five years, the queen had held the custodianship of Edinburgh Castle, a position that allowed her to dispense patronage by nominating her choices for its staff. The keeper of the castle was Lord Darnley, grandfather of the second husband of Mary Queen of Scots. In 1482, the older Darnley acted as the king's jailer. He was, as has been pointed out, Margaret's man. So, too, was James Shaw of Sauchie, keeper of Stirling Castle, who would play a significant role in the final crisis of James III's reign six years later. During the king's detention, Shaw supplied food to the king's half-uncles in Edinburgh Castle. Though this lends credence to the view that the queen knew beforehand of the intention to incarcerate her husband, it does not mean that she wanted him overthrown, even if her eldest boy might become king in his place. In fact, she began to negotiate for James III's release, while discussing with Albany plans for the education and development of Prince James.

Albany sought out the queen and the prince in August or September of 1482 because he needed their support. His aim was to become lieutenant general of Scotland, either ruling for his hamstrung brother or for his young nephew. By now he had accepted that deposition of James III was not acceptable to the queen or the majority of Scots and that any hopes he might have entertained of ruling himself were lost. During his visit to Stirling, Margaret seems to have persuaded him that her husband must be released while being open to his taking some part in the education of Prince James. Well aware of the danger that continued instability posed, and perhaps genuinely concerned to limit the humiliation of her husband, she had to tread carefully in what was an unprecedented situation. The king languished under restraint, frightened that he might be assassinated at any moment, while his rebellious brother sought to influence his wife and eldest son on the future shape of the monarchy.

We do not know what passed between Margaret, Albany and Prince James. No record of their conversation survives and it would, in any case, have been unwise to commit anything to paper. When Albany went back to Edinburgh he rather ostentatiously besieged the castle, thereby securing the release of James III. He then placated the greedy and duplicitous half-uncles with lands and titles and proceeded to style himself lieutenant general of Scotland and earl of Mar, an unsubtle reminder of the mysterious fate of his younger brother. But he was not trusted by many of the nobility. His ambition seemed too vaunting and his involvement with England was hard to stomach. During the winter of 1482–3, as the struggle for power continued, some of the northern lords and the Scottish parliament swung away from Albany, remembering belatedly that their primary allegiance should be to the king. The death of Edward IV of England deprived Albany of a key supporter and for a couple of years, as the English struggled with their own dynastic crisis, James III was left to recoup his position. Not that his flamboyant brother was done quite yet, for the duke made several more attempts to impose himself on Scotland, one of which culminated in a daring escape from Edinburgh Castle, before he met what might be viewed as a fitting end, dying of wounds sustained while jousting in a Paris tournament in late 1485.

The events of 1482 brought home to the young Prince James, in a way that no formal education could have done, the harsh realities of late fifteenth-century Scottish politics. Suddenly thrust into the limelight, he knew how close he was to the throne. It was, though, a realization that was as uncomfortable as it was thrilling. Although he did not live in a bubble in Stirling, his days up until now had been predictable, passed under the guidance of his mother and the precepts of his tutors, with his two younger brothers for companionship and support. We do not know how often he saw his father but there is no reason to suppose that their relationship was in any way difficult before 1482. However, in that year the prince learned that the king had been imprisoned by his own relatives and had seen his mother acting as an arbiter in dealings with James III's captors and his uncle, a potential usurper. In front of this man who had brought an English army to humble his own father, James heard the queen discuss plans for his continuing education, listening as views on the best way to equip him for the throne were exchanged. For a nine-year-old, accustomed to seeing his mother as a gentle but firm shaper of his general behaviour and conduct, witnessing how she handled herself in a time of such crisis must have been a revelation. His own importance to Scotland had been vividly brought home to him. Yet the comforting certainties of childhood had gone, to be replaced by an altogether more complex existence. For though the prince could scarcely be held accountable for what had happened, James III could not forget that his eldest son had been sought out by a traitor and knew well that he had nearly lost his throne. What ambitions might have entered the boy's mind he did not know, but he suspected that they were there and that they would only increase with the passing years. The threat to his throne was contained for the time being but it had not truly gone away.

∽

GIVEN THE SERIOUSNESS of the crisis that had nearly engulfed him, a less stubborn man than James III might have re-examined his policies, sought to build reliable friendships among the leading men of Scotland and strengthened family relationships. Such was not James's way, however. Resentful and suspicious, he would not change. Encouraged by papal support and the improvement of relations with England that followed on the succession of Henry VII, he continued to assume that international success would keep him secure on the Scottish throne. It was later claimed by Margaret's Italian biographer that he never forgave his wife for her role in 1482: 'After his release, he reposed more hatred than previously in the Queen, because of her consent to his arrest; as a result he kept her at a distance of thirty miles ... He was unwilling ever to see her again, either in life or in death – a period of three years.'[4] There is no firm evidence to support this assertion, since Margaret's main residence had been at Stirling for some years. Details of James's itinerary for this period are lost, so we cannot be certain that he never saw his wife or sons again and his dislike of the queen, if such was indeed the case, did not extend to removing her children from her or lessening her influence on their upbringing. When Margaret died in July 1486, she was buried with full regal pomp at Cambuskenneth Abbey and her husband endowed daily Masses for her soul. It is unlikely that he did this merely for form's sake but her death left the king free to marry again, if he chose, and to give serious consideration to the future of his eldest son. And it is in the king's attitude towards Prince James at this time that a clearer picture of the tensions that had grown over four years begins to emerge.

The prince was thirteen years old at the time of his mother's death and her loss was hard to bear. She had raised him carefully, to be mindful of who he was but not puffed up with pride. 'By her wish, he carved at table and gave her water for her hands, although she had plenty of servants. She said she did this so that he might know how to command servants when he grew up.'[5] The deathbed exhortations to her eldest son are no doubt overdramatized, but they probably do express sentiments that she genuinely held:

> James, my eldest boy, I am speeding towards death; I pray you, through your obedience as my son, to love and fear God, always doing good, because nothing achieved by violence, be certain, can endure. Hold your brothers as dear to you as your own soul. When you succeed to your father's Kingdom, above all else love the people as yourself, with justice, mercy, generosity and affection. Be ready to hear them. Do not fear toil. Take care to keep your subjects united and to preserve the kingdom in peace and tranquillity. See that justice is not violated by greed, which vitiates glory ... be generous with moderation, as is the custom of wise Kings ... Finally, see that, as the sun is known by the clouds, you are too; as a King is different from the people in dress, so must he be in conduct and virtue.[6]

There is much in this little homily that seems like an implicit criticism of the boy's father. Prince James would soon learn that his father did not set much store by either the family or national unity that his mother valued so highly.

As heir to the throne, the prince might have expected his father to take a more personal interest and to include him in the life of the court, perhaps even allow him to attend council meetings and gain some direct experience of administration. But no such move was made. Young James remained at Stirling with his brothers, in isolation made more poignant without his mother, under the supervision of James Shaw. It was a quiet existence only occasionally enlivened by talk of a new potential marriage with a niece of Richard III. The battle of Bosworth put paid to such prospects and in the first years of Henry VII's reign the diplomatic negotiations for Scottish royal marriages revolved around James III himself, with Elizabeth Woodville, mother-in-law to the new king of England, as a potential bride for the Scottish king (an intriguing union indeed, but one that never took place) and the marquess of Ormonde, middle son of James III and Margaret of Denmark, who was proposed as the husband of another of Edward IV's daughters, Katherine. Prince James found himself sidelined, left out altogether from discussions in 1486 and linked only to an unspecified daughter of Edward IV the following year – a curious circumstance, since there were no further Yorkist princesses available by then. Possibly James III was considering a grander foreign match for his eldest son but it certainly looked as though the king was ignoring him, especially when the marquess of Ormonde was given the title of duke of Ross in January 1488 in preparation for the match with Princess Katherine. It was almost certainly no coincidence that within a month of his younger brother's elevation, Prince James, duke of Rothesay, slipped out of Stirling Castle without the king's permission, on 2 February 1488, to join a growing band of rebels who once again threatened his father's throne.

⚭

As INTRACTABLE and unpopular as ever, James III had some-how survived for six years after the Lauder Bridge crisis. He would not give up on the English alliance, causing consternation among the Border families, and he was also quite willing to renew long-standing disputes. The most important of these in 1487–8 was with the influential Hume family, who held the prosperous Benedictine priory of Coldingham on the south-east coast of Scotland. James had been trying since the 1470s to get his hands on Coldingham and its revenues, but the Humes resisted. Now, fortified by the award of the papal Golden Rose by Pope Innocent VIII, the king was determined to have his way. But the Humes, aided by their allies, the Hepburns, refused to back down. As the standoff continued, the king added to his list of enemies by dismissing his chancellor, the powerful earl of Argyll, and turned for help to the very men who had held him captive in 1482, his unreliable and deeply unpopular half-uncles. It evidently never crossed his mind that he might have done better to mend fences with his eldest son or even, on a more practical level, to ensure that he knew where the lad actually was. So scant was his interest in the prince that nearly three weeks elapsed before he found out that James was no longer in Stirling. Whether there were those around him in Edinburgh who knew but kept the information from him is impossible to say. James III had apparently been willing to promote the interests of his second son over those of his immediate heir but neither the king nor his advisers had taken the basic step of ensuring that there was a trustworthy keeper of the prince at Stirling. And James Shaw of Sauchie was certainly not that man. His daughter, Helen, had recently married into the Humes, the very family with which the king was now at loggerheads.

The discovery that Prince James was no longer under his control and had joined those opposing his rule was a serious blow to James III. Later chroniclers claimed that the prince had been coerced, but contemporaries did not speculate on his motives and we do not know what the king himself thought of this defection. For another month, he tried to maintain his position in Edinburgh, hoping that a new parliament summoned for early May 1488 would back him and enable him to re-establish his hold on government. Time, however, was not on his side. Mistrust grew and Prince James remained at large – probably at Linlithgow, though his movements between early February and May 1488 are unclear. By the end of March 1488, James III had gathered sufficient money for the fight that now seemed inevitable. Remaining in the capital was too risky, given that the rebels' strength was in the south of Scotland. James had learned at least one significant lesson from the Lauder crisis of 1482 and that was to evade his enemies so that when the confrontation came, it could be on his terms as far as possible. So he left Edinburgh on 24 March for the north of Scotland, where loyalty to the king was more certain and where he could hope to gather military support from among the northern lords. He reached Aberdeen by 6 April and that city became the headquarters for his fight to remain on the throne of Scotland.

Safely out of the reach of the rebels for the time being, the king sought help from Henry VII in England and Charles VIII in France. Both monarchs had a keen interest in Scottish affairs and James's appeal to them, though obviously dictated by circum-stances, is a reminder that it is all too easy to lose sight of the international dimension of events in the British Isles in the late fifteenth century. James III's difficulties were not simply the product of obscure and convoluted rivalries within the kingdom of Scotland itself or the obduracy of a man who could not connect with his subjects. The king's ambition was to make his country greater in a European context and though his method of achieving such success went against the grain of a deep-seated anti-English sentiment in Scotland, as a goal it was shared by his son and grandson. In 1488, though, James III's requests for assistance were not met, mainly because the rulers of both France and England had difficulties of their own.

While the king looked to retain control of the kingdom, the rebels' resolve intensified. Though the situation remained fluid, they established a solid presence in the south of Scotland, where their leaders, the Douglases, the Hepburns and the Humes, were strong. Soon their numbers were swelled by significant defections from the royalist side: Argyll himself and the bishop of Glasgow, Robert Blacader, a man with a grievance against the premier cleric of Scotland, Archbishop Scheves of St Andrews, whose lowly birth and unswerving support of the king made him unpopular. Though diverse as a group and no doubt harbouring a range of individual resentments against their monarch, the rebels presented an increasingly formidable opposition. They were men of substance and experience who knew how to operate on the wider political scene. They, too, made overtures to England for support and began a propaganda campaign against James III, depicting him as the victim of evil counsellors and, more seriously, accusing him of arranging the death of Queen Margaret by poison. There was no truth in this accusation, but the death of his wife at just thirty years old and their separation towards the end of their marriage left the king exposed to such charges in a credulous age. Certainly, the stories were believed in Denmark, where they caused great indignation. Whether Prince James placed any credence in them is impossible to say, but his silence on the matter and his subsequent actions suggest that he did not. What is much more certain is that the prince's continued involvement with the rebels greatly strengthened their position.

Prince James passed his fifteenth birthday in March 1488. His furtive departure from Stirling Castle the previous month may well have been the response of a peeved and anxious adolescent to his father's apparent animosity but it was, whatever his intentions, a decisive action and one that could not be undone. The flight and his association with rebels put him on a collision course with his father, a man who, in the words of historian Norman Macdougall, 'not only had all the prestige of Stewart kingship on his side, but who, in spite of his arbitrary and illegal acts, could still muster armed support within Scotland, who had the friendship of Henry VII and the blessing of the pope.'[7] These latter advantages turned out, of course, to be hollow, but the rebellious prince would not have known that at the time. Deprived of any real training in politics or government, young James had to learn fast. His commitment to the rebels' cause seems to have hardened the longer he stayed with them. It was a mutual dependency, for much as he might personally have longed for a reconciliation with his father, the prince and his supporters had every reason not to trust the king. The prince may have been a figurehead in February 1488. By May, he was as committed to challenging his father as the king was to holding on to the throne by any means. It seemed increasingly unlikely that the dispute could be settled by anything other than military confrontation.

Yet with the underlying misgiving about taking up arms against an anointed king that was felt by most opponents of an incumbent monarch in those days, the rebels did try to reach a negotiated settlement. It was James III, in a response that would be echoed by Henry VIII in his dealings with the Pilgrimage of Grace in 1536 and Charles I in the seventeenth century, who made a mockery of such efforts. The king had no scruples about breaking his word; he would sign anything if it bought him time. But as most of his northern supporters preferred the peaceful solution of a negotiated settlement, James III did put his signature to the nine Aberdeen Articles proposed by the rebels in late April or early May 1488. Though vague (probably deliberately) in specifics, the articles addressed the key issues that underlay the dispute between the monarch and his opponents: the welfare of the king and that of his errant son, and the divisions among the nobility. Those appertaining to the prince are especially interesting for what they reveal of the distance that had grown between young James and his father. The indirect reprimand for the king's neglect of his son is all too apparent: 'the king's highness shall give honourable sustentacion and living to my lord prince his son.' No longer was the training of the heir to the throne to be neglected: 'wise lords and honourable persons of wisdom and discretion' were to be the prince's mentors 'for the good governance of his person in his tender age', and a major point for further discussion was how to improve the relationship between father and son: 'how my lord prince shall at all times to come be obedient to his father the king and how that fatherly love and tenderness shall at all times be had betwixt them.'[8]

While such paternal emotions may have been in short supply, it had by the spring of 1488 become apparent even to as remote a man as James III that he could not solve the crisis without gaining control of his son. Encouraged by his half-uncle Buchan, one of the rebels' most hard-line enemies, James III decided to break the Aberdeen Articles almost immediately. Now was the moment to move south and seek a decisive outcome to a dispute which had festered throughout the previous autumn and winter. Better weather made campaigning easier and the king may also have felt that he had been absent from Edinburgh and the royal jewel house in the castle, in which much of his ready wealth reposed, for long enough. Moreover, he was hopeful that the overtures of the delegation he had sent to London requesting English military intervention might meet a positive response. Indeed, this must have been a crucial element in his decision to leave the north of Scotland. James III's cavalier attitude towards the Aberdeen Articles alienated much of his local support, as the northern earls went back to their estates.

It is probable that the king anticipated English military reinforcements landing near Blackness Castle on the Firth of Forth. The castle's keeper was loyal and it would have been a convenient base for military operations against the rebels, whose main force was probably somewhat to the west, around Linlithgow. But James III's optimism was misplaced. There were no English troops waiting to support his own army, nor would there be. Once more, the king was compelled to temporize with the rebels, who quickly appeared at the gates of the castle.[9] There may have been discussions about renewing a negotiated settlement, but James decided not to wait around and put himself in jeopardy while these took place. Leaving his uncle Buchan and three other prominent men as hostages, he fled by ship across the Forth to Leith and thence to Edinburgh Castle. He was there by 16 May and immediately began preparations to take the fight to the rebels in southern Scotland. He needed to be sure that he could pay an army and there was plenty of money to go around. Boxes of money containing gold coin and jewels were distributed to royalist supporters and considerable amounts were actually taken out with the king's forces when they left Edinburgh. A box containing £4,000 in gold coins was later discovered 'when it was in the mire' by three local men in a field near Stirling.

King James did not stay long in Edinburgh. Early in June 1488, having learned that his son had returned to Stirling Castle and was styling himself 'Prince of Scotland', a clear challenge to royal authority, he left the capital. He may have hoped for northern support still, despite his behaviour in Aberdeen, and also to take advantage of the fact that the rebel forces were not all gathered in one place. Some remained at Linlithgow, uncomfortably close to Edinburgh, and the king and his advisers were not keen to engage them. Keeping to the north bank of the river Forth, the king intended to attack Stirling from the east. The campaign went well at first, when the royal forces inflicted huge damage on the estates of one of the prince's supporters and, more importantly, put the prince and his rebels to flight in a skirmish near Stirling Bridge. This left the king in control of the town of Stirling but not yet of Prince James himself.

This first direct taste of fighting must have been a disconcerting one for the prince. Having issued forth from the stronghold of Stirling Castle itself, he found himself fleeing towards Falkirk. But it was no victory for James III. Once more, his son had evaded him and the prince's escape would prove to be nearly the last act in the fraught relationship with his father. For as he fled south, Prince James and his supporters encountered the other part of the rebel host coming up to join them. Their numbers now certainly matched, if not exceeded, that of the royal army. On 11 June, the two armies clashed close to the site of the battle of Bannockburn, at what was, for a century and a half afterwards, known simply as 'the field of Stirling'. Now referred to as the battle of Sauchieburn, it is perhaps one of the least-known battles in British history, though one that shook Scotland greatly at the time. For, in the laconic words of the parliamentary record, 'our sovereign lord's father happened to be slain.'[10]

Exactly how James III met his end will never be known. If there was anyone at the time who knew the truth of it, they kept silent, and with good reason. Prince James had given strict instructions that his father must not be harmed in any way and it would have been a foolish man who admitted being the murderer of James III. Well after the event conspiracy theories abounded but while the sixteenth-century chroniclers no doubt drew on oral accounts, the only written record that the battle even took place is the brief reference in the proceedings of the parliament of October 1488, some four months later. The chroniclers, notably Robert Lindsay of Pitscottie, produced a much more dramatic and sinister version of events, full of superstitious echoes of the story of Macbeth. According to Pitscottie, James III found himself facing an army of about eighteen thousand men. This sight, and the memory of a prophecy recently made by a witch, unnerved him and brought about his flight and death: 'So the king, seeing his own enemies to come with his own banner displayed and his son against him, he remembered the words which the witch had spoken to him many days before, that he should be suddenly destroyed and put down by the nearest of his kin.' Unnerved by this earlier encounter with the supernatural, the king 'took such a vain suspicion in his own mind that he took hastily purpose to flee.' But James's flight was brutally halted when he was unhorsed 'before the mill door of Bannockburn and so was bruised with the fall, being heavy in armour, that he fell in a deadly swoon.' Helped inside the mill by the miller and his wife, who did not know who he was, the injured king asked for a priest to make his confession, saying 'this day at morn I was your king'. As in the best murder stories, the priest who eventually came to shrive the monarch was an impostor. In reality, he was a servant of Lord Gray, one of the rebels, and he stabbed the king to death.[11]

This account, particularly the details of the king's murder by a false priest, is almost certainly fanciful, though it may contain elements of a broader truth. The likelihood is that the royal and rebel forces engaged in combat in open fields near to the confluence of the two watercourses known as Bannockburn and Sauchieburn but the precise location cannot be pinpointed with certainty.[12] Indeed, as the fighting unfolded, various skirmishes and pursuits probably took place and may have spread over a wider area. The king himself was eager for a decisive confrontation and went into battle carrying Robert the Bruce's sword. Both the ground he chose for the fight, so close to Bannockburn, and the weapon he carried would have had strong emotional and symbolic associations for James III. No doubt he hoped to inspire his followers to fight valiantly and bring to an end the long-festering dispute with the rebels that had engulfed his son. What his intentions were for Prince James, should the royalists be victorious and the prince himself survive the fray, we shall never know. There is nothing to suggest that his previous attitude had shifted. But the day did not go as James III had expected and at some point while the fighting still raged the king, realizing that his own safety was compromised if he stayed, made the decision to leave the field. It is very unlikely that he retreated alone, so Pitscottie's story of an abandoned and injured monarch dying at the point of the assassin's dagger does not ring true. It is, though, much more plausible that James III and a small group of attendants were involved in further skirmishing somewhere close to Bannockburn mill and that the king was killed by persons unknown. Neither the money he had been carrying (almost a third of his annual income) nor Bruce's sword could save him in the end. Like Richard III in England three years earlier, he had been determined to repel a rebel force and had lost his throne and his life.

The Stewart dynasty, however, remained. Despite initial confusion over the whereabouts and identification of James III's body, his son clearly knew that he was dead. On 12 June, the day after the battle, King James IV issued the first charter of his reign. It nominated to the office of clerk register William

Hepburn, a member of a family that would rise steadily over several generations. Like the Humes, the Douglases and other southern Scottish lords, the Hepburns had helped put James IV on the throne. He was barely more than half the age that Henry Tudor had been at Bosworth and, though raised as a prince, for all but the previous eighteen weeks his experience of life outside Stirling Castle was very limited. At fifteen, he was still growing physically and developing intellectually. There are no portraits of the king to tell us what he looked like in his mid-teens but he had already exhibited the bravery and risk-taking that was to characterize his life. He developed into a well-built man of no more than average height but it is his face that is so striking in later pictures. The keenly intelligent eyes and confident gaze show a man who was curious and questioning, good humoured and regal without being unapproachable. Charming and affable, his restlessness found an outlet in the standard outdoor pursuits of kings. In one portrait he holds a falcon, an indication of his love of hunting.

But in 1488, in the first, uncertain days of his reign, the young James IV could not yet spread his wings. The manner of his accession, the fact that his instructions not to harm James III had been ignored, clearly sat uneasily on his conscience. Later he would wear an iron belt around his waist in penitence, adding weight to it every year. But however troubled he was by his own role in the fate of his father, there was no disputing the fact that the Crown of Scotland was his. It was an outcome he had sought quite deliberately and now he would have to live with the consequences. Alone and ill-prepared, James IV had much to learn.

Part Two

✌

The Road to Flodden Field

1488–1513

CHAPTER THREE

Uneasy Crowns

'He was a wise man and an excellent king; and yet the times were rough, and full of mutations and rare accidents.'

Francis Bacon

'Our king hath not hitherto busied himself with state affairs but hath now arrived at a becoming age.'

The Scottish ambassadors to the emperor Maximilian, June 1495

FOR BOTH THE FIRST TUDOR and the fourth James Stewart, gaining the throne was one thing. Keeping it was quite another. Sixteen years separated them in age, and a gulf in experience, but certain key aspects they had in common. Both were highly intelligent, neither had any experience of government and they were equally determined, whatever difficulties might lie in their paths, to hold on to their crowns. In the British Isles of the late fifteenth century this inevitably meant that their domestic security would be critically affected by their own relationship. Scotland and England were neighbours but they had long been hostile ones and that hostility, particularly on the border of the two countries, was deep-seated. It could not be suddenly changed, especially when emotive issues such as family honour and long-standing blood feuds were involved. Henry VII, however, did not share the prejudices of many of his countrymen towards the

Scots. His exile had made him remote from such xenophobia and he had, of course, good reason to be grateful to the Scots who had fought alongside him at Bosworth.[1] As king, he would work painstakingly towards a lasting Scottish peace from the beginning of his reign but his commitment was not always shared by his younger rival in Edinburgh. There were distractions aplenty for both monarchs. And the times were, indeed, rough, as the next few years would amply demonstrate.

As he journeyed south towards London, Henry Tudor passed through a landscape unfamiliar to him, at best, perhaps, half-remembered from his youth, on the rare occasions he had left Wales. He and his new kingdom were strangers to each other. What he saw must, though, have pleased him, as it did outsiders, often somewhat to their surprise. The Wars of the Roses had devastated the English nobility but not the physical face of the country itself. It remained, in the words of a contemporary Venetian visitor, characterized by its 'pleasant, undulating hills and beautiful valleys, nothing to be seen but agreeable woods, or extensive meadows, or lands in cultivation; and the greatest plenty of water springing everywhere.'[2] He was less complimentary about the people, noting their 'antipathy to foreigners', their coldness and mistrust of each other, and deploring the way they treated their children, who, regardless of their social standing, were sent away from home, sometimes as young as the age of seven, either to be apprenticed or to 'learn better manners' in another household. Aghast at this callous disregard for the welfare of the young, the writer concluded that 'they do it because they like to enjoy all their comforts themselves.' The English were a good-looking people with a high opinion of themselves and their country, being 'for the most part, both men and women of all ages, handsome and well proportioned' (though he went on to say that he had heard that the Scots were much handsomer) and 'great lovers of themselves and everything belonging to them; they think that there are no other men than themselves, and no other world but England.'[3] Their love of fashion and finery was legendary.

It was noted, however, that the country appeared to be thinly populated in comparison to its evident fertility and riches. This was true enough, for England had still not recovered its population level from the disasters of the Black Death nearly 150 years earlier. Further epidemics and economic difficulties in the fifteenth century had kept the population down and late marriage reinforced this trend. Henry VII's realm contained fewer than three million souls and few towns of more than 10,000 people. London, at about 50,000, was by far the largest urban centre, but it was not a major European city; thirteen others, headed by Paris at 225,000 and including all the large Italian cities, were bigger. The rise of commerce and trade that would characterize northern Europe in the next two hundred years was not yet apparent.[4] But London impressed those who approached it from across the river Thames, with its vista of church spires and its vibrant atmosphere. It was also, of course, a violent and unpredictable place in 1485, where muggings and tavern brawls were commonplace and life was easily departed. The immodest but immaculately dressed Englishman was ever quick to take offence. And it was to this prosperous but unruly capital that Henry Tudor now hastened.

Henry's immediate priority after Bosworth was to establish himself as king. This was much more of a challenge than it appears with hindsight. We know that Henry was ultimately successful but the day after his victory on the fields of Leicestershire this comforting assurance would not have come so readily to the man himself. No adult king of England since the Norman Conquest had come to the throne in such unlikely circumstances, almost completely without immediate family or so utterly lacking in formal preparation for the task ahead. But training and education are nothing if the individual concerned lacks the basic qualities or intellect to turn them to positive advantage, as the sad figure of Henry VI had shown, and the new king of England was no green boy. The long years of exile in Brittany, impoverished and insecure, had taught him much. His immediate strategy was clear. To bring home the reality of his victory he decided to date his reign from 21 August, thus making all those who had opposed him at Bosworth traitors in the eyes of the law. Yet he was quick to make it clear that the rule of law itself had been properly restored and resided in him, issuing a proclamation protecting the property of returning troops after the battle, commanding that 'no manner of man rob or spoil no manner of commons coming from the field; but suffer them to pass home to their countries and dwelling places, with their horse and harness.'[5]

These preliminary but vital aspects of his reign accomplished, Henry then made for London as quickly as possible to secure the capital, get himself crowned in Westminster Abbey and call a parliament. Once he had underlined the sacred and secular aspects of his rule, he could set about governing, showing himself to the people in the north where there remained a strong groundswell of support for the defeated Richard. There were a great many men of dubious loyalty watching him attentively in these first weeks and months. He would need to choose his advisers carefully, since he could not ignore the fact that the men with the most experience of government had all served the previous Yorkist regimes. A complete replacement of the old order with a trained and reliable staff of his own was impossible – such men did not exist. And, finally, he needed to establish his dynasty and, hopefully, quell the fears of the Yorkist faithful by making good on his promise of Christmas Day 1483 and marrying Elizabeth of York. For the moment, however, that would have to wait.

According to the *Great Chronicle of London* Henry wasted little time in getting to the capital, arriving in the vicinity on 27 August, only five days after Bosworth. His formal entry, however, was not until a week later, on 3 September, by which time presumably the appropriate arrangements for all the ceremonial that accompanied these occasions had been made.[6] Certainly the City of London turned out in force to greet their new king:

> When he approached near the city, the Mayor, the Senate and the magistrates of the same, being all clothed in violet,

met him at Shoreditch and not only saluted and welcomed him with one voice in general, but every person particularly pressed and advanced himself, gladly to touch and kiss that victorious hand which had overcome so monstrous and cruel a tyrant, giving lauds and praisings to almighty God . . . and with great pomp and triumph he rode through the city to the cathedral church of St Paul, where he offered his three standards. In the one was the image of St George, in the second was a red fiery dragon beaten upon white and green sarcenet [a fine silk fabric] and the third was of yellow tarterne [another silk fabric, originally from China] in the which was painted a dun cow.

Offering up to God his victorious standards in this way reinforced the single most important aspect of Henry Tudor's claim to the English throne. It was won in battle, with God's help. This was incontrovertibly true, and presented a stronger claim than the dubious Beaufort line of his mother. God had given him the victory and no man – or woman – could gainsay that.

In these first public acts of his reign we see the Henry VII who had a natural instinct and a flair for performance and show that would characterize all the Tudors. No doubt he had observed and learned much from the courts of Brittany and France but his own love of spectacle was asserted at the very start of his rule. It might be argued that an appreciation of ceremonial was a prerequisite of successful kingship at the time (James IV and the Stewarts practised it, too) but it was remarkable in a man who did not know the English court and customs at all and whose life had been spent largely in hiding rather than as the centre of public display.

∽

THE NEXT STEP in Henry's well-orchestrated debut as king of England was his coronation. This took place on Sunday 30 October 1485 in Westminster Abbey. A considerable body of surviving documentation reveals that this was intended to be a memorable spectacle on a lavish scale. The total outlay for furnishings, decorations and clothing for all those involved, from the king to his footmen and horses, was just over £1,500, or £7.4 million today, a staggering sum for the anointing of a man who had been compelled to raise his own loans to finance his invasion of England just a few months earlier.

The formal ceremonies surrounding the coronation took place over several days, starting on 27 October when Henry dined at Lambeth with the archbishop of Canterbury. After the meal, the king and his entourage rode on towards the city, 'riding after the guise of France with all other of his nobility upon small hackneys [ambling horses for leisure riding], two and two upon an horse.'[7] At London Bridge, the mayor and other city dignitaries, including representatives of the guilds, met him and he then rode on to the Tower of London.

Popular history has given the Tower a sinister reputation, associated as it is with imprisonment, execution and mysterious deaths, so it is easy to forget that it was also a great palace and would have been the natural residence for the new king before his coronation. Within its more luxurious accommodation the next day, Henry bestowed pre-coronation honours on the men who had brought him to the throne. His faithful uncle, Jasper Tudor, already restored to the earldom of Pembroke, was created duke of Bedford and Henry's stepfather, Lord Stanley, whose intervention at Bosworth had spelled the end for Richard III, was made earl of Derby. Bishop Morton would have to wait a little longer for the preferment he so richly deserved. Two key posts came to him in 1486, first the lord chancellorship in February and then the archbishopric of Canterbury in the autumn. This politically astute churchman, a capable administrator of gentry stock, was to remain the closest and most valued of all Henry's counsellors until his death in 1500.

Henry's journey from the Tower to Westminster Hall prior to the coronation was intended to impress. The entourage was arranged in an order set out 'according to a book made by the order of the king's council' – perhaps a reference to the document known as *A little devise of the coronacion of . . . Prince Henrie the vij*, which was itself based on the fourteenth-century order for English coronations, the *Liber Regalis*. The ceremonial importance of these great occasions of state was too important to be left to chance and the weight of historical procedures was needed to emphasize the continuity of kingship, especially as there might be scepticism about Henry's claim to the throne and how long he might survive on it. For the procession was all about the king himself, who was at its very heart. Henry rode bare headed, as protocol decreed, but his attire was striking: 'He was arrayed in a long gown of purple velvet furred with ermines and wore a rich baldric [a decorated belt worn pendent from one shoulder across the breast and under the opposite arm]; the trapper of his horse was of cloth of gold and similarly trimmed with ermine.'[8] At Westminster, Henry was greeted with a collation of spices and wine and then went off to his own chambers to bathe, as was the custom.

For the coronation itself the next day, no expense had been spared. The abbey and the hall at Westminster blazed with scarlet cloth (sourced from six different suppliers) and the king was resplendent in a variety of richly decorated and furred robes, as well as jackets and gowns, changing them for the different stages of the ceremonial. There was a dazzling display of red, blue and white cloth of gold, rich velvets in russet and crimson and satins in similar hues. The precise form of the coronation seems to have followed closely that of Richard III (presumably because of the dictates of time rather than any admiration for the forms used by the detested previous monarch), indicating that the *Little Devise* was a Yorkist manual originally. But in one important aspect, Henry did not follow the earlier script. Richard's coronation ceremony had been adapted to allow for the crowning of a queen alongside the king and he and his wife, Anne Neville, had duly been crowned together. Henry Tudor, having, as yet, no consort, was crowned alone. There were also other more subtle differences, some of them with political overtones. The key roles were performed by those closest to the new king: his uncle carried the crown in front of him, his stepfather held the sword of state and the earl of Oxford carried his train. Though Thomas Bourchier, archbishop of Canterbury, performed the religious heart of the coronation, the anointing and crowning itself, at eighty he was deemed to old to handle the entire proceedings and was therefore assisted by the bishops of Exeter and London.

The lavish coronation feast that followed had its own ceremonial, including the customary challenge issued on horseback by the King's Champion, Sir Robert Dymmock, mounted on a charger trapped with the arms of the Welsh hero, Cadwallader. Clearly, Henry wanted to make a point about his Welsh roots. In all respects, though, this demanding and emotional day (Margaret Beaufort was said to have wept copiously as her son was crowned) went without a hitch and the king's confidence was boosted by its success. The next priority for the newly crowned king was the opening of his first parliament.

This took place on Monday, 7 November 1485, amid the ritual and pomp that was part of its historical tradition.[9] Wearing their parliamentary robes, Henry and the peers of England left Westminster Palace between nine and ten in the morning and walked in procession to the abbey. Here, Mass was celebrated and the king made an offering. Meanwhile, Henry's stepfather, the newly created earl of Derby, supervised the roll call and swearing-in of members of parliament back in the palace. When this was over, everything was ready for the full parliament to convene, probably in the Painted Chamber in the south of the palace.[10]

Proceedings began with a sermon from the chancellor, Bishop Alcock of Worcester, a Yorkist who had swiftly accommodated to the change of regime. His text encapsulated Henry Tudor's life and aims: 'Strive to prosper, go forth and triumph.' Drawing on biblical and classical sources that would have resonated with his audience, the bishop's aim was to establish Henry as the deliverer from discord and the provider of peace and prosperity. When he had finished, the assembly joined in prayer.

When the newly elected Speaker of the Commons was presented to Henry on 9 November, the king made his first speech to parliament. Unsurprisingly, it dealt with a vital but sensitive issue – his own claim to the throne.

The speech itself is not recorded, but is briefly described in the parliamentary roll. Henry asserted the justness of his title and God's supportive judgement by giving him victory in battle. We do not know how much farther he went in developing arguments based on his own Lancastrian lineage but as this was a much more contentious area than the incontrovertible argument of military success combined with divine approbation, as shrewd a man as Henry Tudor would probably not have relied too heavily on his Beaufort descent, no matter how much he loved his mother. Nor can we be certain what language the king used for these first public utterances. He would surely have wished to speak in English if he could but it is possible that Henry was not yet confident enough in a language that he had scarcely used for years, and spoke in Latin, or even in the French that came more easily to him.

So a short bill was introduced declaring the king's title without any explanation, together with another intended to remove any taint from the legitimacy of Henry's future wife, Elizabeth of York. This legislation nullified Richard III's bastardization of the children of his brother, Edward IV, in 1484 and paved the way for another carefully planned piece of political theatre. For when parliament was prorogued on 10 December, the Commons requested that Henry should marry 'that illustrious lady Elizabeth, daughter of King Edward IV', thus enabling 'the propagation of offspring from the stock of kings'. If this was a veiled reference to the lack of such pedigree in his own bloodline, Henry does not seem to have taken it badly. The king assented personally and preparations for the wedding were put in place. The couple were eventually married on 18 January 1486 in Westminster Abbey by the aged Archbishop Bourchier, almost five months after Henry's victory at Bosworth. Some might have wondered why this dynastically imperative union had taken so long but Henry's bride had seen a lot of life in her twenty years. She was used to waiting.

∽

CIRCUMSTANCES HAD made Elizabeth adaptable, if not always patient. She knew that power was dearly bought and easily lost. The spectacle of the court she had witnessed as both princess and bastard, her privileged existence punctuated by the uncertainty of sanctuary in the far less sumptuous surroundings of Westminster Abbey, not once, but twice, had brought home to her the unpredictability of life. Her uncle seized the throne in 1483, declaring that the marriage of her parents was invalid because of her father's pre-contract with another lady. At a stroke, Elizabeth and her siblings found that they were illegitimate, their place in the succession vanished, their status unclear, replaced by an uncertain, dangerous future. Although the former princess returned to court at Christmas the following year and even wore fine clothing that matched that of Richard's queen, a sign of favour, she knew that Henry Tudor had vowed to make her his wife. To counter this, Richard III undertook to find an honourable marriage for his niece, to a 'gentleman born', but this was a far cry from the promise of becoming queen of France that had been Elizabeth's in 1475. A husband was duly supplied for her younger sister, Cecily, but no match was forthcoming for Elizabeth. Her increasing frustration about her situation may explain a letter she wrote to the duke of Norfolk early in 1485. A précis of this document, itself surviving only in fragmentary form, has been the subject of considerable speculation about whether Elizabeth would have been willing – indeed, eager – to marry her uncle himself.[11]

Anne Neville, Richard's wife, became seriously ill in the first months of 1485 and died in March, leaving the king a childless widower. We know that Elizabeth's name as a possible replacement was considered because the king was compelled to make a public disavowal of such an intention: 'in the presence of the Mayor and citizens of London and in a clear, loud voice [King

Richard] carried out fully the advice to make a denial ... as many people believed, more by the will of his counsellors than by his own.' Later, Polydore Virgil would state that Elizabeth had 'a singular aversion' to such a marriage and this became, of course, the official Tudor explanation of what might otherwise have lingered as a stain on Elizabeth's character. All that can be said with certainty is that the surviving fragment indicates that she wanted Norfolk to be a mediator on her part to the king, for a cause that is unknown. Her appeal may well have been to speed up the process of finding a husband, rather than an attempt to push her own candidature as Richard's wife. She was a young woman in limbo, whose concerns are entirely understandable. And the fate of her two younger brothers remained a mystery, a sadness that hung over her but could not be spoken of publicly. Nevertheless, the prevailing image of Elizabeth of York as a sweet and tractable lady of no real character is given the lie by this episode, whatever its actual truth. She could speak up for herself and was not without ambition. The day that she became Henry Tudor's wife and queen of England was no small triumph for the eldest child of Edward IV and Elizabeth Woodville.

We cannot be certain where Elizabeth was living at the time of Bosworth. After the battle, Henry sent for her to come to London, where she was placed in the household of his mother.[12] Here, Henry met his intended bride for the first time. Although it was perfectly normal in those days for royal matches to take place without either party knowing the other at all, the age of chivalry was not entirely dead and the notion that Henry wanted time to pay court to Elizabeth, though dismissed by some historians, is not mere whimsy but fits in with what we know of their subsequent relationship. Both Henry and Elizabeth had known anxiety and heartache and the success of their union would be key to the survival of the new dynasty. No doubt there were wider political considerations, the desire not to appear dependent on his wife's claim to the throne being paramount among these, but Henry also wanted to establish his personal life on a sound footing. Bacon's assertion that the king was cold towards his wife and always mistrusted her Yorkist ancestry has no foundation. Though he loved his mother deeply, he scarcely knew her, either, after so many years of separation, and the placing of Elizabeth in her care enabled him to spend time with both of them.

Margaret Beaufort had been provided with a fine house in London called Coldharbour, overlooking the Thames. It required a number of hasty renovations before the king's mother could move in, probably shortly before the coronation in October. A suite of rooms was specially prepared for Elizabeth and accommodation was also provided for two young boys with their own claims to the throne – Edward, earl of Warwick (son of Edward IV's wayward brother, the duke of Clarence) and another Edward, the duke of Buckingham, descended from Edward III. The two children became Margaret's wards, though in some respects she was closer to being their jailer.

For Elizabeth, the return to London was no doubt welcome, for at last she could meet the man who would become her husband. Although the dictates of politics had brought them together, they made an attractive couple, Henry with his European air, his charm and conversational skills and Elizabeth with her family's acclaimed good looks. At a time when it was customary for poets to fête all royal ladies with elaborate references to their beauty, Elizabeth's physical endowments do seem to have been genuine. She was tall and fair, slender in those days, before frequent childbearing coarsened her figure and features. Like Henry, she spoke French but her Latin was limited – de Puebla, the Spanish ambassador to Henry's court in the 1490s, would later say that neither the queen nor her mother-in-law could converse in Latin, a defect not uncommon in well-born ladies of the time who had perhaps learnt the rudiments of Latin grammar and could follow certain religious rituals and books in the language but were not confident enough to speak or write it.

His future wife's lack of proficiency in the Latin tongue

would probably not much have bothered Henry Tudor. Everything about Elizabeth showed that she had been raised as a royal consort. Well possessed of the courtly skills, she was a fine dancer and loved music and singing, playing the clavichord herself and keeping her own minstrels when she became queen. Other indoor interests, typical of high-born women of her time, were sewing, embroidery and gambling; playing at cards was a major pastime in the lives of both the English and Scottish aristocracy. In her outdoor pursuits, Elizabeth was also a typical noblewoman of the period, competent on horseback, enjoying archery, watching jousts and hunting. As a girl, she and her sister Cecily had read historical romances for pleasure, their horizons no doubt widened by studying the testament of Sultan Nichemedy, emperor of the Turks. So it was a well-rounded, gracious but far from naïve young woman that Henry VII found at his mother's pleasant riverside retreat in the autumn of 1485. They must both have believed that they could put the past behind them and embrace their future with mutual affection and hope.

No descriptions of the marriage ceremony survive and, even if they had, contemporary commentators seldom wrote about bridal gowns in detail, as is the custom today. We have no idea what Elizabeth wore for her wedding day, though indirect evidence from the accounts suggests that an impressive gold wedding ring was provided. As to popular reaction, Henry's personal historian, the Frenchman Bernard André, claimed that there was much rejoicing. This seems plausible – after all, the occasion was one of happiness and optimism – but coming in the dead of winter, the opportunity for extensive carousing in the streets to toast the royal couple was probably restricted. As soon as the spring came, Henry left his new wife to make a vitally important tour of the northern part of his kingdom. No plans were made to crown the queen at this stage but any that might have been considered tentatively would have to wait, and not just for the king's return. When he departed London in March, travelling through East Anglia and the Midlands to York and then eventually down into the south-west, Henry had given his wife a set of splendid furs for the very early Easter. By then Elizabeth was already pregnant, though it is unlikely that the king knew this before he left.

✍

IT WAS TO PROVE a dramatic trip. Henry needed to establish his authority in the north, and especially in York, where ties to Richard III and resentment at the manner of his death remained strong. The loyalty of the northern lords and the gentry in their service was England's chief bulwark against the Scots. The king had already shown that he was not vengeful but that did not mean he had the unswerving devotion of all Yorkist supporters. Despite effusive greetings from the civic authorities on his official entry to York, with crowds shouting, 'King Henry! King Henry! God preserve that sweet and well-favoured face', an attempt was made to assassinate the king on 23 April, St George's Day, and Henry's life was only saved by the personal intervention of the earl of Northumberland.

The king put a brave face on this turn of events, which came shortly after he had learned of what was to be the first revolt against his rule. Three known Yorkist dissidents, Viscount Lovell, Sir Humphrey Stafford and his younger brother, Thomas, escaped from hiding in Colchester and attempted, unsuccessfully, to coordinate risings in the Midlands and North Yorkshire in the spring and summer of 1486. Their ostensible aim was to overthrow Henry and put the young earl of Warwick on the throne. Using a combination of clemency and financial restriction, which meant that men of suspect loyalty had to provide substantial sums to the Crown in return for their freedom, the king dealt with these first challenges to his rule effectively. Yet there did not appear to be widespread opposition to his rule among the English population as a whole. And on 19 September, Henry's hold on power was strengthened when Queen Elizabeth gave birth to a son. The arrival of an heir, Prince Arthur, born in Winchester, was a great boost to Henry Tudor. Both the city of his son's birth and the child's name had been carefully chosen for their associations with Camelot and a distant but glorious age when another Arthur had united the country. Henry's consistent message had been that he would do the same. Elizabeth Woodville, Henry's mother-in-law, was godmother to the child and took part in his christening ceremony, a further public demonstration of reconciliation with the Yorkists. But inside and outside his realm forces continued to gather that would stop him if they could. Less than a year later, England was invaded, the earl of Warwick's claim was reignited and Henry VII was fighting a full-scale battle again.

The Lambert Simnel conspiracy, as it has come to be known, was almost certainly never intended to put a lowly born boy from Oxford on the throne. Though little is known about Simnel himself, nor precisely how he came to have been spirited from Oxford to Ireland by a disaffected priest, he had undoubtedly been trained to pass as a nobleman even before the choice was made to claim that he was Edward, the young earl of Warwick. He also had powerful backers – the indefatigable Lord Lovell, who had evaded capture in 1486, John de la Pole, earl of Lincoln (who almost certainly would, if successful, have put forward his own claim) and, across the North Sea, the dowager duchess Margaret of Burgundy, sister of Richard III. Even Elizabeth Woodville was suspected of disloyalty and her lands were summarily given to her daughter while she retired to a convent.

Accepted as genuine by the Irish peers, Simnel was actually 'crowned' as Edward VI in the cathedral of the Holy Trinity, Dublin, on 24 May (Whitsunday) 1487. This farce was an early indication, and warning to Henry VII, if any was needed, of the lengths to which his opponents would go. Despite having paraded the real earl of Warwick in London months earlier, the king could not avoid military confrontation. Less than two weeks after the impostor's coronation, a force of two thousand German and Swiss professional soldiers, accompanied by a number of diehard Yorkists and a larger but much less well-armed group of some four thousand Irishmen, landed at Furness in north-west England.

This was a serious invasion – indeed, the whole Lambert Simnel conspiracy was more serious than historians have sometimes thought. Henry's opponents hoped to gather support in Yorkshire and then to advance rapidly south before the king could gather sufficient forces to contest them. But they had miscalculated on both counts. The king went north to meet them, via Leicester and Nottingham (where he managed to get lost), and by 15 June he had been joined by the forces of the men who had fought with him at Bosworth: the earls of Oxford, Derby and Devon and his ever-reliable uncle, Jasper. The king had twelve thousand men, the opposing forces only nine thousand, and when they met upstream from Newark, on the river Trent near the village of Stoke, on the morning of 16 June, a short but bloody battle followed. The earl of Lincoln was killed and young Simnel captured. He was allowed to live at Henry VII's court, as kitchen boy and then falconer. But Lovell, a troublemaker who excelled at escaping, got away again. He found his way to Scotland, where both James III and James IV gave him refuge. Thereafter, he disappears from history. It was, however, brought home to Henry VII that his northern neighbour could still give sanctuary to his enemies. The very real threat that this posed became all too apparent in the 1490s, when James IV decided that the time had come to rule for himself.

⚬⚭

IT HAD BEEN a long and sometimes bumpy apprenticeship, especially in the early years of the reign. There were no splendid festivities but James IV was crowned at Scone on 24 June with considerable pomp. Both the place and the date were significant. It was the anniversary of the battle of Bannockburn and the first coronation of a Scottish monarch at Scone, with its sacred and ancient associations, since James I more than sixty years earlier. Resplendent in a series of blue, black and crimson satin doublets, the young king had ridden to his coronation on a horse decked in velvet, supported by eight henchmen in black satin and velvet.

Ahead of him went a man carrying St Fillan's bell, which was supposed to cure the mentally afflicted. This may be revealing of the emotional turmoil of a boy who could not rid himself of the notion that he was being crowned while his murdered father remained unburied. The ceremony was conducted by the bishops of Glasgow and Dunkeld. Archbishop Scheves of St Andrews, the senior Scottish cleric (and loyal supporter of James III), was not present.

It is likely that James IV was crowned by Robert Blacader, bishop of Glasgow, and Scheves's great rival. Once the crown was on the king's head, the lords came forward to swear homage, touching the crown itself and promising to support the king. His own coronation oath followed, in which he promised to be 'a loving father to the people ... loyal and true to God and the Holy Church and to the three estates of my realm' and to govern according to the law and customs of the kingdom, making no changes without the consent of the estates. The clergy and the lords then responded with promises of loyalty and good counsel and thus the ceremony drew to its close.[13] James did not stay long at Scone. Following the interment of his father, probably on 28 June, the young king returned to Stirling, where Masses were said for Margaret of Denmark. These duties to his parents done, James IV could then begin the task of becoming acquainted with his country, its landscapes, people, culture and international relationships, as well as with its structure of government. Over time, he acquired a mastery of all these aspects. In short, he would learn how to rule.

His realm was smaller, colder, wetter and poorer than England. Around 800,000 people lived in Scotland in 1488, less than 5 per cent of whom inhabited towns. Edinburgh, the capital, with a population of 12,000, was by far the largest city, though only a quarter the size of London. Aberdeen and Glasgow were much smaller, with populations estimated at about 4,000 and 2,500 respectively. The geography of this overwhelmingly rural society was described by Pitscottie as very much a divide between the more fertile, prosperous south and the untamed north: 'The

Scots which inhabit in the southern part be well nurtured and live in good civility, and the most civil use the English speech . . . the other part northern, are full of mountains, and very rude and homely kind of people doth inhabit, which is called the Redshanks, or wild Scots. They be clothed with one mantle, with a shirt fashioned after the Irish manner, going bare-legged to the knee.' He went on to describe the area around Stirling (which would have been well known already to James IV) where white bulls, 'long-maned, like lions', had flourished in the Cale-donian forest but were now almost extinct, and moved on to a description of the inhabitants of the island of Orkney, recently joined to the kingdom of Scotland, where they used 'the Goth's speech'. Despite the climate, and the fact that they ate only fish, the islanders were 'lusty of body and mind, living very long'. The Scots, he concluded, were very wise, 'as their learning declareth', brave yet cantankerous. But the poor were very poor, and lazy, too.[14]

Andrea Trevisan, the Venetian commentator, obtained his descriptions of Scotland and its people from the Spanish ambas-sador to the court of James IV, Don Pedro de Ayala. The Spaniard was a great admirer of James and found much that was positive to say about the country, apart from the fact that it was very rainy. The Scottish people were very courteous and the nobility, residing on great, forested estates teeming with game, lived well: 'They have excellent houses, built for the most part in the Italian manner, of hewn stone or brick, with magnifi-cent rooms, halls, doors, galleries, chimneys and windows.' Unlike the English, the Scots 'are extremely partial to foreigners, and very hospitable, and they all consider that there is no higher duty in the world than to love and defend their crown.'[15]

The accounts of both Pitscottie and Ayala are revealing, but not necessarily the whole story. Their emphasis on regionalism is interesting – localism was a vital element of civic and ecclesi-astical life, but the functioning of Scottish government and society operated at local, regional and national level, with kinship and clan loyalty not solely confined to the Highlands, but regarded with equal fervour in the Lowlands and the Borders. At the apex of society was the king, commanding the kind of instinctive loyalty from lords, burgesses and peasants that went with an intensely personal, highly visible style of kingship. In late medieval Scotland, ordinary men and women stood a real chance of seeing their monarch in person at some point in their lifetimes. It was no wonder that James III did not command much popularity, since he seldom ventured outside Edinburgh. The motives of those who had put his son on the throne were far from altruistic and they were eager to reinforce their own legitimacy by parading the king, but, in so doing, they helped ensure that James IV did not repeat his father's mistakes. The boy's upbringing in Stirling, with only occasional visits to the capital, meant that he had much to learn about his country. In the first few months of his reign, James was constantly on the move, learning new skills and developing interests that would remain with him for the rest of his life. In early August, only six weeks after he was crowned king, he was at Leith, Edinburgh's port, watching the ships and learning about naval warfare; his enthusiasm for all things naval probably dates from this visit. A few days later he was at Linlithgow, taking a break from his new duties by watching plays, listening to music and hunting. By 8 August he was back in Stirling and then, less than two weeks later, he was off again, presiding over his first justice circuit court at Lanark. These justice ayres, as the circuit courts were known, were a key feature of the Scottish legal system, bringing the rule of law to the farthest corners of the land. They provided a good grounding for the king in legal matters and an opportunity to be out among his subjects. Early on, they allowed the affable and inquisitive side of James's nature to develop. Travelling was a new experience for him but it came to characterize his reign. Far more than his English counterpart, James IV was always on the move, leading his troops, visiting his castles for rest and enjoyment, dispensing justice, departing on pilgrimage and sailing on the ships he loved.

He was the sovereign of a country that was, like him, neither inward-looking nor isolated. Scotland has a coastline longer than that of the eastern seaboard of the United States and much travel was done by sea because it was quicker and easier than trying to traverse appalling roads, where these existed at all. The Scots had long been determined to play a significant role in Europe and the sea routes naturally made them look outwards – westward to Ireland and, as well as this neighbour with whom there was much cultural and linguistic commonality, to the rest of Europe. Trade and diplomacy were vital. Denmark and Scandinavia were natural allies, through geographical proximity and the intermarriage of their royal families over the centuries. James IV was keenly aware of his Danish heritage and sought to exploit it for Scotland's benefit. Also important were trade links with Flanders, making good relationships with the Habsburgs, soon to be the most prominent dynasty in Europe, vital. The Scottish court and elite watched Europe carefully (as did their English counterparts), copying its fashions, importing its manufactured and luxury goods, and above all in the case of France, drinking its wine. And for the major European powers there was an underlying truth about Scotland that had been voiced by Pope Martin V in 1421, when he remarked that 'the Scots are an antidote to the English.'

Nowhere was this more self-evident than in Scotland's relations with France. The origins of the Auld Alliance, as the Scots had dubbed it, were lost in the mists of time; tradition had it that they went back to Charlemagne. In the twentieth century, General de Gaulle called it the oldest alliance in the world.[16] In essence, the alliance was a fluid military pact. It was not embodied in one overriding treaty, nor, of course, were its details identical from one period to the next. Pragmatic and adaptable, often renewed, it always had the same aim: to contain and control England's position in north-west Europe, to the benefit of France and Scotland. As such, its theatres of war were confined to the Borders, to France and to the maritime routes that all three countries shared across the North Sea and the English Channel. Fuelled by the Hundred Years War, it had fallen into abeyance during the reign of James III, though by that time its deeper effect on Franco–Scottish relations was well established. The Scots were a restless people and the twin disruptions of the Black Death and the Hundred Years War caused them to settle in large numbers in France during the late fourteenth and fifteenth centuries, fifteen thousand arriving in the period 1419–24. They went predominantly to central France – to Berry, the Touraine and Anjou – offering their services as mercenaries. Many prospered, acquiring land, building fine homes and patronizing the arts. The Stewarts who settled around Aubigny in the Berry did especially well. But despite French becoming their first language and their livelihoods being dependent on the French kings, they never forgot Scotland. It was all the more ironic that some of their descendants should have helped Henry Tudor to the throne of England in 1485. This was not a pattern that James IV and his advisers wished to see continued. Firstly, though, they were compelled to deal with domestic problems, for in the early years of James's reign, rebellion, as in England, was never far away.

It was not, however, aimed at deposing James himself. At stake initially was the survival of those who had put him on the throne. The victors of Sauchieburn were forsworn and uneasy. Having broken their oaths to the new king not to lay violent hands on his father, it was imperative to move on quickly. The question was, how to do this? James IV was undoubtedly affected by the manner in which he had come to the throne and his backers could not be sure how he would react in the coming months. Because of his age, he could not rule entirely by himself, yet neither could he be regarded as a mere figurehead. Financial and legal stability were the priorities and once the treasure of James III was located, there was no danger of lack of funds. Personal enrichment in the shortest possible time was a prime motivation for the Hepburn and Hume families, who now formed the core of advisers surrounding James IV. The Hepburn dominance of government offices was overwhelming: half a dozen of them filled key roles, many in the king's household in positions such as master of the king's stable, steward of the household and the quaint-sounding post of master of the royal larder. By early autumn, with his uncle John Hepburn, the prior of St Andrews, appointed as keeper of the privy seal, a role that gave him control of Crown patronage, Patrick Hepburn sealed the family's rise to prominence by acquiring the keepership of Edinburgh Castle and the office of sheriff of Edinburgh. Even more importantly, as the newly created earl of Bothwell, he gained custody of the king and his brothers. This stranglehold of office and influence meant that Bothwell felt confident enough to call a parliament. It might have been a risky step, but the death of James III had shocked Scotland and the earl was a skilled political operator who knew that this must be put on the public record, or the ghost of the man who had died so mysteriously near the Bannockburn mill could yet undo his success. Casting the late king as the villain for having broken the agreement made at Aberdeen in April 1487, it was claimed that the rebellion was justified because Scotland had been 'badly and confusedly governed'. As the Hepburns basically controlled the well-attended parliament, their explanation of events won the day.

It did not convince for long. Too many prominent families felt left out by the Hepburn and Hume ascendancy and there was widespread concern that no real effort had been made to bring the killers of James III to justice. At the same time, law and order began to break down, with local feuds growing unchecked in southern Scotland. The sense of personal grievance and social dislocation fuelled uprisings against the new regime, first in south-west Scotland, where the Lennox family seized Dumbarton Castle, and then in the north-east, where the powerful Huntlys also rebelled. By the autumn of 1489, both groups were working together, producing propaganda to justify their actions and preparing for further military action. In early October 1489, the rebels were ready to make their move. The Lennoxes marched out of Dumbarton towards Stirling, where the king was living, intending to seize James IV himself. 'For the second time in seventeen months, James found himself the leader of a faction at Stirling, waiting to be assailed in an armed struggle, the outcome of which was far from certain.'[17]

Was his very survival as king at stake? It might have seemed so. He had younger brothers who could replace him and the duke of Ross, the nearest to him in age, was with him at Stirling. James seems to have got on well with his brothers, giving them both roles in government in due course, but the fact that his father had appeared to favour the duke of Ross could make this younger brother a viable alternative to his disaffected nobility now. The dangers of seeming to be controlled by an unpopular clique were amply demonstrated to James IV at this time. Yet no one could doubt his determination or physical courage. He had participated in the unsuccessful attempts to raise the siege of Dumbarton and now he took to the field again. On 11 October 1489, his forces clashed with the rebels at what is known as the Field of Gartloaning, a battle probably fought over a wide area in the hills to the west of Stirling and extending into the Trossachs. Here, in a beautiful area of the upper reaches of the river Forth, in fighting that went on over several days, the Lennoxes were betrayed by one of their own side and an assault on Stirling was averted.

James outfaced his opponents, but the conflict had been inconclusive. The Hepburn–Hume alliance did not give up so easily. Summoning a new parliament (the fourth in less than two years) for February 1490, they agreed reluctantly that the king's Privy Council should be more broadly based, and appointed by parliament. But one man who still felt left out of the circle of power was Archibald Douglas, fifth earl of Angus, whose power base in south-east Scotland was given visible presence by the mighty fortress of Tantallon rising above the coast between Edinburgh and Berwick. For while Angus might often be about court, playing dice and cards with the king, this social interaction was no substitute for political power.

Angus did not have to wait too long for the political landscape to shift. In 1492 the Hepburns reconsidered their position, and, looking to the long-term survival of their influence, relinquished a number of offices, including the privy seal, which went to William Elphinstone, a loyal supporter of James III and a man whom Bothwell seems to have always regarded with some confidence, since he had been permitted to accompany James IV on the justice circuits at the very start of the reign. Once returned to high office, Elphinstone proceeded to draw up the first Scottish land registry, an invaluable tool for the management of royal patronage. Elphinstone's elevation indicated that the power base was broadening. Then, at the end of 1492, the death of the chancellor, the earl of Argyll, opened a key vacancy, which the earl of Angus was only too happy to fill.

Angus's return to Scottish politics was important for Henry VII. The English king's initial reaction to the overthrow of James III was a nervous one. Fearing for the security of his northern border, he ordered musters of men at the key fortresses. An attack did not materialize (the new Scottish regime was far too preoccupied to launch an offensive against England at this time) and clarification of the new relationship between the two countries was sought through diplomacy. The English wanted 'perpetual peace' but the Scots commissioners who met them at Coldstream in the early autumn of 1488 would agree only to a three-year truce. Patrick Hepburn and the young king himself were keen to move Scotland back towards France, believing that it was in the country's best interests to restore goodwill with such a long-standing ally. Angus, like all of his family, was an Anglophile and his contacts with Henry VII were already established. This cynical and self-serving old rogue had already offered the English king the key Border castle known as the Hermitage in return for lands in England, if he did not succeed in changing the direction of Scottish foreign policy in Henry's favour. There would inevitably be tension as the Scottish lords vied for power. Angus was by no means the only Scottish aristocrat who could turn to England when it suited. The heir to the earl of Huntly, the most prominent northern lord, had appealed for English help in the 1489 rebellion and in 1491 the earl of Buchan, the same scheming half-uncle of the king's father, was loaned money by Henry VII in return for kidnapping James IV and his brother, the duke of Ross, and handing them over to England. The scheme sounds hare-brained, and it came to nothing, but it was indicative of Henry's opportunism (and perhaps a greater level of concern about his relationship with Scotland at this time than has been supposed), as well as the continued duplicity of members of the Stewart royal family itself. Stability in Scotland, as in England, was elusive. The relationship of the two countries remained a shifting, sensitive issue, its evolution unclear. Meanwhile, as the last decade of the fifteenth century dawned, both kings watched each other carefully, their networks of spies and informers constantly busy. And it was not all politics and battles for James IV as he grew to manhood. The temptations and delights of love beckoned.

∞

DESPITE HIS STATUS as one of Europe's more eligible unmarried kings, there was no rush to find a bride for James IV. The search for a wife could prove useful diplomatically and, meanwhile, there were other ways in which it could be helpful to politicians at home, since the young man himself seemed more interested in romantic liaisons with attractive young women of the court than in finding a queen. His parents married young and he had seen for himself that theirs was not the happiest of unions. The obligations of kingship were serious enough for a teenage king without the added responsibility of a wife. There was no shortage of ladies willing to share the king's bed among the daughters of the Scottish nobility, eager to gain the favour of their monarch. James was to become an inveterate womanizer, his growing charisma and natural charm, allied to a rugged manliness and physicality, bringing him many conquests. He was also the centre of an increasingly cultured court, where poetry, plays, storytelling and music provided a focus for entertainment and the opportunity for dalliances to flourish. Nor were all of these with ladies of prominent families. James had broad tastes in women throughout his reign, as payments to one 'Jane Bare Arse' unashamedly illustrate.[18]

Most, like Jane, did not last long. The king's first 'official' mistress, and certainly the first of any social standing, was Marion Boyd. We know little about her other than that she was the niece of the earl of Angus. This proximity to a man who wished for a greater role in government is unlikely to have been coincidental. As a gambling companion, Angus may well have noted James IV's liking for a pretty face and made sure that Marion was brought to the king's attention. Their affair began in the summer of 1492 and continued for three years. During that time, Marion bore James two children, Alexander and Katherine Stewart, but he had apparently tired of her by the end of 1495, when she was married off to John Muir of Rowallan. A new mistress, Margaret Drummond, was about to enter his life. Though theirs appears to have been a very intense relationship, and Margaret was, for some months, residing at Stirling Castle with the king, it was short-lived. He did, however, make proper provision for their daughter (also called Margaret), who was brought up at Stirling. James never neglected the illegitimate children of these liaisons, ensuring that his sons were well educated and his daughters raised as ladies who could expect to make good marriages.

The end of the affair with Marion Boyd may have been prompted by more than just ennui and the attractions of another lady. Angus's influence was on the wane and the king finally decided in 1495 that he would take the reins of government himself. Over seven years, he had mastered the business of domestic administration and developed a keen interest in military and diplomatic matters. His move towards personal assumption of power was no doubt encouraged by his success in mounting an effective campaign to bring the Western Isles of Scotland firmly into line. This exercise, known as the 'Daunting of the Isles', was intended to break the local power of the highland chieftains, extend effective justice into the region and, eventually, bring the granting of lands and titles under royal patronage, as had been done with landowners in the Lowlands. It was a process not fully completed for almost another decade but this demonstration of power by a king who could himself speak Gaelic, the language of the Highlands, meant that he could now devote his attention to the wider international sphere.[19] This would bring him into direct conflict with England, as both he and Henry VII sought to establish their credibility in Europe. It also led to one of the most extraordinary episodes of James's reign, as he gave extravagant public support to a charlatan who bedevilled Henry Tudor's life for eight years.

CHAPTER FOUR

The Impostor

&

'*By the craft, invention and devilish imagination of that pestiferous serpent lady Margaret, duchess of Burgundy, a new idol was set up in Flanders and called Richard Plantagenet, second son to king Edward IV, as though he had been resuscitated from death to life.*'

Hall's Chronicle

'*Cousin, our bounty, favours, gentleness,*
Our benefits, the hazard of our person,
Our people's lives, our land, hath evidenc'd
How much we have engaged on your behalf.'

King James IV in *The Chronicle History of Perkin Warbeck* by John Ford

THE YOUNG MAN who caused so much friction between Henry VII and James IV did not, however, first come to public attention in Flanders but in Ireland, that 'backdoor' to the Tudor realm that had long been uneasily subject to English government and would continue to cause problems throughout the entire Tudor period. And it was while strolling on the chilly streets of Cork, in November 1491, that a youth of about seventeen years of age, dressed to impress in a fine array of silks, caught the notice of the local populace. He was not, then – or so he later claimed – promoting himself. Instead, he was a walking advertisement for the wares of his master, the Breton merchant, Pregent Meno, whose ship was anchored in the harbour. The citizens of Cork remarked upon the young man's bearing and appearance and their chattering gave rise to speculation that he must be no ordinary crewman. The boy seems to have possessed the instinctive talents of a model, the ability to invest the clothing that he wore with something greater than the quality of the cloth itself. He had a presence and style that quickly attracted attention, and not just from the ordinary townspeople.

In Ireland at that time were many Yorkist sympathizers, who could use the island's traditional recalcitrance towards the English Crown as a fertile base for plots. For these men, Henry Tudor was a usurper and their cause was anything but lost. Two in particular – the Devonian merchant John Taylor and the city of Cork's former mayor, John Atwater – saw in the distinctive young man who had arrived amongst them a potential that went far beyond the demonstration of silk fabric. The boy's bearing and his denials that he was the duke of Warwick (as was first believed) combined to play into the hands of Henry VII's enemies in Ireland. Questions had been raised amid a general stirring of interest that could be exploited. They did not care that this new prospect had been born Pierrechon de Werbecque in Flanders. His past was, indeed, another country. His future, though, would be brilliant. They intended to make him King Richard IV of England.

So was born the Perkin Warbeck conspiracy. History has tended to be rather dismissive of its significance, since we know the outcome, but no one, least of all Henry VII, regarded it as trivial at the time. Faintly ludicrous as belief in Perkin may seem to us now, the late fifteenth century was a credulous age, one where disappearance and reappearance were not impossibilities, where the more open mind of the Renaissance had not entirely replaced the medieval world's love of chivalry, of adventure, of dark imaginings and miraculous rebirths. Europe was a continent a boy could wander in, dependent on the goodwill of others, his past half-remembered, until fate rescued him from oblivion – or so contemporaries might have liked to believe. And why not

Perkin? From 1491 to 1497, this charming, well-schooled and apparently plausible impostor strutted the European stage, plaguing Henry Tudor's life and compromising the security of his kingdom. The Warbeck affair was a protracted nightmare, raising all sorts of questions about recent, unresolved happenings, such as the fate of the Princes in the Tower (Queen Elizabeth's missing brothers) and challenging Henry's very right to rule. At home, it sparked treason in the king's own household and extended family. Abroad, the monarchies of Europe, so much more powerful than Henry himself, watched the outcome keenly, exploiting uncertainties wherever and whenever they could.

The appearance of a rival with an apparently better claim to the English throne was a powerful diplomatic bargaining tool, to be used with varying degrees of cynicism, but always a weapon against a king who knew that if he was to bring lasting stability at home he must be seen as a legitimate, effective ruler by potential allies in Europe. The fate of the fledgling Tudor dynasty was at stake. And all the time James IV, keen to assume the direction of foreign policy in Scotland and make a name for himself and his country internationally, stood poised to seize any advantage that his neighbour's embarrassment might offer. He ruled over a smaller and much less prosperous kingdom, but from an international perspective, it was far from insignificant. Henry's troubles presented James with an opportunity to make a name for himself as a European monarch at the beginning of his personal rule and he took it eagerly. His actions would, eventually, lead to momentous developments for both England and Scotland.

The question of who Warbeck actually was has never been fully resolved. Some might say that it is not altogether relevant, since ultimately it was who he was *not* that mattered. His own confession, made in October 1497 when he was finally captured, may have been made under duress. It goes into greater detail about his early years and background than about his adventures once he was reinvented as a Yorkist prince: 'First let it be known that I was born in the town of Tournai in Flanders [Warbeck clearly considered himself as Flemish though the town was ruled by France at that time and his first language would have been French] and my father's name is John Osbek ... which was controller of the said town of Tournai, and my mother's name is Katharine de Faro ...' He went on to describe his wider family and their role among the civic officials and prosperous small merchants of Tournai, how his mother had sent him to Antwerp to learn Flemish and how, after a long period of illness, he had worked for a number of merchants in Bergen op Zoom and Middelburg.[1] Perkin's solid basis in the mercantile activities of the cloth industry in the Low Countries led somehow to a meeting with Lady Margaret Beaumont, the English wife of a lowly born Portuguese Jew, Duarte Brandao, also known as Sir Edward Brampton, whose conversion to Christianity had been sponsored by King Edward IV. At Easter 1486, Perkin accompanied Lady Margaret on a voyage to Lisbon that greatly expanded his horizons.

The connection with Brampton, a colourful opportunist who seems to have felt little loyalty to anyone except himself, and may even have been a bigamist, was probably more tenuous than conspiracy theorists have wanted to believe. It is impossible to say how well Warbeck knew Brampton but what is certain is that the boy's year-long stay in Portugal, between 1486 and 1487, made a profound impression on him. At the beginning of the great age of exploration, Portugal was a fascinating place and Perkin found work with a son of one of its greatest explorers, Tristão da Cunha. This opened up for him a wider world and the continuing desire to travel. In 1488 Perkin, who could by now speak several European languages, knew the Portuguese court and had probably picked up a good working knowledge of the Yorkists from Lady Margaret and her husband, entered the service of Pregent Meno. It was perhaps ironic that his voyage in 1491 to Ireland, a country well off the beaten track and not known for the wealth of its merchants, should have led to such a startling, and dangerous, change of fortune for this cosmopolitan, well-educated and apparently self-assured seventeen-year-old from a respectable Flemish bourgeois background.

∝

HENRY VII could not expect to make much of a mark in Europe until he had tightened his hold on England and established a dynasty. A family was vital for success; sons gave confidence in the future of the Tudors and daughters were indispensable for marriage alliances with other royal houses. In this respect, Henry and Elizabeth had already done well. Two more children arrived after Prince Arthur: Margaret, born in November 1489, and Henry, in June 1491. A year after Arthur's birth, at the end of November 1487, Elizabeth was finally crowned at Westminster Abbey. This was also the occasion of a magnificent spectacle and the nobility, gorgeously attired and bejewelled, if not, in reality, of unswerving loyalty, paid homage to the eldest daughter of the House of York. By 1489, Henry Tudor's stock also seemed to be rising in Europe. He entered into an alliance with Ferdinand of Aragon and the powerful archduke of Austria, Maximilian, intended to keep France in check. This was a significant development because Henry had sent military aid to Brittany when France cast envious eyes on the duchy following the death of his long-time protector Duke Francis in 1488. It was also agreed with Ferdinand and his wife, Isabella of Castile, that Prince Arthur should marry their youngest daughter, Katherine.

Yet trouble was never far away, either at home or abroad. In the spring of 1489, less than a month after what seemed like a notable diplomatic triumph with the Spanish monarchs, Henry's northern strongman, the earl of Northumberland, was murdered by rebels who were protesting against increased taxation at a time of economic difficulty. The earl had saved Henry from assassination three years earlier but there was no one to perform the same service for him. The king sent the earl of Surrey north to administer this vulnerable part of the kingdom and to keep a careful watch on the Scots. Surrey was in his late forties, a former

Yorkist with a ruthless streak who had served Richard III loyally and been severely wounded at Bosworth. Yet by 1489, when his lands were restored, he had evidently calculated that his future did not lie in rebellion or exile. Putting his devotion to the White Rose firmly behind him, he went on to serve both Henry VII and Henry VIII with distinction. He would also have a major part to play in the life and death of James IV.

By the time of the birth of Prince Henry in June 1491 there were grounds for Tudor optimism both at home and abroad. The advent of Perkin Warbeck cruelly shattered these. In a short space of time it became apparent just how disruptive 'Richard IV' could be. The shadowy conspiracies of widely scattered Yorkist loyalists had not amounted to much before, but now they could begin to coalesce, to have real substance and threat, thanks to the opportunity they offered various European monarchs to keep Henry VII in check. Though Perkin may have posed the greatest danger to Henry when he came to Scotland, he arrived there in 1495 by a circuitous route that took him to the courts of France, Austria and Burgundy.

At the beginning of January 1492 Warbeck was still in Ireland, being heavily coached for his role by John Taylor and Stephen Fryon, a former French secretary to Edward IV. He had much to learn, including a good grasp of the English language, in a short space of time. Why he agreed to this most elaborate of charades remains a mystery. No doubt he was put under pressure, but the advantages offered to him must have seemed worth the effort of transforming himself into someone else. The flattery, the encouragement, the exciting hope that he might actually be believed, must all have outweighed the underlying fear of the consequences of being caught or merely abandoned at some point. And, initially, Perkin was being fed and clothed at the expense of others while being invested with the character of Richard, duke of York. If it came to nothing, he would at least have learned the skills of an actor (something that clearly came easily to him) and could disappear to reinvent himself in another guise. With confidence came plausibility and the self-assurance that he could readily persuade crowned heads of Europe that he was their equal. A vague but heartrending backstory was created for him, and though we do not have evidence for it in writing before 1493, when he appealed unsuccessfully for acknowledgement to the very hard-headed Isabella of Castile, no doubt he had used this story before. He explained that his elder brother Edward V had, indeed, been murdered, and asserted that 'I myself, then nearly nine years of age, was also delivered to a certain lord to be killed.' The unnamed lord had taken pity on his innocence, kept him alive and spirited him to a place of safety:

> First, however, causing me to swear on the holy sacrament that to no one should I disclose my name, origin or family, until a certain number of years had passed. He then sent me therefore abroad, with two persons, who should watch over and take charge of me; and thus I, an orphan [a curious thing to say, since his supposed mother, Elizabeth Woodville, was still very much alive at this time], bereaved of my royal father and brother, an exile from my kingdom, and deprived of my country, inheritance and fortune, a fugitive and in the midst of extreme perils, led my miserable life, in fear, and weeping, and grief, and for the space of nearly eight years lay hid in divers places. At length, one of those who had charge of me being dead, and the other returned to his country, and never afterwards seen, scarcely had I emerged from childhood alone and without means, I remained for a time in the kingdom of Portugal, and thence sailed to Ireland, where, being recognized by the illustrious lords the earls of Desmond and Kildare, my cousins, as also by other noblemen of the island, I was received with great joy and honour.[2]

Taylor and his accomplices were much more than instigators and preceptors. They had a well-thought-out strategy to promote the rediscovered duke of York far and wide. By February 1492, well before the appeal to Queen Isabella, they were already confident enough in Perkin's plausibility to send letters to Maximilian and to Margaret of Burgundy, announcing that the rightful heir to the English throne, Richard Plantagenet, 'King Edward's son', had been found and was seeking their aid. Early in March, the Irishman Edward Ormond arrived at the court of James IV bearing a similar missive. But at this stage, with internal dissent still a problem in his council, James was either unable or unwilling to give support. His interest could well have been aroused but he and his advisers may also have calculated that it would be best to let other European powers take the lead at this point. He wished to improve his relations with the French, who by now had an ambassador in Edinburgh, but he could let them steer events. For that is precisely what happened. Once schooled, Perkin did not stay long in Ireland. The initial interest in him there had not moved to full-scale support and his French backers, now with the added impetus of the outbreak of war with England, did not want to leave him exposed. They sent a fleet of vessels to whisk him to the French port of Harfleur in Normandy and so bring him, now fully fledged as Richard, duke of York, to Charles VIII of France.

The French king did not, however, keep him long. In concert with Maximilian, Henry VII invaded northern France in October 1492. He landed at Calais with a force of fourteen thousand men, in what was, numerically, the greatest invasion of France undertaken by the English in the fifteenth century. After capturing Arras, the campaign was swiftly concluded by the Treaty of Étaples, much to the annoyance of his Austrian ally, who had hoped to regain territory lost to France in 1482 under the Treaty of Arras. Ten years on, Maximilian still had not reclaimed these lands and was further snubbed by Charles's rejection of his daughter, Margaret of Austria, who, as agreed in the Arras treaty, had been brought up in the French court to be Charles's future wife. Charles was young but cunning. He had recently solved the Breton problem by marriage to its duchess and now his sights were set on achieving far greater military glory and the kingdom of Naples in Italy, to which he had a distant claim.

War with England was an unnecessary distraction for him.
Henry VII, on the other hand, may have dreamed of restoring
part of England's lost French empire (his great-grandfather, after
all, was king of France) but military advice told him he could
not even recapture the important fortress of Boulogne, and so
the pragmatist in him settled for peace. But the improvement of
relations with France did not solve the problem of Perkin
Warbeck's imposture, a matter of growing concern for Henry
both at home and abroad. Instead, it moved Perkin on, with
the help of John Taylor's bribery and scheming, towards the
unpredictable and now greatly offended Maximilian, and, more
particularly, to the embrace of Margaret of Burgundy, the 'pestiferous serpent lady' herself.

❧

SHORTLY BEFORE Christmas 1492, Warbeck and his backers
arrived at the court of Margaret of Burgundy at Malines in
Brabant, some fifteen miles south of Antwerp in what is now
Belgium.[3] The dowager duchess was then forty-six years old, the
childless widow of the brave but reckless Burgundian duke,
Charles the Bold, who had died in battle at Nancy in 1477. She
was born Margaret of York, the youngest daughter of Richard,
duke of York, and his wife, Cecily Neville. Sister to two kings of
England, Margaret was Duke Charles's third wife, but her
marriage to him in 1468, when she was twenty-two, represented
a huge diplomatic triumph for her brother, Edward IV. It more
than balanced the disappointment felt by English politicians
when Edward himself married Elizabeth Woodville. The wedding took place amid great pageantry in England and in Burgundy and was celebrated in Bruges with one of the greatest
series of festivities ever seen there. The tall and slim Margaret
would prove herself, in terms of ambition and dynastic determination, a true child of the House of York. As a young woman
she was probably good looking, as were most of her family,
though a later portrait, the only one that can be confidently
attributed, is not flattering.

Margaret of York's marriage to Charles the Bold underlined the close relationship between the British Isles and the Low Countries that had existed at least since the high Middle Ages. Based on the mutual advantages of trade and commerce, the kings of both England and Scotland needed this wealthy and influential neighbour for their own prosperity. Burgundy was definitely the senior partner in these relationships. It was the 'mightiest and richest duchy in Europe' and its dukes ruled over the continent's largest urban population. It was, in every way, a contrast to the overwhelmingly rural nature of the British Isles. Margaret had made a splendid marriage and was expected to undertake the duties that came with it. Well educated and pious, the duchess seems to have carried out her role with aplomb, travelling widely and presiding over a rich and cultured court. Her failure to produce children must have been a disappointment, particularly to a man who pushed himself as hard as Charles the Bold, but he did entrust to Margaret the upbringing of his daughter, Mary, his sole heir. Mary of Burgundy became very fond of her stepmother and was heavily dependent on her in the difficult months after Charles's unexpected death, when both internal revolt and French invasion threatened. Realizing that the best protection for her stepdaughter would be to find her a powerful husband, Margaret was instrumental in arranging a speedy marriage to Maximilian of Austria. In so doing, she helped create the sixteenth-century's most formidable dynasty. Mary's marriage into the Habsburg family would lead to an empire that stretched from the borders of eastern Europe to the south of Spain and eventually to the Americas. Yet though Mary acknowledged Margaret's assistance at this time, saying that she had 'given freely and cordially of her help and shared in and supported all of our affairs with all her might', the dowager undoubtedly had an ulterior motive. Her own survival in Burgundy and, more especially, the granting of her dower lands there, were dependent on her stepdaughter's goodwill and the attitude of Mary's husband. Margaret was accustomed to the grand lifestyle of the Burgundian court and although she might herself have looked for a new marriage, she seems to have preferred comfortable widowhood in her adopted country, a choice not uncommon among ladies of her rank at the time and for which she can hardly be blamed. In fact, she was so concerned about concluding the business of her dower that she apparently irritated Maximilian by bringing the topic up on the eve of his wedding.[4]

This episode reveals an understandable, if not entirely appealing, aspect of Margaret's character. The death of her brother, Richard III, and the advent of Henry Tudor showed a great deal more about her devotion to her family and her capacity to cause trouble. For the dowager was a true Yorkist – ambitious, proud, mettlesome but ultimately lacking in judgement. Her reaction to Henry VII was instinctive but driven by rancour rather than the desire to do England service. Perhaps it has been overstated by Tudor propagandists, who have given Margaret a disproportionate share of the blame for a prolonged campaign to overthrow the man who had defeated her house, but it is hard to find any saving grace in a woman who, in reality, put the idea of dynasty before the interests of surviving members of her own family. But for Margaret it was York that mattered. She was not a woman to sit quietly, however large her library of devotional books might have been. And she was also living in a past that was less glorious than she remembered. Contacts in her mother's household kept her informed, as did spies and Irish priests (Margaret, like Henry VII, had an active network of informers), but she was distanced from England by time as well as geography. It is impossible to say whether her support of Perkin Warbeck was always cynical or whether there was a substantial element of self-delusion in it. One thing is certain, however. When Perkin came to Malines, Margaret welcomed him with open arms.

In August 1493, Margaret, too, wrote to Isabella of Castile, reinforcing her 'nephew's' claim and explaining the process by which she had come to accept him. This had started the previous year with letters written by the earls of Kildare and Desmond, telling her that the second son of her brother, King Edward, had been rediscovered in Ireland. This missive, no doubt similar, if not identical, to the one received by James IV in Scotland, had profoundly disturbed her: 'These things seemed to me to be ravings and dreams.' But when the young man was accepted as Richard, duke of York, at the French court, Margaret explained that she sent 'certain men who would have recognised him as easily as his mother or nurse' and these men confirmed to her with many sacred oaths that the lad was genuine. Presumably these men were among the floating population of Yorkists who fled across the sea after Bosworth, part of what has been called a 'world of displaced men', but Margaret did not name them. And she evaded the inevitable question of how anyone could identify Richard of York with certainty after ten years. Instead, she claimed that she knew him at once: 'I recognised him as easily as if I had last seen him yesterday or the day before,' adding, somewhat less convincingly, 'for I had seen him once long ago in England.' His coming had greatly affected her: 'I indeed, for my part, when I gazed on this only male remnant of our family – who had come through so many perils and misfortunes – was deeply moved, and out of this natural affection, into which both necessity and the rights of blood were drawing me, I embraced him as my only nephew and my only son.'[5]

This letter perhaps reveals more about Margaret and her emotional state – the yearning for the glory days of the House of York, her wistfulness at her own childlessness – than it does about the authenticity of the claimant himself. His plausibility had clearly impressed her and, more than anything, she wanted to believe him. The disappearance of the Princes in the Tower and the absence of any firm evidence that they had both died in 1483, as was widely believed at the time, made it impossible to prove with absolute certainty that Perkin Warbeck was not who he said he was. Maximilian, too, was willing to entertain the idea that Margaret's protégé might be genuine – especially while it served his purpose in European diplomacy. He invited Perkin to accompany him on his travels in Germany and Austria and, in November 1493, at the funeral of Maximilian's father, the emperor Frederick II, in Vienna, the resurgent Yorkists could congratulate themselves on their greatest achievement to date, when all the princes and bishops of the Holy Roman Empire acknowledged the young man as a prince of the House of York. Maximilian and his son, Philip of Burgundy, maintained public support for the impostor for a couple of years, though most of Perkin's financial backing continued to come from Margaret. The dowager duchess never did manage to persuade Isabella or her husband, Ferdinand of Aragon, that the duke of York was genuine and the Spanish monarchs affected to be surprised that anyone could take the whole business seriously. They wrote somewhat indignantly to their ambassador in England that Henry VII had complained 'that they [Isabella and Ferdinand always referred to themselves in the third person] correspond with the person who calls himself "Duke of York"'. They went on, 'The fact is, the so-called Duke of York and the old Duchess Margaret had written to them once at Barcelona, asking their protection. They had sent no answer to the pretended Duke of York, but only to the Duchess, showing her that the whole affair was an imposture. The Duchess made no reply.'⁶ More concerned with the negotiations for a marriage between Prince Arthur and Katherine of Aragon and also keen to gain Henry's participation in the Holy League, their alliance against France, the Catholic Kings believed that their English ally could handle the threat posed by so obvious a masquerade.

Henry had good reason to be less sanguine, though he had known who Warbeck was for some time and his information fits with Perkin's later confession. Writing in 1493, he declaimed against 'the great malice that the lady Margaret of Burgundy beareth continually against us . . . by the untrue contriving of a feigned lad called Perkin Warbeck, born at Tournai in Picardy'. The real purpose of his letter, however, was to request military aid from the prominent men of the shires, in case of invasion or uprising. Indeed, he could hardly have done otherwise, for the support given to Warbeck in the Low Countries had serious repercussions at home. The prospect of an alternative with a better claim to the throne threatened to destabilize England, reviving the Yorkist cause among the English aristocracy and many former adherents of the previous regime who were still at court and even in Henry's privy chamber. The king decided to parade the 'real' duke of York in the first official engagement for the three-year-old Prince Henry, created duke of York on 1 November 1494, in a further display of Tudor pomp and power. Summoned from the calm of his childhood home at Eltham Palace, south-east of London, the little prince rode through the streets of the City of London as part of an impressive procession of the Tudor elite, 'sitting alone upon a courser [a warhorse]'. He was also created a knight and carried himself well through the elaborate ritual that accompanied the ceremony, culminating in his father girding him with the sword and dubbing him in the time-honoured manner. Afterwards, in a gesture that mingled paternal pride and affection with his innate flair for the public gesture, Henry VII hoisted his namesake son onto the table so that all present could see.

He must have wished that all his knights were as reliable as this attentive, dutiful small child. But they were not, and the king knew it. His spies and informers supplied him with all the unwelcome details, their network stretching into the great households of the realm, providing an abundance of information that was hard to sift. Implicated in the plotting were members of the household of Cecily Neville, the old duchess of York, and, a far greater blow, Henry's own step-uncle, Sir William Stanley, the man whose intervention had been so crucial to his success nine years earlier at Bosworth. Stanley was chamberlain of the royal household and said to be the richest commoner in England. He had a high opinion of himself and possibly, as well, a deep-seated loyalty to the Yorkist cause that he had served faithfully in the reign of Edward IV. Perhaps he resented his brother's elevation to an earldom while he remained a knight. For whatever reason, he forgot the golden rule of Tudor England, which was to be very careful where you put your trust. Henry VII had been watching him for some time. Betrayed by a colleague whose life was spared, Stanley was condemned to death at a trial presided over by his own brother in early February 1495 and beheaded a week later. His death demoralized the aristocratic support for Warbeck in England and was a blow to Warbeck's hopes, though by no means a fatal one.

Hoping to exploit discontent in England and Ireland, Margaret and Maximilian eventually produced sufficient finance for Warbeck to attempt an invasion in the summer of 1495. It was, though, too little, too late. Attempting a landing at Deal in Kent in July, Warbeck discovered that the frequently cantankerous inhabitants of the county had no interest in welcoming him. In fact, they fought bravely and the ensuing bloodbath on Deal's steeply shelving beach seems to have made Perkin very queasy about any further personal involvement in fighting. With Maximilian preoccupied by greater troubles in Europe and Margaret's coffers empty, Perkin was now literally at sea. At the end of the month, he reached Ireland, hoping to aid the rebellion of the earl of Desmond that, at one point, seemed likely to tear the island apart. Desmond was besieging Waterford but even the arrival of Warbeck's fleet of eleven ships could not break the determined resistance of the citizenry. This setback turned the 'duke of York' into a fugitive in the very place where he had been invented four years earlier. Yet all was not lost. By the late autumn his faithful backers, aided by the Irish lord Hugh O'Donnell, who met with James IV in Glasgow to plead Perkin's cause, had found a way out and a new sponsor. So Perkin escaped to Scotland and to a warm welcome from James, now firmly in charge of his own destiny and determined to make his Tudor rival's life as difficult as possible.

❧

JAMES IV's motives for supporting Perkin Warbeck were driven, however, by something greater than a desire to embarrass Henry Tudor. His developing self-image and his ambitions for his kingdom were focussed on enhancement of Scottish standing in Europe. By the summer of 1495, his sights were set on entering the Holy League in his own right and he was prepared to abandon the French alliance to achieve this aim, particularly if it meant that he could marry either Margaret of Austria, daughter of the Emperor Maximilian, or one of the daughters of Ferdinand and Isabella. For the time being, Perkin Warbeck was a card he would keep up his sleeve. There was no need to play this hand too soon as the Scottish king, a keen gambler, well knew. James was never a man to underestimate his own worth, nor did he see the need to be subtle in his diplomacy. When he got nowhere with Maximilian, he looked to the south. By September 1495 Bishop Blacader, a stalwart and able negotiator, like most high-ranking men of the cloth in those days, was at the Spanish court in Tarazona expressing his king's wishes for a much closer relationship between Scotland and Spain. He could also point out the disadvantages that might arise if his master was not taken seriously: breaking of the truce between England and Scotland and the possibility of supporting the Yorkist claimant if James did not get his way. Faced with this unexpected overture from a king whom they had hitherto regarded only as a junior partner of France (albeit one who might distract Henry VII from making war on France if the English king found he needed to defend his northern border against a belligerent Scottish foe), the Spanish monarchs played for time by announcing that they would send two ambassadors to Scotland for further discussions with James himself. This ploy went disastrously wrong when the ambassadors, travelling much more slowly than the returning Blacader, found that their instructions to continue stalling had been intercepted and were already known to James himself. His public humiliation of the Spanish diplomats was a calculated insult to Ferdinand and Isabella.

No doubt he was disappointed by their duplicity but he could not have been entirely surprised. It had been a brazen first attempt to catapult himself into the top rank of European monarchs. Yet he was not deterred. He had already spelt out the alternative and now he would proceed exactly as he had threatened. On 16 October 1495 James presided over an unusually large council meeting in Edinburgh. Forty of the country's leading nobles and churchmen, including the king's younger brother and heir, the duke of Ross, were present. Though no record of their discussions survives, it is clear that the main topic was whether to receive Perkin Warbeck. Even if concerns about the true identity of the pretender were raised – and by no means all of James's nobility were keen on a war with England, which seemed the likeliest outcome of embracing Warbeck – the dubious voices did not prevail. On 20 November 1495, Perkin and his small, bedraggled retinue rode through the gates of Stirling Castle to a warm welcome from the king. Perkin was received as 'Prince Richard of England', given a house in the town, royally clothed by his new sponsor in, among other garments, 'a greatcoat of the new fashion with sleeves, in velvet, lined with damask' and invited to tell his story to the lords and barons of Scotland at an especially summoned meeting in Perth. By this time he was so accustomed to repeating the fabricated version of his miraculous survival and wanderings that he probably believed it himself. And Perkin was undoubtedly a fine actor and very persuasive. James seems to have taken to him at once on a personal level. But did he really ever believe that this new arrival at his court, an impecunious wanderer taken up and then abandoned by some of Europe's most powerful rulers, was, indeed, the younger son of Edward IV of England?

Rationally, almost certainly not. James had seen how useful, at least for a while, Perkin had been to others and the time seemed right to derive what advantage he could from supporting the impostor himself. The course of his actions from November 1495 to October 1497, when he effectively abandoned Warbeck, indicates that Perkin's value to him had been cleverly assessed from the start. A document from the end of December 1495 was witnessed by someone described as 'Richard Plantagenet, son of the serene prince Edward, illustrious king of England, as he asserts'.[7] This is hardly a declaration of confidence in the recent arrival. And yet, at this time, the king of Scotland was already preparing for his guest to marry a distant kinswoman, Lady

Katherine Gordon, daughter of Alexander Gordon, the earl of Huntly.

Perkin's Scottish marriage is frequently cited as the major proof that James IV must have believed in him but this is not necessarily the case. If he liked the young man, as he seems to have done, the king probably saw no great harm in providing a bride from the Scottish nobility, without agonizing too much about whether the bridegroom was genuine or not. The gesture was an earnest demonstration of his own sincerity and perhaps also of the romantic side of his nature.[8] This was the stuff of the tales told by the professional storytellers who entertained James and the court through the long nights of the Scottish winter, or of the *makars*, the poets whose output was part of a golden age of Scottish literature. A handsome prince who had narrowly escaped death and lived the life of a fugitive, miraculously rediscovered and come to claim his birthright, was to wed a beautiful and virtuous noble lady. What heart could not warm to this story, or praise the Scottish king as the young couple's benefactor?

In truth, the union was somewhat less glittering than it first appeared. James IV was not offering a close relative to Warbeck. Katherine Gordon is often described as the king's cousin but this was a term very loosely used in the fifteenth and sixteenth centuries; Katherine's mother, Lady Annabella Stewart, was, in fact, James IV's great-aunt. Such a marriage, would, however, undoubtedly add shine to the pretender's somewhat tarnished prestige. It also sent a message to Henry VII that this trouble-some impostor might make things even more difficult by estab-lishing his own spurious dynasty, backed by Scotland. If the earl of Huntly entertained any misgivings about his daughter's future should her husband's identity prove false, he must have quickly overcome them. The young lady's own views are similarly unknown and would not have mattered much in any case. She married at the command of James IV, a man who loved women but, as with all men of his time, viewed them as the weaker vessel and certainly not to be consulted in such matters. At the back of his mind may well have been the realization that he was wedding her to a young man who was a complete fraud but he could equally argue that, impostor or no, if the rediscovered duke of York was successful in his bid for the English throne, then Katherine would become a queen. And he, James, would expect to dictate the future of the entire British Isles.

The marriage was celebrated in Edinburgh, on or around 13 January 1496. This would have been about the earliest time after Warbeck's arrival in Scotland permitted by the religious calendar, which did not allow weddings in Advent or over the Christmas period. Though an arranged union, it appears to have been a happy one. Perkin had every reason to be delighted with this great improvement in his prospects and in his bride herself, who was, by all accounts, a very attractive young woman. Perkin seems to have been enchanted by Katherine, addressing her in the most flowery of language: 'All look at your face, so bright and serene that it gives splendour to the cloudy sky; all look at your eyes as brilliant as stars, which make all pain to be forgotten, and turn despair into delight; all look at your neck, which outshines pearls; all look at your fine forehead, your purple light of youth, your fair hair; in one word, at the splendid perfection of your person; and looking at, they cannot choose but love you.' Perhaps Perkin's ardour did have an effect, for Katherine was to prove a loyal wife, even when the heady days of her husband's wooing were replaced by the eventual realization that his cause was lost.

The Scottish king was pleased with his support of 'the duke of York' and no doubt gratified that the match was acceptable to both parties, but it was a means to an end. James IV was looking for personal glory and he intended to send a message to the English that, from now on, they would have to deal with him. If Henry VII had ever entertained any hopes that the pro-English party in Scotland would prevent war, by the summer of 1496 he was forced to accept that James's intentions were bellicose and that the young King of Scots would not sit quietly in Edinburgh for much longer. The pretender's cause gave James all the excuse he needed for a military confrontation and he would not be deterred. The time for talking was over and the longer Warbeck stayed without matters being brought to a head, the more of a drain he and his followers were on the Scottish exchequer. James could not command Henry VII's financial resources, though he was not the pauper that some have made out.

Here was a real possibility to put England at a disadvantage and to gain territory at the expense of a king preoccupied by the prospect of domestic rebellion and the desire to assure the European powers that he could handle all the threats against him. Henry knew earlier than his fellow monarchs that Perkin had found refuge in Scotland and was keen to persuade them that it was a matter of no importance in his relationship with the King of Scots. In March 1496 his instructions to the Richmond Herald, sent on a diplomatic mission to France, were deliberately nonchalant:

> If it should happen that the French king, or any great personages of his Council, should make any question or enquiry how the king and the king of Scotland accord, seeing that the latter supports and entertains the garçon [Warbeck] in his kingdom ... he may reply that ... the king cares nothing about it and that it is the least of his troubles. For the said king of Scotland is unable to injure him in any manner whatever, except, perhaps, in making him spend his money in vain.[9]

This was not an analysis of the situation that would have appealed to James IV, who did not like to be set at nought in the international reckoning. Six months later things looked very different. In the late summer of 1496, when James and the Scottish host crossed the river Tweed into Northumberland, they had Perkin Warbeck, now calling himself 'Richard IV', in tow. It was James's most public gesture of support for the pretender, though he was fast losing interest. Spoiling for a fight, eager to display the personal valour that he had learned as a young, rebellious prince, James wanted to do damage in the Borders, to raid, attack fortifications and, above all, to see if he could regain for Scotland the town of Berwick. If the north of England rose for 'Richard IV', that would be a bonus but he does not seem to have been surprised when no such support materialized or particularly dismayed when Perkin, who did not share his delight in arms, left the army after just one day in England. For James, the fight was only just beginning.

The proclamation that preceded Perkin's inglorious withdrawal, in which he described himself as 'Richard, by the grace of God, King of England, Lord of Ireland, Prince of Wales', boasted that Henry VII was preparing to flee and put a price of £1,000 on Henry Tudor's head. This piece of rhetoric, describing Henry as 'our mortal enemy [who], agreeable to the meanness of his birth, hath trodden under foot the honour of this nation, selling our best confederates for money, and making merchandise of the blood, estates and fortunes of our peers and subjects by feigned wars and dishonourable peace, only to enrich his coffers' is eloquent witness of the delusions of Perkin Warbeck's Yorkist backers and that their assertion that the King of Scots' support had come without any strings attached, 'without any pact or promise, or so much as a demand of anything that may prejudice our crown or subjects', was either grossly naïve or an outright lie.[10]

Henry VII had initially required the northern lords to defend the border with Scotland themselves, reasoning that they had a very strong incentive to do so as they would suffer James IV's depredations first. Spies kept the English king informed but their information on the level of disaffection in the north-west turned out to be more alarmist than was justified. As Ian Arthurson pointed out in his fine account of the Warbeck conspiracy, 'old memories died quickly in the harsh climate of border defence.' Henry was also being fed information from a pro-English traitor at the Scottish court, John Ramsay, formerly earl of Bothwell, a disgruntled supporter of James III who had seen his lands confiscated and his title passed to the Hepburns in 1488. Ramsay raised the tantalizing possibility that the duke of Ross, James IV's brother, might be won over to the English side.[11] Ramsay was, however, inclined to paint far too rosy a picture of the internal opposition to a war within Scotland itself. His view of James's own reckless desire for confrontation is probably more accurate: 'The young adventurousness of the king,' Ramsay wrote, 'will jeopardize himself, the boy [Perkin] and all his people ... I find him as far out of reason, and so little inclined to goodness, but all to trouble and cruelty without [unless] his will be fulfilled in all points ...'

Ramsay's resentment towards James IV is evident but his depiction of the king's strong will rings true. Others commented on the Scottish king's relish for personal danger. The newly arrived ambassador from Spain, Pedro de Ayala, who became a considerable admirer of James IV, reluctantly accompanied the 1496 invasion of Northumberland, remarking that the king was 'courageous, even more so than a king should be. I am a good witness of it. I have seen him often undertake most dangerous things in the last wars. I sometimes clung to his skirts and succeeded in keeping him back. On such occasions he did not take the least care of himself.'[12] James told Ayala that because it was the duty of his subjects to follow him without question whatever the justness of the cause, he felt that he must lead from the front.

James was undeterred by Perkin's departure. He was not for turning back. He destroyed five fortified houses in the valleys of the rivers Tweed and Till and laid siege to Heton Castle. How long he would have stayed is open to doubt. By now it was late September and the end of the campaigning season was fast approaching. The chance to show the world his bravery, embarrass Henry VII and try out his artillery (James was keenly interested in new military developments) all spurred him to continue for a while. But his plans did not include full-scale confrontation. In the event, the decision to raise the siege and return to Scotland was made for him, when he learned on the night of 25–6 September that an English army, commanded by the earl of Surrey, had left Newcastle that day. James did not delay. He abandoned the siege and took his entire army back across the Tweed into Scotland in the space of eight hours. It had scarcely been a war – more of a classic raid in the Borders, in time-honoured fashion. Henry VII, though, did not see it that way. If James IV wanted a war, he would give him one.

Angered by this display of Stewart bravado, Henry prepared for a serious fight. While James went hunting in the autumn, the English king sought the financial backing that would enable him to wage a full-scale war, on land and sea, with his Scottish rival. By January 1497, parliament had ratified a grant of £120,000, a huge sum by late fifteenth-century standards, equivalent to about £64 million today. This was twenty times the annual revenue of James IV and gives a sobering indication of the very differing financial resources of the two kings. It also showed that Henry's thoughts of revenge were on a disproportionate scale to the insult he had received. James IV may not have known the full scale of English preparations but his anxiety grew. Though no one expected fighting before the summer, the Stewart king spent Christmas 1496 at Melrose Abbey, only ten miles from the English border. Throughout the winter months he continued with his own preparations, including a pre-emptive strike in February which was perhaps intended to test out English strength in the Borders but did little other than to annoy Henry VII even more. By Easter, when he had originally intended to call the muster of his lieges to bring together his army, the Scottish king's artillery was being prepared for action. The famous gun Mons Meg, given to his grandfather, James II, was readied for action. She had not been used since 1489 and was the most deadly offensive weapon in the British Isles, able to fire an eighteen-inch stone ball more than a mile and a half. By providing her with new wooden wheels, James, who may have known by then considerably more about the extent of the preparations by Henry VII, and therefore the odds he faced, was making a statement of intent. He would not sit idly by and wait but take the attack to the English. A further, brief flurry of diplomatic activity in May 1497, when Henry again demanded that Perkin Warbeck be handed over, came to nothing. For though James's support of Perkin had lessened, and the pretender does not seem to have been at the Scottish court for many months, he had not yet entirely abandoned him as he believed Perkin might still be a useful tool in a struggle of uneven strength. James did not back down. The army was summoned to meet in the Borders in early June and the Scottish king continued as bold as ever, summoning his falconers and musicians to meet him and preparing to ride to war in a new green coat. This, he believed, was what kings should do. It is a highly arresting image of a fearless, energetic young man prepared to confront a formidable foe. But for the full-scale conflict, the cut and thrust of sword and the chance to gain new territory, he would have, once again, to wait.

⚶

HENRY VII had good reason to fear Perkin Warbeck, an impostor who, despite numerous setbacks, had still not gone away. But, in the summer of 1497, it was not the Flemish boy who halted the Scottish war in its tracks. Instead, the danger came from the far west of England, where the men of Devon and Cornwall rose in revolt against the king. Originally led out of Cornwall by a local blacksmith who soon found many sympathizers in his objection to the exorbitantly high taxes being raised by Henry's government to fund the war, the rebels gathered support from the local gentry as they moved east towards London and also sent messages to Warbeck in Scotland offering to help him. By the start of June the rebel army, now led by a West Country nobleman, Lord Audley (who had been expected to participate in the northern campaign but was still a Yorkist at heart), camped outside the cathedral town of Wells in Somerset, its numbers swelling all the time. As the rebel forces split in two, still moving quickly towards London, Henry VII faced one of the greatest crises of his reign. A force variously reckoned at between fifteen and forty thousand men was bearing down on him. Fearing an assault on the capital and with

significant parts of his army already dispersed in preparation
for war in the north, Henry moved his wife and family into
the Tower of London for their own protection. The battle of
Blackheath, fought on 17 June 1497, has been called the defining
moment of his reign. Yet though he won a decisive victory, this
was largely thanks to the expertise of his most durable supporter,
the earl of Oxford, and the bravery of his chamberlain, Giles
Daubeney, a Somerset man himself, whose loyalty was put to a
severe test. The Spanish ambassador to the Flemish and imperial
courts conveyed the uncertainty that engulfed England and
perfectly captured the scale of the threat to the Tudors when he
described 'a time when the whole kingdom was against the king,
and when Perequin [Perkin] had entered the country calling
himself king, and the king of Scotland was coming in by another
way, and the whole country was in rebellion, and the men of
Cornwall were giving battle at a short distance from London;
when, had the king lost the battle, he would have been finished
off and beheaded.'[13] No wonder de Ayala, writing the following
year to Ferdinand and Isabella in Spain, remarked that 'the king
looks old for his years, but young for the sorrowful life he has
led.'[14]

Blackheath was a decisive victory in military terms, crushing
the rebels and leading to the summary execution of their leaders.
But it did not mean the end of discontent in the south-west of
England, nor did it immediately solve the problem of Perkin
Warbeck. In fact, the pretender would make one last attempt to
exploit the situation in England and to add to Henry Tudor's
discomfiture. It is hard to say how much encouragement he was
given to leave Scotland – the Spanish later took credit for having
brokered his departure – but in the second week of July 1497,
Perkin and his Scottish wife set sail from Ayr, on the west coast,
in a Breton ship appropriately named the *Cuckoo*. James had been
compelled to spend £150, more than Perkin's monthly pension,
to provision his voyage, so even getting rid of him was costly.

On 7 September, having stopped for a while in Ireland,
Perkin finally set foot on the soil of the kingdom he claimed as

his. Landing at Whitesands Bay on the western tip of Cornwall, he moved on to Bodmin and pressed east with a growing force of men. Ten days after his arrival he was at the gates of Exeter with an army of ten thousand but found, after a day of fighting, that the citizens were even less inclined to support him than they were the Cornishmen earlier in the year. It was at Taunton in Somerset that the king's forces finally caught up with him. With John Taylor, who had started him on his amazing career of deception six years earlier, Warbeck and a few close followers tried to make their escape. Abandoning those who had risen for them, they took refuge in Beaulieu Abbey in Hampshire, still hoping, presumably, to get away yet again by sea. But the abbot alerted the authorities and Warbeck was captured.

Perkin was taken back to Taunton, where Henry awaited him. His life would be spared, but he must make and sign a full confession. For a year he was allowed to live at court under supervision but an attempt to escape from his locked quarters brought him public humiliation in the stocks and then far stricter captivity in the Tower of London. Despite these setbacks, the cause of the 'duke of the York' was not quite defeated and a further plot in the last year of the fifteenth century cost Perkin and the innocent earl of Warwick, his fellow prisoner in the Tower, their lives. Only then was the Yorkist threat seriously diminished, though far from destroyed. It rumbled on for years. The disaffected west of England also suffered, feeling Henry's displeasure for much of the rest of his reign. But there was one notable survivor of the Warbeck conspiracy. Lady Katherine Gordon was treated as befitted her rank and attached to the household of Queen Elizabeth. She lived on well into the reign of Henry VIII, marrying three more times. If the opportunity to return to Scotland was given when her husband was put to death, Katherine did not take it. She adapted well to her new life and it is doubtful, given all that had happened to her, that she would have wanted to go back.

Yet if she had done, it would have been to a less warlike Scotland. For unknown to Perkin and Lady Katherine, two days before they arrived in England a seven-year truce had been signed by Scottish and English diplomats at Ayton in Berwickshire. It followed a brief flurry of military activity in the previous month, in which James had besieged Norham Castle, the stronghold of the bishop of Durham, and the earl of Surrey had attacked Ayton Castle, a property of the Hume family. But this kind of Border skirmishing could hardly be viewed as a war and neither side had the will or the means to turn it into one. James IV's invitation to the earl to settle the fate of Berwick in hand-to-hand conflict was a fine chivalric flourish, typical of the king, though unfair to Surrey, who was more than fifty years old, whereas James was only twenty-four. It was never going to happen and Surrey politely declined, thanking the Scottish king 'that he would put him to so much honour that he being a king anointed would fight hand to hand with so poor a man as he [referring to himself in the third person]', though he went on to add, more forthrightly, that 'his commission was to do the King of Scots all the harm he could and so he had done and would do'.[15] In 1497, James IV had no concept of just how much harm Surrey might one day do him. But for now, Henry VII urgently wanted peace and James was running out of men and money. A brighter prospect beckoned. Instead of remaining Henry Tudor's rival, James Stewart would join the family. His future lay, not as an enemy, but as Henry's son-in-law.

CHAPTER FIVE

A Summer Wedding

⚭

'Now fair, fairest of every fair,
Princess most pleasant and preclare,
The lustiest one alive that been
Welcome of Scotland to be queen.'

Verses attributed to the poet William Dunbar,
welcoming the new queen to Scotland

'I would I were with your grace now and many times more.'

Margaret Tudor, Queen of Scots, betrays the homesickness of
a thirteen-year-old bride to her father, Henry VII

THE GIRL WHO WOULD become Scotland's queen was ten years old at the time of Perkin Warbeck's execution. The second child and eldest daughter of Henry VII and Elizabeth of York, the princess had been born at Westminster Palace on 28 November 1489 and named after her paternal grandmother, Margaret Beaufort. Her early years were spent in the royal nursery at the palace of Sheen, on the banks of the Thames, with a growing band of brothers and sisters, though only three other children, Arthur, Henry and a younger sister, Mary, would survive infancy. In 1497 a serious fire at Christmas time destroyed much of Sheen and the royal children were moved to Eltham. Set in beautiful grounds and well away from the unhealthy air of London, Eltham had been popular with the English royal family since the early fourteenth century and Margaret's grandfather, Edward IV, added a splendid great hall, which can still be seen today.

Margaret grew up in an affectionate family setting, surrounded by privilege and luxury unimaginable to the vast bulk of her father's subjects. Though affairs of state inevitably meant that the princess spent more time with her mother and grandmother than her father, Henry VII seems to have been genuinely fond of his children and was an indulgent parent, showering them with gifts. The information that survives about Margaret's upbringing and education shows that she was well prepared for the role that would inevitably be hers: that of the wife of a European prince or king. For while her father faced down constant threats to his fledgling dynasty and lived daily with the chronic insecurity this engendered, Margaret's preparation for queenship continued tranquilly in safe surroundings. It is often asserted that she was less studious than her brothers and her rather shaky signature on the voluminous correspondence that emanated from her in later life suggests that writing was not her strong point. But ladies of high birth were accustomed to dictating their letters, sometimes adding brief comments in their own hand at the end, and there was, besides, no need for Margaret to receive an education comparable to that of her brothers, or so contemporaries would have thought.

She was certainly not neglected and among her tutors were the foremost English scholars of the day, Thomas Linacre, John Colet and William Grocyn. With these men, she studied Latin and learned to speak French, essential accomplishments for a Renaissance princess. Perhaps more to her taste were her lessons in archery and dancing, as well as her music. Like all the Tudors, Margaret was very musical and she could play the lute and clavichord. Her love of fine clothes and rich jewellery was another Tudor trait, though it was also a statement of rank and expected of royalty at the time. All these facets of her character and training combined to make her an attractive prospect on the European marriage scene, once she reached the required age of twelve years. Until that time, she was rarely seen in public, though she did present a gold and diamond ring to Edmund de la Pole at the jousts to celebrate the creation of her brother, Henry, as duke of York in 1494.[1]

The possibility of a match between James IV and Margaret was first raised by Henry VII in 1496, when he was trying to detach James from Perkin Warbeck. The King of Scots did not take up the offer at this point, perhaps because he was still hoping for a grander Spanish marriage. Margaret's age was also a stumbling block and would remain a cause of concern to Queen Elizabeth and Margaret Beaufort. Henry himself voiced their worries (though he was also playing politics) when he told Pedro de Ayala:

> I am really sorry that I have not a daughter or a sister for him [James IV]; for I have loved him most sincerely since the conclusion of the peace ... but I have already told you, more than once, that a marriage between him and my daughter has many inconveniences. She has not yet completed the ninth year of her age, and is so delicate and weak that she must be married much later than other young ladies. Thus it would be necessary to wait at least another nine years.

This was surely an exaggeration. Margaret may or may not have been small for her age in 1498 when this conversation took place, but waiting a further nine years seems excessive. But the king went on to explain that his concerns were shared by his wife and mother, saying that they were 'very much against this marriage. They say if the marriage were concluded, we should be obliged to send the princess directly to Scotland, in which case they fear the King of Scots would not wait, but injure her, and endanger her health.'[2] There spoke the voice of Margaret Beaufort, who did not want her granddaughter to endure the kind of sexual trauma that had been visited on her at too young an age.

Henry VII also had another, more glorious, union to negotiate and he made this his priority in the closing years of the fifteenth century. His heir, Prince Arthur, was being prepared for the throne in his own household at Ludlow. A marriage had been arranged between Arthur and Katherine of Aragon, youngest daughter of Ferdinand and Isabella. This union was vital to Henry's foreign policy. Scotland and England were officially at peace, Margaret was still too young to live with James IV as his wife, and her brother's future was more important. Arthur and Katherine were married at St Paul's Cathedral in November 1501, amid great rejoicing. The way was now clear for completion of the prolonged diplomatic discussions between England and Scotland that would, it was hoped, bring to an end years of hostility between the two countries and send Princess Margaret Tudor to Scotland as its queen.

Margaret's future husband does not seem to have minded the delay, nor does he seriously appear to have considered looking elsewhere for a wife. This may be because domestic disorder was now well in the past and he ruled over a stable kingdom that had seen its stock rise internationally. He had two brothers as potential successors, though most rulers in those days wanted sons, rather than siblings, to inherit their thrones and his growing brood of bastard children were proof of his ability to beget legitimate offspring once he did marry. More tellingly, he had also taken a new mistress, with whom he seems to have been very happy, and she would prove more durable than any of her predecessors.

Her name was Janet Kennedy. This cousin of Lady Katherine Gordon was probably born around 1480, making her about twenty years old when she became the mistress of James IV. She had grown up in the south-west of Scotland, in Ayrshire, where the Kennedy family, proud of their Gaelic background and traditions, lived. Janet came from a well-off family with connections to the court but she probably received little formal education, though she may have been able to read. Wed by the age of sixteen to a Gordon kinsman of her mother, Janet had a daughter in 1496. The marriage did not last long. The concept of marriage in fifteenth and early sixteenth-century Scotland was much more fluid than might be supposed; divorce was very rare but the ending of relationships and the taking up of new partners was not. It was even possible to remarry while a previous spouse was still alive and the Church seems to have turned a blind eye to this flagrant sin, especially if the parties involved were well connected politically. By 1498, Janet had moved on to become the mistress of the forty-seven-year-old Archibald, earl of Angus, a much more important and influential man than her first husband. He was also married but this did not stop him from making generous grants of land to Janet which, it was noted in the official documentation, were because of his 'singular affection and love for her'. But the earl's devotion to his teenage mistress was not returned for long. Perhaps because she was often about the court with Angus, Janet came to the attention of the king. In 1499 she abandoned Angus for a greater lover, James IV himself. At about this time, Angus fell out with his monarch, though it is not clear whether Janet was the cause of their disagreement. He remained out of favour for a decade. But Janet Kennedy had definitely arrived.

No portrait of her survives but she was evidently a young woman whose looks and personality attracted attention and she had won the king's heart. James was never shy of acknowledging his amours and was a responsible parent to the three illegitimate children he had already sired. Janet lived openly with him at Stirling Castle throughout all the time that diplomatic discussions were going on for his English marriage and she travelled to other parts of Scotland in his company as well. James paid her expenses, gave her costly clothes and gifts and the castle of Darnaway in the north-eastern part of the country. She was a feminine influence in what was otherwise a very masculine court. Janet appears to have been a keen horsewoman and James's gifts of a black horse and sumptuous riding clothes allow tantalizing glimpses of her life and interests. She was, like most women of her background, a keen embroiderer, a pastime that she shared with the king himself. For James was also handy with a needle and thread, as Janet's biographer has pointed out, and the treasurer's accounts show that gold threads, sewing silks, needles, thimbles and linen cloth were purchased, 'for the king to broider with'.[3] This conjures up a delicious image of the physically restless, daredevil King of Scots sitting quietly with his mistress on a light-filled summer's afternoon, both with their heads bent over their needlework in an unexpected picture of domestic bliss.

As the new century dawned, James IV was confident and eager, a king well in control of his country and always looking to enhance its prestige. The Spanish ambassador, like other foreign visitors, was much taken with Scotland and its king. The country was, he noted, 'very old and very noble and the king possesses great virtues and no defects worth mentioning'. Ferdinand and Isabella had asked to know more about this distant northern land and its monarch, a young man who could potentially jeopardize their aims in Europe if he distracted England too much. And it is to Pedro de Ayala that we owe the detailed description of James IV that brings him very much to life:

> He is of noble stature, neither tall nor short, and as handsome in complexion and shape as a man can be. His address is very agreeable. He speaks the following languages: Latin (very well), French, German, Flemish, Italian and Spanish. He likes, very much, to receive Spanish letters. His own Scotch language is as different from English as Aragonese from Castilian. The king speaks, besides, the language of the savages who live in some parts of Scotland and on the islands. It is as different from Scots as Biscayan is from Castilian. His knowledge of languages is wonderful. He is well read in the Bible and in some other devout books. He is a good historian. He has read many Latin and French histories and profited by them, as he has a very good memory. He never cuts his hair or beard. It becomes him very well.

Ayala went on to comment that James was a good son of the Church, saying all his prayers, not eating meat on Wednesdays or Fridays and not riding on Sundays 'for any consideration, not even to mass ... he gives alms liberally but is a severe judge, especially in the case of murderers ... his deeds are as good as his words. For this reason and because he is a humane prince, he is much loved.' Temperate in eating and drinking, neither prodigal nor avaricious, he was also blessed with good judgement. But he was not perfect: 'I can say with truth that he esteems himself as much as though he were Lord of the world,' and he was very fond of war, which was profitable to both James and Scotland. Even allowing for Ayala's partiality, for he was clearly entranced both by the country and its king, this is a portrait of an impressive man.[4] No longer the uncertain boy who felt guilty for having brought about his father's death, James had blossomed into one of the leading monarchs of his day. An extensive and ambitious building programme at the major palaces of Scotland visibly underlined his success and was certainly on a par with Henry VII's own achievements in this respect. Scotland might be smaller and chillier than England but its royal homes were magnificent and James spent generously on Linlithgow, Stirling, Edinburgh Castle and Holyrood Palace. He was a fitting husband for an English princess from a new dynasty, even if the nobility of England were convinced of their own innate superiority over the Scots.

Although she could never be his wife, Janet Kennedy's love affair with the king may partly explain why James was in no hurry to finalize his own wedding. Romantic historians of the past, taken in by lurid tales of the demise of his earlier mistress, Margaret Drummond, who died with two of her sisters in mysterious circumstances in 1502, have wrongly assigned the king's slowness to an affair that was over some years before. Yet even as Janet gave birth to a son, later created the earl of Moray, and another daughter by the king, James and she must both have known that she could not continue by his side indefinitely. When the three agreements known as the Treaty of Perpetual Peace were signed in London on 24 January 1502, Margaret Tudor's arrival in Scotland was still eighteen months away, but that she would become, at last, the wife of James IV was no longer in doubt.

The signatories at Richmond Palace that winter's day were four churchmen and two soldier-politicians, a mix typical of the time, when most diplomats were also men of the cloth. The Scots were represented by Bishop Robert Blacader, Lord Patrick Bothwell and Andrew Forman, soon to be bishop of Moray. The English signatories were Henry Deane, archbishop of Canterbury, Richard Fox, greatly experienced in Scottish matters and now holding the see of Winchester, and Thomas Howard, earl of Surrey. These men all knew one another from previous negotiations or diplomatic exchanges and it was they who hammered out the details of the agreements that would unite James IV and Margaret Tudor.[5] There were also two other treaties. One, for 'Peace and Friendship', supported by interested European parties including the kings of France and Spain, the Austrian emperor, Maximilian, the Hanseatic League and the Brandenburg merchants, demonstrated the importance attached to an Anglo–Scottish peace by Europe's key players.

There was also a connected, and less well known, third treaty, dealing with the highly contentious area of the Borders as well as introducing measures to police the seas, where piracy was rife, and to regularize naval traffic. For while the overriding aim of these treaties was to bring about a royal marriage, the importance of day-to-day justice in the Borders could not be forgotten. This was where the reality of the new Tudor and Stewart friendship would be put fully to the test. The established system of Border courts and their regular meetings had managed to continue even with the interruption of war in the 1490s but there was a residue of bad blood on both sides. New, detailed legislation set out procedures governing the apprehension and punishment of cross-border raiders and those accused of homicide would be tried by a mixed panel of Scottish and English jurors. There would be regular supervision of the Border courts with greater involvement of local lords and appointments of men learned in civil law. Despite the popular impression of continued lawlessness in the

Borders, this legislation did lead to a period of comparative tranquillity in the final years of Henry VII's reign, with considerable cross-border cooperation in dealing with gangs of marauding thieves.[6]

The marriage treaty itself dealt with loftier matters. Margaret's dower was set at £10,000 (the equivalent of nearly six million pounds in today's money), one third of which was to be paid on her wedding day and the remainder two years after. This was a welcome sum for the always cash-strapped Scottish treasury. James's financial obligations to his wife were also set out: he was to endow her for life with lands and other income yielding £2,000 per annum (just over a million pounds today) and she was to have £1,000 Scots or the equivalent of just over £300 sterling at her own disposal (about £174,000 in today's money).* A healthy income and the twenty-four English attendants she was permitted as part of the agreement would help keep Margaret in the manner to which she had become accustomed.

This all seemed well and good but there was a more serious underlying issue that exercised the minds of Henry VII and his advisers as the treaty discussions neared completion. It was a question that was bound to be raised but could not really be answered except hypothetically. Supposing that the marriage led to the eventual succession to the throne of England by the children of James and Margaret? At the time the treaty was signed, Henry VII had two apparently healthy sons and Arthur, the elder, was just married and expected, in due course, to produce heirs of his own. The possibility that Margaret's line might one day rule England seemed remote but could not be entirely discounted. Interestingly, the English king did not see this outcome as necessarily undesirable. The Scottish historian John Leslie reported that Henry said that if such a thing did happen – which God forbid – England would be unscathed: 'in that case England would not accress unto Scotland but Scotland

---

* The Scottish pound was worth about one third of the English pound

would accress unto England, as the most noble head of the whole isle.'[7] Henry went on the give the example of Normandy coming into English hands centuries earlier, a disingenuous parallel surely and not one that the Anglo-Saxons would have recognized. But then a marriage between Margaret and another foreign prince might produce an even less desirable outcome, with England the satellite of some European power. Henry was not in the mood for further speculation and voices of opposition to the Scottish match were silenced. All was ready for the first public and ceremonial aspect of the treaty, a further show of Tudor display that would set the seal on twelve months of glorious diplomatic achievement, the high point of Henry VII's reign.

Margaret's proxy wedding to James IV took place at Richmond the day after the treaty was concluded, on 25 January, St Paul's Day, in the year 1502. Though not as splendid an occasion as the wedding of Arthur to Katherine of Aragon two months earlier, it was still a considerable spectacle. In attendance were ambassadors from Spain and Venice, papal and French diplomats, three archbishops of the British Isles – Blacader of Glasgow, Deane of Canterbury and Savage of York – as well as the bishops of Winchester, Chester, Rochester and Norwich. The English nobility was headed by the young duke of Buckingham, who was accompanied by nineteen earls and lords, including Lord Stanley, Henry VII's stepfather, and a further twenty-eight bannerets and knights. The ladies present included the six-year-old Princess Mary, younger daughter of the king and queen, and Elizabeth's sister, Katherine, as well as Lady Katherine Gordon, who had hoped to be a queen in England but was now witness to the betrothal of a young English princess who would become Queen of Scots. Surprisingly, missing from the roll call is the king's mother, now countess of Derby. Since Margaret Beaufort's husband was present, we can only assume that her health or extremely difficult travel conditions kept her away, since she had always taken a keen interest in family matters and in Margaret's marriage in particular. The newly wed Arthur and his Spanish wife were already established in their separate household in Ludlow, leaving Prince Henry as the senior royal male present after his father. The prince had appeared enthusiastic at his brother's wedding but a story was put around subsequently that he was much less enthralled by the realization that his sister, as Queen of Scots, would take precedence over him. Theirs became a difficult relationship and the seeds of their rivalry and mistrust may have been built on this childish resentment of a sister's elevation to a position that Henry did not, at this stage, believe he would ever occupy. And on this day it was Margaret, twelve years old and destined to wear a crown, who was the focus of attention.

The royal family first heard High Mass together in the chapel of Richmond Palace, followed by a 'notable sermon' made by the bishop of Chichester. From there, they proceeded to the Queen's Great Chamber, a magnificent room in Henry VII's newly built palace, where the details of the betrothal ceremony itself were enacted. Once it had been formally established that papal dispensation was given (Margaret and James were distantly related) and that there was no impediment on either side, Margaret was asked by the archbishop of Glasgow whether she was content to undertake this marriage without compulsion and of her own free will. Well-rehearsed, the princess answered: 'If it please my Lord and Father the King and my Lady my Mother the Queen.' Henry indicated that she had both their blessings and Blacader read the words of the betrothal, by which Lord Bothwell undertook marriage with Princess Margaret on behalf of his sovereign, 'James, by the grace of God King of Scotland'. Margaret replied:

> I Margaret, the first begotten daughter of the right excellent, right high and mighty prince and princess, Henry, by the grace of God King of England, and Elizabeth, Queen of the same, wittingly and of deliberate mind, having twelve years complete in age in the month of November last be past, contract matrimony with the right excellent, right high and mighty prince James, King of Scotland, the person of whom

Patrick, earl of Bothwell, is procurator; and take the said
James, King of Scotland, unto and for my husband and
spouse, and all other for him forsake, during his and mine
lives natural; and thereto I plight and give to him, in your
person as procurator aforesaid, my faith and truth. [8]

Margaret was now technically Queen of Scots, though she knew
that another, greater ceremony awaited her on her arrival in
Scotland. But the date of that was still some way off, as it had
been agreed that she would not cross the border into Scotland
before 1 May 1503. Meanwhile, there was much to celebrate.
This first stage of the marriage in Richmond was followed by
anthems and peals of trumpets and two separate feasts, one for
Henry VII and the Scottish dignitaries and another, more
intimate and affectionate, for Elizabeth of York and Margaret.
'The queen,' it was reported, 'took her daughter the Queen of
Scots by the hand and dined both at one mess covered.' Bells
rang in London to celebrate the betrothal; there were street
bonfires and wine supplied to the citizenry, giving an air of
festivity despite the winter season. On the afternoon of 25
January was the first in a series of jousts at which the duke of
Buckingham and other courtiers figured prominently. One of
these gentlemen, perhaps half-noticed by the little Princess
Mary, was Charles Brandon, who would one day become her
second husband. Margaret herself, in her first official act as a
queen, gave out the prizes.

After further pageants, dancing and disguisings, which were
the essence of court entertainment at the time, there was an
elaborate exchange of costly gifts, with the Scottish representatives going home weighed down with gold and silver plate and
the lesser gentlemen of their delegation receiving velvet gowns.
The heralds of both countries, too, fêted each other and Bothwell
left behind the gown of cloth of gold he had worn to represent
his king at the betrothal. This display of ceremony, entertainment and largesse at the palace on which Henry VII had lavished
money was intended to honour his daughter but also to bring

home to the Scots the power and wealth of their new queen's family. It was a lesson not lost on James IV, who strove mightily to compete when it came time to celebrate the actual wedding in Scotland in the summer of 1503.

For Henry VII, those early months of 1502 were the public witness of the success of a constant battle for survival. He had established his dynasty and safeguarded its inheritance. Alas, it had been very much a false dawn, for the year 1502–3 was to bring unimagined personal tragedy and loss to a monarch who, despite increasing signs that his health was now suffering as the result of the constant rigours of rule, must briefly have entertained the hope that the worst was behind him.

THERE WERE indications as early as 1501 that Henry's health was a concern. In July of that year he wrote a very loving but rather troubling letter to his mother, apologizing that he did not write to her in his own hand more often, 'wherefore I beseech you to pardon me, for verily, Madame, my sight is nothing so perfect as it has been'.[9] Failing eyesight became a Tudor characteristic: Henry VIII towards the end of his life and Mary I and Elizabeth throughout theirs had poor vision. But the woes of Henry VII in the spring of 1502 were far greater than his restricted sight. At the beginning of April came wholly unexpected and dreadful news from Ludlow. Prince Arthur had died after a short illness. Arthur was Henry and Elizabeth's firstborn and all their hopes had been invested in him. A dutiful son, carefully educated and prepared to succeed his father, recently married to a Spanish princess as part of an important diplomatic alliance, was suddenly gone. The shock was immense.

The news was broken to the king at Greenwich by his confessor before dawn on 4 April. Stunned, Henry sent for Elizabeth so that they could face this tragedy together. They had come through years of uncertainty as they tried to establish their dynasty and had outfaced or outlasted each new challenge, but the death of their eldest son was a blow almost beyond endurance. In truth, neither of them had spent much time with Prince Arthur, as was the custom in royal families in those days, but this did not mean that their affection for him as their son was necessarily any the less. And on him they had pinned their hopes for the future, even as their family grew. They lost several children in infancy, including a third son, Edmund, who had been born and died in 1499. Now their family consisted, as the queen reminded her husband, of 'a fair prince' and two princesses. She sought to alleviate the king's distress by reminding him that they were both still young and could yet have more children. When she felt she had calmed Henry sufficiently the queen retired to her own chamber, where the strain and sorrow brought about a complete collapse: 'Natural and motherly remembrance of that great loss smote her so sorrowful to the heart that those about her were fain to send for the king to comfort her. Then his Grace, of true gentle and faithful love, in good haste came and relieved her, and showed her how wise counsel she had given him before, and he for his part would thank God for his son, and would she should do in like wise.'[10]

It is a rare glimpse of the human pain that afflicted the great as well as the common man in those times when the unpredictability of life was ever present. Henry VII is often depicted as a cold, strange, avaricious man but such generalizations fail to do him justice. The need for the support of his wife and their efforts to comfort each other are touching witness to the depth of their sorrow and to all they had endured as a couple. Elizabeth was no longer the elegant beauty Henry had married for dynastic security in 1486. Childbearing had coarsened her figure and endangered her health, particularly during her last pregnancy and delivery. But she was determined to try once more, to be as good as her word to her husband. A couple of months later she was pregnant again.

During the summer she seems to have spent considerable time in the company of her daughters. Her accounts show a series of items purchased for the young Queen of Scots: a black velvet dress, several pairs of sleeves, furs and more mundane items like strings for Margaret's lute. They are a touching witness to a mother's love for a daughter she knew would soon be leaving her. The queen also travelled a great deal in 1502, including a visit to her Stafford relatives in Wales, despite her advancing pregnancy. It was part of her duty as Henry's queen but it must have taken its toll. Yet there was no immediate cause for concern. The king and queen spent Christmas and New Year of 1502–3 at Richmond, where they were perhaps reassured by the confident prophecy of the Italian astrologer William Parron that Elizabeth would live to be eighty years old. It was to prove a disastrous miscalculation.

There are conflicting views among historians as to where Elizabeth had planned her lying-in before the birth but the queen was in the Tower of London on 2 February 1503 when she gave birth prematurely to a baby girl. Henry had sent urgently for the queen's physician, Dr Hallysworth, to come from Gravesend in Kent and later summoned another doctor from as far away as Plymouth. He obviously feared for his wife's health and sought desperately to give her the best care available. But Elizabeth could not, this time, be saved. She died on 11 February, her thirty-seventh birthday, and her last child, Princess Katherine, died just one week later. In the space of less than a year, Henry VII's world had disintegrated. Overcome with grief, he placed the funeral arrangements in the hands of the earl of Surrey and the financial controller of the royal household, Sir Richard Guildford. Then he left for Richmond to mourn in solitude, there to 'pass his sorrows and would no man should resort to him but such his Grace appointed, until such time it should please him to show his pleasure'. The king did not, though, forget his wife's servants at this difficult time, sending them 'the best comfort . . . that hath been seen of a sovereign Lord with as good words'.[11]

Elizabeth was given a lavish funeral, costing the equivalent of over a million pounds today. Custom dictated that the king did not attend (the principal mourner was Princess Katherine, the queen's sister) and, even if it had been otherwise, Henry was himself seriously ill. A severe throat infection, possibly quinsy, left him unable to eat or drink for nearly a week. Weakened by his loss, the king nearly succumbed. For more than a month he could not perform any official duties. When he did return to court, he was a changed man. And he knew that another parting was yet to come. For, as Thomas More had written in *A Ruefull Lamentation* on the death of Elizabeth of York, Margaret Tudor was going to leave him as well, to go where they 'should seldom meet'. The death of her mother could not be allowed to delay the journey of the young queen to her new kingdom, as the marriage treaty stipulated.

Henry was determined that his daughter should have the best of everything to sustain her in her new role. He spent unstintingly on clothing, carriages, furniture and all the trappings of royalty, eager to demonstrate his financial clout, his commitment to his daughter and English prestige. Great care was given to display Henry's armorial bearings; his badge (the portcullis) and the red rose of Lancaster were displayed everywhere: on Margaret's bed, chair, litter and liveries. She was provided with a magnificent bed 'of cloth of gold estate', with a yellow damask lining for the valance, silk and gold for the fringe, curtains of crimson sarcenet and fifteen yards of green velvet for a counterpane.

The accounts are as minute in detail as one would expect from this most meticulous of kings. No item was too small to be overlooked, including pins, needles and threads. There were warrants for hose, shoes, sheets and bedclothes, for dresses, hoods, riding boots and slippers, as well as altar cloths and a needlework crucifix. Margaret's staff were to be appropriately arrayed, her ladies in gowns of damask and velvet while her two footmen were supplied with doublets of black velvet and green damask, with 'the portcullis crowned', jackets of green and white cloth of gold, crimson hose, two hats and two bonnets and a generous twelve pairs of shoes. Nor were her horses forgotten. Their collars and bridles were listed, as were stirrups of copper and gilt and harnesses of black and crimson velvet. The queen's litter, in which she would be transported for much of her journey, was covered in cloth of gold. Musicians and heralds were appointed to accompany her as she journeyed north.[12] Henry clearly intended that Margaret's progress to Scotland would afford the opportunity for a great display of Tudor pomp and magnificence. It was a boost sorely needed in the sad summer of 1503.

On 27 June, Margaret and her father left Richmond for her grandmother's estate, Collyweston, in Northamptonshire. There the Queen of Scots spent eleven days in a comfortable family setting while her grandmother supervised the final preparations, before she began her long journey to Edinburgh. Although father and daughter must have hoped they would see one another again, they knew that such occasions would be rare and might, in reality, never happen. As a parting gift, Henry gave Margaret a beautiful prayer book, inscribed from 'your kind and loving father'. He asked her to pray for him and reminded her that 'at all times' she carried with her God's blessing and his own. In the circumstances, these words were all the more poignant.[13]

Henry VII took leave of his daughter on 8 July, entrusting her to the earl of Surrey and his wife, who were to accompany Margaret to Scotland and see her safely and properly installed there. Surrey was, of course, primarily a soldier, and he organized the journey with a military precision that Margaret came to resent long before she crossed the border. The progress was a considerable challenge for a thirteen-year-old, no matter how well trained she was. Margaret was on display relentlessly for three weeks of tiring public events, required to look her best at all times, changing outfits frequently, being gracious to cheering crowds and dining with the great and the good of the towns she passed through. Once in Scotland, she would finally meet her husband, a man more than twice her age, get to know him slightly in carefully orchestrated meetings and then marry him amid great displays of public rejoicing. Thereafter she would be crowned and take up all the new duties that came with queen-ship. If the prospect daunted her, she did not show it as she set out.

We know a great deal about Margaret's journey into Scotland because it was faithfully recorded by the Somerset Herald, John Young, who was appointed by Henry VII to accompany her. His detailed descriptions of the procession itself, the lords and ladies who went with Margaret, and her reception in the places she passed through, are a rich source of information about one of the most significant celebrations of Tudor England and Stewart Scotland. Young begins with a description of the Queen of Scots leaving Collyweston, 'richly dressed, mounted upon a fair pal-frey', and arriving, on the first night of her journey, in Grantham in Lincolnshire. After what was to become a customary greeting from local dignitaries, Margaret spent two nights in Grantham before moving on to Newark. 'Through all the towns and villages where she passed, all the bells were rung daily. And by the way came the habitants of the country for to see the noble company, bringing great vessels full of drink . . .'

By 14 July, Margaret was in Yorkshire, where she had a major public engagement at York. Only twenty years previously, England's second city had been staunchly Yorkist, proud of its association with Richard III. Now it was to receive the daughter of the usurping Tudor and underline Henry VII's success in establishing a new dynasty. The principal player here was the earl of Northumberland, who now joined the queen's progress and was to accompany her over the Scottish border. He met her two miles outside the city, resplendent upon a fine horse, 'with a foot cloth to the ground in crimson velvet, all borded of Orfavery; his Arms very rich in many places upon his saddle and harness, his stirrups gilt, himself arrayed of a gown of the said crimson. At the opening of the sleeves and the collar, a great border of stones.'[14]

Northumberland was the foremost nobleman of the region and he came supported by many knights in his livery to greet the queen. Margaret and her ladies changed clothes before she entered the city, not on horseback this time, but in her litter. On the next day, Sunday 16 July, she left the archbishop's palace for the minster to hear High Mass. Margaret was dressed in 'a gown of cloth of gold, a rich collar of precious stones and a girdle wrought of fine gold, hanging down to the earth' and her train was carried by the countess of Surrey as she entered the church, which was packed with an attentive congregation of local aristocracy. After hearing Mass, Margaret made an offering and returned to dine at the archbishop's palace, where the countess of Northumberland was presented to her and received a welcoming kiss.[15]

The next day Margaret left York with many of the populace straining to see her: 'the streets and the windows were so full of people,' wrote the Somerset Herald, 'that it was a fair thing for to see.' She continued north towards the Scottish Borders, stopping four days in another cathedral city, Durham. There, after the now customary ceremony in the cathedral (the religious obligations of Margaret's journey were scrupulously observed), she spent her time in the castle, the abode of the bishop of Durham, at his expense. This outpouring of adulation and costly entertainment also gave the northern aristocracy, frequently looked down upon by their worldlier London counterparts, an opportunity to demonstrate their own importance and power and to have a rare glimpse of a member of the Tudor royal family. Margaret's mission was not merely the apotheosis of Anglo–Scottish diplomacy. She was also her father's representative to the northern nobility who had, for centuries, borne the heavy burden of defending the border and deserved the recognition that Margaret's presence among them indicated. Their loyalty was sometimes suspect and would, if anything, become more so in the reigns of Henry VIII and Elizabeth. It was not easily bought and the Queen of Scots' progress into her new kingdom presented a valuable opportunity for fostering a spirit of commitment.

Continuing at a leisurely place, Margaret went via Newcastle (where Northumberland gave a magnificent feast with 'dances, sports and songs') and Morpeth to the earl's fine castle at Alnwick. This stop allowed her a little time for recreation and, proving that she was handy with her bow and arrow, she killed a buck in the earl's deer park. Berwick, the fortified town on the river Tweed that was held by the English but desired passionately by the Scots, was Margaret's last stop in England. She stayed here between 29 and 31 July. There she 'had great cheer' and the streets of the town, presumably somewhat to the consternation of its inhabitants, were turned into a hunting ground 'with other sports of bears and of dogs together'.[16] This kind of risky brutality was a great entertainment for the Tudor elite. It was also Margaret's farewell to her native land. On 1 August she and her train passed into Scotland, to go to Lamberton Kirk, as the 1502 treaty specified. There Margaret was greeted by up to a thousand Scots, headed by Bishop Blacader of Glasgow and the bishop of Moray. These Scottish dignitaries bowed down and acknowledged her as their queen. This was Margaret's first official ceremony in Scotland, exactly a week before the date of her wedding. Once it was over, Northumberland and several other northern lords took their leave, returning into England. But hundreds of horsemen remained to accompany the queen on the final stage of her journey.

Margaret attracted a great deal of attention in her new land. On 2 August, en route to Haddington, she passed by the castle at Dunbar. There were so many people gathered to see her that a way through had to be made by force. Keen, perhaps overly so, to celebrate, the Scots brought with them plenty of drink. The next day the queen arrived at Dalkeith Castle, home of the powerful earl of Morton. She may have been relieved to be away from the press of crowds but by far the most important meeting of her journey awaited her. James IV, in the convention of the day, just happened to be hunting locally when he heard of her arrival and came, as if on a whim, to visit.

In reality, there was nothing unexpected about the king's arrival and Margaret was well aware that she was about to see her husband for the first time. She and her company were

These superb panel paintings in the Royal Collection show the family of
James III at worship. The king is kneeling, watched over by St Andrew, the
patron saint of Scotland. His eldest son, the future James IV, stands respectfully
in the background. Margaret of Denmark, James III's queen, is also praying,
splendidly robed, and with the figure of St George guarding her.

James IV as a young monarch, holding a falcon. Hunting was one of
his favourite pastimes. Restless, energetic and physically brave,
his charisma inspired loyalty and affection.

Henry VII. The first Tudor king was an unlikely victor at Bosworth in 1485. He had no previous experience of government and years of exile meant that he was unfamiliar with England. This portrait hints at the personal cost of surviving the many challenges he faced.

Margaret Tudor. The elder daughter of Henry VII and Elizabeth of York married James IV of Scotland in 1503, aged only thirteen. Despite James's philandering and Margaret's temper, the marriage was a success. Only one of their six children, the future James V, survived, but it was Margaret's great-grandson, James VI and I, who united the Crowns of England and Scotland a century later.

The Treaty of Perpetual Peace signed between England and Scotland
in 1502 formed the basis of the marriage agreement between James IV
and Margaret Tudor. Its title was optimistic. England and Scotland
were at war again in 1513.

Henry VIII, Margaret Tudor's younger brother, aged about twenty-eight and still some years from seeking to divorce his wife, Katherine of Aragon. His rivalry with his sister exacerbated strained relations between England and Scotland.

This beautifully illuminated Book of Hours is thought to have been a wedding gift from James IV to his English bride. The illustration shows Margaret at prayer.

Above This unusual contemporary illustration shows James IV ceding his crown after being defeated at Flodden in 1513 by an English army led by the earl of Surrey. In fact, James had been cut down in a desperate attempt to slay Surrey, knowing full well that his army was suffering a catastrophic defeat. He would never have surrendered.

Below The battlefield of Flodden today, peaceful agricultural land in a remote corner of England.

A nineteenth-century depiction of Margaret Tudor at the gates of Stirling Castle (wrongly shown by the artist as Edinburgh Castle), refusing to hand over her sons to a deputation of lords sent to remove them from her custody.

Archibald Douglas, sixth earl of Angus, was the second husband of Margaret Tudor and father of her youngest child, Lady Margaret Douglas. The marriage cost Queen Margaret the regency and soon became acrimonious. Angus himself was largely Anglophile and determined to dominate his stepson, James V, who hated him. Towards the end of his life, Angus rediscovered his Scottish patriotism.

James V of Scotland came to the throne aged seventeen months and survived a troubled minority to become a competent ruler. Cultured and pro-French, his adult rule was characterized by a deepening rivalry with his uncle, Henry VIII. He died of illness contracted during the Solway Moss campaign in 1542.

Madeleine, the first wife of James V, was the daughter of Francis I of France. James went to France to seek her hand and was much influenced by the magnificence of Paris and the French court. His wife, alas, was already dying of tuberculosis when they married and lived only seven weeks in Scotland before dying there in the summer of 1537.

carefully dressed and prepared for the occasion. James arrived wearing a crimson velvet jacket edged with cloth of gold, grand gear, even for a king, for a casual hunting expedition. He was accompanied by his younger brother, James, duke of Ross, the earls of Huntly, Argyll and Lennox and many other Scottish lords, making a total of about sixty people.[17] The king's lyre, rather than the hunter's crossbow, was slung over his back, in a romantic gesture that signified that he would play music for his lady. Margaret and James met for the first time at the door of the Queen's Chamber in Dalkeith Castle. After exchanging the 'great reverences' of deep bows and curtseys that the occasion required, they kissed, and then took stock of each other.[18]

Margaret saw a well-built and obviously very fit man of nearly thirty, bare headed but with a long beard, totally unlike her increasingly thin, self-contained and clean-shaven father. Whereas Henry VII was already showing signs of the long illness that would eventually kill him, James Stewart was the picture of active good health. He was not conventionally handsome but there was a brightness in his eye, an evident good nature (though he did not like to be crossed) and an undeniable charm. James knew how to put this little English lass at her ease. For all her grand clothing, jewellery and mastery of the forms and behaviour that were expected of her, she was still very young.

The only picture we have of Margaret Tudor at this point of her life is in the wonderful collection of ink and chalk drawings held in northern France called the *Recueil d'Arras*. This shows Margaret at the time of her marriage, still slim and modestly dressed, with rather prominent eyes and a full mouth. Although lacking the beauty of her younger sister, the Princess Mary, she is still a personable girl in this picture. A better known later portrait of Margaret with a monkey is from a copy, and shows that she may have begun to put on weight with childbearing, as her mother had done. Later in life she simply looks fat. But in 1503 there is still more of the girl than the woman in the drawing. And James, who must surely by that time have been a good judge of women and their moods, probably realized that, though proud and gracious, she was also uncertain. After a hearty greeting to the earl of Surrey, the king took Margaret aside and they talked together for a long time. Then they sat side by side to dine and watch the entertainment that accompanied the meal. For Margaret, it was the first opportunity to show off her dancing skills, which she did, partnered by the countess of Surrey. 'This done, the king took licence [leave] of her – it was late – and went to his bed in Edinburgh very well content of so fair a meeting.'[19]

Over the next two days Margaret and James met again at Dalkeith, amid much festivity. She performed several dances and the king demonstrated his musicianship by playing for her on the clavichord and the lute. This no doubt proved a welcome distraction from the distressing loss of several of Margaret's favourite horses, killed in a stable fire. James speedily supplied replacements and impressed his young bride by leaping into the saddle of his own mount without using the stirrups when he took his leave of her. A superb horseman of great skill and endurance, these visits to Margaret were merely pleasant jaunts for a man who could ride from Stirling to Aberdeen and on to Elgin in northern Scotland, a staggering distance of 156 miles, in one day.[20] He came, of course, superbly dressed, as was Margaret throughout these proceedings, where cloth of gold and richly embroidered velvet were worn to dazzle the assembled company. It was later reported by the chronicler Edward Hall that the English visitors were studiously unaffected by Scottish ceremonial and spectacle, but contemporary accounts suggest otherwise and John Young, in his continuing narrative, showed every sign of being greatly impressed. Proceedings were clearly going well and a rapport had definitely grown between the earl of Surrey and James IV, though Margaret seems to have found this increasingly irritating.

It did not, however, detract from the final act of her arrival in Scotland before the marriage ceremony itself, which was her official entry into Edinburgh, mounted behind James on horseback, in time-honoured Scottish fashion. A more amenable palfrey was a last-minute replacement for the high-spirited courser that James had intended to convey himself and Margaret through the streets of her new capital. Both king and queen were superbly dressed – she in cloth of gold and a magnificent necklace of pearls and precious stones (perhaps not the most comfortable outfit for being perched on a horse behind the king) and James himself regally splendid in a purple velvet jacket edged with fur, a doublet of violet satin, scarlet hose and a shirt edged with a glittering array of jewels, 'his spurs gilt and long'. Pageants for the queen's entertainment began with a joust, in which two knights fought for a lady's love until parted by the king. As the company moved on, an angel in a specially constructed gatehouse delivered the keys of the city of Edinburgh to the queen and wine spouted from fountains, to the delight of the crowds who had gathered to witness the spectacle. Eventually the procession reached the abbey of Holyrood, where the king's brother and all the Scottish bishops waited to receive their new queen.[21]

Throughout a long and demanding day, James had deferred constantly to Margaret, insisting that she kiss the holy relics he was offered first and that they kneel down together at the altar. He guided her throughout, his arm around her waist, leaving us a touching image of his sensitivity to her youth and vulnerability, as well as providing an opportunity for her to experience the closer physical contact that awaited her once they were formally united in marriage. The night before their wedding he danced for her at his palace of Holyrood House and then 'the king took his leave and bade her goodnight joyously.' The next day would see a Tudor princess married at last to a Stewart king.

James had stretched his exchequer to the limit in his preparations for this historic wedding. There had been a frenzy of building work at Holyrood itself and no expense had been spared on its furnishings. The greatest attention was given to a new chapel and the Queen's Great Chamber, which was probably constructed of Scandinavian timber. The building work came to about three quarters of a million pounds in today's money. The wedding celebrations themselves came to just over £1 million, a very great deal of money for such a small country. It has been estimated that the king spent more than a quarter of his annual income on wine alone.

Very little of James IV's palace remains at Holyrood. His son, James V, would take up the work again in 1528, though much of what we see today was not completed until the latter part of the seventeenth century, by Charles II. Yet one most beautiful artefact does survive from all the splendour and pageantry of the occasion, though sadly it cannot be seen in Scotland. This is the *Book of Hours of James IV and Margaret Tudor*, a superbly decorated late medieval manuscript now held in the Austrian National Library in Vienna.

We can be certain that this was a gift to Margaret when she became queen of Scotland and though the person who com-missioned it cannot be identified conclusively, the probability is that James had it made for his wife, not just as a sign of his religious convictions but also of his commitment to their life together as king and queen of Scotland. Two prominent Flemish artists, Gerard Horenbout and Simon Bening, have been identi-fied as the illuminators and scribes of the work.[22] It begins with a monthly calendar depicting landscapes without people, very unusual for a book of hours at the time. The scenes are ones of richness and tranquillity. Yet beyond this pastoral opening, when it came to the all-important pride of two great families joined in marriage, the artists had clearly done their homework. The depiction of the English and Scottish heraldic devices was correct to the last detail. The arms of Scotland, with the motto 'In my defens God us Defend', and the initials I and M (for Iacobus and Margaret), tied with love knots around the edge, are superbly executed. There are nineteen full plates in the work, depicting scenes from the life of Jesus, various religious commemorations and, importantly, two showing the king and queen separately, at prayer. James is depicted as clean-shaven (an indication that the book might date from shortly after his wedding), his long, reddish-brown hair and distinctive eyes making him immediately identifiable. Margaret, in her picture, kneels before an altar, dressed in gold, with a blue velvet jacket and train. She looks, as indeed she was, very young. As with her husband, the likeness would appear to be consistent with the few other portraits we have of her.

We cannot be sure of the emotional significance Margaret attached to her Book of Hours. At some point after she became a widow, she gave it to her sister, Princess Mary Tudor, who may, in turn, have passed it on to their niece, later Queen Mary I. By the mid-seventeenth century it had found its way into the hands of Leopold of Austria, Holy Roman Emperor. It remains in Vienna, the tangible and sumptuous witness of sixteenth-century Britain's most important royal marriage.[23]

Margaret and James were wed in the beautiful chapel of Holyrood. Now an imposing ruin, it is still possible to gain an impression of what the richly decorated church must have been like that summer's day more than five hundred years ago when, as the Scottish historian Robert Mackie has written, 'the sunlight, streaming through the unshattered glass, glittered on the sculptured figures of saint and angel, and added a richer dye to silks and damask, to velvet and cloth of gold.'[24] And for descriptions of what took place we have again to thank John Young, whose fulsome prose can sometimes become repetitive but who did not stint in his narrative on this, the most important day of Margaret's life.

The young queen and her party arrived first at the abbey and stood by the font in the north aisle. Margaret was supported by the archbishop of York, Thomas Savage, himself a larger than life figure who loved to hunt and swear great oaths, and the overbearing earl of Surrey. Close by, and perhaps helping to keep up Margaret's confidence in this company of so many flamboyant males, was her lady mistress, Elizabeth Denton, who was reported as being 'always nigh her'. Arrayed in white damask, with crimson velvet border to match her husband's wedding outfit, Margaret wore a crown of gold specially made for her by the Edinburgh goldsmith John Currour. Her hair, caught in a very rich coif, hung loose all the way down her back. A necklace of gold, precious stones and pearls gleamed around her throat. Her train, carried by the countess of Surrey, was so heavy that the countess needed the help of a gentleman usher to handle it. Behind Margaret were the great ladies of England who had journeyed north with her, each one paired, by the earl of Surrey's order, with a Scottish lady of equal degree.

Next to arrive was Blacader, the archbishop of Glasgow, who would conduct the ceremony, accompanied by all the hierarchy of the Church in Scotland. Finally came the king himself, supported by his brother and followed by his council and his nobility. Though he had given his queen every reverence and would continue to do so, that day it seems that James IV equalled and perhaps outshone his wife in the splendour of his apparel. Beneath his robe of white damask he wore a doublet of cloth of gold and a loose jacket of crimson and black. But he did not wear a crown. Instead, on his head was a bonnet of black velvet, adorned with a large ruby.

James and Margaret passed under the rood screen into the choir of the abbey church, where Blacader joined them as man and wife. The archbishop of York's role in the ceremony was to read out the papal bulls permitting the marriage. After hearing the Litany and Mass, the queen was anointed and James gave her his sceptre. 'Te Deum' was then sung, after which the king took his bride by the right hand and led her out of the church. They returned to their own chambers for a time, before the wedding feast, at which wild boar's head, hams and many other meats were served. Minstrels played, the king and queen danced and there was much festivity. James heard evensong without his wife and after supper, as the night approached, the company withdrew to their various lodgings.[25]

Despite her public demeanour, which seems to have been at all times regal, Margaret was not yet fourteen years old and a long way from home. The precise date of her famous letter to her father, showing both childish petulance at Surrey's treatment of her chamberlain and resentment at her husband's preference for the crusty old earl's company over her own, is unknown, but it betrays an insecure and exhausted girl. 'God send me comfort,' she wrote desperately to Henry VII, 'that I and mine that be left here with me be well entreated.' Then she added in her own, sloping and ill-formed handwriting: 'For God's sake, sir, hold me excused that I write not myself to your Grace, for I have no leisure this time, but I wish I were with your Grace now and many times more, when I would answer. As for this that I have written ... it is very true, but I pray God I may find it well for my welfare hereafter. No more to your Grace at this time, but our Lord have you in his keeping. Written with the hand of your humble daughter.' The letter is signed simply 'Margaret'.[26]

The Somerset Herald drew a veil over the wedding night. No doubt the queen's ladies prepared her in the time-honoured way, dressing her in a splendid nightgown and brushing her red-gold hair lovingly. Whether James was led to her bed amid the often ribald merriment that accompanied such proceedings we do not know. All that John Young said is that 'the king had the queen apart, and they went together.' The king, of course, knew a great deal about women, though Margaret was probably the youngest high-born lady he had ever had in his bed. Whether the marriage was consummated immediately only James Stewart and Margaret Tudor knew. But both would have been well aware, as they lay beside each other on the night of 8 August 1503, that if something happened to her brother, Margaret would be heir to the throne of England. The prospect of the Stewarts ruling the entire British Isles had moved a significant step closer.

CHAPTER SIX

Brothers in Arms

'*Now we perceive the king of Scots, our brother-in-law and your master, to be the same person whom we ever took him to be, for we never esteemed him to be of any truth.*'

Henry VIII's contemptuous response to James IV's herald
in the summer of 1513

'*The Flowers of the Forest, that fought aye the foremost,
The pride of our land lie cold in the clay.*'

Eighteenth-century lyrics describing the battle of Flodden,
set to an ancient Scottish lament

THE NEW QUEEN OF SCOTS may have felt herself overlooked but in one thing she immediately got her way. She did not like her husband's long, untrimmed beard. Her father was clean-shaven and she evidently preferred that fashion. The day after his wedding, James submitted himself good-naturedly to the skills of the countess of Surrey and her daughter, who removed his facial hair and were amply rewarded for their services with costly textiles, cloth of gold and damask. It has been remarked that their combined fee of over £500 (the equivalent of just over £100,000 pounds today) may be the largest barber's bill on record. James was clearly happy with both the cost and the result. Perhaps he also felt that it was appropriate to make a distinction in his appearance between the days of his bachelorhood and his

150

new status as a married man. He also gave Margaret a 'morrowing' gift for the day after their wedding, a tradition for new Scottish queens, of Kilmarnock in Ayrshire to add to her impressive list of lands and properties. The king was committed to treating his wife as befitted her status but there was one aspect of his own life that he would not have shared with her immediately. At the time of their marriage, his mistress, Janet Kennedy, was pregnant with their third child.

How and when the subject of James's illegitimate family was broached with Margaret Tudor is not known. Janet had been at Stirling Castle until a matter of weeks before her lover's marriage, when she was moved to Darnaway in northern Scotland, where a daughter was born towards the end of 1503. The name of this child is never revealed in the accounts but her father provided for her and visited her as she grew up. Janet's second child with James, also a daughter, died at Stirling shortly after her mother left the castle. James had made no secret of his children, but given Margaret Tudor's age and, one must suppose, innocence of such matters, the discovery that Stirling had been used for years as a nursery for her husband's children by various women must have been at least disconcerting. The only indirect evidence for her displeasure is that Lady Margaret Stewart, the daughter of Margaret Drummond, was moved at about this time to take up residence at Edinburgh Castle. If the queen was angry, she seems to have known better than to make a fuss in public.

For despite the difference in their ages and the continued philandering of James, the marriage was apparently a successful one. James was indulgent and attentive as a husband, ensuring that his wife wanted for nothing. Soon after their wedding he and Margaret left Edinburgh so that she could see something of her new country and he could continue the roving lifestyle that he so loved and that was a vital component of his kingship. They were not, of course, always together and he managed to fit in a visit to Janet in Darnaway during the latter stages of her pregnancy, while still being back in Edinburgh in time for Margaret's fourteenth birthday celebrations at the end of

November. Carefully, he eased his little queen into her role, ensuring that she was secure in the knowledge that she was his lawful wife and anointed consort and that she would always be respected as such.

His affair with Janet Kennedy was brought to a close two years after his wedding, when a marriage was arranged between 'the lady', as the Scottish treasurer's accounts always called her, and John Ramsay. This was the same John Ramsay who had been one of the closest companions of James III and the traitor who sold himself (or, at least, his information) to Henry VII in the 1490s. James, however, like Henry, knew that loyalties were fickle and the aggrieved needed to be encouraged as well as constrained. By the beginning of the new century, with most of his forfeit lands restored, Ramsay was back at court and close to the king. James may well have thought that having a former enemy married to a discarded mistress was a neat way to bind them both to him, allowing them to be at court without scandal. The fact that Janet was still, in the eyes of the Church, married to Alexander Gordon was irrelevant. But Janet's new marital arrangement did not last more than a few years. By 1508 Ramsay was recorded as the spouse of another lady. Janet herself lived on for many years, perhaps as late as 1545, careful of her property and in genteel retirement. She saw her son, the earl of Moray, become a loyal and competent adviser to his younger half-brother, King James V.

Margaret, for her part, put her homesickness behind her and set herself to learning the language of her new realm. She would eventually become fluent in Scots, dictating her correspondence in it, albeit in her characteristic jerky rather than elegant style. James responded well to her efforts to adapt. She had arrived in Scotland basically as a child, and he formed her into a woman. If they did not exactly come to love one another, there does appear to have been a deepening fondness. James and Margaret were both strong-willed and proud, but they knew what was expected of kings and queens. And James was a hard man to dislike. The measure of his consideration for his wife can be seen in his restraint when it came to the procreation of their own children. Like all monarchs at the time, James wanted a legitimate heir. But he was mindful of Margaret's age (and, no doubt, her proximity to the English Crown) and he did not rush things, even though both his brothers died within a year of one another in 1503–4. It was not until the beginning of 1507, when she was seventeen, that the queen gave birth to her first child, a son. The king was delighted, though concerned by his wife's health after a difficult birth and lengthy recovery. Sadly, the prince lived for only a year. Margaret's pregnancies were hazardous affairs but from this time onwards she did her duty valiantly. Babies arrived at regular intervals: a daughter, who was born and died the same day in 1508; Prince Arthur in 1509, who died the following summer; another daughter, born prematurely in late 1512. Only the child who would become James V, born at Linlithgow, Margaret's favourite palace, in April 1512, was strong enough to survive.

As Queen of Scots, Margaret's main responsibility, apart from producing heirs, was to preside over James IV's court. The king spared no expense in ensuring that his wife was regally dressed to fulfil her role. A master of the wardrobe was appointed for her after her arrival in Scotland and soon she was being equipped for her first winter in her new land.[1] Six packages of furs, each containing forty skins of calabar (furred grey squirrel) are recorded in her accounts. The sleeves of her winter dresses were in miniver, the white fur from the winter coat of the red squirrel. And as the temperature dropped, the queen took heart from her surroundings, and her homesickness receded.

She would have discovered that her husband's ambition for his country, his determination to put it on an equal footing with other European states, meant that she had arrived in Scotland at a time when there was a great flowering of court life. This was a golden age of Scottish literature, steeped in the Celtic traditions of poetry and storytelling. The culture was both aural and visible; James IV himself participated in plays and masques staged for court entertainment. There was nothing fusty or restrained about the life into which Margaret Tudor had stepped. Clad in the splendid gowns, furs and glittering jewels with which he so liberally provided her, the young queen watched as her husband took to the stage himself. They shared a love of dancing and music and Scotland had been long without a queen. Her presence added an extra dimension to the splendour that James was encouraging.

Few direct descriptions of James IV's court survive, but one of the greatest Scottish poets, or *makars*, of the period, William Dunbar, has left us a wonderful, if somewhat jaundiced, account of those who served the king honestly (such as himself) and their much less desirable counterparts, the army of hangers-on. It reads better in the original Scots but for ease of understanding has been rendered into modern English as follows:

Sir, you have many servants
And officials with different responsibilities:
Churchmen, lawyers and fine craftsmen,
Doctors in law and medicine,
Soothsayers, rhetoricians and philosophers,
Astrologists, artists and orators,
Men of arms and valiant knights
And many other excellent people,
Musicians, minstrels and merry singers,
All kinds of soldiers,
Makers of coins, carvers and carpenters,
Builders of barques and small ships,
Masons dwelling on the land,
Shipwrights cutting wood on the shore,
Makers of glass, goldsmiths and jewellers,
Printers, painters and apothecaries;
And all skilled in their craft,
And all at once together labouring
Who pleasing are an honourable
And to your highness profitable,
And most fitting to be
With your high regal majesty,

> *Deserving of your grace most worthy*
> *Gratitude, reward and support*

But what of the ne'er do wells?

> *But you so gracious are and meek*
> *That on your highness follows also*
> *Another company more miserable,*
> *Though they be not so profitable:*
> *Dissemblers, hypocrites and flatterers,*
> *Shouters, clamourers and chatterers,*
> *Parasites and gunners,*
> *Monsieurs of France, good claret tasters,*
> *Inopportune beggars of Irish race*
> *And stealers of foods, as if out of their wits,*
> *Scroungers and spongers in the corner*
> *And hall hunters of drakes and ducks,*
> *Pushers and thrusters, as they were mad,*
> *Rogues not known to any respectable man,*
> *Shoulderers and shovers without shame*
> *And no skill can claim,*
> *And know no other craft or duties,*
> *But to crowd, sir, your doors.*[2]

Dunbar was angling for a larger annual stipend. It is not clear whether this memorable evocation of the court of James IV and Margaret Tudor produced the desired result. No doubt it came close to describing the reality of many European courts at the time.

James IV marked his wife's first pregnancy with a great musical celebration at Christmas 1506, summoning sixty-nine different musicians to play for the court. In the summer after the prince's birth a great tournament, one of the best documented of the period, was arranged. At its centre was a chivalric theme but with a new twist: 'the jousting of the wild knight for the black lady'. There were two women described as Moorish ladies at the court by 1507, living at Edinburgh Castle in the household of Lady Margaret Stewart. One of these, 'my lady with the mekle [large] lips', was the centre of the tournament organized by Janet Kennedy's husband. A large crowd watched as the king, dressed as a 'wild knight', his followers decked out as 'wild men', enacted a story whose symbolism is lost to us now, defending the honour of an exotic lady. James liked novelty and scored a notable triumph in the arranging of this joust, ensuring that the 'Moor lass', as she was known, had her place in history. Clad in 'a gown of damask flowered with gold and trimmed with green and yellow taffeta', the lady rode to the tournament in Edinburgh in a 'chair triumphal', with two female attendants and two squires. Whether she enjoyed being the centre of attention we do not know. The king, of course, had added to his reputation as 'the very pattern of a Paladin of chivalry'.[3]

Pageantry was important to James IV, as it was to his rivals, but there was much more to the mature king that Margaret Tudor had married than a mere love of show. James embraced the times in which he lived. Though he would probably not have thought of himself as 'a Renaissance man', he could lay claim to being a polymath. He was certainly interested in new ideas and new developments, while never questioning the role of religion in his own daily life or that of his subjects. He prayed, heard Mass diligently, was strict in his annual visits to various shrines and sites of pilgrimage, some of which he went to on foot. All of this clearly meant a great deal to him, but it was not enough. He was fascinated by science, studying both medicine and dentistry. There are records of his having extracted teeth from his subjects while on his travels throughout his kingdom and he was keen to attract medical practitioners to his court. Several came from outside Scotland and are known either by their place of origin ('the Ireland leech') or their appearance ('the leech with the curly hair' and 'the leech with the yellow hair'). But, above all, the king was fascinated by military matters.

Though James was keen to follow all the latest developments in artillery and military strategy, his great love, perhaps more than any woman, was the navy. Ever since he had been taken to Leith shortly after his accession, the desire to build up his naval defences had burned within him. The Scottish historian Norman Macdougall has called it his obsession. In the summer of 1506 he wrote to Louis XII of France telling him of his determination to develop a fleet that would be the key to defending Scotland from her enemies. He was as good as his word and by the second decade of the sixteenth century expenditure on ships was the largest item on the royal accounts. James moved the centre of Scottish shipbuilding from its traditional home at Dumbarton in the west of Scotland to two newly created dockyards in the Firth of Forth, on the east coast. This may have been prompted by the disastrous expedition to Denmark just a year before the marriage to Margaret Tudor, when an attempt to aid his Uncle Hans, the Danish monarch, went disastrously wrong. Smarting and embarrassed by this failure, James did not waste time. He realized that his existing fleet was not fit for purpose and that he needed skilled labour to build more ships. In pursuing the ideal of a navy that would rival any in Europe, a remarkable aim in itself for a small country, the king imported French shipwrights (the best, it was believed, were to be found in England but there were obvious difficulties in trying to entice his father-in-law's subjects to assist) and came close to denuding the royal forests of Scotland, whose trees were liberally felled to meet the requirements of the shipbuilding programme.

By 1505, the first great warship was completed. She was named the *Margaret*, after the queen, a pleasing gesture to his then sixteen-year-old wife. In size and armaments she rivalled the English *Mary Rose* of 1509 and had cost James the equivalent of over a million pounds. But six years later, in October 1511, an even larger and more formidable vessel, the *Michael*, was launched. The English referred to this as 'the great ship' and the chronicler Robert Lindsay of Pitscottie described her as 'the greatest ship that ever sailed in England or France'. Contemporaries were overawed by the size of the *Michael*. The French ambassador de la Mothe must have described it in superlatives to Louis XII, for the French king was keen to avail himself of its services in support of his struggle with England and Spain in

1513. Louis called it a ship 'so powerful that none other like it is to be found in Christendom'. Boasting a crew of 300, weighing 1,000 tons and probably about 180 feet long, the *Michael* carried twenty-seven bronze cannon, a slightly larger number than Henry VIII's *Great Harry*, a ship which modelled itself on this crowning achievement of James IV's ship-building programme. During his reign, James 'built, hired, received as gifts or seized as prizes a total of at least thirty-eight ships'. He was justly proud of all this and the huge boost it gave to Scottish prestige in the eyes of the world and of his own subjects.

Yet while the Scottish nation may have basked in the reflected glory of their energetic and determined monarch, his poorer subjects relishing the opportunity to come face to face with him as he travelled his realm and his lords vying with each other for a place at court, there was a price to be paid – often literally – for his style of kingship. There was much that was endearing about James, but he could be ruthless when needed. Queen Margaret's dowry gave a welcome boost to Scottish finances and encouraged James to live beyond his means but it was all spent by 1508. The king looked for other sources of income and found, like Henry VII in England, that his better-off subjects could be squeezed for much more. In his pursuit of feudal dues the king and his advisers showed no mercy. The dispute with the elderly earl of Angus, viewed romantically as a quarrel over the lovely Janet Kennedy, may have been given an extra edge by their rivalry for the lady's affections but was essentially a tussle over land and money. Extensive searches were made to discover tenants of the Crown who had failed to obtain legal title for their estates, sometimes going back centuries. James did not spare anybody in his quest for financial security. Eleven earls, sixteen lords, sixteen knights, two clergy and one royal burgh were pursued for being unable to show legal title to lands that they claimed. Nor was the Church, for all James's piety, exempt. The king already had control of the revenues of the archbishopric of St Andrews, first through his brother and then, when he died in 1504, through his own illegitimate son, Alex-

ander Stewart, who was speedily nominated as a replacement at
the age of eleven. Alexander was too young to be consecrated, so
the moneys from his diocese, as well as those from the wealthy
abbeys of Holyrood, Arbroath and Dunfermline, all went to the
Crown. James IV's financial exactions are less well known than
those of Henry VII but they caused considerable hardship and
anxiety to a significant number of his subjects. Most accepted
the situation, being powerless to fight against the king's will, but
there was a further rebellion in the Western Isles in 1506, put
down by the earl of Huntly.

Neither was James overly fond of summoning parliament.
Between 1496 and 1504 it did not meet at all, nor did it sit for
the last four years of the reign. The favoured method of government for most of his personal reign was the general council, a
body similar in size and composition to a parliament, but usually
summoned at much shorter notice to deal with specific issues
that had arisen. There appears to have been little opposition to
this style of government and James was not inclined to support a
forum that might encourage more organized opposition to his
policies. As in Tudor England until the Reformation, parliament
was a tool to be used at the king's pleasure and not to serve the
ends of its constituent members. But James was certainly more
profligate with money than his father-in-law. The relationship
with England, though subject to the inevitable tensions in the
Borders, remained quiet in the main while the first Henry Tudor
lived. He had never been an aggressive king and, besides, he had
other preoccupations as his reign was drawing to a close.

⚬⚭

IT IS CUSTOMARY to think of the last years of Henry VII's reign,
certainly from 1503 onwards, when personal tragedy brought
him to his knees, as a period of almost unrelieved gloom for the
king and his subjects. A recent work has underlined this view of
Henry as a 'dark prince', an embittered, unloved, avaricious
monarch, marked by the scars of years of insecurity, a mistrustful
man who found comfort only in the collection of punitive

exactions from a terrified aristocracy and a resentful commercial class.[4] Everyone, from dukes to City of London merchants, dreaded the assaults on their purses, and sometimes their liberty, carried out with increasing callousness by a new group of men around the king. In this reading, in which Henry is portrayed as ill and withdrawn from the world, it seems as if the first Tudor is struggling to come to terms with what he has achieved, as if survival, peace, international recognition and the establishment, however shakily, of his own dynasty were not enough. His only pleasure is derived from putting his heel on the necks of his subjects, reducing them to penury and fear. England was a police state, rife with spies and informers, presided over by a miser ill in body and spirit. There is, of course, much truth in the detail of this terrifying vision of early sixteenth-century England, but it is not the whole story and to focus on it, without taking a more measured view of what Henry achieved, is to do him an injustice. None of us today would have liked to live in Tudor times. Good Queen Bess ran a better oiled, more hideous regime than her grandfather but little enough mention is made of this in the biographies of Elizabeth that continue to appear with predictable frequency.[5]

While his elder daughter was adapting to life as Queen of Scots, Henry VII was not just sitting in his counting house. His style of government, like his son-in-law's, was intensely personal and though the mechanics of it were carried out by men despised by the aristocracy (or what had survived of it after the Wars of the Roses) he was, in this respect, following a trend begun by Edward IV. There were few executions of opponents because there was no need. Like James IV, Henry knew how to hit his subjects where it hurt but he had a similar sense of theatre. He had built his public image on processions, triumphal entries, receptions, tournaments and a lively, cultured court. Despite the absence of a queen, all that did not suddenly disappear. He could put on a splendid show when he felt the occasion warranted it, as he did when a violent tempest delivered an extremely reluctant Philip of Burgundy and his hapless wife, Queen Juana of Castile, to English shores in February 1506. Philip was essentially Henry's prisoner, but the king was determined to take full advantage of the diplomatic opportunities so unexpectedly opened up and to finally scotch the threat posed by the rebel Edmund de la Pole, then skulking in exile in the Low Countries, by inducing his visitor to return the earl to England. Henry entertained Philip with very public displays of extravagance at Windsor, housing him in his own recently refurbished apartments. A carefully orchestrated programme of entertainment, of wining, dining, hunting and tennis (Henry had himself been a keen player of the game but his worsening eyesight meant that he was more often a spectator now), produced the desired result. There was even a role for the overlooked Katherine of Aragon, who was enduring the creeping years of her widowhood in England and abandonment by her father with a mixture of ill grace and desperation. Philip's boorish refusal to dance with Katherine only added to her humiliation.

Henry VII was also fortunate in Princess Mary, Margaret's younger sister, who was frequently at court with her father. An attractive and gracious child, she was better looking than Margaret and seems to have inherited their mother's social skills as well as her beauty. As she grew, Mary took a much more active role in court life. She was definitely the star of Henry's reception for Philip of Burgundy and the king was determined not to lose the opportunity of concluding a splendid marriage alliance for her with the archduke's son, Charles. Henry was always a skilled opportunist and had not lost his touch. Philip was powerless to resist him. This match, had it ever come about, would have seen Mary occupy a place on the European stage far greater than that of her sister, but Mary's fate lay elsewhere.

The king, meanwhile, had certainly not ruled himself out of the marriage market, no doubt mindful of the fact that other heirs would be a welcome insurance for the future. Yet though several ladies – Margaret of Austria, Margaret of Angoulême and Joanna of Naples – were considered, the king's heart does not seem to have been too deeply engaged in the process. The diplomatic possibilities opened up were useful but nothing came of any of these discussions. Henry had grown more particular with age and his detailed instructions in respect of Joanna were so fastidious as to be ungallant: he wanted to know whether she had any hair on her lips and whether her breath was bad. His diplomats' valiant attempts to make Joanna sound reasonably presentable, when she clearly was not, make amusing reading.[6]

The king's other major concern after the death of Prince Arthur was the preparation of his surviving son, Henry, to succeed him. The prince had been brought up with his mother and sisters, spending most of his time in recent years at Eltham. He made occasional visits to court and had participated in several great ceremonies of state: his own creation as duke of York, the marriage of Katherine of Aragon and Prince Arthur, and the proxy wedding of his sister Margaret to James IV at Richmond. He seems to have been something of an extrovert, especially at his brother's wedding, but then the expectations of him as second in line to the throne were quite different from those on the slender shoulders of Arthur. He had been well educated, as befitted a prince, but, again, without pressure. Life at Eltham was pleasant and he was close to his mother. Her death, when he was not quite twelve, dealt him a considerable blow, and one which lingered. Writing to the Dutch scholar Erasmus some years later, he described 'the news of the death of my dearest mother' as 'hateful intelligence'.[7]

Preoccupied with his losses, of Arthur, Elizabeth and then Margaret to her new life in Scotland, Henry VII took his time to decide how best to proceed in respect of his new heir. Precedent would have suggested setting him up in an independent household where he could learn the skills of kingship within his own personal court. But there were always problems with this rarefied approach and the experience of sending Arthur off to Ludlow had been such a miserable one that the king decided not to repeat it. Perhaps he also recalled what had happened to Edward V, whose isolation in the Welsh Marches had greatly facilitated the coup d'état of Richard III in 1485.

If his own health was to fail suddenly, Henry VII did not want his son several days' journey from the centre of power. He had subdued Yorkist claimants but not entirely erased them and Buckingham was ever conscious of his own proximity to the throne.

So it was that in June 1504, when England was in the grip of a terrible heatwave, Prince Henry and his retinue arrived to take up permanent residence at court. In the remaining five years of his reign, the king would keep his son close by his side. With the help of his own mother, whose talent for such organization was unsurpassed, the king had introduced a number of changes into his son's household, one of the most notable being the retirement of his tutor, John Skelton, who was replaced briefly by John Holt and then William Hone. Another main influence in the prince's education was William Blount, Lord Mountjoy, an admirer of Erasmus. This connection with one of the greatest humanists of the age was to have a profound influence on the course of Prince Henry's development and education.[8] The king and Lady Margaret chose Sir Henry Marney, from an old Essex family, to be chamberlain of the prince's household and the king also gave a court pension to Arthur Plantagenet, Edward IV's illegitimate son and half-brother to Queen Elizabeth, who had been a member of her household. Both the king and his son were very fond of Plantagenet.

The young prince suddenly found himself constantly in his father's company, watching as he dealt with day-to-day matters of state, sitting in on council sessions, receiving ambassadors, learning first-hand what it meant to rule. His father intended to mould him very much in his own image. It was an intense schooling that the prince found stifling as time went by. His contemporaries regarded him as a virtuous prince, a good son of the Church who loved learning but was open to new ideas. Although he and his father shared an interest in physical activities such as hunting and loved the tournament and the tennis court, they were, in many respects, very different. The younger Henry had been shielded from the threats to the throne that had so plagued the first fifteen years of his father's reign. He knew nothing of financial hardship or exile. Together with the young men who were his companions at court, he inevitably began to form a focus of attention that may not have been in overt opposition to a style of government that was increasingly resented but did certainly provide a vision of a different future. Sadly, in seeking to bind his son so close to him in order to ensure that the succession passed smoothly, Henry VII alienated him. Young Henry, like Shakespeare's Prince Hal in *Henry IV*, wanted the crown himself.

From 1507, it became obvious that his wait would not be interminable. The king's health was deteriorating badly. Three successive springs brought on severe illness, which may have been tuberculosis though we do not know the precise cause. By February 1509 it was apparent that Henry VII did not have long to live. Still, with the strong will and courage that had character-ized his life, he lingered until after Easter, having literally crawled from his bed to his private chapel to receive the sacrament on Easter Sunday. He died, emaciated, unable to breathe and in great pain, on the evening of 21 April. Twenty-four years after his improbable victory at Bosworth, he left his son a full treasury and a peaceful country. Perhaps he did belatedly repent of the harsh manner in which he had achieved financial security but one suspects that even if he acknowledged that he had been unnecessarily severe in the latter years of his reign, he believed it had brought stability for his heir. He had successfully established the Tudor dynasty.

Lady Margaret Beaufort lived on for a scant two months after her son. She saw her grandson crowned but succumbed soon afterwards. At the time, this was put down to overeating at Henry VIII's coronation feast, an explanation that sounds entirely out of character with her careful, measured approach to life. She was sixty-nine, a good age for the times in which she lived, and had become increasingly frail. Perhaps her end was hastened by the mixture of joy and sorrow she would have felt, but she had every reason to be proud of what she had achieved since she was taken in, as a pregnant and frightened thirteen-year-old widow, by her concerned brother-in-law.

The new king sought immediately to distance himself from his father's style of government by beheading two of its most loyal servants. Eager and full of fun as the young Henry VIII is often depicted, these were but the first of many political executions that came to characterize his reign. He started early. He was also determined to make his mark in Europe. When he finally married the neglected Katherine of Aragon a few weeks before his coronation, he took England once more into the orbit of Spain and the Habsburgs and away from the peaceful relations with France that his father had maintained after the early 1490s. This course, underpinned by his addiction to the old medieval ideals of chivalry and warfare, would also bring him into direct conflict with his brother-in-law, James IV of Scotland, with tragic consequences for his elder sister, Queen Margaret, and the entire Scottish nation.

✢

IT WOULD BE misleading, however, to put the blame for the deterioration in Anglo–Scottish relations entirely on Henry VIII. There had been concerns about Scottish intentions towards the north of England as early as 1505, shortly after the last portion of Margaret's dowry was paid. Three years later Henry VII had been sufficiently concerned about the possible renewal of a treaty between France and Scotland to send his almoner, an able young diplomat named Thomas Wolsey, to Edinburgh on a diplomatic mission to avert any such rapprochement. Wolsey was made to wait after his arrival until the persuasion of the queen managed to get him an audience. James, in a wonderfully dismissive snub, had claimed he was too busy making gunpowder and shooting. When the king and English envoy did meet, James assured him that all his council were keen on renewing the French alliance but when his brother-in-law agreed to release the earl of Arran, who was imprisoned in England for travelling without an official safe-conduct, the surface tensions died down.

Despite renewal of the 1502 Treaty of Perpetual Peace on the accession of Henry VIII, and James's public avowal at the end of November 1509 that he would abide by the terms of the agreement, it soon became apparent that friendly relations would be subject to severe strain by Henry VIII's determination to renew the conflicts of the Hundred Years War. For despite the image he undoubtedly wanted to project of a young, vigorous Renaissance prince, Henry VIII's foreign policy and his obsession with past feats of English glory looked backwards, not forwards. The Europe into which he now intended to thrust himself was, though, a complex and unpredictable place. New dynastic alliances, a belligerent pope, the encircling Habsburgs and the ever-present threat of Ottoman incursions were a highly combustible mix. Britain sat on the fringes of this continent, both its kingdoms wanting to exert influence in it while trying to deal with their own conflicting aims. By 1511, when Henry VIII entered into the Holy League, he had already signed an alliance with Spain. Now he joined with the Emperor Maximilian and the Warrior Pope, Julius II, whose resentment of French land-grabbing in Italy fuelled the general opposition to France. Louis XII had caused revulsion by allying with the Turks and attempting to undermine papal authority by calling a general council of the Church to meet in Pisa in May 1511. Isolated and defiant, Louis called upon the support of his ancient ally, Scotland. James IV's military support, particularly his fine navy, might be crucial in defending French interests.

Thus were Henry VIII, 'an egocentric teenager whose tantrums and petulance bespoke an inferiority complex',[9] and the middle-aged James IV, successful king and hardened fighter, drawn into the European drama. But there was another, more personal edge to what happened. The exchange of 'loving letters' that followed on Henry's accession was soon replaced by an underlying rivalry. The English king and his Spanish wife, nearly six years his senior and inclined to think that she could direct him, ostentatiously set up a court modelled on the Arthurian legend of Camelot, full of brave knights, fair ladies and endless amusement, intended to eclipse anything that James and Margaret could aspire to in Edinburgh. The English court feasted, laughed and jousted its way to war, while anti-French diplomats like Christopher Bainbridge, Henry's highly partial envoy to the papal curia, fuelled the flames. And on New Year's Day 1511, Katherine seemed to have trumped the still childless king and Queen of Scots when she produced a son. But he lived less than six weeks and the following year it was Margaret who proved the better breeder, when she at last gave birth to a healthy boy of her own. She was almost immediately pregnant again, losing a premature child at the end of 1512. By the summer of 1513 she was expecting once more, in what seems like an increasingly concerted effort by her and James and to establish their dynasty and its wider future in Britain. Henry and Katherine could only wait. Until they were successful, Margaret was her brother's heir. No doubt mindful of this, Henry was determined not to acknowledge it.

His resentment found expression in ways that hurt his sister and infuriated her husband. Margaret had been left money and goods in the wills of Prince Arthur and her father, but these were never paid, despite repeated requests. Though the money would undoubtedly have been welcome to the depleted Scottish exchequer, the principle irked as much as the cost. At the end of 1512, Margaret told Lord Dacre, a Border lord with whom she would have much contact in coming years, that she was 'sorry for any grudge between you [Henry VIII] and her husband'. The following spring she expressed herself more strongly in a letter to her brother:

> We cannot believe that of your mind or by your command we are so unkindly dealt with in our father's legacy, whereof we would not have spoken nor written had not the doctor [Nicholas West, Henry's envoy] now spoken to us of the same ... Our husband knows it is withholden for his sake

and will recompense us . . . We are ashamed therewith and
wish God word had never been thereof. It is not worth such
estimation as in your divers letters of the same and we lack
nothing; our husband is ever the longer the better to us, as
knows God.[10]

This was written in May 1513, when Margaret was with her son
at Linlithgow. It gives a clear picture of her anger and her loyalty
to her husband. Henry had evidently been disparaging about
James's ability to support her in an appropriate manner, but she
would have none of this. She was firmly on his side.

England and France were, by then, at war, and though
Ferdinand of Aragon had already backed out and made a separate
peace with France (the first of many betrayals that Henry VIII
would suffer from his allies in the course of his long reign), the
conflict continued. Indeed, Henry was about to lead an invading
force of some thirty-five thousand men across the English
Channel in person. James IV, meanwhile, having avoided a final
commitment to France for nearly a year and sidestepping any
involvement with Louis XII's attempts to undermine the pope,
waited until he had promises of sufficient money and weaponry
to be confident that he could enter the war on the French side.
So the treaty of peace between England and Scotland was finally
shattered and James prepared to invade his brother-in-law's
kingdom.

⁂

ALTHOUGH THERE RAN a deep undercurrent of mistrust and
even hatred between England and Scotland, it had ebbed and
flowed over time. Now it was resurrected as part of a European
war. The priorities of the early sixteenth century were different from those of the thirteenth, when the Scots had fought
Edward I for their independence. James IV was not trying to
keep the English out of Scotland as he made his military
preparations in the summer of 1513 but rather to undertake a
diversionary tactic intended to embarrass and limit Henry VIII,

keeping to his part of the bargain struck with the king of France. Of course, it was a move James relished – he saw himself as a warrior king and he had taken the Scottish host over the border with considerable success in support of Perkin Warbeck in the 1490s – but he was now the ally of a major European power and the context was much broader. The stakes were also higher and James had already suffered the indignity of being excommunicated by the choleric Pope Julius II at the start of 1513 because of his renewal of the treaty with France. He does not, however, seem to have been unduly distressed by this, viewing it, no doubt correctly, as a manoeuvre by the English that would, in time, be overturned – by the early sixteenth century, excommunication was more of a political tactic than a spiritual attack.[11]

Fuelled by the colourful and doom-laden texts of the Scottish chroniclers written after the event, hindsight has painted an entirely misleading picture of the background to the Flodden campaign. James was no hothead bent on glory. There was widespread support in Scotland for war with England and the king, far from haranguing his dubious advisers into submission, consulted at length with a general council before the final decisions were made. The stories of portents – of a mysterious man in a blue gown appearing to James as he prayed in the church of St Michael at Linlithgow, warning him not to go to war, or of Queen Margaret's dreams of disaster – have no contemporary corroboration. James's preparations were considered and orderly and he had every reason to believe that he would succeed.

The die was effectively cast at the end of July. On three successive days, the king despatched his fleet to aid Louis XII, sent the Lyon Herald to Henry VIII's camp at Thérouanne in northern France with an ultimatum to desist in his designs against the French or bear the consequences and then, presupposing the young English king's negative response, summoned the Scottish host to muster at two points – at Burghmuir, the moorland to the south of Edinburgh, and Ellem in Berwickshire. Seventeen years had passed since King James last brought his army together. This time it was nearly forty thousand strong, probably the largest force of men ever assembled to fight the English.

James's personal commitment was everywhere evident. He accompanied the fleet on the first part of its voyage, sailing on his pride and joy, the huge warship the *Michael*, as far as the Isle of May in the north of the Firth of Forth. The ships, under the command of the earl of Arran, continued north and then down the west coast of Scotland, making a foray across to Ireland, where they bombarded the English stronghold of Carrickfergus. This diversionary tactic may or may not have been authorized by the king but it had the effect of delaying the fleet's progress. Subsequent bad weather meant that the combining of the Franco–Scottish navy did not take place until September. It was unable to inflict any damage on Henry VIII and played no further part in the war of 1513.

The last diplomatic exchange took place when Lyon Herald, Sir William Cumyng of Inverallochy, arrived at Henry VIII's camp on 11 August bearing an uncompromising message from the King of Scots. Henry was required to 'desist from further invasion and utter destruction of our brother and cousin the Most Christian King' to whom James was 'bounden and obliged for mutual defence the one of the other . . . and we will,' he went on, 'do what thing we trust may cause you to desist from pursuit of him.'[12] It was further pointed out that Henry's invasion had caused the French king to withdraw his army from Milan and that this should be a sufficient cause of satisfaction to warrant the return home of the English army.

Henry was not impressed. He was twenty-two years old, his blood was up and he was revelling in the campaign, the sur-roundings of his 'rich tent' and his alliance with the Emperor Maximilian. 'The king, standing still with sober countenance, having his hand on his sword, said "Have ye now your tale at an end?" The herald of arms said "nay". "Say forth then," said the king. "Sir, he summoneth your grace to be at home in your realm in the defence of his ally."' But Henry VIII was not about to be pushed around and told to go home by his brother-in-law. His indignation overflowed. He told Lyon Herald:

> It ill becometh a Scot to summon a king of England. And tell your master that I mistrust not so the realm of England but he shall have enough to do whensoever he beginneth; and also I trusted him not so well but that I provided for him right well, and that he shall well know. And he to summon me, now being here for my right and inheritance! It would be much better agreed with his honour to have summoned me being at home, for he knew well before my coming hither that hither would I come. And now to send me summons! Tell him there shall never Scot cause me to return my face. And where he layeth the French king to be his ally it would be much better agreed and become him, being married to the king of England's sister, to recount the king of England his ally. And now for a conclusion, recommend me to your master and tell him if he be so hardy to invade my realm or cause to enter one foot of my ground, I shall make him as weary of his part as ever was man that began any such business.

He finished with a flourish aimed at rekindling the ill feeling over Margaret's legacy, claiming that 'I care nothing but for misentreating of my sister, that would God she were in England on a condition she cost the Scottish king not a penny.' Lyon Herald, however, knew Queen Margaret better. He retorted: 'If your grace would give her your whole realm, she would forsake it to be entreated as she is.' Henry did not believe him and further insulted James IV by asserting that he had, in effect, been bribed by Louis XII, 'anointed with the crowns of the sun', a literal translation of the French gold coin, the *soleil d'or*. [13]

So now there could be no backing down on either side. All Henry's pent-up hostility, his resentment of his sister and her husband, can plainly be seen in these contemptuous words. The English king knew full well that if he died, Margaret would ascend his throne and her husband would become ruler of both

Scotland and England. This truth was very raw. For his part, the King of Scots was goaded beyond endurance by his brother-in-law's posturing and by the claim he made that, as king of England, he was also overlord of Scotland. Henry's French adventure was the occasion, rather than the root cause, of the deep dislike that had taken hold between them. In truth, they aspired to be players on a wider European stage where both had limited influence. But their quarrel, heightened by personal animosity, would reach its climax far away from the larger conflict, on a hillside in north-eastern England, on a windy and wet autumn afternoon.

❦

AS PREPARATIONS for the campaign began in earnest, James IV visited Linlithgow to take his leave of Queen Margaret and Prince James. The palace there was one of his finest and had been much improved during his reign. Even today, with its roof long gone and its great hall and once splendid chambers open to the sky, it remains an impressive structure. The beautiful church of St Michael, where James prayed before his departure, stands close by. The queen may well have been nervous. Certainly the words attributed to her – 'Ye go to fight a mighty people' – are not implausible but it is unlikely that she brought any major pressure on her husband to desist. After ten years of marriage, she must have known him well enough to realize that he would not change tack merely to assuage her anxieties. We cannot be certain that she knew she was again pregnant when she and James parted, though by the time of the battle of Flodden this would have been confirmed. Perhaps she did remind him that their son, though reportedly 'a right fair child, and large of his age', was still less than two years old and that Scotland would be vulnerable if things went badly, but the king's confidence was at its height. He was assembling a large force, adopting the latest continental military skills and tactics, all backed up with a formidable artillery train. He had no thought of failure. But he had made a will, as did most men going into battle in those days.

In it, he named Margaret regent in the event of his demise, a sign of his confidence in her ability. They bade each other farewell and she remained at Linlithgow to await news of her husband's expected success.

James returned to Edinburgh to supervise arrangements for the campaign. By 19 August 1513, all was ready in the capital. A signal gun was fired to mark the start of the march, followed by the command to move. The line of men moved forward out of Scotland's capital, dragging twenty pieces of artillery behind them. This ordnance, much of it made of brass, the very latest innovation and much lighter than iron-cast guns like Mons Meg (left behind in Edinburgh), would, the king believed, be crucial to victory. Full of confidence, he took his men south, through Dalkeith and over the Lammermuir Hills, heading for the second mustering point at Ellem Kirk, where they joined another substantial force. Though estimates have varied wildly over the centuries, and cannot be verified because the official records are missing, the Scottish army that combined in Berwickshire was probably between 30,000 and 40,000 strong. But as many as 25 per cent of these men had deserted by the time they engaged the English force in September and although they still outnumbered their opponents, the numerical advantage had lessened. Accompanying James IV were most of the nobility of Scotland and their levies. It was still a feudal system but it produced the nearest thing to a national army that Scotland had seen.

The king did not appoint a second-in-command and he has been criticized for this omission. In reality, it did not sit well with his own, or his people's, view of himself as a military leader and might have led to ill feeling among the Scottish lords who had answered their sovereign's call because he was a powerful king and because England was the traditional enemy, but who would not necessarily have taken kindly to any one of them being singled out above the others. The most important of the aristocrats who rode with James in the Flodden campaign were the Border chieftain Lord Alexander Hume; the northern magnate Alexander Gordon, the earl of Huntly; Matthew Stewart, the earl of Lennox; Archibald Campbell, the earl of Argyll and Adam Hepburn, the earl of Bothwell (Patrick Hepburn's son). All these men wielded tremendous local power and influence in the regions of Scotland. But when it came to assigning them roles in the order of battle itself their rivalries could yet turn out to be counterproductive. The presence of a European commander might have alleviated some of these tensions and given James a more detached perspective but his foreign advisers were gone with the fleet across to France. He had followed their training methods and military advice, believing that this would give him the advantage of the newest techniques, but how effectively these could be put into practice remained to be seen. But though they may have disliked one another, the personal bravery of his nobility and the vast majority of their men was never in doubt.

In persistently damp weather, the Scottish host crossed the river Tweed, the border with England, at Coldstream on 22 August, making for the bishop of Durham's fortress at Norham. James had been this way before and knew the country. Norham Castle itself had been the scene of many attacks over the centuries and though it was probably lightly manned at this time, its Constable, John Ainslow, held out for six days of heavy barrage by Scottish guns before surrendering on 29 August. James won his first victory of the campaign and as his soldiers plundered the supplies and costly furnishings of Norham, he turned his thoughts to further successes. There was, as yet, no sign of an opposing English force, and the Scots were able to take the castles of Etal and Wark easily. James moved on to Ford Castle, defended by Lady Elizabeth Heron, whose husband was being held hostage in Scotland for the murder of the Scottish warden of the East Marches, Sir Robert Ker, by a bastard relative. Lady Elizabeth surrendered the castle to the Scottish king on 1 September and for the next four days he made it his headquarters. The subsequent scurrilous tales of James's dalliance with Lady Heron, and of a similar liaison involving her daughter and James's son, the archbishop of St Andrews, have no contem-

porary corroboration. James was certainly a womanizer but we
have no way of knowing how tempting Lady Heron actually was
and, besides, James had more serious preoccupations while he
waited at Ford Castle. His own troops were growing tired and
increasingly hungry, worn down by the relentless rain and strong
winds, and he was obliged to send back to Edinburgh for supplies
of ammunition and new wheels for his guns as well as fresh oxen
to pull them. And now he had to deal with a much greater threat
than relatively defenceless Border castles. The English army,
commanded by the earl of Surrey, the man who had brought
him his bride ten years earlier, was fast approaching.

∾

SURREY WAS, at first, devastated to have been left behind in
England while almost every other commander of note accompanied Henry VIII across the Channel to wage war on Louis
XII. Now seventy years old, his entire life had been one of
military service and it seemed he was to be denied a brilliant
finale in France. Being charged with the defence of northern
England was insufficient compensation and early reports of the
size and equipment of the Scottish army were scarcely encouraging. The earl was at Pontefract Castle in Yorkshire when the
Scottish host was being assembled but he had begun his own
preparations already. As Commander of the North, he was
responsible for organizing the levies of men and mobilizing the
English lords and gentry who would form the backbone of his
troops. When he set off for northern England he had already
arranged for his artillery to be sent up from London to Durham.
A further source of assistance was likely to be the English fleet
once it returned from escorting Henry VIII to France. Surrey's
elder son, also called Thomas, was Lord Admiral and could be
counted on to provide well-trained men and sailors.[14]

The government of England had been left in the hands of
Queen Katherine, advised by a council led by the archbishop
of Canterbury, William Warham. Officially, Surrey answered
to Katherine, who took a keen interest in the preparations and

was ready to lead a second army up from the south in person if necessary. The queen's warlike demeanour may have been a conscious copy of her mother, Isabella of Castile's, militant spirit but her role in the war of 1513 has probably been overemphasized. In the event, she never got further than Buckinghamshire with her troops.

On 25 August, word was brought to Surrey that the invading Scottish host had crossed the Tweed into Northumberland. The next day, having sent out a signal for the northern levies to be amassed, he moved to York, where the Lord Mayor called out the city's defenders and provided him with a generous war chest of over £4 million, in today's money, to fund his expenses. In atrocious weather, the earl reached Durham on 29 August. He stayed overnight and when he left for Newcastle he took with him the banner of St Cuthbert, kept in the city's cathedral and regarded with awe as a surety of victory since it had been used in the great defeat of the Scots in 1138. Here was a move clearly intended to inspire and unite the English forces.

When Surrey got to Newcastle the next day, he found the northern commanders waiting for him as arranged: Lord Dacre, with his elite force of cavalry well used to fighting in the Borders, Sir William Bulmer, who had already given Lord Hume a bloody nose when the latter ill-advisedly undertook a raid of his own into England before James IV had even left Edinburgh, and Sir Marmaduke Constable. The weather remained so bad, with gale-force winds, that Surrey feared for the fate of his son, the admiral, still at sea. Thomas Howard managed to ride out the storm and eventually joined his father on 4 September, greatly raising Surrey's spirits.

He had moved out of Newcastle the previous day, realizing that he could wait no longer. When he raised his standard at the village of Bolton-in-Glendale, near Alnwick in Northumberland, he may have had as many as twenty-six thousand men, brought together from across the shires of northern England. As with the Scottish host, we cannot be certain of the figures, but Surrey was definitely outnumbered. He was not, however, outwitted. And he knew that he must make some quick decisions if he was to gain the initiative.

The English war council reviewed their options on 4 September. It was decided that their best hope lay in engaging the Scots while the English forces were still fresh. There were few supplies to be found in the bleak countryside and rations would be running out by 9 September. Better, then, to challenge James to fight by that date. It was a risky strategy but it held the attraction that, at the very worst, it would inflict considerable inconvenience and some losses on the invaders. Surrey would have been content with harassing his opponent and causing James to withdraw. He believed he could do this without suffering outright defeat, even if he could scarcely anticipate full-scale victory. Nor would he put himself at risk. He would command the rearguard. James IV, however, was determined to lead from the front.

✂

SURREY HAD the advantage of knowing the King of Scots already. During his time in Scotland, they had seen much of each other (too much, it will be recalled, for Margaret Tudor's liking) and the earl had the measure of James. He believed he would not refuse a challenge. This was issued by Surrey's Herald, Rouge Croix, who went to Ford Castle on 5 September to deliver it to James. Surrey did not yet know that the Scottish king had already moved his army across the river Till, a tributary of the Tweed, to take up a commanding position on Flodden Hill and James was not about to reveal this by letting the English herald return immediately with such crucial strategic information. Rouge Croix remained with the Scots and Islay Herald, his Scottish counterpart, was detained by the English.

James could not let Surrey's challenge, and the accusation that he had 'unnaturally, against all reason and conscience . . . entered and invaded this his brother's realm of England, and done great hurt to the same, in casting down castles, towers and houses, burning, spoiling and destroying of the same, and cruelly murdering the king of England his brother's subjects' go unanswered.[15] He was further angered by a much more strongly worded missive from the younger Thomas Howard, taunting him that the Scottish navy had fled before his ships and asserting that he would take no Scottish nobles, except for the king himself, as prisoner when battle was joined. This provocative claim ran counter to accepted forms of diplomacy at the time and would have caused great indignation among the Scots.[16]

Surrey's challenge named Friday, 9 September 1513 as the proposed date of battle. James, however, was not minded to budge from a nigh impregnable position on Flodden Hill. At this point he and his advisers may well have considered the possibility that they did not need to fight at all. So they stayed put and waited for Surrey's next move. It was not long in coming. Frustrated by James's unresponsiveness to his challenge, Surrey and his commanders decided to play on the King of Scots' sense of honour, one of the key aspects of his character. They would lure him off Flodden by suggesting that his behaviour, his refusal to meet Surrey's challenge, was unchivalrous. James was furious. 'Show to the Earl of Surrey,' came the reply, delivered by one of his gentlemen, 'that it beseemeth him not, being an Earl, so largely to attempt a great prince. His grace will take and hold his ground at his own pleasure and not at the assigning of the Earl of Surrey.' He remained true to his word, forcing Surrey to take the initiative. But if he thought the earl would be cowed, he was wrong. Surrey could not face the prospect of withdrawal and Henry VIII's displeasure. In the end, it was he who brought matters to a head. On 8 September, the day before the suggested date of battle, he made an inspired move. Starting at noon, he took his entire army across to the eastern bank of the Till and marched north and west through the ceaseless rain, arriving the following afternoon at the foot of Branxton Hill. Hidden by the terrain from the sight of the Scottish army, Surrey had out-flanked them and cut off their retreat to Edinburgh. James would now be compelled to fight.

THE BATTLE which ensued actually took place on the slopes of Branxton Hill and contemporaries often referred to it by that name. Over the centuries, it became known by the name of James IV's first encampment at Flodden. Today it is peaceful farmland, in a remote and beautiful corner of England, about four miles from the town of Coldstream and an hour and a half's drive from Edinburgh. It has been claimed that the battlefield is one of the best preserved of its period in Europe.* The position of the various English and Scottish divisions, or 'battles', as each individual unit was then known, are clearly shown on markers that explain the course of the fighting. On a clear day it seems a tranquil spot, with little trace of the terrible events that took place there five hundred years ago.

But on the afternoon of 9 September 1513 the weather was atrocious, as it had been for weeks, and the hillside was blanketed in low, swirling cloud and smoke from the fires set when the Scots had abandoned their first camp, all blown about by a blustery wind as the rain continued to fall. Atop Branxton Ridge was the entire Scottish army, having swiftly moved the mile and a half from Flodden Hill to meet Surrey's threat. Though the ground was not of James IV's original choosing, his larger numbers and commanding position should have given him the advantage. His guns had been hurriedly dragged over the wet ground and now stood ready to fire at his command. The Scots were compelled to react quickly to Surrey's bold seizing of the initiative but they did not lack confidence as they peered downhill at the smaller English force.

At the Scottish army's centre, commanding the largest division, was the king himself. There would be no place in the rearguard for James Stewart. The counsel of some of his commanders that, for the sake of his kingdom, he should stay back until the course of the fighting became clear, was angrily dismissed. James believed that he must be visible to his soldiers and

---

* The site is well worth visiting, though the steep climb up to the top of Branxton Ridge might challenge the unfit, especially if it is rainy.

he may have had some concerns about the reliability of the Highland and Border troops. There had been a significant number of desertions after the fall of Norham Castle. His presence would unite and, he hoped, inspire the entire Scottish force. More fundamentally, his character and the principles by which he had always lived, the very fabric of his belief in kingship, would not allow him to skulk in the rear. He believed that his honour would be forever diminished if he did not enter the combat with his troops. Surrey had read him well.

James and his commanders drew up their troops in a diamond formation, 'four up and one in reserve, with each of the forward units just a bowshot distance from its neighbour'. On the left were ten thousand men commanded by Lord Hume and the earl of Huntly, a combined force of Highlanders and Borderers, with the latter more numerous. In the left centre three earls, Errol, Crawford and Montrose, commanded seven thousand men from central Scotland and the Lowlands. The main 'battle', fifteen thousand strong, was to their right and led by James IV himself, with the royal household troops at their core, fighting under the banners of St Andrew and St Margaret. To the king's right were five thousand men commanded by Argyll and Lennox, Highlanders and their chieftains, and a small group of Frenchmen. In reserve, and originally on the extreme right but eventually moved behind the king, were five thousand men from the Lowlands and Borders led by the earl of Bothwell.[17] It was as impressive an array of unity behind their sovereign as Scotland would ever see.

The battle began in the mid-afternoon with a great volley of fire from James IV's artillery aimed at the English army below. The Scottish king hoped to inflict severe casualties in the heart of the opposing force and, essentially, to pound it into a state of such weakness that it would be overwhelmed by his superior numbers in any subsequent hand-to-hand fighting. The admiral, Surrey's son, who had arrived at the foot of Branxton Ridge before his father and the rest of the English forces, took his men back down to the other side of the small intervening ridge and desperately called for his father's aid. The sound of the guns and the glimpses of the Scottish army, tightly drawn up in pike formations, convinced him that he would be wiped out if the rest of the English did not arrive swiftly.

Yet King James's beloved cannons faced difficulty from the outset. They had been hurriedly positioned on soft ground and were firing downhill, making it difficult to gauge the range that they needed to inflict real damage on the English. Most of the shot flew over the heads of Howard's men. And the Scottish gunners, under their master gunner, Robert Borthwick, were inexperienced. It has been suggested that James did not order the use of sighting rounds at this point because he did not want to reveal his position but the guns were, in any case, unstable and their position could not be quickly changed. When Surrey and his younger son, Lord Edmund Howard, arrived with Dacre's men to back up the admiral, it became clear that they would have to combine their formations in a manner that could match the Scots. This they achieved impressively. The admiral retained the largest group of English soldiers in the vanguard, a total of about fourteen thousand men, his brother to his right and Sir Marmaduke Constable to his left. The rearguard, probably somewhat under twelve thousand men, was commanded by Surrey himself, with Lord Dacre's cavalry behind him, ready to move as needed. Yet to appear was the Lancashire magnate, Sir Edward Stanley, whose detachment was still struggling to reach Branxton.

The English had smaller guns but their lighter ordnance was far more easily moved and their gunners were quick and accurate. They also had the advantage of firing uphill. Soon they began to inflict considerable casualties on the Scottish gunners and some of the men in the centre, under James IV's direct command. Surrey, meanwhile, had moved the English army forward. They stopped in a marshy area at the foot of the main climb up to Branxton Ridge, where a small stream ran. The line where they halted can be plainly seen today and the ground is still damp, even in dry weather. In 1513, it became the site of a terrible slaughter.

James IV now decided that he must commit the Scottish host to the fight. The English guns were making a mockery of his state-of-the-art technology and his losses were mounting. He would defeat the English with his pike formations and their French captains and he himself would take the field. Although it may seem obvious with hindsight that he could merely have refused to give battle, or at least ensured that he personally had a safe route back into Scotland if things went awry, the character of James Stewart meant that such considerations would never have entered his head. It would be a memorable contest, the greatest test of his generalship and a timely demonstration to the rest of the world that he had mastered the latest arts of warfare. Above all, it was to be a vindication of his very personal style of kingship, an inspiring example to be recounted and admired through the long winter nights. He was forty years old and the grey was beginning to show in his reddish hair. This was his supreme moment. And so, at about five o'clock, he gave the order to advance.

On that gloomy and cold autumn afternoon, the English army at the foot of Branxton Ridge saw a fearsome sight. The Scots were moving down the hill towards them, in complete silence, as they had been trained by their king's French advisers. There were no battle cries, no Gaelic screams or imprecations. Clutching their fifteen-foot-long pikes, the Scots, many of whom were barefooted in order to get a better grip on the slippery slopes, moved remorselessly towards their foe. None would have anticipated what transpired over the next couple of hours.

First of the Scottish divisions to move was the vanguard commanded by Hume and Huntly. Engaging Edmund Howard's forces, the weakest in the English formation, it met with immediate success as many of the younger Howard's men took flight and his standard bearer was cut down by the Highlanders. Eventually, he was rescued by the bastard John Heron but by that time his part in the fighting was effectively over. Determined to press home his advantage, James IV now committed his second division to commence their descent; he intended to follow them closely. He did not know that Hume, who had been harried by Dacre's Border cavalry, was about to retire to the top of Branxton Ridge and would take no further part in the fighting. Whether or not an agreement had been reached among the Borderers on both sides to hold back from further combat, the truth is that when the king needed Hume's help, it was not forthcoming. Without it, the king and his troops faced a much more difficult task. Nor was it yet apparent that the second division, trapped by a small stream at the foot of the main hill and the slight rise behind it, were about to be cut to pieces by Englishmen wielding a weapon far deadlier than a pike in hand-to-hand fighting: the shorter agricultural hedging implement known as the brown bill, or halberd. For it was on these two factors – the uneven, boggy ground and the deadly use of a weapon that the Scottish had underestimated – that the outcome of the battle of Flodden was to hinge.

Even at this point, there were those among the king's advisers who implored him not to risk himself. They pointed out that if he entered the fray he would not be able to command effectively but this very salient point was not what James IV wanted to hear. For him, there was now no going back. Yet even as he moved off it must have been apparent that things were not going according to plan for Errol, Crawford and Montrose, though the full extent of the disaster being wrought on the second Scottish division was not yet apparent. Hemmed in and unable to use their pikes, the men fought heroically but all three earls and hundreds of their followers were cut down by the English.

James's huge 'battle' advanced down the slopes of Branxton Ridge, crossed the stream and mounted the small hill beyond. It was a stirring and colourful spectacle, even on a day without a hint of sunlight. The king himself, under his red and gold royal banner, was clad in full armour, over which he wore a gold and scarlet surcoat decorated with the royal arms of Scotland. His household knights and nobles who fought with him that day were richly dressed and armoured, too, partly for show but also to protect them from English arrows. But at Flodden this much feared weapon, the staple of English armies for centuries, inflicted far less damage than the continued volleys of shot and the viciously wielded bill. Soon there were many dead in the king's division but it continued forward without breaking, intent on making a conclusive breakthrough of Surrey's lines. But the English fell back at key moments of the Scottish advance, regrouping and luring their opponents ever onwards into tighter and tighter combat, cutting them down remorselessly. This brutal fighting continued for upwards of two hours, as the Scots tried unsuccessfully to counter with their swords and James, caught in the thick of the encounter, could neither summon his reserve under Bothwell nor compel the Highlanders, watching from the top of the ridge, to come to his aid.

In the end, Bothwell moved first, probably without orders, since James was not in a position to issue any. His intervention made matters worse, since he attacked Surrey's rear with five thousand men and inadvertently put pressure on the Scots engaged in close-quarters combat ahead of him. The Highlanders, perhaps riven by internal disputes about the best course of action and dissuaded at first by one of James IV's French commanders from charging down the hill to his aid, eventually realized that they must commit in order to save the day for Scotland. But they were prevented from doing this by the belated arrival of Sir Edward Stanley and his troops. Mounting the hill, Stanley's men loosed their arrows in great numbers at the Highlanders, shooting most of them in the back. Lacking the protective clothing of the royal division, the Highlanders were mowed down before they could come to James's assistance.

Without hope of rescue, James and his men fought on with great bravery. Eventually, their bulky armour and ineffective weapons told against them. As his losses mounted, the king probably realized that he could not win. But he would not surrender. He would not allow himself to be taken prisoner, to sit in London at the king of England's pleasure, or even to try to flee. How could he return to Scotland after such a defeat? In one last desperate effort, he gathered his household troops and made for Surrey's banners, apparently hoping that if he could kill the earl, the English might yet concede. But the carnage intensified and, as his own banner-bearer was killed beside him, he knew what he must do. Thrusting himself forward into the midst of his enemies, he made his final charge. In the press of men and weapons he must have realized that he had only moments to live. His armour could not save him now. Pierced below the jaw by an arrow, his throat gashed by the unforgiving English bill, he fell dying, choking on his own gore. He had got to within a spear's length of Surrey. And as the blood of the last king of medieval Scotland seeped into the muddy earth of Northumberland, his magnificent guns stood deserted on the hill above, the mute witnesses of his destruction.

�֍

As MANY AS ten thousand Scots and four thousand Englishmen perished with James IV at Flodden. Close to the king fell his eldest illegitimate son, Alexander Stewart, archbishop of St Andrews, the bookish short-sighted pupil of Erasmus. Among the dead were a bishop, two abbots, twelve earls, thirteen lords, five eldest sons of peers and up to three hundred other men of rank, whether in the Church or aristocracy. Almost every Scottish family of note lost a father, brother, husband or son, sometimes all four. But, personal tragedies aside, it was the loss of their king that hurt the most. There were those who did not want to believe him dead and rumours began to circulate that he had somehow escaped and become a wanderer, a pilgrim to Jerusalem, an eternal traveller seeking forgiveness and peace. The truth was much less fanciful and pathetically undignified.

The king's naked body, stripped, like all the Scottish casualties by scavenging English troops, was identified the day after the battle by two of his servants captured by the English and by Lord Dacre, who knew him well. It was then sent to Berwick and onward to Richmond but because James IV died excommunicate, he was never given the state funeral befitting a king. Henry VIII sought papal permission to bury his brother-in-law

in St Paul's Cathedral in London, but tombs there were vandal-
ized during the Reformation and in the seventeenth century the
Great Fire of London destroyed the old cathedral. So the last
resting place of James IV is not known and he has no memorial.

The battle of Flodden itself, too painful for the Scots to
remember and little known in England, became largely forgotten
except by military historians, a mere footnote in centuries of
Border hostilities. It was not until 1910 that a cross to the fallen
was erected at this scene of a slaughter so terrible that in intensity
it rivals some of the actions of the Battle of the Somme. The
memorial carries the simple but poignant inscription 'Flodden,
1513. To the brave of both nations.' It does not need to say
more.

History is not, of course, kind to the vanquished and over
the years the fate of King James IV and his army at Flodden left
a deep scar on the Scottish psyche. His death, coming when he
was apparently at the height of his power, seemed the result of
unnecessary posturing by a man seduced by an empty chivalric
notion of honour. Yet this is to misunderstand both James and
the times in which he lived. On the day that his life ended,
James made mistakes. He lacked experience of commanding such
a large force in such trying conditions, had never put his new
weapons to the test before and was out-generalled by a clever
professional soldier. The king and his country paid dearly for a
series of misjudgements and an element of sheer bad luck. But
the manner of his brutal death and the devastating loss to
Scotland has overshadowed his achievement as one of Britain's
great kings. James had come hesitantly to the throne as an
untried boy of fifteen. He was to occupy it with the full vigour
of the remarkable man he became. Yet his achievement in
putting Scotland firmly on the map of Europe and the love and
regard with which he was held by most of his subjects cannot be
denied. In marrying Margaret Tudor he had also introduced the
possibility that his heirs might one day unite the kingdoms of
England and Scotland, to create a greater Britain. Time would
show that this was not merely the product of an overactive Celtic

imagination but the solution to a long-running conflict between two families vying to control one island.

James IV is almost unknown now outside his native land. Even popular television histories of Scotland pass over his reign in a few sentences. This neglect does not do him justice. Perhaps the final word should go to the poet Sir David Lindsay of the Mount, who called him 'the glory of princely governing'. It is a fitting tribute.

Part Three

❧

Half a Tudor

1513–1542

CHAPTER SEVEN

Queen and Country

'To my thinking, this battle hath been to your grace and all your realm the greatest honour that could be, and more that ye should win all the crown of France.'

Katherine of Aragon to Henry VIII

'Brother, all the welfare of me and my children rests in your hands.'

Queen Margaret to Henry VIII

IT IS UNLIKELY that Henry VIII agreed with his wife's estimate of the significance of Surrey's victory over James IV. All his efforts were bent on France. His Spanish queen, however, saw things differently. On 16 September 1513, one week after the death of the King of Scots, she wrote to Henry telling him that she was sending him a piece of James IV's bloodied surcoat as a trophy: 'In this your grace shall see how I can keep my promise, sending you for your banners a king's coat. I thought,' she continued, with unseemly relish, 'to send himself unto you, but our Englishmen's hearts would not suffer it. It should have been better for him to have been in peace than have this reward. All that God sendeth is for the best,' she concluded. Yet even at this time of triumph, she knew that her most pressing duty lay elsewhere. She was twenty-seven years old and after four years of marriage still she had not borne her husband a child who survived. There was now no need to lead her troops north in person. Instead, she intended to visit the shrine of Our Lady at Walsingham in Norfolk, 'that I promised so long ago to see'.[1] There she would pray to remain fertile and produce a healthy heir. It is a poignant footnote to an otherwise strikingly repellent missive.

Yet both Katherine and the earl of Surrey knew that, in reality, it would not be wise to present Flodden as the major victory of the war against the French. The only successful action involving the English in France had been the minor cavalry pursuit grandiosely titled the battle of the Spurs and, even then, Henry VIII had not taken part. But the siege and capture of the city of Tournai was a much greater prize and no doubt one that the king himself considered far greater than the defeat of the Scots. Too much crowing by those left behind in England would earn royal displeasure. Besides, the campaigning season was drawing to a close and Surrey lacked the resources to follow up his victory. He had neither the men nor the authority to invade and occupy Scotland. His job was done. Henry VIII did not tarry long in France, either, returning home in October 1513.

King Louis XII of France, meanwhile, was dismayed by the defeat of his ally. It came at a bad time, though the reversals he had suffered in fighting the Habsburgs and Henry VIII were far from being major defeats. Writing from Amiens in northern France at the beginning of October, he made sure that the Scots understood how deeply he regretted the loss of their king, instructing the diplomats who were to be sent to Scotland to assess the state of that country to 'tell of the king's great sorrow at the misfortune said to have happened to the late king of Scots, at which he grieves so much that he will never be content till he has shown the love he bore to the late king, which he will try to show also to the young king, his son.' As Queen Katherine had not held back in gloating over James IV's death, so Louis XII could not be restrained from an outpouring of affection which, it is fair to say, was unsuspected by those who knew this cold and calculating man well. 'The king's love to the late King of Scots,'

Louis said, 'was so great that he cannot hide it, and, though he cannot bring him back from the dead, yet he would wish to make his memory everlasting in all the world as a great and virtuous king, worthy of all honour and glory, and to raise, preserve and guide his noble descendants and preserve them from their enemies.' These were fair words, but at the end of his instructions he revealed his true concern: 'to know the truth and the condition of the young king and kingdom and to learn what help he can give for the preservation of the kingdom and resistance to its enemies.'[2] By now he possessed the better part of the Scottish navy, including the great ships the *Michael* and the *Margaret*, but if French influence in Scotland was to be maintained, he could not afford to sit on the sidelines. The country had an English queen regent but where the balance of power might lie was not yet apparent.

Yet within a year, as the alliance between Henry VIII and Emperor Maximilian finally unravelled, Louis XII would make a peace with England and marry Margaret Tudor's younger sister, Mary, leaving the Scots out in the cold. And by then much had changed in Scotland itself.

∽

RUMOURS OF the defeat of their army and the death of their king reached the citizens of Edinburgh the day after Flodden. The fear that the English would now stream across the border and attack the capital city itself prompted a call to arms but it soon became apparent that the enemy army was moving back to Berwick. Precisely when the news reached Queen Margaret at Linlithgow is not known, nor is her immediate reaction. The story that she had kept watch for a messenger in a room at the top of one of the towers of the palace is unsubstantiated and the idea that her screams of anguish echoed around the palace when she was told of her loss is fanciful. Yet she must have known that her life would never be the same again.

Margaret Tudor was not quite twenty-four years old when she was widowed. She had been ten years the consort of a dynamic king. In that time she had wanted for nothing and, even if James was not a faithful husband, he had treated her with the respect due to her rank and they had worked together to enhance the Stewart monarchy. Eventually, after the sad loss of several babies, she had born him a bonny son to carry on his name. By now, she knew for sure that she was pregnant again and believed that this would make her more secure. Still, her situation was very far from enviable. Although she had watched James rule, she had no direct experience of government. And her husband's will contained one notable restriction. Margaret's regency was contingent on her never remarrying. This was not because James IV wanted to tie her to some lifelong devotion to his memory but because he realized that a second marriage would inevitably compromise her position. A foreign husband of appropriate rank would surely mean that she had to leave Scotland and could have no further role in her son's upbringing and preparation for adult rule. A spouse drawn from the Scottish nobility, on the other hand, might lead to civil war. The rival great families would not sit quietly by while one of their number effectively dominated Scottish politics.

Doubts about the queen's marital intentions were, for the time, put aside or, at least, subsumed in a greater area of concern. Margaret may have learned Scots and tried in every way to demonstrate her commitment to Scotland but she was English by birth. Her brother's declaration that he was overlord of Scotland was very ill-received by her late husband and his lords and could not be forgotten. There was suspicion that the queen did not know where her true loyalties lay. This, and the fact that women rulers were regarded with hostility and suspicion throughout Europe, would prove a severe challenge now that fate had compelled her to step out of her husband's shadow and try to lead Scotland in his stead.

History has not been kind to Margaret but the view that she was an oversexed whinger who was always more concerned about her wardrobe and the company of handsome young men than the well-being of Scotland overlooks the complex reality of her life after the death of James IV. Her immediate response to personal tragedy and the country's overwhelming loss was one of determination and dignity. Leaving Linlithgow, she travelled to Stirling, her dower palace, taking the little King James with her. She summoned a general council to meet there on 19 September, called a parliament for December and oversaw the arrangements for her son's coronation. He was, and would remain, the focus of her life, a love that cost her dearly and one that James V himself never really appreciated.

The Mourning Coronation, as the crowning of James V is known, took place on 21 September 1513. It was a sad affair and nothing is known about the ceremonial or those who attended beyond the council records that outlined the arrangements, in which it was noted:

> The lords think it expedient and it please the queen's grace that the king our sovereign lord be crowned on Wednesday next to come, the twenty-first day of this month of September in the church of the castle of Stirling and that my lord of Glasgow [Archbishop James Beaton] be *executor officii* and provide therefore, and that all other necessary provision be made for the said coronation again the same day.[3]

Apart from Beaton and James V, the names of the other participants remain unknown, although we can be reasonably certain that the holders of the great hereditary ceremonial offices – William Keith, the earl marischal, and William Hay, earl of Errol, the constable of Scotland – would have been present. So, too, would the queen mother and some of the lords appointed to advise her, such as the earls of Angus, Huntly, Morton, Argyll and Lennox.

The king himself was only seventeen months old and cannot have understood the ceremony. He would have been anointed with oil and given the regalia – his sword, sceptre and spurs – to touch, but could not take the oath himself; someone else had to speak it on his behalf. It has been suggested that he was carried into the church by a trusted servant, perhaps Sir David Lindsay

of the Mount, the poet and courtier who was his master usher
and who played an important part in his upbringing. The little
king might have been more startled than gratified by the oath of
loyalty made by the congregation, the peers of the realm kneeling
before him to declare their fealty individually, followed by the
singing of psalms and playing of trumpets. But when the ceremonial, however hastily convened and adapted to circumstances,
was over, there could be no doubt that James V was King of
Scots in the eyes of God and man.

Those around him were still struggling to come to terms with
what had happened to their country and to contemplate what its
future might be. As 'tutrix' (her official title in James IV's will),
his mother expected to play a major role in his upbringing and,
in so doing, effectively to rule Scotland on his behalf, through
what would be a long minority. If the child she was carrying
proved to be another son, then this should, in theory, strengthen
her position. The reality, however, would turn out to be much
less straightforward and the physical restrictions of pregnancy
itself somewhat limited Margaret's options in the months after
Flodden. She did attempt to take as active a part in the business
of government as her health permitted, though, attending council
meetings and issuing instructions and requests even shortly
before she gave birth.[4] No one could deny the terms of James
IV's will but this did not mean that it would be acceptable to the
magnates of Scotland or that Margaret's comprehensive interpretation of her role would go unchallenged. Indeed, it very soon
became apparent that there was an alternative and one that was
far from palatable to the queen or to her brother, Henry VIII.

The tradition of a near male relative acting as regent for a
king during his minority was more acceptable than placing a
woman in this role, despite the fact that Mary of Gueldres,
mother of James III, had performed this task competently in the
1460s. But the underlying suspicion that Margaret would promote English interests and essentially become an agent for her
brother had not gone away. Given these considerations, some
Scottish lords began to look elsewhere. The closest male relative

to James V was his cousin once removed, John Stewart, duke of Albany, son and heir of the rebellious exiled brother of James III. But choosing Albany would bring problems of its own. He was French by birth, loyal servant of the king of France and had never set foot in Scotland. Pitting him against Queen Margaret was to personify the stresses of Scottish history. For it seemed that, whatever the outcome, the kingdom would become the tool of larger countries engaged in a European conflict. Yet both Margaret and Albany had much more concern for Scotland itself than their detractors realized.

John (or Jehan, as he always signed himself) Stewart, second duke of Albany, was born in the Auvergne region of France, probably in the year 1482. His errant father had married a rich heiress after his flight to France. Although the extensive Scottish lands that came with the Albany title were forfeit, the title was still used at the French court. John Stewart was very young when his father died in a jousting accident and he was sent to court at an early age, where he learned the manners and diplomatic *politesse* that were to characterize his approach to governing the troubled realm of Scotland. Like all young courtiers of his time, he was also trained in military matters and his prowess was well regarded. After serving with some distinction in the Italian Wars, a highly advantageous match was made for him with his first cousin, Anne de la Tour, heiress to the count of Auvergne, in the year 1505. This made Albany a rich landowner and placed him firmly at the centre of those who served Louis XII. It would also give him a significant and often overlooked role in wider European politics when his sister-in-law, Madeleine, married the Italian duke of Urbino and gave birth to a daughter, Catherine de Medici. The deaths of both of her parents within a month of her birth meant that John Stewart was the closest surviving French male relative of a child whose wealth and connections made her a very attractive marriage prospect. As time would show, Albany took his responsibilities to his niece seriously. Yet though he grew up speaking only French, he did not forget his Scottish heritage. During the reign of James IV, he corresponded with the king, also his first cousin, and undertook a couple of diplomatic missions to the pope on James's behalf. Perhaps he hoped this would restore him to favour in Scotland because, at the end of 1512, Louis XII formally requested his Scottish ally to restore John Stewart to his father's dukedom. It says something about the continuing doubts of the elder branch of the Stewart line about the younger that James IV did not respond.

After Flodden, John Stewart's position was fundamentally changed. Until Queen Margaret gave birth to her husband's posthumous child, he was the heir presumptive to the Scottish throne. Even if Margaret produced another son, the proximity to the throne of an adult male who was close to the old ally, France, made Albany a serious contender for the role of regent, or 'governor', as he was officially styled. The queen may not have liked this at all but it presented an alternative that a considerable number of Scots involved in the political process found appealing.

And those members of the Scottish polity who either survived Flodden or had not taken part in the battle were evidently keen to make their voices heard in the uncertain circumstances that their country faced. Some of this may have been prompted by self-interest and jockeying for position but there was genuine concern for the future of their country as well. The disaster at Flodden had left Scotland reeling and thrust a new and inexperienced generation into government but it did not bring to a halt the functioning of government itself. The general council meeting called by the queen at Stirling for 19 September was attended by twenty-three lords, twelve of whom were spiritual peers and the rest lay peers. Ten more lords, making a rather unwieldy total of thirty-three, were nominated to sit daily on the general council but it was soon decided, for the facilitation of the smooth functioning of political life, that the queen would be advised by a permanent body of six councillors.

The emphasis was on continuity and filling roles caused by deaths on the battlefield. Lord Hume remained as chamberlain, despite his doubtful behaviour at Flodden, and was entrusted with keeping peace in the Borders. Patrick Paniter, James IV's secretary, continued in that office. William Elphinstone, bishop of Aberdeen, whose service to the Scottish Crown went back to 1479, carried on as keeper of the privy seal and was named as 'guardian' to the infant king. Elphinstone was the natural choice for the vacant archbishopric of St Andrews but Pope Leo X, ever obstructive in Scottish ecclesiastical matters, refused to confirm him. For the time being the senior churchman in Scotland was the bishop of Glasgow, James Beaton, who crowned James V and was now propelled to the top rank of Scottish politics when he was appointed chancellor. This was a role that had declined in influence during the reign of James IV and the appointment of the pro-French Beaton, who had met Albany at the French court and favoured a role for him in Scottish politics, cannot have been welcome to Queen Margaret.

As the months passed and her pregnancy progressed, the queen found herself increasingly preoccupied about if and when her authority (as she perceived it) would be challenged by the arrival of a French-born Stewart, the duke of Albany. Louis XII was happy to extend French influence in Scotland by parting with one of his most loyal courtiers but only when the moment suited France, and certainly not until the duke's responsibilities and powers were clarified. From across the sea, Albany scented divisions arising within a month of the defeat at Flodden. In October 1513, he made his first intervention in Scottish politics, writing to the queen and her council to beg them that they 'keep in agreement for the sake of the young king and his kingdom, since misfortune from outside may be remedied, but not internal misfortune. It seems therefore that they must be united and abandon all quarrels, for a united kingdom cannot be defeated or subjugated.' He went on to beg his emissary, Alexandre de la Bastie, to remind Queen Margaret 'to assist in the above matter which touches her more than any other'.[5]

This measured plea was typical of Albany. It is all too easy to label the duke and his supporters as pro-French and Queen

Margaret and hers as pro-English, but the truth was not so simple. And it is worth noting that the only letter that the queen received from England at this time was from her sister-in-law, commiserating with her on the death of her husband. In sharp contrast to the self-congratulatory epistle sent to Henry VIII, Katherine of Aragon had been moved, whether through genuine concern or because propriety demanded it, to acknowledge the blow dealt to Margaret. She even sent a friar north to offer spiritual comfort. The Queen of Scots thanked her politely but without warmth. There were no words of advice from Henry VIII, no call to his sister to foster unity in her country. Indeed, Henry may well have found it difficult to accept that Margaret could rule effectively in Scotland. He could never entirely overcome his resentment of her and the fact that a Tudor brother and sister now had the opportunity to decide the future of the British Isles was lost on him. Naturally, he did not want French influence to supplant her altogether but he wanted to remind her that it was his judgement of the Scots that would prevail in their mutual dealings. The Borders remained unstable, with Dacre undertaking frequent raids, and when Margaret wrote to Henry asking for a permanent peace he replied dismissively that 'the Scots should have peace or war with him according to their own choice and behaviour.' Thus reinforcing that he held the power and the Scots must essentially conform to his view of them as a subservient nation, Henry left his sister at the mercy of events at a time when she was most vulnerable, and opened the door to Albany.[6]

That door had been ajar since 26 November 1513, when the general council held at Perth proposed the continuation of the Auld Alliance between France and Scotland and requested Albany to come with men and munitions to defend the country from continued English attacks. The council also suggested that there could be a division of power between the queen, as the physical keeper of the little James V, and Albany himself, as governor responsible for the day-to-day government of Scotland. This scheme had a precedent in the minority of James I of

Scotland and it would have made Margaret, in theory at least, a figurehead not tainted by association with any particular family or interest. It would have been a difficult but not necessarily unrewarding role with perhaps more power than Margaret perceived. The only problem was that, with true Tudor spirit, the queen did not want to share control of Scotland in this ill-defined way. As the spring of 1514 arrived her thoughts were, however, directed to the approaching birth of her child.

∞

ALEXANDER, DUKE OF ROSS, was born on 30 April 1514 at Linlithgow. He appeared to be a healthy baby and his arrival made the question of the succession in Scotland less pressing but it did not give his mother the boost to her authority that she was seeking. In fact, returning to the business of government and attending council meetings once she was recovered from the birth (apparently one of the more straightforward of Margaret's deliveries) seems to have brought home to the queen her vulnerability. Yet even as she mulled over how to proceed, her councillors made it clear that they were still willing to accept her as regent under the terms of James IV's will: 'Madame, we are content to stand in one mind and will and to concur with all the Lords of the realm to the pleasure of our master the king's grace, your grace, and for the common weal, and to use none other bands now nor in times to come in the contrary.'[7] This declaration was made to the queen on 12 July. Evidently it did not inspire sufficient confidence in Margaret that she could continue alone. Within a month she had married for a second time, to Archibald Douglas, sixth earl of Angus, in a secret ceremony at the church of Kinnoull in Perthshire. It was to prove the biggest mistake of her life.

Margaret knew very well the terms under which her children were entrusted to her care and guidance but she had not been able to live with the continuing uncertainty regarding her own ability to rule outright rather than live as a figurehead. Pressure of circumstances and a strong Tudor desire to obtain and exercise power propelled the queen into taking a fateful step. The parallels between her situation in 1514 and that of her granddaughter, Mary Stewart, in 1567 have not always been adequately appreciated, but if Margaret was not physically coerced by the Douglases and their family allies, the Drummonds, in the way that Mary was by Bothwell half a century later, she may well have felt psychologically pressured to choose Archibald Douglas and his kin as protection in uncertain times. Clearly, she did not want to be entirely reliant on her brother, Henry VIII, nor was she anticipating that her actions would cause her to lose control of her sons. This second marriage was undertaken to ensure quite the opposite. Margaret did not want to leave Scotland. Henry VIII was in the process of marrying his younger sister, Mary, off to the ancient king of France and even if Margaret's personal pride might have been piqued by being passed over in this way, she did not want to remain a disposable asset for her brother in the European marriage stakes.

Seeking to control her own destiny, Queen Margaret had therefore to find a Scottish husband. There was no one who would have been universally acceptable – rivalries among the nobility were simply too great for that. Nor was there a wide selection of possible candidates. The duke of Albany might have been ideal but he was already married and even complete control of Scotland was unlikely to be sufficient inducement to divorce his enormously wealthy wife, with whom, in any case, he seems to have been reasonably happy. James Hamilton, earl of Arran, was next in line in the succession after Albany, but the legality of Arran's divorce from his first wife was in doubt. Divorce in Scotland was a murky area, as Janet Kennedy's career shows, but for those close to the throne the difficulties it threw up could not be so readily disregarded. Archibald Douglas offered the protection and influence of a long-established family (albeit one whose loyalty was first and foremost to themselves rather than the Crown of Scotland), powerful in southern Scotland and largely Anglophile in outlook. It is likely that expediency, rather than any great sexual passion on the queen's part, made him the only choice for her. Their courtship was, of necessity, brief because Margaret felt that her ability to influence Scottish politics was diminishing fast and the Douglases did not want her to change her mind.

The marriage of Queen Margaret and the earl of Angus has fuelled the imaginations of historical novelists, who have portrayed a woman in her mid-twenties intoxicated by a handsome teenager. In fact, they were the same age and Angus was already a widower himself, though engaged to marry someone else before he wed the queen. He may well have been reasonably presentable in appearance but the flaws in his personality that became so obvious within a short time of his second marriage had already been spotted by an uncle, who called him a callow young fool. He was to prove a difficult and unreliable (as well as unfaithful) husband, keen on expanding his power, a willing tool for Henry VIII, a greedy and incompetent regent and a stepfather much hated by James V as the lad grew. He was the absolute antithesis of James IV and, for Margaret, marriage to him was full of stress and shouting matches.

Henry VIII's reaction to his sister's remarriage (which had taken place without his permission) was to wait and see what would transpire. As it happened, he did not have to wait long. In Scotland, the response to Margaret's union with Angus was swift and unfavourable. Margaret was deposed from the regency on 21 September 1514 when the lords, meeting at Dunfermline, announced that 'the queen's grace has forfeited the office of tutrix of the king's grace our sovereign lord her son and shall cease from using of the same in times coming and shall not interfere with any matters pertaining to the crown ... because she has contracted marriage ... through which the office of tutory ceases in her, conformable to the laws of the realm.'[8] Before this, however, they had required the queen, 'with the consent of her husband', to agree to letters being sent immediately requesting that the duke of Albany 'as governor of Scotland' should come across from France 'in all goodly haste'. Margaret had little option but to agree. She clung to the hope that, despite earlier exhortations, there would continue to be no sign of Albany, who remained firmly in France and was likely to stay there under the terms of the new friendship between Henry VIII and Louis XII.

As the autumn of 1514 progressed, it seemed that divisions in Scotland would settle into an uneasy stalemate. Margaret had lost her official position but would not give up without a struggle. Not all the lords wanted Albany and the queen still had physical possession of her two sons. She was not without support but she was becoming increasingly concerned. The queen could not collect her rents and her financial resources were dwindling. Marriage to Angus, far from improving her position, had complicated it. In a letter of November 1514, she poured out all her troubles to her brother, pleading for his assistance, via military intervention if necessary:

> I commend me to you with all mine heart. I have received your loving and comfortable writings from a man of Lord Dacre's ... wherein I perceive your fraternal love and kindness. I and my party were in great trouble of mind, till we knew what help you would do to us ... My party-adversary continues in their malice and proceeds in their parliament, usurping the king's authority, as I and my lords were of no reputation, reputing us as rebels, wherefore I beseech that you would make haste with your army by sea and land.

This was, of course, treasonable and it was also unrealistic. Henry VIII was not about to commit forces against Scotland again so soon after Flodden, while he was at peace in Europe and at the start of winter. Margaret also wanted her brother to send money, saying she was 'at great expense' and would soon be 'super-extended'. She implored him to try and prevent Albany's coming in any way he could. The letter, so typical of Margaret's rambling style and tendency to accentuate the negative, did, however, end on a more positive note. Her children were both well – 'right life-like', she called them – and she would remain in the safety of Stirling Castle.[9]

Help from Henry VIII, whether financial or military, did not come. As the year 1515 dawned he had other preoccupations, for on New Year's Day Louis XII of France, worn out, some said, by the attractions of his young wife (though, in reality, he had been in poor health for some time), died. The throne of France passed to his cousin and son-in-law, Francis of Angoulême, who became King Francis I. The new monarch wanted to make a name for himself and reassert France's role in Europe. He viewed the Auld Alliance with Scotland favourably and was not afraid to put the cat among the pigeons when it came to Anglo–Scottish matters. He authorized Albany's departure to Scotland and the duke arrived in the land of his forefathers for the first time on 16 May 1515. Ten days later he was in Edinburgh, determined to try to bring stable government to Scotland after nearly two years of dissent and uncertainty among the political class. It was a charge that he laboured to fulfil with dignity and impartiality and which was to cause him immense frustration in its execution. But if he was to have any real effect on Scottish government, he knew from the outset of his tenure of office that he must secure the person of the king.

THERE WAS A high level of attendance at the first council meetings following Albany's arrival and a good turnout for the parliament called for July 1515. Much of this may have been prompted by a mixture of curiosity and a desire to be noted in the first months of the new governor's regime. Even Margaret was, on a personal level, favourably surprised. Albany's courtly French manners and personal deference to her rank appealed to the status-conscious queen. But Albany was also determined to reinforce his own standing, knowing that his effectiveness would in large part depend on his success in gaining acceptance of the executive powers of his role and his right to govern. He knew he must be given the right to exercise the powers of an adult king or he would get nowhere. The ceremonial surrounding his own entry to parliament was of crucial importance and he made a

duly impressive entrance on 11 July, noted by Dacre in his report
to the council of Henry VIII: 'At the beginning of the Scotch
parliament . . . the sword was borne before Albany to and from
the Parliament by the earl of Arran, and a coronet set on his
head by Angus and Argyll, and he was appointed protector till
the king came to the age of eighteen.'[10]

The arrival of Albany did not please Henry VIII and the
English king was already taking steps to destabilize the duke
before he could grasp the sceptre of Scotland too firmly in his
hand. At the beginning of his report, Dacre noted that his
instructions from London were 'to foment quarrels between
Albany and Angus and between Albany and the Chamberlain
[Beaton] so as to drive the duke out of Scotland'. This kind of
stirring had long been a feature of English policy towards
Scotland – Dacre boasted that he had had spies in Scotland for
the last three years – but it did not necessarily bring about instant
results. Albany's move to seize James V came swiftly and could
not be pre-empted.

At the end of July, the Scottish parliament approved a scheme
which would remove the king and his brother from their mother
and place them in the care of a group of eight lords, four of
whom could be chosen by Margaret. Angus appears to have been
willing to give up the children immediately. He was then at
Stirling with the queen and was apparently more concerned
about what might happen to his estates if there was a confrontation. The future of his stepsons was of secondary importance.
Margaret was not prepared to give in so easily. She countered
with the nomination of four lords of her own choosing (one of
whom was her husband) but they were unacceptable to Albany.
The duke had learned quickly who his opponents were. Nor was
he inclined to prolong debate on this issue. He wanted control
of James V and the little duke of Ross. When Margaret defied
the lords sent to remove her sons by lowering the portcullis of
Stirling Castle in their faces as she stood with the king by her
side and the duke in his nurse's arms, Albany had had enough.

He sent an army to besiege the queen and compel her to hand over her sons.[11]

Angus had, by now, slipped out of the castle and returned to the south-east, the beginning of a pattern of his seldom being there when his wife needed him. Dacre, supported by Lord Hume, who resented not being given a prominent role by Albany, cooked up a desperate scheme to kidnap the King of Scots and his brother and spirit them across the border to England but Hume's small force was trounced by the besieging army and the plot failed. It must surely have had at least the tacit support of Henry VIII.

On 4 August, Albany arrived in person in Stirling with a large artillery train that included the famous cannon Mons Meg. Margaret realized that she could not hold out against such odds. Although 'left desolate', she behaved with great dignity and demonstrated a considerable flair for the public occasion, a strong Tudor trait. She gave the keys of the castle to her three-year-old son and told James V to hand them to Albany, thus reinforcing that the child was king and only he had the authority to dispose of the castle itself. She then begged Albany to 'show favour to the king and his brother and her husband Angus'. The duke reassured her that he would honour her and the children but pointedly refrained from making any reference to Angus, saying that 'he would not do with no traitors'. But it was to be more than a year, with considerably more treasonable activity in between, that justice finally caught up with the Hume family. Lord Hume and his brother William were executed in October 1516 and their heads displayed on the walls of Edinburgh Castle. Margaret herself had given up the fight much earlier.

❧

THE WORLD COLLAPSED around Margaret Tudor when her sons were officially removed from her care. In the space of two fraught years she seemed to have lost everything that mattered to her. She had been unwilling or unable, perhaps both, to think coherently about how she might turn the position of queen mother to her advantage merely by biding her time. As Catherine de Medici was to discover half a century later, it was not necessarily an empty role and a more cunning person than Margaret might have realized the advantages of staying aloof from Scottish politics. Yet against that it must be acknowledged that her Englishness was always going to be perceived as a problem by some of her son's leading subjects and her brother was determined to interfere whenever an opportunity presented itself. But the arrival of Albany in Scotland really was a hammer blow, determined as he was to have control of the king. The autumn of 1515 was a dismal time for the queen, who was further hampered by being in the final stages of what would prove to be her last pregnancy. She was carrying Angus's child but he had already demonstrated that his primary loyalty was to himself.

In England, disconcerting parallels were now being drawn with the fate of the sons of Edward IV more than thirty years earlier. The disappearance of Edward V and his brother, Richard, duke of York, had taken place after the seizure of power by an older male relative. Could the duke of Albany be another Richard III? Whether Henry VIII believed that his nephews were genuinely at risk or not is uncertain but it clearly suited his purpose to spread such rumours abroad.[12] This merely added to Margaret's agony of mind. In these circumstances, she was increasingly dependent on Dacre, the conduit to her brother, who became her chief adviser. He seems to have had more influence on the queen than her husband, but that impression may have been precisely the one that this hard-nosed Border magnate wanted to convey in his dealings with London. The weakness of the Queen of Scots provided Dacre with an opportunity to take centre stage in Anglo–Scottish affairs. It was a part he relished.

Then aged fifty, Dacre was the most formidable of all the northern English lords. No one else could match his knowledge of Scotland and its chief men, or his experience of Border government, in which he played such an active role. It was second nature to him to act as Margaret's Tudor's mentor and sometimes to foist on the queen schemes that were as much his own as London's. Kidnap and raiding were in his blood and he had abducted his own wife, a notable heiress and royal ward, in order to secure her hand in marriage. Small wonder, then, that he felt it completely feasible to bundle the royal children of Scotland across into England, though he had wisely left it to Lord Hume to try and achieve this. Not a sentimental man, like all aristocrats in England and Scotland at the time he was determined to promote the interests of his own family. He does appear to have had some genuine sympathy for Margaret, though reading between the lines of his voluminous correspondence he seems always to have thought of her as a woman to be directed rather than a monarch to be respected. And at this point, as the queen considered her future and the safety of her unborn child, he persuaded her into a course of action that would embarrass Albany and inadvertently bring about an irreparable breach in the queen's second marriage, already under strain after barely a year. Encouraged by Dacre, Margaret resolved to flee from Scotland and place herself squarely under the protection of Henry VIII.

By early September, a plan was in place, agreed by the queen, who accepted that its actual success would depend on her own resourcefulness. Accompanied only by Angus and a few servants, she slipped away from Linlithgow where, as custom dictated, her lying-in before giving birth was to take place. At first she went to Tantallon Castle, the great Douglas family fortress high above the sea on the east coast. But Albany learned of her being there and made moves to intercept her, so she left hurriedly, abandoning her baggage and much-prized jewels. By 16 September she was safe in Blackadder Castle, the Hume stronghold. Just over a week later she had managed to cross the border into England at Coldstream, where the nuns of the priory gave her shelter. Angus was now proscribed as a traitor.

The secret departures and constant need to evade capture took a heavy toll on Margaret. The intention had been for her to ride as far as Morpeth but the advanced stage of her pregnancy made further travel on horseback impossible. On 8 October, worn out and anxious, she survived a difficult labour to produce a healthy daughter. The arrival of the child, Lady Margaret Douglas, was splendidly announced by the queen in a letter to Albany in which she said she had given birth to 'a Christian soul, being a young lady'. This particular young lady would have her own significant part to play in the drama of the Tudors and the Stewarts but, for now, her mother lay desperately ill at Harbottle Castle in Northumberland. It took Margaret many weeks to make a full recovery from the birth, in a castle ill-equipped for a queen or a newborn. Dacre's residence at Morpeth had been prepared for the birth and Henry VIII and Katherine of Aragon sent a complete wardrobe of beautiful dresses for Margaret and clothing for the baby there, but the queen was not strong enough to appreciate their gifts until mid-November when she was moved by litter. And though she had not forgotten her ambitions for Scotland or her claims to her sons, writing to Albany soon after giving birth to Lady Margaret Douglas that she still claimed 'the whole rule and governance of my children', it seems to have been the sight of the twenty-two gowns sent by her brother that caught her imagination at this emotional time. The courtier Sir Christopher Garneys, sent by the king to deliver all these fine things, reported her reaction: 'Her grace was borne in a chair out of her bedchamber into the great chamber ... When she had seen everything, she bid the Lord Chamberlain and the other gentlemen come in and look at it, saying, "So, my lord, here ye may see that the king my brother hath not forgotten me and that he would not that I should die for lack of clothes."[13] Given Margaret's circumstances, this sounds frivolous and has contributed to negative depictions of the queen as a woman who was more concerned with her own personal appearance than matters of state. Yet she was still badly affected with sciatica brought on by riding when heavily pregnant. 'Her grace hath such a pain in her right leg', reported Garneys, 'that this three weeks she may not endure to sit up while her bed is a-making, and when her grace is removed it would pity any man's heart to hear the shrieks and cries that her grace giveth.'[14] Margaret was not one to suffer in silence but the pain of sciatica can be excruciating and she was generally in very weak health. As for her clothing, she had left everything behind in Scotland and Margaret Tudor (and, indeed, other members of her family) did not expect to be taken seriously as a queen without the trappings that went with majesty.

Amidst all the cloth of gold, silk, satins and crimson and purple velvets, Margaret passed Christmas at Dacre's home, where 'a great house' was kept for the festive season. Garneys commented that he 'never saw a baron's house better trimmed in all my life'. Dacre and his wife had spared no expense for their royal guest, her husband and small entourage. But even as it seemed that she might eventually recover from the prolonged stresses of flight and childbirth, fate dealt Margaret another blow. Her younger son, Alexander, on whom she seems to have doted, speaking with great maternal pride of his achievements, proved sadly less 'life-like' than she had reported to Henry VIII the previous autumn. The little duke died in December and the news was kept from Margaret for a while because it was feared that the shock might kill her.

It was not until early spring that Margaret was ready to move south to London, for a reunion with the brother she had not seen for thirteen years. As she recovered, she began, with prompting from Dacre, to put together a catalogue of her complaints against Albany, who was still hoping that she could be induced to return to Scotland, since her presence in England, though it removed her as an obstacle on one level, raised serious problems of its own. He feared that the queen's sense of grievance would be nurtured at her brother's court and that if she determined to return on her own terms, it might be with an English army at her back. The duke urged Margaret to 'be a good Scottish woman, as it accords her to do'. The queen did not rise to this bait.

Margaret travelled slowly down to London, arriving at the

beginning of May 1516. She was accompanied by the charming Sir Thomas Parr (father of Katherine, who would later become her brother's last wife) and if the journey was not as memorable as her progress to Scotland years before, there was still a triumphal entry into London, the sort of occasion Margaret loved. The reunion with Henry VIII and Katherine of Aragon, as well as her sister Mary, always known since her brief time in France as 'the French Queen' and now married to the duke of Suffolk, was a joyful time for the children of Henry VII. Mary's marriage was, however, a sharp reminder to Margaret that her own marital affairs were not so happy. Angus had not accompanied her to London. His duty to his wife had been done in Northumberland. Now he felt that he must safeguard his own and his family's interests in Scotland. He needed to preserve a degree of detachment, which would give him more room for manoeuvre if Albany's position weakened or the duke was compelled to return to France. Angus's quest for independence would cause pain to his wife, complications for Henry VIII and long-lasting resentment from his stepson, James V, as he grew.

CHAPTER EIGHT

The Young King

❧

'And, ay, when thou came from the school
Then I behufft to play the fool.'

Sir David Lindsay of the Mount, poet and master usher to James V,
recalls the lighter moments of a troubled childhood

'Before going, it would be well to find out what England
will do for Scotland, telling them that Albany has authority
to treat, if they think fit . . . If Henry refuse these overtures,
it will be evident that he does not wish to treat France as
a friend.'

Memorandum prepared for Francis I before his meeting
with Henry VIII at the Field of Cloth of Gold, 1520

JAMES V was only three years old when his mother fled to
England. The episode marked a decisive break in their relationship and led to a distance, both literal and metaphorical, that
could never fully be bridged thereafter. He had lived with Queen
Margaret in various palaces, principally at Stirling and Linlithgow, cared for by his own team of retainers but very much under
maternal supervision and with frequent contact. Suddenly, she
was gone and his world changed. The impact that this had on
him at the time can only be imagined but the unpredictable and
occasionally frightening course of his childhood helped shape the
man he became.

His father dead and bereft of his mother, James V grew up without family ties. His younger brother died before the age of two and he never became close to his half-sister, Lady Margaret Douglas, who was in the custody of her father, the earl of Angus, and spent considerable parts of her childhood outside Scotland. It is unlikely that James was deprived of the company of other children – Alexander Gordon, fourth earl of Huntly, son of James V's much older half-sister, Lady Margaret Stewart, became a close companion when both boys were in their teens – but the names of his playmates are not known.[1] He was a child but also a king and this set him apart. As the long years of his minority went by, the struggle for 'the person of the king' became the one constant in Scottish politics and a matter of considerable interest in England. Many wanted to control James V – Henry VIII, Albany, Francis I, the Hamilton faction under the earl of Arran and their sworn enemies, the Douglases. Queen Margaret herself, through initial exile, ill health and fraught relations with her brother and second husband, never abandoned hope that she would regain direction of her son on her own terms. Half a Tudor James may have been (and his portraits show a strong resemblance to Henry VIII as a young man), yet the fact that he seemed to belong to everyone developed in the young man the belief that he was beholden to no one. It is a facet of the king and his reign that has not been adequately recognized.

His childhood, though sometimes chaotic, was by no means unpleasant. Carefully nurtured in the 'safe' castles of Edinburgh, Stirling and Craigmillar, his security was in the hands of a rota of nobles deemed trustworthy by regent Albany (initially Lords Borthwick, Fleming and Erskine), men who could reasonably be relied upon to put the national interest and the king's well-being above that of personal or family ambition. It is worthwhile remembering that such men did exist and not to tarnish the entire Scottish nobility with the failings of the better known few. But it was James's fiercely loyal and affectionate household staff who gave him the day-to-day comforts that any small child, even a king, holds dear. And the man who was closest to him in these difficult times, who supervised the domestic arrangements and was ever present, was Sir David Lindsay of the Mount.

Lindsay was a member of an old family from Fife in eastern Scotland. Although little is known about his formal education, he was at court by 1508 and attached to the household of the first son of Margaret Tudor and James IV, who died young. The contact he had with the queen and his friendship with the man who became her secretary in 1515, Sir James Inglis, suggests that Margaret and her entourage had confidence in Lindsay. This link may have made it easier for James V to cope with the absence of his mother. His relationship with Lindsay was close and warm: 'when thou was young,' wrote Lindsay, 'I bore thee in mine arms, full tenderly, till thou began to grow.' He also sang sweetly to lull the little king to sleep, 'with lute in hand', taught him music and dance, told him tales, dressed up and acted for James's entertainment. 'So, since thy birth, I have continually been occupied, and always to thy pleasure.'[2] It is a touching testimony of someone who cared deeply for his charge and was conscious of the need for warmth and continuity in the upbringing of a child, especially one born into such a demanding role.

Albany took seriously his obligations towards the king, ensuring, as much as his interrupted presence in Scotland permitted, that the boy was trained appropriately. James seems to have liked and respected him but circumstances made it difficult for them to develop a really close relationship. Albany also saw his role primarily in political terms. But there was another aspect to kingship that needed to be addressed as the king grew and this was in the hands of churchmen.

It was a deeply religious age and the king's understanding of his quasi-spiritual responsibilities called for nurturing under sensitive guidance. Several chaplains attended on him, supervised by his master almoner, Sir James Haswell. At the beginning of 1517, with his mother still absent in England, it was felt appropriate to appoint a full-time tutor and the post was given to Gavin Dunbar, the future archbishop of Glasgow and a staunch supporter of Albany. Dunbar remained in this post until

1525 when the earl of Angus, by then back in power, dismissed him and effectively brought to an end the formal education of James V.

Given Renaissance views of learning and study as a lifelong process, especially for the upper classes, this was an extraordinarily truncated education. In the young king's case, it was all the more serious because he does not seem to have been a natural scholar. His apparent struggle to read a letter in English when he was twelve years old was noted by the English ambassador, though this may have been more a response to the pressure of a public occasion and the fact that he was being watched by his councillors than a problem of basic literacy.[3] Later on, it was remarked that his Latin and French were both deficient and, for a monarch who was to commit himself firmly to the French alliance, this was a drawback. Henry VIII was fluent in French, conducting much of his diplomacy in it, and his son, Edward VI, admittedly educated twenty years later and in much more stable circumstances, was viewed as something of a paragon for his prowess in the schoolroom.

To be fair to James, he was brought up and educated in a way that helped him connect with his Scottish subjects on a much closer level than mastery of French or Latin would have done. He inherited the love of music common to both his parents and seems to have been an able musician. He loved hunting and riding and wrote poetry in the Scots language. Acquiring the courtly, chivalric qualities of kingship appealed to him more than the schoolroom, a testament to his dual heritage. He was delighted when his Uncle Henry sent him a jewelled sword and hunting paraphernalia and let it be known that what he really wanted was a full-sized English buckler, the round shield used in fighting to ward off blows, not the miniature version for children. His social prowess and love of aristocratic pastimes were praised: 'His said grace,' it was reported, 'stirred his horses and ran with a spear, amongst others his lords and servants, at a glove. And also . . . we have seen his said grace use himself otherwise pleasantly, both in singing and dancing, and showing familiarity among his lords. All which his princely acts and doings be so excellent for his age, not yet of thirteen years ... that in our opinion it is not possible they should be amended.'[4]

⤜⤚

IT WAS, as it would always be, European imperatives that ended Albany's first period as governor of Scotland in the spring of 1517. Francis I, like Charles VIII before him, wanted mastery of Italy and had achieved a great victory at Marignano in the autumn of 1515, a glorious beginning to his reign but not one that he was destined to repeat. He was, naturally, loath to compromise his position by giving too much offence to the English and if that meant that new treaties of friendship with Scotland could not be ratified, then he was willing to sacrifice his smaller ally, at least for the time being. The upshot was that the Scots were backed into agreeing a truce with England, whereby Albany, his job apparently done for the time being, nominated a council deemed competent to govern Scotland without his presence. Retaining the title of governor of Scotland, he left on 8 June 1517, intending to return in five months. In fact, it would be more than four years before he reappeared on Scottish soil. But one thing that he did bring to fruition, soon after he got back to France, was to rectify the diplomatic humiliation felt by the Scots when their overtures for a binding treaty with France had been rebuffed the previous year. A new treaty of friendship and alliance, negotiated by Albany for the Scots and the duke of Alençon for France, was signed at Rouen on 20 August 1517.

The treaty of Rouen has been called one of the most important in sixteenth-century Scottish history. Certainly, it reconfirmed the Auld Alliance, giving Scotland the security of knowing that the French were committed to coming to their aid in the event of an English invasion, though, of course, it also tied the Scots to a similar undertaking if England attacked France. And in agreeing in principle to the future marriage of

James V with a French princess, it determined the emphasis of Scottish foreign policy when the king reached his majority. The wider, long-term implications were even more important, since Scotland was set firmly on a course that would lead to dependence on France and cause deep divisions in Scottish society.

Meanwhile, it was confirmed that Queen Margaret should end her exile in England and come back to Scotland, to be reunited with her son and the earl of Angus. She left London on 18 May 1517, little more than two weeks after some of the most serious rioting the capital had witnessed for many years, when property of foreigners was attacked in a xenophobic outburst badly handled, at first, by the authorities. The king's advisers sought to put Tudor spin on this debacle, which resulted in the public hangings of many predominantly young people, aggrieved by the belief that their livelihoods and prospects were being undermined by foreign workers, distrust and jealousy of immigrants certainly not being confined to modern times. By depicting the unrest as a mass outbreak of treason, the authorities were able to cover their own slack response to the early signs of trouble and allow the king to appear magnanimous in his treatment of the perpetrators. Further summary punishment was halted, often at the gallows themselves, by the supposed spontaneous intervention of the three queens, Katherine of Aragon and Henry VIII's sisters, Margaret and Mary. But as Margaret well knew, when she left the troubled city behind and made her way northwards once more with her jewels, dresses and money provided by her brother, Henry could be ruthless when he felt it necessary. He had made it clear that she could not expect to live out the rest of her life in England at his expense. He wanted her in Scotland. It was her duty to go back. Yet she could not rely on him to support her unequivocally (indeed, by that time she must have realized that his support, when he chose to give it, would always be on his terms), nor could she be certain of what lay in store for her in Scotland. The truth was far worse than she could have anticipated.

Henry VIII had been assured by Albany that the Scottish

lords 'have granted all that he demanded in the name of his sister, the Queen of Scots, and never had any other intention than to honour her.' But the regent either did not know, or felt that it was not his place to point out, that the same could not be said of the earl of Angus, Margaret's husband. During his wife's absence, the earl had taken up again with his former fiancée, Lady Jane Stewart, and was openly living with her while appropriating Margaret's rents to fund himself and his mistress. The liaison resulted in the birth of a daughter and Margaret was, understandably, furious when she found out. The queen had probably regretted her second marriage from very early on, but now the relationship foundered completely. Margaret was not the sort of person to forgive meekly the infidelity of a husband who had not brought her the political power she craved and was also a social inferior. She had no wish to live with him again but did not raise the question of divorce until the spring of 1519, when she wrote to her brother that her husband 'had done her more evil, that I shall cause a servant of mine to show your grace, which is too long to write.' And now she thought of ending the marriage altogether: 'I am so minded, that, an I may by law of God and to my honour, to part with him for I wit well he loves me not, as he shows me daily.'[5] Henry VIII was horrified. The idea of his sister trying to obtain a divorce was completely unacceptable and Queen Katherine joined him in urging Margaret to abandon all thoughts of bringing such a disgrace to the family, a sad irony in view of what the future had in store for her. More pragmatically, Henry put considerable store on the usefulness of the Anglophile Angus and so he urged Margaret towards reconciliation. This took place briefly, but Angus soon abandoned Margaret for his unofficial family again, all the while blatantly spending her revenues. So Margaret's marital problems were a further complication in Henry VIII's policy towards Scotland.

Margaret's position was unenviable. She had little income, was not allowed to live with her son because the Scottish regency council feared she would remove James V to England and her brother refused further requests for money and armed support. At one stage she was reduced to borrowing money from her financial controller and dismissing household servants to economize. Some of the Scottish lords affected to sympathize with her, but their sympathy did not amount to hard cash or an improvement in her standing in Scotland. Their reluctance, however, was understandable given the wider political problems that threatened to engulf Scotland in Albany's absence. They had more to occupy them than the wailings of a dowager queen.

For though Angus might have been playing fast and loose with his wife and her money, he was not so successful in dominating the government of Scotland at this time. Albany had left a council of no fewer than seven regents to govern in his absence. Angus sat with the other three leading earls, Argyll, Huntly and Arran, as well as the still useful Andrew Forman, archbishop of St Andrews, and James Beaton, archbishop of Glasgow. Most had some reason to dislike Angus and to chafe at the seventh appointee, Antoine d'Arces, Seigneur de la Bastie, the trusted French lieutenant of the duke of Albany.

The council did not hold together long. De la Bastie's influence in south-east Scotland, where he had been given administrative responsibility by Albany, upset the great local families and none more than the troublesome Humes, who contrived to ambush and assassinate the Frenchman on 17 September 1517. But it was Angus who felt the most aggrieved when the regency council voted to hand de la Bastie's role to the earl of Arran, thus effectively making him head of the Scottish government. For several years, the two earls circled each other, vying for power and influence, particularly in the capital, until there was an armed confrontation in Edinburgh known as 'Cleanse the Causeway', when Angus and Arran supporters fought each other along the High Street on 30 April 1520. Small wonder that Queen Margaret described Scotland as 'evil-governed' at this time, but she never gave up her struggle for restitution of her rights. And then, towards the end of the following year, in November 1521, the duke of Albany at last returned to Scotland. War with England was again on the horizon but perhaps the most remarkable aspect of the duke's second period of direct Scottish rule was that it was supported wholeheartedly by the woman who had previously opposed him so vigorously six years earlier. Abandoned by her brother and overlooked by the Scottish lords, Margaret Tudor now threw in her lot with Albany. She believed he alone could get her what she wanted. No amount of cajoling by one of the succession of friars that either Henry VIII or Katherine of Aragon kept sending up to Scotland over the years, to offer soft words of comfort and keep Margaret on the path of duty (as they saw it), could prevail. The queen had heard it all before and she was at breaking point. Her brother, her husband, even Lord Dacre, always so free with advice that provided little practical solution to her problems, had all let her down:

> As to my lord of Angus [she wrote to Dacre], if he had desired my company or my love, he would have shown him more kindly than he hath done. For now of late when I came to Edinburgh to him, he took my house without my consent and withholding my rents from me which he should not do. I had no help of his grace my brother, nor no love of my lord of Angus and he to take my living at his pleasure and despoil. Methinks, my lord, that ye should not think this reasonable, if ye be my friend. I must cause me to please this realm [Scotland] when I have my life here.[6]

Henry was aghast at his sister's volte-face. Showing the streak of ruthlessness that all the Tudors possessed when it came to their own interests, she had surprised him. Never mind the fact that he had turned down her pleas to be allowed to return to England, heartlessly requiring her to stay in a marriage that was humiliating and effectively condoning the loss of dignity she suffered; Henry felt himself the wronged party. It has been said that Henry and Wolsey, his chief minister, did not allow themselves to be distracted by Scotland but it could be argued that a distraction is precisely what Scotland always was for the English king. His policy towards his northern neighbour was often incoherent and always opportunistic. Margaret's support of Albany (and, by extension, French interest in Scotland) came at a particularly delicate time for the king of England. At home, he had just executed an overmighty subject, the duke of Buckingham, for treason, thus ridding himself of a potential rival for the throne but also highlighting the weakness of his own dynastic position. Buckingham was but the first of many high-profile victims of the English king's jealousy and concern about the survival of his dynasty. And abroad, as the pattern of European alliances was frequently being reconfigured, Henry was facing the prospect of war with France. Merely a year before it had all been so different.

For while Scotland suffered domestic upheaval and uncertainty as the long minority of James V continued, the young king's English uncle (his nearest male relative, an uncomfortable reality for the Scots) was determined to cut a figure on the European stage. Best remembered for his six wives and for establishing the Reformation in England, the thirteen years of Henry's reign between the ending of the French war in 1514 and the decision to seek an annulment of his marriage to Katherine of Aragon in 1527 are something of a lost period in the general perception of his reign. The long-held view that Henry was lazy in matters of government, preferring the company of a small circle of hangers-on and flatterers who hunted, jousted and caroused with him, has been challenged by recent historians. Henry undoubtedly liked the chivalric and physical aspects of kingship, the bravado and bonhomie of a clique of followers, as much as he liked to dabble in writing music and verse. He was also a good, if slightly pompous, son of the Church, keen to take up his pen against the renegade German monk Martin Luther. Henry's 1521 treatise against the early stages of the Reformation in Europe, the *Assertio Septem Sacramentorum* (*In Defence of the Seven Sacraments*) was the first book published by a king of England. It won him plaudits from Rome and the title of 'Defender of the Faith' while also opening up an ongoing controversy with Luther and his supporters. Henry, who probably did not write all of the work personally, had established himself as a ruler who was not afraid to engage in theological debate, though he was, for the moment, on the side of the conservative religious forces in Europe.

But there was much more to him than intellectual aspiration and personal braggadocio. Henry was a man of formidable intelligence, closely engaged in political decision-making. He never abdicated the responsibility of rule for personal pleasure. It was during this time that the king's style of government evolved and matured and foreign policy dominated. As such, the significance of these years should not be underestimated. While it is not necessary to rehearse the changing alliances and lengthy diplomatic proceedings that lay behind them, there are a number of constants. England was not irrelevant to what was going on in Europe but neither was it as important as Henry VIII liked to think.

The developing struggle between the Habsburgs, originally a German family but now ruling much of western Europe, and their enemies, the French Valois kings, defined the first half of the sixteenth century in Europe. England and Scotland both had a part to play in this contest but were not the major protagonists. Henry VIII, throughout his reign, saw himself as a new Henry V, a king who would restore England's glory in France and regain at least some of the territories lost in the Hundred Years War. He had resurrected the old English claim to the throne of France when he went to war in 1513. But it was always a dream and only in his youth and then again in old age did the king make any effort to make the dream come true. This meant that his natural predisposition was to support the young Holy Roman Emperor, Charles V, the nephew of Katherine of Aragon, against France. Charles's grandfather, the wily and unreliable Maximilian, died in 1519. In theory, the role of Holy Roman Emperor was elective and not hereditary and, for a while, both Henry VIII and Francis I harboured thoughts that it might come their way. But Maximilian had distributed enough money among the seven German electors that there was only ever going to be one outcome. He told his cautious grandson: 'If you wish to gain mankind, you must play at a high stake.' This cynical but prescient remark might be taken as a watchword for how diplomacy and politics have long been conducted.

Henry had never, realistically, stood any chance of gaining the imperial Crown so he and his advisers sought to maximize English influence by looking to their advantage as events unfolded. If this meant abandoning Charles for a while, they were perfectly happy to pursue a better relationship with France. The 1520s saw a succession of treaties in which the pendulum swung one way and then another. When relations with France improved, then there was less tension with Scotland, its natural ally in the British Isles. When they deteriorated, the prospect of a renewed outbreak of hostilities in the British Isles was never that far away.

Yet Henry was not solely preoccupied with being taken seriously as a European monarch, much as this appealed to his ego and sense of theatre. The Buckingham episode was intended to underline his kingly power at home. European rivals could be friends or enemies, depending on circumstances, but in England Henry would brook no opposition. Underneath this determination lay an uncomfortable reality. Henry's only legitimate child was a daughter, Mary, born in 1516. Katherine of Aragon's childbearing years were behind her as the new decade of the 1520s dawned. Both of Henry's sisters had produced boys but the king himself had only an illegitimate son, Henry Fitzroy, born to Elizabeth Blount, one of Queen Katherine's ladies, in 1519.[7] Though this birth gave confidence that the king could produce boys, it did not alter the fact that Katherine of Aragon was now extremely unlikely to present the king with a male heir.

Her last pregnancy was in 1518 and the king's anxiety about it gives us a glimpse of how seriously he regarded her situation. He wrote to Wolsey that he was fearful of Katherine miscarrying: 'the chief cause why I am so loath to repair to London were, because about this time is partly of her dangerous times, and because of that I would remove her as little as I may now. My Lord, I write this unto you not as a ensured thing but as a thing wherein I have great hope ... and because I do well know that this thing will be comfortable to you to understand.'[8] Alas, for the king and queen, all Henry's care came to nothing. The child was a stillborn daughter. There would be no more pregnancies, though a further nine years went by before the king resolved to end his marriage to his Spanish first wife.

Throughout this period, Henry was supported by his immensely able minister, Thomas Wolsey, archbishop of York and later cardinal. An experienced diplomat who had been on a mission to Scotland under Henry VII but who knew France better, Wolsey was undoubtedly the major figure of Henry VIII's reign until he came unstuck when he failed to deliver a speedy annulment of Henry's marriage to Katherine of Aragon. Before that, he had seemed the perfect servant, sharing Henry's human-ist agenda and interests while consistently striving to enhance the regal majesty of his sovereign. If Wolsey chose to live superbly as well, Henry did not mind; the sumptuous state and palaces of his adviser reflected the king's own glory. The fact that Wolsey was the son of a tavern-keeper-turned-butcher from Ipswich in Suffolk did not bother Henry, though it raised eyebrows among the old aristocracy of England, who disliked Wolsey's airs and graces. While he had the king's favour, no one could touch him and many importuned him. And perhaps his greatest hour came in France in the summer of 1520.

Wolsey was given the task of organizing the meeting that took place between Henry VIII and Francis I that was known as the Field of Cloth of Gold. Today we would call this a summit, though its ostentatious magnificence certainly makes modern international gatherings look positively grey. The temporary en-campment that was set up for Henry and Katherine at Guisnes, on territory that was still held by England, made contemporaries marvel and fall over themselves with superlatives. This was, of course, the intention. Henry VIII inherited his father's belief in public display as a means of reinforcing the monarchy, but he exercised it on a far more lavish scale. As a statement of wealth, luxury and conspicuous consumption, the Field of Cloth of Gold surpassed expectations. Five thousand people, including almost all the high nobility, accompanied the king and queen across the English Channel. Henry was seeking to impress and to impose himself on his own aristocracy every bit as much as he wanted to demonstrate his power and wealth to his French rival.[9]

Strangely left behind, however, was the four-year-old Princess Mary, who, as the betrothed of the French dauphin, might have been expected to attend. Certainly Francis I was perplexed by her absence and sent a trio of French diplomats to London to ascertain whether the child had some impediment that the king of England wished to hide. Mary soon quashed any fears by handling her first international audience with great aplomb for one so young. James IV's old adversary, Surrey, by now elevated to the dukedom of Norfolk, was the most prominent noble left behind to attend to the business of government. He reported to the king that the princess 'is right merry, and in prosperous health and state, daily exercising herself in virtuous pastimes.' The reasons for her staying behind in London remain unknown but might possibly have had something to do with Katherine of Aragon's known opposition to the meeting with Francis I.[10]

The temporary palace constructed at Guisnes was decked out with cloth of gold and precious stones. Fountains ran with red and white wine, prodigious quantities of food (over two thousand sheep were slaughtered) and drink were supplied and the ladies wore their richest clothes and costliest jewels. Indeed, the role of ladies at the meeting had been deemed important from the outset. Sir Richard Wingfield, Henry VIII's ambassador to France, reported that a major search was underway at the French court to find the fairest women. He hoped that Queen Katherine 'would bring such in her band that the visage of England, which hath always had the prize' would be appropriately represented. Francis I himself told Wingfield that he hoped Henry would not be displeased if he brought a good number of ladies along, to which Wingfield, no doubt well aware of his monarch's weakness for the fair sex, replied that he had never seen the English king 'encumbered or find fault with an over great press of ladies'.[11]

The French court, encamped nearby at Ardres, which was on French territory, could not be seen because the valley between the two camps had been artificially widened. Great care was taken to ensure that one side could not intimidate or outdo the other. Francis, typically, had not held back in his own preparations. The French king's tent was twelve feet high and covered with gold brocade and three wide stripes of blue velvet 'powdered' with gold fleur-de-lis, the symbol of France. It had taken one French official no fewer than seven visits to Florence to obtain the right cloth of gold. The sight of all this finery prompted one observer to say that it surpassed the pyramids of Egypt and an Italian commentator, who felt that the English camp actually outdid the French, noted that Leonardo da Vinci could not have done better than the design of Henry VIII's tent.[12]

Proceedings started with the meeting of the monarchs in the vale of Ardres, where the two kings alighted from their horses and embraced, Henry telling Francis that 'I never saw prince with my eyes, that might of my heart be more loved.' These fair words were rendered somewhat hollow by the fact that, just before embarking from Dover, he had entertained the emperor Charles V with a similar outpouring of affection and pageantry. But Henry was not to be deterred from his immediate aim in France: to establish a personal rapport that might avoid an outbreak of war in the future. So he dined, jousted and wrestled, at one point throwing Francis to the ground in an exhibition of English prowess that had to be quickly hushed up. And while Queen Katherine entertained Francis in her quarters, Henry dined with the delicate but clever French Queen Claude in hers. Claude was no beauty (but then neither was the overweight and puffy Katherine of Aragon by this time) but she had borne sons and her husband, though consistently unfaithful, was actually rather fond of her. With his large nose and swarthy colouring, Francis was himself less handsome than the golden king of

England, but a string of high-ranking mistresses bore witness to his other attractions and, of course, his supreme power in France.

Yet when all the festivities, lasting from 7 to 24 June, were over, there was no treaty of alliance and uncertainty still hung over the future of relations between England and France. There was never going to be more than a temporary respite in hostilities between Francis I and Charles V, and Henry was torn. His natural instinct was to side with his wife's nephew but he did not wish to abandon the Treaty of London, the non-aggression pact signed by seven European powers, including France and the Holy Roman Empire, in 1518. But in the end even the largely pro-French Wolsey, the master of ceremonies at the Field of Cloth of Gold, knew that the treaty was doomed to failure. At Bruges in 1521, Wolsey signed a new alliance with Charles V on Henry's behalf. It would lead to war with both Scotland and France within two years.

∞

THE DUKE OF ALBANY's second period of residence in Scotland came at a time of heightened tension and was especially displeasing to Henry VIII. The duke's standoff with the earl of Angus ended in submission by Queen Margaret's estranged husband, who went off to exile in France, taking his daughter with him. There he stayed until 1524. The choice of France as opposed to England as his place of retreat has never really been explained but must, presumably, have been dictated by Albany. Angus was hardly known as a French sympathizer and his uncle, Gavin Douglas, was already in England trying to get more support for the Douglas family, so fleeing across the border would have been the more likely choice. Margaret had initially been a supporter of the elder Douglas, nominating him to the Highland bishopric of Dunkeld in happier times, but her rift with Angus had long since extended to the rest of the family. When Gavin died of the plague in London in 1522 he had already spread salacious rumours about Margaret's relationship with Albany, rumours which Henry VIII was quite willing to believe.

The idea that his sister might now marry Albany (whose French wife did not die until 1524) was taken seriously by the king of England. In January 1522 he wrote to the three estates, the body politic of Scotland, in high dudgeon. Albany had, he asserted, given 'the charge of [King] James to a stranger of inferior repute, intending to sever the queen from her husband and marry her himself, to the great danger of the king, the ruin of the queen, and Henry's honour.' Frustrated by the duke's continued influence over Scottish affairs, Henry was ready to believe that Margaret was having an affair with Albany and he held forth on the subject in a letter delivered to the Scottish queen by the Clarencieux Herald the month after his separate missive to the Scottish government.

Margaret was, at first, reduced to tears by what she termed her brother's 'sharp and unkind letter' but her considered response was feisty enough. She had written in favour of Albany only for the sake of peace and 'could do no less'. 'Nothing', she stated, 'is dearer to me than the weal and surety of my son.' She accused Wolsey of slandering her in front of Henry's council when he claimed that she 'loved the Governor to my dishonor'. The idea that Albany intended to harm the king she dismissed as ridiculous and she chided her brother with his apparent intention to make war on herself and her son, while at the same time upbraiding him for his neglect of her personal interests: 'As to her treatment in this country, which she had hoped Henry would have got remedied, she has found a better friend in Albany than any other.' James V, she said, was being looked after 'by as good and true lords as any in the realm' and she demanded to know what greater security for the young king her brother thought he could offer. If his unreasonable demands and accusations continued, 'the world will think he aims at his nephew's destruction.'[13]

This war of words constituted the most bitter exchange of correspondence between the Tudor siblings. Their relationship, never tender, was permanently damaged. Henry's mistrust of his sister, his willingness to believe that all her doings were really the result of feminine weakness and selfishness, took little regard of her situation. Perhaps, more than anything, the episode underlines Henry's inability to see things from her perspective. But then, as God's representative on the throne of England, why should he? And his anger was no doubt coloured by the fact that he was once more allied with the Habsburgs against the French and was planning a further invasion of northern France. His mood cannot have been helped by the uncompromising response of Chancellor James Beaton and the Scottish estates to Henry's lecture, pointing out that 'if as appears by Henry's letters, the good done by Albany is taken in evil part by the king and the sinister reports of Scottish traitors easily believed, they see not what love can subsist between him and his nephew.'[14]

Albany shuttled between Scotland and France in the period 1521–4 but though he came with four thousand soldiers, eighty-seven ships and six hundred horses in the autumn of 1523, he failed to persuade the Scots to give wholehearted support to his campaign. The memory of Flodden was too raw and even the Scottish lords who admired him were reluctant. At the end of October 1523, his only serious military endeavour against England ended ignominiously when he abandoned his siege of Wark Castle in Northumberland after just three days.

The final realization that the Scots wanted his presence but would not commit to fight for him struck the duke hard. At heart, he was always a servant of France, but he had done his best for a troubled land and its boy monarch. Now his thoughts turned to returning home for good. Even the pleas of Francis I's mother could not keep him in Scotland for much longer. On 31 May 1524, he set sail from the port of Dumbarton for the last time, having, as he believed, 'reduced the kingdom into excellent order'. Though he might have thought that he could always come back yet again if needed, his days of influence were gone. In July 1524 Queen Margaret, supported by the powerful Hamilton family and their senior representative, the earl of Arran, effectively engineered a coup d'état by declaring King James of age to rule. The lad had been chafing for some time under the restrictions of his life at Stirling Castle and, at twelve years old, was keen to assume at least some of the mantle of kingship. His mother, however, had every intention of exercising power through him, as she had tried to do more than a decade before.

~

THE MAN determined to frustrate this ambition was her second husband. The earl of Angus returned from France via England, where he held talks with his brother-in-law and received sufficient assurance of support to enable him to confront his wife. This he did shortly after the opening of a new session of the Scottish parliament in mid-November 1524. Supported by the earls of Lennox and Buccleuch, Angus and a band of four hundred followers scaled the walls of Edinburgh, opened the city gates and, proclaiming themselves the loyal subjects of James V, demanded to be able to take their seats in parliament as was their right. Margaret was no longer minded to trade arguments about precedent with her husband. She ordered guns to be trained on his forces and after a volley killed four innocent bystanders, the earl withdrew at the king's command. Advised by her brother's ambassador, the quavering churchman Thomas Magnus, not to do anything so unwifely as shooting at her own husband, Margaret responded by telling him to 'go home and not meddle with Scottish matters'. Poor Magnus was stymied by his own consciousness of his social inferiority – lecturing a queen was something that came less easily to him than it had to Lord Dacre – and the indecisiveness of Wolsey and Henry VIII. Even before Angus got back to Edinburgh, they were having second thoughts. Wolsey wrote:

> Everything depends now upon one of two points: whether the queen and lords will train their king to the amity of England, or of France. These things are far more material than the sending of ambassadors, pacification of private quarrels, or entertainment of guards. The King thinks that Margaret, notwithstanding her wilfulness towards her husband ...

should not be sharply dealt with . . . reconciliation of Angus
with the Queen of Scots and Arran is not to be insisted on
. . . no evidence has appeared, since he [Angus] came to
Scotland, that he is so well loved there as was reported.[15]

The acknowledgement that Angus did not enjoy the sort of
support they had been led to believe is typical of the confusions
of English policy towards Scotland at this time. The realization
that there were two largely pro-English groupings in Scotland,
one led by the queen and her allies and one by Angus, was
confusing. Henry VIII had favoured his brother-in-law for the
simple reason that he did not trust his sister to do his bidding.
He was afraid, as a definitive peace between England and
Scotland remained elusive, that Margaret might still ally with
France. But in 1525 his old rival, Francis I, suffered a catastrophic defeat on the northern plains of Italy at the battle of
Pavia and was taken prisoner by Charles V. While he might have
been frustrated by Scottish politics, Henry VIII now had every
reason to congratulate himself on his alliance with the emperor.

He would have been less pleased if he had known that
Francis I's doughty mother, the regent Louise of Savoy, was
offering Margaret an attractive pension in return for a French
alliance. Margaret did not accept but her days as regent were
numbered. Parliament recognized Angus's right to sit alongside
Arran, Lennox and Argyll in a new scheme that would see
control of the king and the administration of Scottish affairs
rotate between these four earls quarterly from July 1525. Quite
how anyone genuinely believed that this well-intentioned but
totally impractical approach to handling the political tensions of
the country would work is a good question. Perhaps the fact that
the lords previously responsible for James V's upbringing had
behaved honourably in the execution of their office inspired the
hope that this new policy could succeed. Arran had been at least
partially reconciled to his old adversary, Angus, and may have
believed that he could derive an advantage from acquiescing.
Margaret, who remained a member of the council but had

effectively lost the regency, was very unhappy but lacked a sufficient power base to impose an alternative.

Warning bells should have sounded when the first period of guardianship of the king was given to Angus, on the grounds that he was best placed to negotiate a truce with England. The opportunity was too good for Archibald Douglas to miss. We do not know if he planned his coup from the outset but when the time came for his period of authority to end, he simply kept control of the person of the king. On 2 November 1525, he entered Edinburgh with James V firmly under his physical control. He now had the capital and the monarch in his grip. For the teenage James, who had grown closer to his mother in recent years and, through her encouragement, yearned to rule in his own right, the most difficult period of his life was about to begin.

CHAPTER NINE

Uncle and Nephew

'You are to remind her of her son's possibility of succession
of the Crown of England.'

Henry VIII's instructions to the Carlisle Herald prior to
a meeting with Queen Margaret in November 1531

'But of his marriage made upon the morn,
Such solace and solemnization
Was never seen afore, since Christ was born,
Nor to Scotland such consolation
There sealed was the confirmation
Of the well kept Ancient Alliance,
Made betwixt Scotland and the realm of France.'

Sir David Lindsay of the Mount in his poem
The Deploration of the Death of Queen Magdalene

HENRY VIII'S SUPPORT for the earl of Angus and his evident
preference for the Douglas family as more reliable than his own
sister cannot have endeared the English king to his beleaguered
nephew. Early adolescence is an impressionable time and James
V, though influenced by his mother, was showing clear signs of
wanting to make his own decisions. His uncle's interference was
an obstacle, adding to his feeling of resentment and rebellion,
and though Margaret would not have wished to drive a wedge
between her brother and her son it is unlikely, given her
temperament, that she concealed her displeasure at Henry's

stance. If James V did not view his Uncle Henry as an enemy, he was by no means certain of his friendship and a coldness developed between them as the King of Scots grew into adulthood. There were close ties of blood but there was no real affection and, despite repeated efforts, the two men never met. The reluctance was more on James V's side than Henry's and it could not be overcome. A relative who has tried to kidnap you as a child does not inspire confidence and this particular fear haunted the Scottish lords and their king throughout his life. James's proximity to the English throne was equally uncomfortable for his uncle, who did not wish to see Margaret's heirs assume control of the entire British Isles.

This possibility seemed a distant one while King James could not govern his own land but must chafe under the restrictions of Douglas rule. The king having been declared of age, it was not possible for Angus to claim the regency but, if he lacked the title, he was determined to exercise a regent's powers in reality. The simplest way to achieve this, even with the unpredictable earl of Arran temporarily reconciled, was to promote his own family members (and there were many of them) to positions of high office. Queen Margaret and James Beaton were sidelined, though not necessarily silenced, and Angus relied heavily on his younger brother, the energetic and fiercely loyal George Douglas, to ensure that the family's interests were maintained. Yet it soon became apparent that the earl's heavy-handed approach would not go unchallenged.

In the summer of 1526 John Stewart, earl of Lennox, challenged Angus's control of government and attempted to free the king from the men who were, in reality, little more than his captors. The Lennox Stewarts stood next in line in the succession to the earl of Arran and were less inclined to accommodate the Douglases.[1] James V, desperate to assert himself, signed a bond with the earl of Lennox in June. The bond would have made Lennox chief counsellor to the king – effectively taking over Angus's role – but the notable thing about this unusual document is that the king appears to have agreed to give such sweeping powers to Lennox of his own volition. We cannot be sure how much pressure he was put under and Margaret herself, consumed with hatred for the husband to whom she was still legally married at this point, may have exerted maternal pressure, but the episode underlines James V's desperation to remove himself from the 'thralldom', as he perceived it, of the Douglases.[2]

Unhappily for the king, Lennox's attempted coup was a failure. A battle took place involving substantial numbers of men (about three thousand on each side) near Linlithgow on 4 September 1526. The king himself was present at the field. This policy of bringing the king into physical danger was a deliberate one on the part of the Douglas brothers, who were basically using him as a hostage. As George Douglas is reputed to have said to the unwilling king during the fighting, 'Before the enemy shall take thee from us, if thy body should be torn to pieces, we shall have a part.'[3] Such bloodthirsty impudence to an anointed monarch illustrates the lengths to which at least one family would go in its hunger for power. Small wonder that James detested the entire Douglas family. Over a decade later, he would have his revenge on one of them in a particularly vindictive and cruel way.

The young king's despair when Lennox and his supporters were routed at Linlithgow can only be imagined. The earl himself was killed, in circumstances that have never fully been explained, though later chroniclers claimed that he had tried to surrender and was then murdered in cold blood by Sir James Hamilton of Finnart, the eldest illegitimate son of his rival, the earl of Arran. But whatever the truth of Lennox's fate, his son, Matthew Stewart, inherited his father's title, and his ambition to become, in the course of time, a major player in the politics of both England and Scotland. But, for the meantime, James V was compelled to accept Angus's domination of his country and his life. Angus's opponents, sensing that he was better in a crisis than in the day-to-day running of government, decided to bide their time and look for a more favourable opportunity. Among them was the king's half-brother, Janet Kennedy's son, the earl of Moray, pro-French and much praised by the duke of Albany when he was in office. The twisting, troubled history of the minority of James V suggested that Moray and men like him would not have to wait too long before the tide turned again.

Throughout the period of his domination, Angus sought to both inhibit and distract the king. When James V appeared in public, the earl was always with him – at justice ayres, at council meetings and when James was moved between residences, as happened quite frequently. Though not literally kept under lock and key, James was easier to control if he was not kept in one place for too long. There was, indirectly, some positive benefit to Angus's peripatetic approach to his charge's life, in that it enabled James to get to know his country, meet some of its people and understand how justice and administration worked, much as his father had done before him. And it must have already been apparent to James V that a visible ruler is a popular one. In the years of his personal rule, he was keen to go out and about, sometimes in disguise, to learn more about his subjects. They called him the Red Fox and the epithet captures his appearance and his ability to survive well. Often pursued, even cornered, he nevertheless managed to shake off his tormentors to become a force in his own right.

Realizing that hunting, chivalric pursuits and travel were insufficient in themselves to quell the king's resentment, Angus attempted to curb James's growing appetite for power by awakening his sexuality. In this, it must be admitted, he was spectacularly successful. James had a weakness for the ladies from a very early age. His father had been a great lover of women and whether through encouragement or natural inclination, the son more than matched him. James V had nine known illegitimate children, all by different mothers, and as the majority of those he acknowledged were boys there is the possibility that a considerable number of daughters may have been missed from the overall tally. It does, as has somewhat laconically been remarked, 'constitute a notable extension of personality on the part of an early modern British ruler.'[4] Henry VIII's extramarital dalliances, not to mention the English king's fertility, pale into insignificance besides the amours of his nephew. This was an aspect of their rivalry in which James was a clear winner. But as all of the recorded illegitimate children were born after 1529, when James had begun to rule in his own right, we cannot be certain whether any of these very early teenage affairs produced offspring. James was handsome and cultured and he was the king. These were more than sufficient attractions for his many mistresses.

Angus might have encouraged such liaisons but, in the end, he could not hold on to his pre-eminent position in Scottish politics. His financial management was poor, his much vaunted acceptability with the English had not stopped raiding across the Borders, where law and order seemed once more to be breaking down, and the Douglas stranglehold on high office had caused widespread disquiet. Nor had he, a man without any male heirs of his own, given any thought to planning a strategy for the future. In the early summer of 1528, the sixteen-year-old king, exhibiting a winning combination of bravery, cunning and determination, was finally able to break free of his hated stepfather.

It was not easy to throw off the Angus yoke but a combination of factors played into James V's hands. The precise timing of the king's physical escape from the Douglases, and his whereabouts at the time, made a fine tale for the chroniclers but there is much that remains uncertain about his movements in the early spring of 1528 because the Treasurer's Accounts for the years 1527–9 are lost. What seems much more certain is that a series of events, some foreseen and some not, enabled the king and his supporters to develop the elements of a plan, the final success of which would have to wait on circumstances.

On 12 April, James celebrated his sixteenth birthday, which happened to coincide that year with Easter. At a meeting of the council held in Edinburgh a disagreement arose between the king and Angus. The young king gave a clear enough description of this to English diplomats subsequently, saying that he had summoned Angus to answer for various governmental abuses and that the Douglas brothers had then gone away to plan a series of raids in the Borders during which their enemies on the council would meet untimely deaths. It looks, however, as if this explanation was fabricated as a convenient way to discredit the Douglases in the eyes of their English backers and to underline James's own responsible attitude to government. But although a raid had been planned for June, and was subsequently cancelled by the king in one of his first independent acts, it seems unlikely that the course of events was exactly as James described retrospectively. Angus would not have waited two months to move against his critics. There was another, more significant development that worked in James's favour. His mother's divorce from Angus had finally come through at the beginning of April and James now devised an effective way of turning it to his advantage.

Margaret had fallen in love with Henry Stewart, a member of her household, and may have married him secretly before the official pronouncement of her divorce reached Scotland. Now she was free to make this union public, with the permission of her son. Angus's reaction to news of Margaret's remarriage was to deprive Henry Stewart of his freedom (to 'ward' him, as this type of confinement was known) but James had other ideas. He would give his blessing to his mother's new marital arrangements if she would sign over to him her rights in the important, strongly defensible castle of Stirling, her chief dower property. Given Margaret's sensitivities about her lands, it says something about the extent of her passion for her third husband and her love of her son that she agreed to this proposal. In so doing, she gave the king a stronghold from which he could, if necessary, take the fight to Angus.

By the end of May, James had somehow managed to escape from the Douglases. Pitscottie's romantic tale of a daring night ride from Falkland Palace to Stirling, prompted by the king's being left temporarily unguarded, has no known basis in fact and it seems more likely that James was in Edinburgh when he managed to get away.[5] He then raised the royal standard at Stirling and prepared for what would be his final confrontation with the earl of Angus. Success was not a foregone conclusion –

Angus still held the capital, Edinburgh – nor was it achieved without hard work and persuasion. During the next month, the king and his mother managed to gain sufficient support for him to declare that he would now rule in his own right, free of guardians or regents. On 6 July 1528, James returned to Edinburgh and a week later he felt confident enough about his own position to write to Henry VIII with details of the wrongs Angus had done him and the earl's mismanagement of Scottish government. He reminded his uncle that Angus had been 'put in high authority at Henry's request' and had then proceeded to apply 'all the commodities of the realm to his own use'. He had used the king's authority to make war on those who opposed him in the Borders 'to make him more powerful than the Crown' and now he and his brother were refusing to obey orders that they enter into house arrest.[6]

For, in truth, James might now be fully in charge of Scotland but he was not quite done with the Douglases. They refused to ward themselves and were declared traitors but the royal army's efforts to besiege them in their seaside fortress of Tantallon failed. They were never subdued by military might, despite the Scottish lords vowing to pursue them to their 'utter destruction', and it was a diplomatic agreement between Henry VIII and his nephew, the Treaty of Berwick of December 1528, that gave James the Douglas lands while allowing Angus and his brother refuge in England. The treaty was ratified three months later and only then, in April 1529, did the earl of Angus cross into England. There he remained, living mostly in Berwick-upon-Tweed, just across the border from Scotland, using his extensive network of informants and carrying out various bloody border raids on behalf of his patron, Henry VIII. He did not return to Scotland until 1543, by which time James V and Queen Margaret were both dead and another royal minority had just begun. Whatever one thinks of him – and it is mostly his enemies that have had the strongest say – he was a doughty survivor.

His daughter, Lady Margaret Douglas, fared rather differently. Taken in by Henry VIII, she entered the household of

Princess Mary, and the two girls became very close; their friendship endured even the end of the Katherine of Aragon marriage and Mary's banishment from court for three years. During that time, the adaptable Margaret had served Anne Boleyn but Mary does not seem to have held this against her cousin. The English king was genuinely fond of his niece, whose vivaciousness made a favourable impression at court. A French diplomat described her as 'beautiful and highly esteemed'. But Margaret was her mother's daughter in unwise affairs of the heart and when she secretly became engaged to Anne Boleyn's uncle, Sir Thomas Howard, Henry had them both confined in the Tower of London. Margaret was too close to the Crown of England to be allowed to follow her own inclinations without the king's permission. Her mother was horrified but far from sympathetic. 'She shall never have my blessing and she do not all that you command her,' the queen wrote to Henry VIII in October 1536. Preoccupied with a serious uprising in the north of England that came close to threatening his throne, Margaret Douglas's misdemeanour could scarcely have come at a worse time for her uncle. Just after Christmas he responded to his sister, noting that her daughter had 'so lightly used herself, as was both to our dishonour and her own great hindrance.'[7] Yet he made it clear that if Margaret Douglas would behave herself, he would continue to favour her. He was as good as his word, though he did not find a husband for his niece until 1544.[8] Meanwhile, the ailing and lovestruck girl was released from the Tower into the unwilling custody of the nuns at Sion Abbey, to the west of London, where she recovered rapidly and was soon driving the abbess to desperation by her never-ending stream of visitors.

Margaret was compelled to wait for her independence, but her half-brother, at last, could savour his. In 1528 James V had managed to break free from a guardian who he detested and, having been king for all but the first seventeen months of his life, began to rule for himself. He was considerably younger than his father had been when James IV assumed personal control of Scotland and his upbringing had been even more dysfunctional.

But his desires to bring good government and international prestige to his realm were values very much inherited from the father he had never known. His assumption of power also distanced him from his mother, whose third marriage had provided him with important leverage but also diminished his respect for her. From now on, James V was determined to be his own man. He can have had no illusions that his relationship with his Uncle Henry would play a major part in his life, even as an independent monarch. Their rivalry would become more personal as James grew into his role. But for now Henry VIII had troubles of his own.

⸎

IT IS A LITTLE-KNOWN irony that Margaret's divorce from Angus was pronounced in Rome by the pope within two months of Henry VIII taking the first public steps to annul his marriage of eighteen years with Katherine of Aragon. The king of England, who had taken such a high-minded view of his sister's attempts to free herself from an unfortunate *mésalliance*, was even then instructing his ministers and men learned in Church law to find a way for him to put his Spanish wife aside. He had no legitimate male heirs apart from James V and his younger sister's son, and he would not entertain the idea that either of them should inherit from him before he tried much harder to produce male offspring himself. And while Katherine saw no difficulty in their daughter, Mary, succeeding, the prejudices of the time, fully shared by Henry, made this a disturbing prospect. If the princess married a foreign husband of appropriate rank, as had always been intended, but then inherited the throne of England herself, the country's independence would most likely be compromised. If, on the other hand, Mary married an English nobleman, would he not assume the powers of king, since women were considered unfit to rule by themselves? Such an eventuality might lead to civil war.

Henry also had a massive ego, wounded by his failure to beget a son, and a conscience troubled by the fact that he had married his brother's widow. The Bible sent confusing messages on the acceptability of such an act, but the couple's failure to produce males seemed like an indictment to a troubled king. He was also much taken with one of his wife's ladies, the alluring and ambitious Anne Boleyn, a diplomat's daughter who had spent time at the French court and absorbed its style and manners. Henry had probably thought about putting his wife aside before he noticed Anne and he might have been content, in the early stages, to make her his official mistress, while he looked for a bride of suitable rank and diplomatic benefit to replace Katherine. The difficulty here was Anne's refusal to fulfil such a role.

When he instructed Wolsey, in the spring of 1527, to find a way out of his marriage, Henry had no idea of the difficulties he would encounter and the momentous events that would follow. He had just signed a new agreement with Francis I, the Treaty of Westminster, which seemed to assure peace with France for the foreseeable future. It was unlikely that Francis would tackle him over his divorce. The French king, who married his second wife, Eleanor, sister of Charles V, in 1530 might, however, have raised an eyebrow at the idea of a king wedding his mistress. But the emperor, Katherine of Aragon's nephew, was unlikely to take kindly to his aunt's removal as Henry's consort. And since the Sack of Rome by the imperial army in 1526, the freedom of decision that the pope could exercise was severely compromised. This was an obstacle not fully appreciated by Henry when he started proceedings, known in England as 'The King's Great Matter', in the summer of 1527. By the following year, the battle between King Henry and Queen Katherine was well and truly joined and the impact spread far and wide. In July 1528, even as young James V was finally throwing off his restrictions, Henry was finding that marital liberty was hard to obtain.

Katherine appealed directly to the pope via the imperial ambassador in Rome. In her statement, Katherine asked that Clement VII 'forbid the suit, and impose perpetual silence', as the marriage was 'contracted in accordance with an apostolic ordinance, and consummated by the cohabitation of many years and the birth of children.' She foresaw a grim outcome if Henry VIII persisted: 'Wars between Christian princes will be the result. It is intended to separate what God has joined, mutual will has confirmed, and the Holy See has ratified; to impugn the decrees of the Roman church, and restrain the pope's power.' Here Katherine was cleverly ratcheting up the pressure on the pope, at a time when new religious ideas were spreading across Europe.

> The enemy of man will profit much from this seed of wickedness and discord. No marriages will be secure if this is dissolved. The cause should on no account be decided, except at the court of Rome, because of its importance and because it turns upon the interpretation of a papal dispensation. Least of all should it be determined in England, where the Queen fears the powers of the King, and there will be no security for her defence.[9]

The divorce would leave many casualties in its wake but its first major victim was Cardinal Wolsey, who had feared all along that he could not make things happen with anything like the speed or simplicity that his king desired. Anne Boleyn turned against him, believing that he stood in the way of the king ever obtaining a divorce. It was necessary to find some excuse to bring about his downfall and the means were soon found. Accused of the offence of praemunire (obeying the jurisdiction of a foreign, in this case papal, court over that of the royal courts of England), Wolsey was forced to hand over his great wealth and fine palaces to the king. But his enemies were not content to stop at anything short of his utter destruction. Wolsey may have considered plotting with France and Charles V against Henry, though these stories were put around by his opponents and cannot be verified. But he was never put on trial, dying at Leicester on the way to London to answer charges of treason. His death removed someone who had given Henry unmatched service over many years and though Katherine of Aragon had never liked him and considered him an opponent, her cause was not helped by his passing.

For nearly six years, Henry clung to the hope that a legal solution to his difficulties, acceptable to both God and man, could be found. He certainly did not give up easily, to the frustration of the woman waiting to be his true and proper wife. But while Anne Boleyn saw her twenties disappear, and with them perhaps the most fruitful years in which she could bear children, Katherine of Aragon refused to budge. She would not go quietly; even the option of entering a nunnery was spurned. The English queen's defiance forced Princess Mary to take her mother's side in the dispute, with devastating consequences for the seventeen-year-old. Henry, ever the stickler for propriety, invested considerable sums of money in trying to get a consensus among the great European universities that his marriage was unlawful. Charles V made threatening noises but never seriously contemplated going to war on his aunt's behalf. And eventually it dawned on Henry VIII that there could only be one way out. He would have to break with Rome and establish his own authority as Head of the Church in England. The proud defender of the old faith now found his salvation in the new religious ideas, where anticlericalism and denial of papal authority were becoming increasingly vocal. Henry's will would be done, whatever the consequences, and those who opposed him would feel his wrath.

Early in 1533, impatient and infuriated by Rome's intransigence, he married the pregnant Anne Boleyn. Just two months earlier he had paraded her as queen in all but name, in front of Francis I at his second and last meeting with the king of France, in Calais. The new archbishop of Canterbury, Thomas Cranmer, a reformer, finally found for the king (as he was expected to do) at the end of May 1533, allowing just enough time to complete the arrangements for Anne's coronation in June. She gave birth to a daughter, Elizabeth, in September. The long wait had not produced a male heir but Henry was now on a course that he saw no reason to reverse. The dispute with the papacy had brought home to him the advantages of bringing the Church in England directly under his own control. The Act of Succession in 1533, which declared Mary illegitimate and replaced her with her half-sister, was swiftly followed by the Act of Supremacy of 1534, declaring Henry Supreme Head of the Church. Henry was ruthless with those whose consciences could not accommodate themselves to the changes. His chancellor, Thomas More, and the bishop of Rochester, John Fisher, were two of the most famous names to lose their lives for opposing the king. Many others less well known, including members of the religious orders such as the Carthusians, who could not accept the break with Rome, also suffered and would continue to be persecuted throughout the 1530s and beyond.

In pursuit of an heir, Henry VIII had unleashed a force that could not be contained. Towards the end of his reign, he acknowledged what he believed to be the negative effects of this great revolution in belief and its impact on society as a whole. Yet despite the assistance of an army of civil servants, the support of parliament, the collusion of an aristocracy and rising gentry who grew rich on the profits of former monastic lands when Henry decided to dismantle monasticism in England, this was always the King's Reformation. Though the king was advised by councillors, who by no means always agreed among themselves, until 1540 there was one man above all others who helped Henry transform England. His name was Thomas Cromwell and he would try to influence affairs in Scotland as well as England as the tumultuous decade of the 1530s progressed.

❧

NORTH OF THE BORDER, James V watched as his uncle was branded a heretic and became the pariah of Europe. Henry's preoccupations allowed James to establish himself in Scotland and to forge his own style of kingship, though the two monarchs were ever conscious of their geographical proximity and their ties of blood. But James was determined to demonstrate that, despite the vicissitudes of his long minority, Renaissance monarchy had survived in Scotland and would flourish again. He also realized from very early in the period of his personal rule that his relationship with the Church in Scotland would be a vital element in the success he was so keen to achieve. But he did not follow his uncle's path, no matter how much Henry VIII urged him to do so. In fact, Henry's break with Rome worked largely to James's advantage. The King of Scots could present himself as a good son of Rome while simultaneously working towards a greater fusion of Crown and Church, as James IV had intended. Many clerics were also trained lawyers and diplomats and the king was able to use their expertise to underpin a new, more cohesive approach to the exercise of justice in Scotland, so essential for effective government. In 1532 he created the College of Justice, in which lawyer-clerics played a crucial role. And while this was intended to work to monarchical advantage on the domestic front, it also earned James V approval from both Clement VII and Charles V at the very time that Henry VIII's troubles with the papacy and the Holy Roman Emperor appeared more and more intractable.

This success, in which James's chancellor, Dunbar, and the king's secretary, Sir Thomas Erskine, played a significant part, was more than just a feather in the king's cap. It meant that he had very much arrived on the European stage. The pope authorized taxation of the Scottish clergy to pay for the new legal set-up in Scotland, giving James access to Church finances without the more brutal methods employed by Henry VIII. Charles V, meanwhile, in a move that signalled a notable improvement to Scottish–Imperial relations, admitted James to the Order of the Golden Fleece. Founded in 1430 by Duke Philip the Good of Burgundy, this knightly order was highly regarded in Europe. Henry VIII and Francis I were already members and James was joining an illustrious company. More than that, he and Charles V were both mindful that, despite Scotland's long history of diplomatic alliance with France, the trading routes across the North Sea to Flanders were important for Scotland's economic well-being.

Henry VIII was irritated by his nephew's international success. It had been reported to Henry, admittedly by the unreliable earl of Bothwell, that the emperor had told James V that he should style himself 'Prince of England and duke of York'. This was calculated to meet the same rebuff from Henry as Queen Margaret's earlier suggestion that her son should be acknowledged as the English heir and made Prince of Wales. For his part, Henry had not given up his claim of overlordship of Scotland that had so rankled with James IV in 1513. Now England's Habsburg ally seemed to be stirring up further trouble between the two countries. Henry was angered and decided to test his nephew by ordering raids in the Borders.

Some of James's first actions as king had been to try to bring better order to this continuously lawless region. Between 1529 and 1536 he personally led seven military campaigns in the Borders to try and contain, if not permanently annihilate, the threat posed by recalcitrant families like the Armstrongs, who were either local heroes or murderous brigands depending on your standpoint. Like his father, James was not afraid to face danger and he acted with determination. In 1530, he summoned the notorious John Armstrong to appear before him in Teviotdale and promptly ordered the Border ruffian's execution, as well as that of many of Armstrong's gang.[10] Nor was he going to be bested by a peevish uncle. The Scottish host, under the command of his half-brother, the earl of Moray, was summoned in the spring of 1533, while the earl of Bothwell and the archbishop of St Andrews, both suspected of treasonable contact with the English, were placed under house arrest. James also decided to mount an attack on the English in Ireland and raid the Isle of Man. Finally, an end to these hostilities was brokered by the French and a peace treaty signed in 1534. It has been said that 'the costly war of 1532–33 exemplified the short-sighted and unpredictable nature of Henry VIII's Scottish policy.'[11] One man who was certainly troubled by this episode was Thomas Cromwell, who now committed himself, over the next three years, to improving Anglo–Scottish relations.

Cromwell had risen to power in the service of Wolsey and had managed to come through the difficult period of his master's fall from grace unscathed. A lawyer with a remarkable talent for administration and a shrewd head for business, his initial reputation had been that of a 'fixer' rather than a politician, but he certainly aspired to statesmanship and while his role in the Reformation in England may have been overstated in the past, he was a man of great ability and energy, as well as being increasingly and genuinely interested in religious reform. A prodigious worker, Cromwell is not especially known for his interest in foreign policy at this time and yet his dealings with the imperial envoy to England, Eustace Chapuys, show a man at pains to be viewed as having unparalleled access to Henry VIII, with his finger absolutely on the pulse of affairs of state. He had also, much earlier in his career, provided an interesting insight into his own views by stating his support for unification with Scotland, though via military invasion rather than diplomatic means: 'who that intendeth France to win,' he wrote in a speech for parliament as early as 1523, 'with Scotland let him begin.' He went on to point out that Scotland was 'joined unto us in nature all in one island, into which we may have recourse at all times when we will.'[12]

In the autumn of 1532, as Henry VIII's views on the divorce and his own relationship with the English Church were hardening, letters concerning the financial management of the Scottish war were being regularly addressed to Thomas Cromwell. He had become master of the jewels in the spring of that year, a post that sounds ceremonial but gave access to the management of royal finances. Cromwell was also developing a spy network in Scotland so that he could make his own judgements on what was going on there. Favouring a diplomatic solution over a military one, and mindful of the likelihood that Scotland would be used by continental powers in the event of war with England, there was a sudden flurry of diplomatic activity. Sir Adam Otterburn arrived from Scotland as the new resident ambassador and Cromwell cultivated his company, as he did that of other foreign diplomats in London. As the Act of Succession was being prepared in 1533, tempting promises were held out by

Cromwell and Henry VIII. James V might be named heir if Anne Boleyn's children did not survive. Yet when the legislation finally went through parliament, James was not named. The Scots would have been dismayed, but not entirely surprised, if they had seen the notes which Cromwell wrote for himself, his 'Remembrances', in which he observed that 'the King of Scots should in no wise be named, for it might give him courage or else cause him to take unkindness.'[13]

There was, however, one idea that came up for repeated consideration for the next eight years that seems to have originated with Cromwell. This was the desirability of a meeting between the two kings. First suggested to the bishop of Aberdeen in April 1534, it was raised again during successive English missions to Scotland. James V, not wishing to alienate either his European allies or his uncle, repeatedly stalled during 1535. Cromwell tried to involve Queen Margaret, whose counsel James no longer took, and he also sent a diplomat of more overtly reforming views to bring pressure on the King of Scots, but James would not be drawn.

He could not, however, ignore the fact that his own orthodox religious views were no longer shared by all of his countrymen. Scotland prided itself on its links with Europe and was no more impervious to the arrival of new religious ideas than was England. Scottish believers in reform may have lacked the springboard of the divorce and they faced the opposition of a king who did not share his uncle's desire – or need – to change the status quo, but they were as passionate and committed as their counterparts in England. The first Scottish religious martyrdom of the Reformation had taken place early in 1528, just before James assumed power in his own right, and was a high-profile case. The victim was Patrick Hamilton, a younger son of one of Scotland's leading families, nephew to both the duke of Albany and the earl of Arran. A young man of gentle disposition and considerable learning, he had lived in Germany and been much influenced by Martin Luther. His fearless preaching and Lutheran ideas were unacceptable to the authorities and particularly to Archbishop James Beaton. Hamilton was brought to trial, found guilty of heresy and sentenced to immediate death by burning. His shockingly bungled and prolonged execution – it took him more than six hours to die with a fortitude that profoundly moved even those who had not agreed with him – did not quell the spirits of those Scots who shared his beliefs, but it did make living in England an attractive option. Many decided to base themselves there and were welcomed by Henry VIII.

Similarly, English Catholics who could not accept Henry's changes found themselves drawn to the idea of moving to Scotland. So there arose a new element to add to border tensions, the so-called 'Confessional Border', which compelled both Henry VIII and James V to face the truth that a new kind of opponent would be harboured in each other's country. The importance of this development is easily overlooked but it caused further friction in the already uneasy relationship of Henry and James. For while, in these early days, it constituted a further barrier between the kings of England and Scotland, it also pointed towards the development of a more profound underlying change in the relationship of the two countries. They were 'so near neighbours, dwelling within one land, compassed within one sea, allied in blood and knit in Christ's faith.'[14] The prospect was already there that, in the future, religion might act as a unifying force between peoples that would be as significant for the history of the British Isles as the personal rivalries of the Tudor and Stewart dynasties.

Henry might have bought his nephew's goodwill by agreeing to give him a place in the succession and marrying him to Mary, though James himself pointed out that an illegitimate daughter is damaged goods. But such an offer was never seriously on the cards. The Treaty of Rouen had promised James a French bride, but Francis I did not, for some time, offer one of his daughters. Instead, he proposed Marie de Bourbon, duchess of Vendôme, a member of the junior branch of the French royal family. Even negotiations for this match stalled for a while and James, in the

spring of 1536, intimated a startling change of plan. He would
not pursue a French marriage but instead intended to wed his
mistress, Margaret Erskine, mother of his illegitimate son, James
Stewart.[15] This sudden petulance may have been inspired by a
real love of Margaret, who appears to have been one of his more
serious amours, coupled with annoyance at Francis I's continued
prevarication and some resentment of the attitude of his own
council, who were pressing him to find a wife.

In taking this step the Scottish king had, perhaps, followed
more closely his uncle's marriage difficulties than was wise, for
there was a considerable impediment: Margaret Erskine was
already married. James readily obtained a Scottish divorce for
Margaret from her husband, Robert Douglas of Lochleven, but,
like Henry VIII, did not want to proceed to a marriage that
would have legitimized his bastard son as the heir to the Scottish
throne without full papal authorization.

But James's nerve did not equal that of his uncle. When Pope
Paul III declined to give a dispensation for Margaret Erskine,
James swiftly abandoned the idea of marrying her. It had been
tempting but he would not put his throne at risk. Besides, he
was a king and no doubt his own pride told him that the woman
who was to become his queen should be of appropriate rank, and
preferably French. Prudently, he had made no official announcement to the French of his intention to marry within Scotland, so
negotiations could be resumed without embarrassment. Margaret
Erskine's reaction to this change of heart is unclear but it seems
that she smarted because of it for many years. Both she and her
son were to play significant parts in the downfall of Mary Queen
of Scots, James V's only legitimate offspring.

King James did not hesitate to put Margaret Erskine aside
once the pope refused her a divorce. He did not want to face a
debacle like the one that had overtaken his Uncle Henry. The
Boleyn marriage had failed to produce a male heir and foundered
on tensions between the couple that grew bad enough for Henry
to decide she must be removed. Anne went to the block at the
end of May 1536, accused of adulteries that she probably had

not committed, and Henry was left with two illegitimate daughters as his sole offspring. He was also beset by a Catholic rebellion, the Pilgrimage of Grace, that threatened the progress of religious reform, the security of his border with Scotland and, indeed, his throne. Once again, his nephew, young, ambitious, healthy and confident, was his heir whether he liked it or not. And it was high time that the King of Scots found a wife. Small wonder, then, that Henry was anxious about James V setting out in person to find a French bride.

∞

ON 23 JULY 1536, King James V embarked from the port of Leith with a small flotilla, apparently heading north. He had told very few people of his real destination and had not taken his mother into his confidence. In reality, he was headed for France, but by a circuitous route that would take him around the northern and western coasts of Scotland, thus avoiding the possibility of being intercepted by Henry VIII's vessels. But as the ships passed the Hebrides and sailed south a tremendous Atlantic storm blew up, scattering the vessels. Faced with the real danger of shipwreck, Sir James Hamilton of Finnart, who was accompanying the king, took the decision to make for safety at the port of Whithorn in Galloway. James, evidently a good sailor, had slept throughout the worst of the tempest and was greatly annoyed by Hamilton's actions. Yet he was not deterred from his original intention. The king made his way back to Edinburgh, visited a shrine near the city to pray for a better voyage, gathered more men, ships and supplies and set sail again from Kirkcaldy on 1 September. This time he was better equipped, with a fleet of six ships and five hundred soldiers for protection. He was also accompanied, as befitted a king, by the earls of Arran, Argyll and Rothes, by Lord Fleming, his chamberlain, and by a rising star in Scottish politics, David Beaton, nephew of James Beaton and keeper of the privy seal, as well as a number of other lords and high-ranking churchmen. This time James was not hindered by adverse weather conditions. He sailed

unobstructed down the east coast of England and out into the
Channel, landing at Dieppe in Normandy on 9 September. He
would be absent from Scotland for nine months.

It says a great deal about how successful James had been in
establishing royal authority since 1528 and his confidence in the
state of his realm that he was able to leave his country for such a
long period. He nominated a regency council which consisted of
his chancellor, Gavin Dunbar, and five other leading churchmen
and nobles to govern while he was away and administration
functioned perfectly well under their guidance. So James was
able to begin his French adventure without any domestic worries.
This was an exciting time for the King of Scots. Between
September 1536 and May 1537, at the height of his powers and
physical health, he was able to enjoy himself as a much fêted
visitor to a foreign land, the respected monarch of a small country
that had suffered through the uncertainties of his minority but
was now asserting itself once more in Europe. During his time
in France he learned much and was greatly influenced by the
monarchical style of Francis I and his brilliant court. He returned
to Scotland full of ideas and enthusiasm for absorbing the best
of what he had seen into his own culture. And his success, which
culminated in a marriage with Madeleine, the French king's
elder daughter, would surely have greatly pleased his father,
James IV.

Matters did not, however, go so well at the outset. James's
intended bride, the one with whom a marriage contract had been
negotiated in March 1536, was Marie de Bourbon, daughter of
the duke of Vendôme. Although the Treaty of Rouen of 1517
had stipulated a daughter of Francis I as future wife to the King
of Scots, Francis had been nervous about honouring it. Unwilling
to cause offence to Henry VIII (to whom he had actually
promised that there would be no union between one of his
daughters and James V), Francis no doubt thought that he had
dodged the issue altogether when he suggested Marie as an
acceptable alternative. After the marriage contract was prepared,
with the Duke of Albany representing James V in his last service

to his cousin, Francis must have hoped that all would now proceed smoothly.[16] But he had not counted on James's own desires entering into the equation. For whether spurred on by his interest in chivalry or possibly uneasy about accepting a second-string wife, however well connected, James determined to go and visit the lady incognito, and to do so without loss of time. The day after he landed in Dieppe, he set out for St Quentin, in Picardy, where Marie was living with her father, the governor of the region.

James apparently arrived at the Vendôme court in St Quentin wearing the clothes of one of his servants. This would have allowed him to inspect Marie, at least briefly, without formality, but such disguisings were also part of a long chivalric tradition of how fair ladies should be wooed. Henry VIII disastrously employed an identical tactic at his first meeting with Anne of Cleves in 1540. On that occasion, Anne failed altogether to recognize the bulky figure dressed as Robin Hood but Marie de Vendôme was not so easily fooled. She had already been sent a portrait of James V as part of the marriage negotiations, and immediately made him a deep curtsey of reverence. Evidently observant and, of course, well trained, we know little else about Marie. But despite James and his entourage being generously received over a period of eight days, the meeting did not go well. There was something about Marie, or her father's court, or maybe simply the strength of James's underlying determination to take no wife other than the daughter of a French king, that meant that James decided he could not go ahead with the marriage to Marie. So this unfortunate French noblewoman became the second lady to be built up for consideration and then rejected by James within a year. Some commentators afterwards said that he had dismissed her because she was lame or deformed and that she had been so overwhelmed by the loss of her suitor that she became a nun, but there is no firm evidence for any of this speculation.

James went back to Rouen, where the Scottish royal party had based itself during the Picardy escapade, and then set out for Paris. He was now determined to marry Princess Madeleine, but he could not take matters further while the French king was away from his capital. Continued fighting with Charles V in northern Italy had threatened southern France and, in an attempt to deny any succour to an invading imperial army, the French had laid waste to Provence, much to the fury of its inhabitants, who saw their livelihoods destroyed as the price of the long-running struggle between Francis and Charles. Francis had gone south to inspect the damage his army had wrought on their own countrymen and to try to calm feelings in the region. He was also much afflicted by the sudden death of the dauphin, his eldest son, who, it was believed, had been poisoned. The arrival of James V on French soil was unexpected but could also be turned to Francis's advantage, since it seemed to send a clear signal to Charles V that Scotland was keen to renew the Auld Alliance and that the days of rapprochement between James V and the emperor were over.

In Paris, while awaiting the return of Francis, James appears to have acted like any visitor seeing this fine city for the first time. The population of Paris was about half a million, perhaps more, in the mid-sixteenth century, whereas that of James's capital, Edinburgh, was a mere fifteen thousand. James had never seen anywhere like it. He was greatly impressed, not just by its size and scale, but by the huge array of merchandise, food and drink available. He shopped almost compulsively, purchasing quantities of rich textiles and jewellery, still trying to hide his true identity. An ill-humoured observer reported to Sir George Douglas back in England that he was 'running up and down the streets of Paris, buying any trifle himself, he thinking no man knows him',[17] when they were all only too aware of who he was. For a time, James fell ill, as tourists who overindulge often do. When he recovered, impatience to meet with Francis got the better of him and he set off south, eventually coming across the French king in the Loire, at Chapelle near St-Symphorien-de-Lay, on the road between Lyon and Roanne. Greeted and treated like a son, the personable and eager James was at last able to persuade Francis that he should be permitted to marry his daughter.

Apart from the diplomatic difficulties that might ensue if he broke his word to Henry VIII, Francis I had good reason to be reluctant about marrying Madeleine to James or, indeed, to marrying her outside France at all. Aged sixteen, she had long suffered from very poor health, with recurring debilitating fevers, and her delicate constitution gave rise to anxiety. How would she stand the long journey to Scotland and the cold, damp climate when she got there? In fact, the princess was already mortally ill with tuberculosis and was probably not long for this world wherever she lived, though in an age when deep religious belief and medical ignorance combined to make hope triumph over despair, no one, including Madeleine, was willing to acknowledge that she might not last another year. Despite his misgivings, and considerable internal opposition to the Scottish marriage from the powerful Guise family, who wanted Madeleine to marry the nephew of the cardinal of Lorraine, Francis finally gave the match his blessing after taking James to meet Queen Eleanor and his two daughters at Amboise. He still hoped that the King of Scots might be persuaded to take Marguerite, the more robust younger daughter, but James was determined and so, it appears, was Madeleine. She apparently said that she wanted to be a queen and she got her wish.

This does not mean, despite flowery contemporary poems and fulsome descriptions of the young couple's mutual devotion by Victorian writers, that James V's marriage to Madeleine of France should be seen as a love story. The idea that the pair fell passionately in love is the stuff of historical fiction. James had calculated that she would bring him political advantage and, in so far as she had any real say in the matter, Madeleine no doubt would have preferred to be Queen of Scots than to make a less prestigious political marriage in France. The young couple do seem to have liked one another, as might have been expected given James's good looks and Madeleine's grace and charm. The only surviving portrait of her from this time, which may be more stylized than accurate, shows a rather dumpy young woman who certainly does not look as if she is at death's door. Facially, however, there is a strong resemblance to her father, whose prominent nose Madeleine had evidently inherited. She was not a beauty and the state of her health did not suggest that she would easily give James the legitimate heirs he needed, but still he pressed ahead.

Once Francis had assented, the marriage contract was quickly drawn up and signed at Blois on 26 November and the wedding day set for 1 January 1537. The contract stipulated Madeleine's dowry – a matter of probably as much interest to James V as his bride herself – at 100,000 gold crowns (around £16 million in today's money), with a further 30,000 francs (over £2 million today) a year for the King of Scots. In return, Madeleine was given two Scottish earldoms, Falkland Palace and other lands. Henry VIII knew all about these developments from his resident ambassadors in Paris but, his throne under threat from the Pilgrimage of Grace, had been powerless to influence his nephew or halt the course of events.

James had outmanoeuvred his uncle and his victory was almost complete. On 22 December, Henry wrote, perhaps through gritted teeth, a letter of formal congratulation: 'Having certain knowledge from those parties of your determination and conclusion for marriage with the daughter of our dearest brother and perpetual ally the French king, our office, our proximity of blood and our friendship towards you have moved us to congratulate with you in the same and to desire Almighty God to send you that issue and fruit thereof that may be to your satisfaction and to the weal, utility and comfort of your realm.' Coming from a man who, at that time, had broken with Rome, divorced one wife and executed another, yet was still without a legitimate heir, these set phrases have a certain poignancy.

His nephew made a formal entry into Paris on the last day of 1536 and was received by the parliament of Paris, where his almost complete inability to understand the native language, or utter even a few gracious words of thanks, was duly noted. The lawyers who made up this assembly were not the only ones to find the Scottish king very taciturn. Stephen Gardiner and Sir John Wallop, the English ambassadors, commented on the uncommunicative James by indulging in a little witticism at his expense: 'His wife shall temper him well, for she can speak, and if she spake as little as he, the house should be very quiet.'[18]

The wedding of James V and Madeleine of France took place in the cathedral of Notre Dame in Paris, amid much pomp and festivity, on New Year's Day 1537. The bride, on her father's arm, walked on a raised platform hung with cloth of gold into the splendid Gothic nave, where all the French royal family and James's Scottish entourage witnessed the ceremony and nuptial Mass. But though no description survives of what bride or groom wore, the overall splendour of proceedings was captured by Sir John Wallop. Writing to Lord Lisle, the governor of Calais, he commented: 'The King of Scots' entry and marriage was very triumphant; the entry on New Year's Eve and the marriage the next day. That night there was a banquet at the palace and the lady princesses of France were never in so rich apparel ... the King of Scots never saw such a sight.' And he went on to add, more ominously, of James, that 'the honour showed him here makes him set more by himself.'[19]

Festivities followed over many days, with jousts, tournaments, balls and masques. James was evidently in no hurry to leave France. He loved the châteaux of the Loire and Fontainebleau and his keen intelligence and artistic eye took in everything that he was seeing. His kingdom was tiny and poor compared with France but he knew for sure that he wanted to model his court and palaces on what he saw during his long stay there. But finally, once the spring came and the weather for travelling improved, he knew that it was time to go. So he prepared to take his delicate young wife and the rich array of gifts – the jewels, tapestries and plate – that her father had lavished on her back to her new home. When all was ready, King James and Queen Madeleine set sail from Dieppe in the second week of

May 1537. Even then, the conditions were unkind. Storms delayed them and they had to anchor one night off Scarborough on the north-eastern coast of England, waiting for the high winds to moderate. It had been a difficult four-day crossing for Queen Madeleine when she at last set foot on Scottish soil on 19 May. She took up residence in Holyrood Palace, but it was soon apparent that her health was deteriorating and her French attendants began to fear for her survival.

James, too, could not fail to notice that his new wife was in a serious condition. He sent for her French doctor to attend her, cancelled the summer progress, delayed her state entry into Edinburgh and postponed her coronation. Plans were made for the queen to visit Balmerino Abbey in Fife, which had 'the best airs of any places in the kingdom', but by now Madeleine was beyond any help that fresh air could give her. Confiding in the young French poet Ronsard, who was one of her pages, that she found Scotland 'very different from her sweet France', Madeleine clung on to life, as brief days of remission allowed some respite, while her underlying condition inexorably worsened. She finally breathed her last at Holyrood on 9 July 1537, having been James's wife for seven months and resident in Scotland for just seven weeks.

The story that she died in James V's arms is probably fanciful. Royalty stayed away from deathbeds in those days. But on the day of her death James wrote at once to notify Francis I of the sad news – and to assure him that 'I wish never to be anything but your good and humble son.' He also informed Francis that he was sending David Beaton on a diplomatic mission but he did not mention that, however much he grieved for Madeleine, 'my most dear companion', he had already instructed Beaton to find him a new French wife.

⚓

THE DUCHESS of Longueville had been one of the ladies whose rich clothing and glittering jewels were remarked upon by Wallop in his report on the wedding of James V and Princess

Madeleine. Marie de Lorraine (or Mary of Guise, as history knows her) was the eldest of the twelve children of Claude, duke of Guise, and his wife, Antoinette de Bourbon. She had an impressive pedigree, being a descendant on her mother's side of the crusading French king Louis IX (St Louis), and the family were becoming increasingly powerful. Competent and highly ambitious, the Guises were a dynasty unto themselves and, as such, aroused feelings of resentment as the older noble families of France watched their seemingly inexorable rise at the French court. Their enemies viewed them as upstarts and questioned their loyalty. Some said they were not really French at all, for their lands lay in what is now eastern France, in territory that had been part of the Holy Roman Empire for many centuries and was not, in fact, formally joined to France until the eighteenth century.

These considerations did not stop the Guises as they continued to gain power and influence. Mary had made a splendid marriage in 1534 to Louis d'Orléans, duke of Longueville, and their relationship appears to have been a happy one. Longueville was a considerable landowner in the Loire and Normandy and he settled on his wife the castle at Châteaudun which she seems to have particularly favoured. A son was born in 1535 and Mary was again pregnant in the spring of 1537, living at Châteaudun while her husband travelled through his estates in western France. From there, he wrote to her that he was unwell and that his doctors had diagnosed chicken pox. Alas, his illness was much more serious and he died in early June 1537. Mary gave birth to another son in August of that year and learned soon afterwards, to her considerable shock and displeasure, that she would not be a widow for long. Francis I had offered her to James V as his new wife. But while negotiations were continuing – and it was still unclear where the dowry demanded by James would come from – Henry VIII entered the contest for the duchess's hand.

Recently widowed himself when his third wife, Jane Seymour, died after giving birth to the long-awaited heir, Prince

Edward, in October 1537, Henry VIII was definitely interested in Mary of Guise as a possible queen consort. And why should he not have been? The lady was renowned for her beauty and wit, had spent some years at the French court and acquired all the requisite skills to carry off the role of queen with grace and dignity; she was intelligent and well educated and had already shown that she could produce sons. If all this were not enough, she was a member of a leading European family whose stock was on the rise. Henry had serious reasons to woo her and, despite the impression sometimes given that the Guises were horrified by this unexpected suitor, Henry's approaches were taken seriously. Claude de Guises, though a close friend and brother-in-arms of Francis I, was a younger sibling in the Guise family and the possibility that his daughter might become queen of England was a very attractive one. Francis I, however, did not see it that way. Conscious of resentment among the French aristocracy towards the Guises, he did not want to give them too much power. There was no telling where things might stop if Mary married the king of England. In his mind, she was an ideal choice for James V, keeping the Scottish monarch close to France without Francis having to offer his younger daughter as a replacement for her dead sister. He had lost one child to Scotland and was not inclined to lose another. And, preoccupied as he was with the struggle against Charles V, he wanted this marriage question settled as soon as possible.

Nevertheless, as a desperate search continued to find the money for Mary's dowry, the duchess was able to stay longer with her son, Francis, and to mourn his baby brother, who died at the age of four months. This was a difficult time for Mary, who had lost a husband and child in the space of six months and now found that her future was decided without any account being taken of her own feelings. This was, of course, the lot of most noble ladies at the time. When it came to marriage they were valuable goods to be disposed of and their desires, generally considered fanciful if not downright improper, were completely disregarded. For the House of Guise, her second marriage was an opportunity to advance the family's fame and fortune. The fact that she was being sought by two kings was no doubt flattering to Mary herself, but she had no say over the outcome. All that she knew was that she would be a queen in a foreign land who had once enjoyed a brief, affectionate marriage as a French duchess.

Once the haggling over the dowry was settled (Mary's father, in a sign that the Guises were not enthralled by the Scottish match, had initially refused to give any money at all towards his daughter's marriage portion), a betrothal ceremony took place at Châteaudun in the spring of 1538. But James V was not going to come to France for a second time to bring his wife back home in person. His role at the spousing ceremony was taken by the Borderer Lord Maxwell, who gave Mary a ring considerably less impressive than the one that had adorned the slender finger of the consumptive Madeleine. The bride's mother, meanwhile, attempted to encourage her daughter with gushing comments on the physical attractions of James V, saying he was so handsome that she was in love with him herself.

Mary of Guise took a tearful leave of her little son in early June 1538. She knew that it was unlikely that she would spend much time with him again. His dukedom and the role of grand chamberlain which he had inherited meant that his future lay in France and he was brought up by his grandmother in the castle at Joinville, on the banks of the river Marne, where Mary had spent part of her childhood. Mary's destiny lay elsewhere, in a role she could never have envisioned when she married the duke of Longueville, expecting to enjoy the life of a French noblewoman. On 10 June, accompanied by her father Claude and sister Louise, she set sail from Le Havre and landed at Balcomie Castle on the coast of Fife in eastern Scotland six days later. James V was waiting with a large party of noblemen to give his new wife an appropriate greeting: 'The whole lords, both spiritual and temporal, many barons, lairds and gentlemen ... received the Queen's grace with great honours and merriness, with great triumph and blitheness.'[20] A long period of uncertainty was finally coming to an end and on 18 June James and Mary were married in the cathedral of St Andrews. Great celebrations followed and then the new queen was taken on the traditional tour of her Scottish lands, as the young Margaret Tudor, Mary's mother-in-law, had been thirty-five years before.

Mary of Guise adapted speedily to her changed situation. She expressed delight at Linlithgow Palace, saying it was as fine as any castle in France, and was tactfully positive about everything she saw in Scotland. Though homesick in the first few months, she was too busy to become depressed and her deep religious faith supported her throughout the period of her adjustment. She made a formal entry into Edinburgh in mid-November, entertained by pageants similar to those that had been devised by Sir David Lindsay for her unfortunate predecessor. The Scots were well pleased by their French queen, a tall, healthy young redhead who celebrated her twenty-third birthday shortly after her formal entry into the capital. It was expected that she would continue her success in producing sons, thus ensuring the stability of the Stewart dynasty.

Though James V and Mary of Guise made a handsome royal couple, there does not seem to have been any great warmth between them. James could charm quite readily but he was not going to change a lifestyle of philandering for monogamy, no matter how attractive his French wife was. Like Margaret Tudor, Mary was forced to accept her husband's illegitimate children and the realization that he would not give up his mistresses for her. Perhaps it was this shared experience that drew the two women together, for Mary was considerate and respectful in her dealings with James V's mother, restoring Margaret to something like the role of official queen mother. Margaret had continued to correspond regularly with Henry VIII and to complain about her diminished standing and financial difficulties, to the point that Henry disregarded these as habit rather than a reflection of his nephew's neglect. Her third marriage failed as her second had done, though with somewhat less acrimony, and Margaret felt very overlooked until her daughter-in-law's arrival. She was pleased to be godmother to the first child of James and Mary, Prince James, born in early 1540. In that year, which saw Henry VIII make a brief and disastrous diplomatic marriage of his own to Anne of Cleves, it seemed that the King of Scots, secure on his throne, successful in his government and presiding over a richly cultured court, had much reason to rejoice.

CHAPTER TEN

Solway Moss

~⌘~

'*Finally mine espial sayeth that the said king will not make war against any other realm, but liveth in fear to defend his own, for the king's nature, his disposition and his qualities are not given to war; but daily labouring in his mind covetously for profit.*'

The report of an English spy on James V's intentions,
May 1542

THE VISITOR TO THE VILLAGE of Falkland in Fife is immediately struck by the sight of a fairy-tale Loire château in miniature. A typically French Renaissance exterior is matched by an elegant interior and lovely gardens. This distinctive residence, the courtyards of which have been described as 'a display of early Renaissance architecture without parallel in the British Isles', is grand yet still intimate. Given to Mary of Guise on her marriage to James V, it was well equipped for both leisure and more active pastimes such as hunting in the nearby countryside. The palace was also favoured by Mary's daughter, Mary Queen of Scots, who would later scandalize her male courtiers by donning breeches to play tennis on what is now the oldest surviving tennis court in Europe.

Mary of Guise soon discovered that, while the climate of her new country might be less forgiving than the milder airs of the Loire, there was much to please in Scotland. French influence was everywhere and this gave her hope for the future. James made an effort to improve his ability to speak her language and to impress her with the magnificence of his court and building programme. Falkland was part of a major effort of restoration and improvement at the Scottish palaces. In the year 1539, more than sixty masons were employed at the palace each month, under the watchful eye of John Scrymgeour, the king's principal master of works, who was a local man. But continental craftsmen were used as well: the sculptor of the statues for the chapel buttresses was Dutch and one of the plasterers was French.

The architectural programme of James V achieved a great deal in the fourteen years of his personal rule and encompassed all the leading residences. But it was at Stirling that James V's vision of his dynasty and Scotland's place in the European order was perhaps most fully realized. A new palace block was constructed, the features of which owed something to both Burgundian and French styles, and its interior was sophisticated and magnificent. James's palace has been superbly renovated and is one of the finest examples of a sixteenth-century interior in Britain. Reopened in 2011, anyone who seeks to understand this king's desire to leave his mark and hold his own with the great continental courts should go and see it. The ceilings are particularly fine, as are the tapestries, specially commissioned to match the originals which adorned the walls in the 1530s and 1540s. All of this would have been admired by the elite of Scottish society and politics, as well, of course, as the representatives of foreign powers waiting in the presence chambers of the king and queen for that all-important interview that might change their fortunes or cement diplomatic negotiations.

Also on display in the palace is the superb sequence of wooden carvings known as the *Stirling Heads*, which show us the faces of real people at the court, including jesters, and a succession of kings and queens. The carvings, roundels of oak cut from trees in distant Poland, probably date from around 1538, when construction on the new palace commenced, and appear to have been the work of several talented woodcarvers – one French

and at least two of whom were Scottish. They originally adorned
the ceiling of the King's Inner Hall. Most of them survived a
near disastrous removal in the late eighteenth century and today
they remain as a unique testament to the court of James V.

In Scotland's capital, rebuilding continued apace. The palace
of Holyrood House was extensively remodelled. Disliking Edinburgh Castle, which had uncomfortable reminders of the period
of Angus domination and was largely used as an arsenal during
James V's reign, the king started work at Holyrood within
months of his assumption of power in 1528. Over several phases,
he spent a total of about £12,000 (nearly £2 million in today's
money) on this, his main residence. At Linlithgow, he made a
new entrance from the south, constructing an outer gate beside
the church of St Michael, where his father had worshipped
before the battle of Flodden. Above it were the insignia of the
chivalric orders to which James belonged, evidence, in the words
of sixteenth-century historian John Leslie, of how important this
was to his self-image: 'for an evident sign and token to all
posterity, the king's arms [were displayed] upon the port of the
palace of Linlithgow, with the rest of the arms from whom he
received them, with the ornaments of St Andrew which are the
proper arms of our nation, our king himself caused there to affix
very artificiously with cunning craft . . .'[1] It is not clear whether
the Order of the Thistle was one of those originally displayed at
Linlithgow. Some historians trace its origins as a piece of Stewart
iconography to the fifteenth century, when it appeared on the
coins of James III, and a portrait of James V (admittedly not
from life, but probably based on an earlier painting) shows him
wearing a collar with the thistle badge. But whether he founded
a formal order of chivalry or not, the thistle as a Stewart emblem
became increasingly common during the sixteenth century.[2]

Situated above a sea loch and influenced by both English and
Burgundian styles, Linlithgow became Mary of Guise's favourite
palace, though its style was closer to the palaces of Henry VIII
than those of Francis I and it was not part of her jointure. The

magnificent fountain in its courtyard, which can still be seen today, may, however, have been completed to please her.

All of James V's palaces had extensive gardens, managed by a substantial staff of gardeners, and were well provided with flowers, walks, archery butts, pools for fish and wildlife – mostly birds, but there were two bears and a wolf at Stirling and a fox and some French wild boar at Falkland. Fresh air and exercise were considered beneficial to health and the surroundings of a royal residence were an important part of the enjoyment of those who lived there. But in the winter it was the interior furnishings and entertainments that mattered more.

The king also spent freely on tapestries and hangings, though his tapestry collection, French-influenced and depicting a variety of classical, chivalric and biblical themes, was one area where James V simply could not compete with his uncle. Henry VIII owned over two thousand tapestries and James about two hundred. The Scottish king did, however, have hangings in rich materials such as cloth of gold and damask, as well as rugs to cover the tiled floors of his homes. There were thick curtains for beds and even a Turkish carpet.

James also found a way to compensate for dark nights and dreary weather in the decoration of his palaces and the patronage of a rich literary and musical tradition. Everywhere there was brightness and colour. The window frames at Linlithgow, long since without glass, were painted in red lead and vermilion. And though the wind now blows cold through the roofless great hall and private apartments of this splendid ruin, during the reign of James V they would have echoed with the sound of music and song. For although the classical and linguistic aspects of James's education may have been truncated, his musical abilities were outstanding. Music was an essential part of Renaissance court life in Europe and James inherited his passion and his talent from both his parents. Accomplished on the lute (the instrument his father had used to woo Margaret Tudor during their early meetings), James was a proficient sight-reader. 'The king,' it was said, 'had a singular good ear and could sing that he had never seen before.' He was not endowed with a melodic voice, however, his singing being described as 'rawky and harske' (raucous and rough).[3] But he did expect high standards from the musicians he employed to entertain him in his private apartments and those who sang liturgical pieces in the royal chapels at his residences. Players of soft instruments had a higher status than musicians such as trumpeters and drummers. The latter were more often involved in state and military occasions, decked out in the red and yellow colours of the Stewarts, and many were foreigners. Musicians who played the lutes, viols, virginals and spinets – the 'softer' instruments favoured for more intimate evening entertainment – came from France and Scotland. They also performed the music for stately dances such as the pavane and more lively dances like the galliard. James was definitely eclectic in sourcing his musicians and his instrument makers, ordering viols from an English maker in 1535. This rich-sounding bowed instrument was gaining in popularity at the time.

Equally important in Scotland was sacred music, though little of it survived the Reformation, which is regrettable as the works that remain, notably those of Robert Carver, an Augustinian friar at the Abbey of Scone, suggest considerable complexity and depth. There were organs in the chapels of all the main palaces, and the chapel royal at Stirling, in particular, was a centre of musical life at this time. James was determined that his court should reflect his love of music and hold its own in this area with the other major courts of western Europe.

The king's cultural interests also supported a flowering of literature. Two massive histories of Scotland, in Latin, by John Mair (Major) and Hector Boece, were presented to him during his minority, but it was only the strongly nationalistic Boece's work that James favoured as an adult. Both men had taught at the University of Paris and were influenced by the European humanism of the period, though the emphasis of their work was very different. While Mair argued that the union of England and Scotland would bring prosperity to Scotland and suggested that James V was uniquely placed to bring this about by his Anglo–Scottish heritage, his argument sat uncomfortably with James's commitment to the Auld Alliance. Much more palatable was the reasoning of Boece, who stressed the historic animosity between England and Scotland and saw the role of the King of Scots as exemplifying the heroic armed resistance of the smaller of the two British states against the larger. This account of Scotland's past clearly appealed to James V, who commissioned John Bellenden, one of his clerks, to translate it into Scots for him. In his preface, Bellenden reinforced Boece's message by noting that 'this realm . . . was never subdued to uncouth empire, but only to the native princes thereof, howbeit the same had sustained great afflictions by Romans, English and Danes.'[4]

James V's court also produced fine poetry, most notably that of his long-time confidant Sir David Lindsay of the Mount, and William Stewart, both of whom wrote in the moral vein that was considered appropriate for addressing princes at the time. James was exhorted to lead an upright personal life (something he clearly was not doing), to rule justly and act on good counsel from his advisers.

In his fine palaces, the king was able to demonstrate the strength of his monarchy and offer his courtiers a focus for their own aspirations. Pageantry and ceremonial and the continued observance of a chivalric tradition added to the effect that James wished to make and the new queen consort, gracious and attractive, enhanced his international standing. The Scottish court was hardly on the same scale as that of France (as Mary of Guise would soon have realized) or of England, but it was both civilized and vibrant. And while James V's second wife missed some of the comforts of her French upbringing, she could still, at least, enjoy its cuisine. Her household accounts show that her patissier provided delicacies such as salmon pasties and plum and raisin tarts to tempt her.[5] If she ever wondered what her life would have been like as the fourth wife of Henry VIII, she kept such thoughts to herself.

James V's uncle, not surprisingly, was able to demonstrate his

kingly power and magnificence with a gusto and expenditure that
Scotland and the Stewarts simply could not command. Henry's
fifty-five palaces epitomized his wealth and status but they also
demonstrated something more, for, as Simon Thurley has written, 'Henry VIII was certainly the most prolific, talented and
innovative builder to sit on the English throne.'[6] One suspects
that the king would far rather be remembered for this than the
constant harping on about the fact that he had six wives but even
a king as dominant as Henry could not manage his image from
beyond the grave. During his lifetime, however, he was able to
erect monuments to his kingship in bricks and mortar and to
take a very personal interest in design. Indeed, design in all its
aspects fascinated Henry VIII, whether the subject matter was
jewellery, armour, tiltyards or coastal fortifications. Henry loved
plans and maps and he kept copies of plans, as well as drawing
instruments, in his studies. But his site visits must have been
dreaded by the workforce and his architects, who frequently
found themselves being obliged to make considerable changes at
short notice. The king did not like to be kept waiting and he
was an impatient builder.

It was in the decade of the 1530s, when his nephew James V
was embarking on his own building programme, that Henry
VIII's involvement in royal building works became much more
active. Before that, he had completed the new palace of Bridewell, near Blackfriars, on land that had once belonged to
Cardinal Wolsey, in 1523. The palace of Westminster had been
destroyed by fire in 1512, leaving the king without a residence in
the heart of his capital. There had also been extensive alterations
to Greenwich Palace, a countryside palace on the river Thames
where Henry was keen to ensure that he could enjoy the
recreations that pleased him most: jousting, hunting and general
revelry. It was a place to entertain and be entertained. A new
tiltyard, stables and viewing towers were constructed but so, too,
was a library, for Henry liked intellectual as well as physical
activities.

But Greenwich and Bridewell were really only the beginning.

The disgrace and death of Wolsey, followed later in the 1530s by the dissolution of the monasteries and a steady acquisition of property from courtiers who had fallen out of favour, provided Henry with a property windfall. Until this point, Wolsey had been something of an architectural mentor. His disappearance from the scene scarcely fazed Henry, or, indeed Anne Boleyn, at that point perhaps more influential than when she actually became queen. Wolsey's new London house, York Place, was transformed into the palace of Whitehall and the cardinal's other riverside residence, at Hampton Court, extensively converted. The king was keen to have more privy lodgings, to develop a retreat from the crowded outer rooms in which lawyers and politicians thronged, and to move his day-to-day living quarters on to a horizontal rather than vertical plan, which meant the demolition of the stacked lodgings of the early sixteenth century, when the king's apartments tended to be above the queen's. The overall appearance of Henry VIII's homes owed a great deal to contemporary Burgundian architecture but French influences were also becoming apparent. The English king did not, however, have an equivalent of Falkland Palace. He wanted to preside over a European court, but that did not mean that he wished to copy all things French. His emphasis was on creating his own unique court and culture that could bear comparison with those of his European counterparts.

To help him achieve this goal he needed information about the palaces of his great rival, Francis I. Some of this was drawn from the reports of his own ambassadors. In 1540, for example, Sir John Wallop, his long-serving diplomat in France, gave a detailed description of Fontainebleau, the main residence of the French court just outside Paris, its galleries and decorations and, most notably, the impressive surroundings of the royal bedchamber: 'and so we went into his [the king's] bed chamber, which I do assure your majesty is very singular, as well with antique borders, as costly ceiling and a chimney right well made.' The paintings and stucco work above the wainscoting were of the highest quality and Wallop was encouraged to clamber up on a bench to examine them at closer quarters. Francis even gave him a helping hand in his climb.[7] Much of Francis's great building programme, in the Loire, in the Île de France and in Paris itself (he also did a great deal of work in the Louvre) coincided with Henry's. It was a boom period for the skilled craftsmen of Europe, the masons, plasterers, painters, glaziers, experts in stucco and wood, who laboured to fulfil the visions of these two master egoists. Henry already knew a considerable amount about the splendour of the French court and Francis's personal style from Nicolas Bellin of Modena, a former valet of the wardrobe to the French king. Implicated in fraud, Bellin fled France and was given refuge at the court of Henry VIII. In England, his talents as artist and designer were put to good use at Nonsuch Palace in Surrey, allowing Henry to demonstrate to Francis that he had 'stolen' one of the French king's leading artisans.

Henry shared with James V a love of music. Francis I did not have their talent, but the English king could both read and write music and was particularly fond of part-singing, which he apparently did to more mellifluous effect than his nephew. The possession of a good voice was an important prerequisite for gentlemen of the king's privy chamber. Henry played the organ, virginals, lute and recorder and he supported substantial numbers of musicians – more than fifty by the middle of his reign. As in Scotland, these instrumentalists often came from overseas and the King's Musik, as the royal orchestra was known, was said to the finest in Europe.[8] When he died, Henry VIII possessed three hundred musical instruments.

His collection of books was equally impressive – perhaps as many as a thousand volumes and manuscripts, some of them travelling with the king as he moved between palaces. James V had nothing like this vast library. This may reflect the difference in scale between the courts of Scotland and England but it also serves to underline the contrasting educational experiences of Henry VIII and his nephew. James does not seem to have been a great reader but his uncle was, even when failing eyesight meant the need for spectacles. Henry loved his books and the world of literature, just as much as he enjoyed disguisings, the performance of masques and the tennis court. Few monarchs of England have equalled the range and depth of the second Tudor's cultural life.[9]

∞

YET DESPITE the richness of court life and his own personal splendour, unforgettably captured in the portrait by Hans Holbein that has passed into national consciousness as our image of this man of overwhelming presence and sheer physical bulk, all was not well in England as the decade of the 1540s dawned. The previous two years had been full of alarm. There were fears of foreign invasion, of a deadly threat to English shores posed by the unlikely temporary rapprochement of Charles V and Francis I, who might target Henry VIII as a heretic without legitimate rule. To safeguard his coastline, Henry embarked on a massive programme of fortification. The greatest of his coastal forts, at Deal in Kent, can still be seen. At home, Henry moved against the remaining upholders of the White Rose, the descendants of Edward IV's brother, the duke of Clarence, when he quashed the so-called Exeter conspiracy. Abroad, he looked for allies elsewhere – among the Protestant princes of Germany who continued to disrupt the Holy Roman Empire and plague Charles V. Encouraged by Thomas Cromwell, Henry embarked on the fiasco of his fourth marriage, to Anne of Cleves (who was actually a Catholic, but whose brother was an important player in German politics), a lady for whom he seems to have felt it impossible to feel any sexual attraction. Henry was clearly humiliated by his inability to consummate the marriage and a humiliated king was a dangerous proposition. Anne of Cleves, a discreet and canny woman, survived the debacle of her speedy divorce unscathed but Cromwell, the faithful servant who had helped Henry VIII transform England in the 1530s, did not. As with Anne Boleyn, there are many things still unclear about the fall of Cromwell but, again, Henry's personal animosity, so unpredictable and so deadly when aroused, seems to have played a major part. Perhaps he really did believe the charges of heresy brought against Cromwell. There may have been a genuine parting of the ways for them over the pace of religious reform and, if so, it was not an argument Cromwell was going to win. He had seemed the perfect servant, but, like all masters, Henry viewed servants as dispensable. For whatever mix of reasons, Cromwell, a remarkable man whose character still eludes historians as it may have eluded contemporaries, went to the block in July 1540.

In Scotland, James V was also getting rid of opponents and strengthening his rule during these years. There were three high-profile cases, beginning with the trial and execution of the Master of Forbes in July 1537 and culminating with the death of Hamilton of Finnart three years later. Though James's record of reprisals is nothing like that of his uncle, there was a vindictiveness in his treatment of at least one of these victims that may be perfectly explicable when one considers the king's past (and the accepted punishments of the time) but it still had the power to shock contemporaries. Within two weeks of the death of Queen Madeleine in July 1537, Janet Douglas, sister of the exiled earl of Angus and George Douglas, was brought to trial in Edinburgh to face two charges of treason. One was that she had conspired to poison the king; the other was that she continued to communicate with and give assistance to her brothers. Always known as Lady Glamis, from her first marriage, Janet was, in fact, the wife of Archibald Campbell of Skipness, who was charged along with her, as was her son. Found guilty, Lady Glamis was sentenced to be burned on Castle Hill in Edinburgh immediately. There was to be no commutation of her sentence nor delay in carrying it out. The following day her husband tried to escape from Edinburgh Castle, where he was imprisoned, but he fell and broke his neck. He, at least, was spared the dreadful death endured by his wife, a good-looking woman in her early thirties, who was the highest-ranking victim of James V.

The manner of her death may seem unbearably cruel but was

standard for women convicted of treason in both sixteenth-century England and Scotland. Anne Boleyn would have suffered the same fate had Henry VIII not shown some mercy and agreed that she should be executed by a swordsman. And though the charge of attempted poisoning seems to be more the product of a superstitious age (it is not at all clear how Janet Douglas would have been able to achieve such an outcome since she was not at court), the accusation that she had sought to aid her brothers and had kept in touch with them carries more weight. She had been suspected before, in 1529 and 1531. Newly returned from nine months in France and having so recently lost his wife, it is not surprising that James V was disinclined to moderate Janet's sentence. If he wanted to make an example and send a message to any other members of the Scottish aristocracy who contemplated treason, Janet Douglas provided him with the perfect excuse. He hated her family and while he could not touch her traitorous brothers, he could strike against their sister.

In 1540 he underlined his determination to be rid of unsatisfactory elements from his past when he executed Sir James Hamilton of Finnart, the bastard son of the first earl of Arran and the man who had murdered the third earl of Lennox at the battle of Linlithgow. Hamilton's career had actually prospered during the 1530s and his role as master of the king's works meant that James V's ambitious building programme was delivered largely through his own architectural expertise. But James had a long memory and he could not overlook the fact that Hamilton did not come out firmly on the king's side back in 1528, when the young James was desperate to impose his authority after his escape from the Douglases. By 1540, Hamilton was yesterday's man. Most of the rest of the nobility hated him, he potentially stood in the way of James V's determination to annex all of the Douglas lands, and he was, as has been said, a soft target for a confident king, who, like Henry VIII, had no compunction in demonstrating that those he had built up could just as easily be destroyed.[10] Accused of treason, Hamilton was

convicted by a jury that included Margaret Tudor's third husband, Henry Stewart, and was duly sent to the block.

✌

WHILE HER SON stamped his authority on his magnates, Margaret continued her long life of regret. Her third marriage turned
sour as Henry Stewart, Lord Methven (the nephew of Janet
Kennedy), spent her money and started a family with his mistress, Lord Atholl's daughter, Janet Stewart. In 1537, Margaret
tried to obtain a divorce but though she was thought to have
sufficient grounds, her son stepped in to halt proceedings. James
had had enough of his mother's marital adventures. Eventually,
a reconciliation of sorts was achieved with Methven and in
Scottish national life Margaret was not entirely overlooked.
When the English diplomat Sir Ralph Sadler, a protégé of
Thomas Cromwell, was sent to Scotland on a mission at the
beginning of 1540, he found the queen dowager installed at
court. Asking permission of the king to visit her, he was told: 'ye
need not to ask my licence for that, but ye may boldly see and
visit her at all times.'

Duly emboldened, Sadler found Queen Margaret still resentful of her brother's treatment of her. The envoy had opened on
a positive note, saying that Henry was 'healthful and merry' –
something of an exaggeration, as the king was deeply unhappy
about the Cleves marriage – and had given him 'special charge
to visit and see her and also to know how she was used and how
all things went there'. Margaret was not impressed by this display
of brotherly concern, noting that Henry could not be bothered
even to write to her:

> She took it the most unkindly that might be, that she had
> no letter from your highness, saying that she perceived that
> your grace set not much store by her. But, quoth she, though
> I be forgot in England, shall I never forget England. It had
> been but a small matter . . . to have spent a little paper and
> ink upon me and much it had been to my comfort; and were

it perceived that the king's grace my brother did regard me,
I should be the better regarded of all parties here.

After this crotchety outburst, which illustrates how deep-seated
was the rift between the Tudor siblings, Margaret went on to
acknowledge that 'she was well treated and made much of, of
the new queen, with such other things of light importance',
concluded Sadler dismissively.[11]

In the last year of her life, Margaret played a significant role
in comforting the grieving James and Mary of Guise when both
of their infant sons died in May 1541. It was to prove her final
service to James V. She was taken ill, apparently the victim of a
stroke, in the autumn of 1541, and died at Methven Castle near
Perth on 18 October. Not at first realizing how close she was to
death, Margaret did not ask for her son until too late. He could
not make the journey from Falkland Palace in time. Her last
thoughts, strangely, were with her second husband, the earl of
Angus, and she asked her confessor to beseech James V to be
'good and gracious unto the earl . . . and did extremely lament
and ask God's mercy, that she had offended unto the said earl as
she had.' What prompted this change of heart is unknown.
Perhaps she hoped such a declaration would ease things for the
daughter she hardly knew, Lady Margaret Douglas, but, if so,
she was sadly mistaken, since Angus cut his daughter out of his
will when he died sixteen years later.

Margaret Tudor was buried in St John's Abbey in Perth, to
lie among other Scottish monarchs. Her rest did not last long.
Twenty years after her death the abbey was desecrated by
Calvinists and Margaret's skeleton removed from its coffin and
burned. Her ashes were contemptuously scattered around and so
she, like her first husband, James IV, has no monument. It
seemed a sad and ignoble end for the young Tudor princess who
had progressed so magnificently up to Scotland in 1503. But
time would give her memory a greater prize.

ONE OF MARGARET'S overriding aims was always to seek for better relations and amity between England and Scotland without compromising her son's position. Yet in the year of her death there were growing signs of friction between the two countries, of rivalries and deep-seated doubts that, once more, seemed to herald war. The causes were to be found in the always uneasy relationship of James V and Henry VIII and, as had so often been the case before, in the shifting relationships of the great European powers, which neither of the British kings could ignore. But it is certainly true that Henry's attitude towards his nephew had become one of growing impatience at the start of the 1540s and he believed he had good reason for his displeasure. For in the autumn of 1541 James had spectacularly snubbed the king of England, and Henry VIII was not a man to forget insults in a hurry.

The cause of this deterioration in personal relations was the famous summit-that-never-was at York, planned for September 1541. Accompanied by his new wife, the teenaged Katherine Howard, who had speedily replaced Anne of Cleves the previous summer, Henry set off on a major progress to the north of England. It was the longest, costliest and most sumptuous travel he ever undertook outside the south of his realm and its culmination was to be a great occasion of state when he would finally meet with the nephew he had never seen in York. But Henry's journey was not solely motivated by family considerations and a desire to improve Anglo–Scottish relations. The north of England was still recovering from the Pilgrimage of Grace six years earlier, support for the old religion remained strong and there was a further conspiracy, known as the Wakefield plot, involving a small group of laymen and priests that had caused him anxiety. It has recently been argued that this disaffection was not, in itself, a sufficient cause for the king to head to Yorkshire. Henry's presence was intended to reinforce his authority but the northern aristocracy and gentry may also have hoped it signalled a new beginning for a troubled region that had never really established a successful relationship with the Tudors. They were to be sadly disappointed by the king's uncompromising attitude.[12]

The royal party began its journey on the last day of June 1541. It included the French ambassador Marillac, who would have been keenly interested in any meeting between Henry and his nephew. As the king journeyed north through Lincolnshire (the inhabitants of which county he had long regarded as ignorant rebels) and into Yorkshire, he received grovelling delegations of local worthies and accepted their protestations of loyalty – and their gifts of money – in a demonstration of regal might: 'When he entered into Yorkshire,' wrote Edward Hall in his *Chronicle*, 'he was met with two hundred gentlemen of the same shire, in coats of velvet, and four thousand tall yeomen, and serving men, well horsed; which on their knees made a submission, by the mouth of Sir Robert Bowes, and gave to the king nine hundred pound.'[13] Thus did the once recalcitrant men of Yorkshire make amends for their region's continued animosity towards the religious policies of Henry VIII. This was a king who had come to humiliate, not to offer his northern subjects a distinctive role in his realm. Taking comfort in collective amnesia of the indignities of 1541, Yorkshire chose in succeeding centuries to remember instead the progress of Henry's sister, Margaret Tudor, and her glorious reception in their city. Henry would not have been pleased by his sister upstaging him once again.

It was not so simple, however, to bring the King of Scots to do his bidding. The Scottish view, as held by the king and his advisers, was later summed up in verse by Sir David Lindsay of the Mount:

> *Soon after that, Harry of England King,*
> *Of our sovereign desired a communing.*
> *Of that meeting, our king was well content,*
> *So that in York was set both time and place;*
> *But our prelates nor I would never consent*
> *That he should see King Harry in the face;*

But we were well content howbeit his grace
Had sailed the sea, to speak with any other,
Except that king, which was his mother's brother:
Where through there rose great war and mortal strife,
Great hardships, hunger, dearth and desolation.
On either side did many lose their life
Of which I would give a true narration,
I caused all that tribulation;
For to talk peace I never would consent,
Without the king of France had been content.[14]

Lindsay clearly played up his own part in the outcome of this episode, probably to exonerate James V from any charge of having been duplicitous or indecisive. There is no evidence that the Scottish king was 'well content' to meet his uncle, except in the politely vague terminology that characterized diplomatic exchanges with Henry VIII's ambassadors. Much of what we know of James V in this respect comes from the lengthy despatches of Sir Ralph Sadler, who suspected that he was being courteously held at arm's length but could find no actual offence in James's stance. No doubt this was the intention. In Sadler's reports, James comes over as a consummate politician, well versed in saying the appropriate thing. He was welcoming, sophisticated, knowledgeable – and cleverly inscrutable. In 1540, Sadler told James that, in his opinion, 'such a meeting might now redouble all; and it should be a great comfort both to the king's majesty your uncle and your grace, the one of you to see the other.' James was not going to deny this, of course, but his response was to muddy the waters. 'By my truth,' quoth he, 'I would be glad to see the king mine uncle, but I would wish that the French king might be at it [the meeting] that we three might meet and join together in one.'[15] But such a tripartite summit was, as James well knew, beyond Sadler's commission. Neither was he impressed by the gift of several horses sent by his uncle, supposedly as a mark of respect. James was a good judge of horse flesh and he knew (as did the embarrassed Sadler) that the English king could have done better.

Henry VIII continued to hope and press for a meeting during the summer of 1541. Although, as we have seen, he had other reasons for making a show of strength in the north, his prestige would be further enhanced if he could persuade the King of Scots to meet him on English territory. He was preoccupied with the so-called Confessional Border and the fact that English heretics posed a threat to his national security. This and foreign policy issues, notably Scotland's continued closeness to France, were items that he wished to address when he met his nephew. But James faced significant distractions within his kingdom, not the least being the deaths of his two sons. If he left to go to York, he would do so without an heir. There were concerns for his safety and mistrust of Henry VIII's intentions. Kidnap was genuinely feared as a possibility and if this sounds paranoid, it is worth remembering that abduction was not an unusual occurrence in Scotland, as James V's daughter would find to her cost in 1567. There was not universal opposition to the idea of a meeting in York among James's counsellors, but there was little enthusiasm and the king seems to have accepted the view that, on balance, he would have little to gain and potentially much more to lose if he committed himself. He was more willing to offend his uncle than Francis I of France and so, while never formally giving Henry VIII a yea or a nay, he simply stayed put in Scotland.

This decision was evidently made by the beginning of September, when Cardinal David Beaton, a strong opponent of England and a man increasingly hated by Henry VIII, wrote from the French court to James V saying that Francis I 'thanks him that he has not condescended to a meeting with the king of England'. There was also confirmation from Sir Thomas Wharton, one of the northern wardens and captain of Carlisle, that the meeting would never happen. He told the Privy Council: 'I did send my espial to know as he could whether the King of Scots would come or did mind to come into England to the king's majesty or no ... which espial sayeth that the king and queen [of Scotland] was upon the last days of August at Falkland with a small company ... and that there was no likelihood of his coming into England nor preparing therefore that could be perceived.'[16] Henry continued to cling to the hope that James might appear until October 1541, when he eventually left York in considerable displeasure. Within a matter of weeks, however, he had far greater heartache when the infidelity of Katherine Howard, his far too lively young queen, was revealed to him. Scottish affairs seemed, suddenly, far less pressing than those that had been going on under his nose. The evidence of the queen's loose living was incontrovertible and her fate unavoidable. She went to the block in February 1542, leaving Henry VIII, for a while, broken by her betrayal. His depression did not, however, mean that he lost all interest in government. Henry was a resilient man.

∽

IN THE MONTHS that followed, neither the English nor the Scottish governments ever made any formal announcement that the idea of a conference between their two kings had been abandoned altogether. It continued to be mooted into 1542 but as the year wore on, events on the European continent made its likelihood even more remote. In the summer, the Habsburg–Valois struggle resumed and Henry VIII reverted to his old dream of victory in a war with France that would enable him to emulate his ancestor, Henry V. The emperor Charles V again appeared as a natural ally and was, needless to say, more than happy to have Henry join him, especially if the English would supply men and money. Almost thirty years after the battle of Flodden, the question of what Scotland might do in such circumstances could not be ignored.

By the autumn of 1542, relations between England and Scotland were deteriorating, with Henry VIII intransigent on the question of English religious rebels being harboured in the Scottish Borders, and there was no consensus on exchange of prisoners held by either side. There had been a series of raids and counter-raids in August, with the Scots successful in a serious skirmish at Hadden Rig near Kelso in the Borders, where Sir Robert Bowes, who had knelt before Henry VIII in York the previous year, was captured. But before they even knew of this defeat, the English were already mustering for war against Scotland, under the command of the duke of Norfolk. Norfolk, the old earl of Surrey's son who had fought at Flodden, had a low opinion of the Scots and was an enthusiastic lieutenant for Henry VIII in the north. It was he who called James V the 'ill-beloved' in an attempt to paint a picture of an unpopular and greedy king, aloof from his nobles and people.

But neither James nor his council wanted war and Henry VIII also thought that continued talking was preferable to outright hostilities, despite English pride being dented by what had happened at Hadden Rig. Commissioners from both countries were still in earnest discussions about ransoming prisoners and arranging a meeting between the two kings early in October 1542. But progress could not be made and on 22 October Norfolk left Berwick with an army of between ten and twenty thousand men. James V and foreign ambassadors gave wildly excessive estimates for this force but it was sufficient to cause the bridge over the Tweed at Berwick to collapse as Norfolk's soldiers marched across. Burning and destroying as they went, the English reached Kelso four days later before turning back into England at the end of the month. They were short of supplies and sickness was rife. Even Norfolk himself became seriously ill with dysentery and was compelled to rest. He had, however, done enough to inspire Henry VIII to continue what he had begun. The English king justified his stance in a document entitled 'A declaration containing the just causes and considerations of this present war by the Scots', adding, ominously, 'wherein also appeareth the true and right title that the king's most royal majesty hath to the sovereignty of Scotland.' The blame was laid squarely at James's door: 'Being now enforced to war by his nephew, the king of Scots, the king notifies his nephew's provocation of it, whom he maintained and protected in minority, and from who he has received letters, embassies, etc., as gently devised as possibly could be.' Henry went on to cite James V's missing the meeting at York the previous year and to accuse the Scots of refusing to ransom prisoners and of misrule in the Borders. But it was the repetition of Henry's claim to Scotland that was always going to cause the most offence, especially couched in the altruistic language of English justification: 'if the king had minded the possession of Scotland, he had the opportunity during his nephew's minority, and yet he has just claim to Scotland, recognised by the kings of Scotland, but would not move war at a time when all Christendom should be united to resist the Turk.'[17] Such sweeping claims were never going to be acceptable in Edinburgh. Faced with this ultimatum, James V did what his father had done three decades before. He prepared to fight. And to his own timescale – not his uncle's.

In late October, James summoned the Scottish host to be ready to fight with supplies for twenty days. Arms and provisions were already being sent south. Far from James being unpopular and isolated, the nobility and clergy were solidly behind the king. Although Scottish records for the time are fragmentary, it appears from the reports of English spies that James may have been trying to raise two armies, one under the earl of Huntly, his boyhood friend, to keep Norfolk tied down and away from Edinburgh, and the second, led by the earl of Moray, the king's half-brother, to come down from Lauder, the traditional mustering place for Scottish armies, and catch the duke in a pincer movement between the two forces. The numbers of those involved were probably exaggerated, as was often the case, though it is no doubt true that the 'wild Irish' counted among the earl of Argyll's Highlanders were much feared, even by other Scottish troops. The fact that neither the Scottish forces engaged the English army under Norfolk later gave rise to rumours, reported by English spies, of accusations of cowardice, particularly against Huntly, and assertions that James V was displeased by his army's failure to take on the English before they withdrew. But Norfolk did not stay in Scotland for long and the Scots may have faced the same difficulties of lack of supplies and disease that he did. Certainly it was late in the season for campaigning on a large scale. A full-scale offensive foray into England was never really on the cards at this time. The Scots had learned something from Flodden and James V realized that Norfolk's retreat meant that he would have to rethink his military strategy.

James decided to strengthen his border garrisons and redeploy his forces. He could be reasonably confident that his fleet would give a good account of itself if there were to be any naval engagement, as he had resumed his father's programme of shipbuilding and constructed a new harbour in Fife. In terms of technological warfare, he could match his uncle. He and his advisers expected, however, that the war would be decided by armies, not navies, and so he continued to prepare accordingly. His plan, from what can be pieced together from the often inaccurate reports of English spies and the fragmentary records of the Scottish Treasurer's Accounts at the time, suggest that he hoped to persuade the English commanders, Norfolk and Hertford (Henry VIII's brother-in-law), that he would concentrate his forces in the east, on the Northumbrian border, when, in fact, he intended to surprise them on the western border with Cumbria, where the English forces were much smaller. If successful, such a raid might be matched by an eastern attack led by the earl of Moray, accompanied by the propaganda coup of a papal interdict against the heretic English king. It was a bold and clever idea that would have given James an advantage in negotiations with Henry VIII without committing to the pitched battle that his father had fought and lost at Flodden. But on 24 November, amidst the swirling waters of the river Esk and the boggy lands along the shore of the Anglo–Scottish border, James V's forces were to suffer a wretched defeat at Solway Moss.

There are no surviving Scottish versions of what happened at this battle, which was, in truth, a raid that went disastrously wrong. The English had learned of Scottish intentions in the west in the nick of time, and Sir Thomas Wharton had left Carlisle with a force of no more than three thousand men to meet a Scottish army that may have been as large as seventeen thousand. The difference in odds did not overawe Wharton, a man highly experienced in border warfare and whose knowledge of the local terrain at Solway Moss was probably better than that of the Scottish commanders. Wharton was also confident in the ability of his lancers (his 'prickers', as he called them) to harry the Scottish forces. He spread his troops out along the water's edge, to give the impression of a larger force, and set his lancers to work on the eastern flank of the Scots.

His tactics paid dividends. Trapped between the bog and the river and hemmed in by their own troops, the Scots were soon in disarray, defeated, as has been said, 'by those eternal enemies of time and tide'. In the absence of coherent leadership – for there appears to have been confusion if not outright disagreement among the Scots under the command of Lord Maxwell – many saw that their situation was hopeless, though the English acknowledged that they fought valiantly. Eventually, preferring surrender to drowning in the Esk (though this fate awaited a considerable number of Scottish soldiers who tried to swim back to their side of the river), many gave themselves up. Among them were the earls of Cassilis and Glencairn and half a dozen lords, including Maxwell himself and Oliver Sinclair of Pitcairn, a favourite of James V. The English estimated that they took over 1,200 prisoners. The Scottish lords were sent south to London, to await negotiations for their release. This unexpected windfall of prominent prisoners would be put to good use by Henry VIII in his subsequent dealings with the Scots, as the king made clear when he wrote to Wharton on 30 November, giving him 'our condign thanks' for the victory 'against our enemies the Scots'.[18]

Solway Moss was by no means the disaster for Scotland that Flodden had been but it was humiliation on a large scale, more than cancelling out the victory at Hadden Rig. James V himself, harkening to the pleas of his queen and no doubt mindful of what had happened to his father, took no part in the fighting. The English reported that he had watched the encounter from nearby Burnswark Hill but his precise whereabouts during the battle are unknown. He was certainly back in Edinburgh four days after Solway Moss and met his council in early December. The business of government continued but seems to have slowed thereafter. The reason for this was not pique on the king's part or overwhelming depression at what had happened. He had not given up mentally.

James managed to visit Linlithgow to see his wife, who was in the latter stages of another pregnancy. We do not know what passed between them and it was fortunate for Mary of Guise that she did not contract the disease that was shortly to kill her husband. She gave birth to a daughter, Mary, on 8 December, in the midst of a spell of intensely cold weather. There is no record that James ever saw his daughter, though he might have had time to do so before he was laid low by severe illness. We cannot be sure of the sickness that afflicted him but he was probably a victim of dysentery or cholera, both illnesses that stalked armies, and James had been among his troops for some weeks. His half-brother, Moray, was also ill and the earl of Atholl was in fact dying during the war of 1542. James V could have been infected by either of them. The king had been unwell previously during his reign but recovered on each occasion. This time the outcome would be different. By 12 December he had retired to Falkland Palace and taken to his bed. He would not rise from it again. Suffering greatly and aware that the end was imminent, he signed a notarial instrument early in the morning of 14 December which appointed Cardinal Beaton, the earls of Moray, Huntly and Argyll and his wife to act as governors to his daughter during her minority. He knew it would be even longer than his own; she was just six days old.

James V died later the same day. Many legends sprung up after his passing, including the famous saying that his last words, about little Mary Queen of Scots and the future of the Stewart dynasty, were 'it cam' wi' a lass and it'll gang wi' a lass'. This is good, dramatic stuff, but someone dying of a virulent disease is unlikely to think that clearly or romantically. His hopes for his daughter were encapsulated in the provisions he made for her (subsequently set aside) and in the knowledge, which must have offered him some comfort in the extremity of his life, that he had governed Scotland effectively and well after the most difficult of starts to his reign. Until more balanced judgements appeared in recent years, James V was dismissed as the most unpleasant of the Stewarts, a rapacious, priest-ridden seeker of international recognition, disliked by his subjects, who had dared to oppose his uncle, Henry VIII. In this interpretation, he suffered a nervous collapse after Solway Moss and left his country in disarray. But such a view overlooks his achievements, the cultural richness of his court and the importance he placed on good government. There is considerable work still to be done on his reign and he awaits a worthy biographer. Meanwhile, it can be said that James V, though half a Tudor by birth, was entirely a Stewart in his approach to kingship and more than equal to the prolonged rivalry with the uncle that he never met. Yet even as the bitter winter closed in on Scotland, that uncle had plans for the little girl that James had left behind.

Part Four

✌

'The Most Perfect Child'

1542–1568

CHAPTER ELEVEN

'Rough Wooings' and Reformation

'Our greate affayre of Scotland.'
Henry VIII to Viscount Lisle, January 1543

'So was the Princess sold to go to France, to the end that in her youth she should drink of that liquor, that should remain with her all her lifetime, for a plague to this realm, and for her final destruction.'

John Knox looks back in anger on the departure of
Mary Queen of Scots for France in 1548

THE DEATH OF JAMES V and the fierce winter weather brought a halt to the English military campaign against Scotland. As John Dudley, Lord Lisle, an English soldier and politician who would rise, by the end of the decade, to a position of supreme power in England, told his king shortly before Christmas:

> seeing that God hath thus disposed his will of the said King of Scots, I thought it should not be to your majesty's honour, that we your soldiers should make war or invade upon a dead body or upon a widow or upon a young suckling his daughter, and specially upon the time of the funeral of the said king, which time all his realm must lament the same. Wherefore . . . I have thought it good to stay the stroke of

your sword until your majesty's pleasure be further known to me.[1]

Dudley's attitude was surprisingly humane. He had a large family of his own and seems to have felt for the widowed queen and her daughter, whose sickliness had been exaggerated by the reports of the exiled Douglas brothers. Henry VIII did not disagree but he was determined not to lose the advantages so providentially delivered to him by battle and nature. Often presented in popular literature as the prey of factions and his own ill health in the 1540s, Henry was still very much in charge of government and policy in England. He was now fifty-three years old and if his body was failing through overweight and bone disease, his mind remained alert and his ambitions lofty. At the beginning of 1543 he seemed to be coming back to life after the depression that had followed the disaster of his marriage to Katherine Howard and was shortly to fall in love for a sixth and final time, with the attractive and intelligent widow Katherine Parr. And now the untimely death of James V at just thirty years old presented Henry with a wonderful opportunity to orchestrate the union of England and Scotland.

Henry's intention was to achieve this through diplomacy rather than warfare, aided, he hoped, by growing religious dissent in Scotland as the ideas of the Reformation began to divide his northern neighbour more seriously than they had done while James V was alive. A full-scale military assault followed by occupation was never part of his policy towards Scotland – if, indeed, he had anything amounting to a carefully considered policy before 1543. Circumstances now allowed him to fashion something more coherent that would avoid the difficulties of trying to impose direct rule on a largely hostile country. Lacking the resources of the modern nation state, this was not an option for the English king. And yet he never had a better opportunity to impose himself on Scotland than in the winter of 1542–3. That he did not do so, in effect repeating what had happened after Flodden, can most readily be explained by events on the wider European stage. For, once again, Henry was preoccupied with France and the prospect of one final chance of glory there. The Habsburg–Valois struggle had moved away from the Italian theatre of war and was now threatening France's northern and eastern borders. Henry VIII hoped that, in allying with Charles V, he could reclaim at least Boulogne and increase the English footprint on French soil. Scotland was significant but it was always France that captured his imagination.

At the beginning of 1543, however, he held two very strong cards. The debacle at Solway Moss had delivered to him a pack of Scottish nobles who were brought south to face honourable captivity and who would not be allowed to return to their native land until they had given signed assurances that they would support English dynastic policy and push for religious change. These 'assured lords', as they were known, were a key part of Henry's strategy: they were to make palatable to their own countrymen Henry VIII's underlying goal. For his second card was his own son, five-year-old Prince Edward, and the wily old Tudor was determined to marry the boy to the infant Mary Stewart. Thus, the joining of the two kingdoms of the British Isles could be achieved without bloodshed. It seemed a perfect match, at least from the English perspective. There was never any doubt in Henry's mind who the dominant partner would be in this arrangement and in this he echoed his father's views, expressed at the time of Margaret Tudor's marriage to James IV. The details would be hammered out in lengthy diplomatic discussions, culminating in a treaty that, it was hoped, would shape the future of Britain.

Henry had a clear vision of what he wanted to achieve but he had overlooked one vital element – the response of the Scots themselves. Reliant as he was on the information supplied by pro-English and often disaffected members of the Scottish nobility, he did not have a well-informed picture of attitudes north of the border. The extent of opposition to his plans was not fully appreciated even by Sir Ralph Sadler, sent up to Edinburgh once more as ambassador, who failed to read the complexities of Scottish politics or understand the play of personalities involved. And too much confidence was invested in the 'assured lords', who could not necessarily sway their fellow Scots and whose loyalty to Henry VIII may have been bought but was by no means certain. Thus the scene was set for a year in which triumph turned to disaster as Henry saw his aims for Scotland negated by the survival of French influence and a deep underlying aversion to English dominance. He was to discover, to his cost, that when it came to a stark choice between the English or the French having the upper hand in Scotland, the Auld Alliance could best him yet.

∞

IN SCOTLAND, despite the uncertainty of yet another long minority, the humiliation of Solway Moss and the grief of a nation that had lost a firm and competent ruler, the proprieties of a monarch's death were fully observed. James V's obsequies were not carried out amid the murky uncertainty that had clouded those of his grandfather, James III, and though his death was a shock it was not accompanied by the gut-wrenching sense of loss that had accompanied his father's demise at Flodden. James V had died amidst the effluvia and pain of a foul disease, but his mortal remains were buried with pomp and dignity. It was a full heraldic and chivalric funeral, befitting his regal status and the honours he had accrued during his brief lifetime. Probably organized by the faithful Sir David Lindsay of the Mount, who had been in James V's service since the king's childhood, the funeral took place on 8 January 1543 at Holyrood, more than three weeks after James's death. The Christmas season had delayed arrangements but on the day before his burial the late king's body was removed from Falkland Palace and taken overland and then by ferry across the Forth to Edinburgh to await interment:

whatever could be devised in solemn pomp, or honourable decorum, or doleful dolour, mourning and grief, here all was done filled with all due ceremonies and due diligence: torches lit, places spread with tapestry, with notable cloth and well-painted, lamentable trumpets, cardinals all in sadness ... the earls of Argyll, Arran, Rothes and Marischal, and others in great number of the nobility ... were all in the meantime so dressed that albeit you may marvel much of their pomp in order, in colour nonetheless easily mourning you might see (for all were dressed in black), when in Edinburgh in the abbey of Holyrood House, in the same sepulchre where Madeleine, his first wife, was buried, was he laid.[2]

The infant Mary, his only surviving legitimate child, had become Queen of Scots at six days old. She was Scotland's first queen regnant and the first in the British Isles; it would be more than ten years before another Mary, Henry VIII's elder daughter, became the first queen of England. Though looking back we may see the sixteenth century as an age of women rulers, contemporaries were not comfortable with the concept, which seemed to them unnatural. In such a patriarchal society, women were meant to bear children, not to rule. Mary's inheritance was thus made doubly difficult, by virtue of her gender and her age. It is true that the Stewarts claimed descent from Robert the Bruce through his daughter, Marjorie, the wife of Walter Stewart, the hereditary Lord High Steward of Scotland (hence the surname), but the only other female who had been viewed as having the legitimate title of Queen of Scots was the ill-fated Maid of Norway, Margaret, granddaughter of Alexander III. In the late thirteenth century, this seven-year-old had been destined as a bride for the future Edward II of England, and might have united the two crowns but for the fact that she died at the age of seven on the Isles of Orkney, after a stormy journey from her Norwegian home. It was not a happy precedent and the prospect of another interminable minority, this time with the unexplored difficulties of raising and training a girl as sovereign, seemed daunting.

The baby queen was, however, immediately accepted as

James V's heir and the rightful monarch. There was no question of rejecting her, despite the fact that she had several illegitimate half-brothers of an age to rule. The principle of legitimacy was the bedrock of monarchical government in Britain and Henry VIII had changed the course of history in pursuing it. Nor would the Scots abandon it now, however capable James V's bastards might be. But several men and one remarkable woman were to engage in a prolonged struggle for the right to rule in the name of Mary Queen of Scots from the moment of her birth. This, like the minority of Mary's father, is a complex period, though somewhat easier to unravel. At its centre is the intriguing figure of the queen dowager, Mary of Guise, who would eventually make a fateful decision on her daughter's behalf after five years of warfare and strife. Her time as queen consort of Scotland had given the widowed queen insights into the functioning of Scottish politics and some understanding of the difficulties that would lie ahead if she were to make a bid for power. Unlike Margaret Tudor, she had not been nominated as regent, was still recovering from childbirth when her husband died, and so had no clear role. She knew that if she was to protect her daughter effectively, she would have to bide her time. And it was the fierce determination to uphold little Mary's rights to the Scottish Crown and safeguard her future that underpinned everything that Mary of Guise now did. Not of royal blood herself, she was, nevertheless, the daughter of one of the most ambitious families of the sixteenth century and a true dynast. Remaining at Linlithgow with her daughter during the first months of 1543, she watched and waited, using her intelligence, good looks and marriageable status to brilliant effect as the Scottish lords quarrelled and the English king tried to lay down the law to them. In particular, she sought to charm and use for her own ends the gullible Sadler, whose support she felt necessary in achieving one of her major short-term goals: the removal of her daughter from Linlithgow to the much more defensible castle at Stirling. Mary of Guise did not entirely trust the Scots and was already well aware of the ill feeling between

Arran and the Lennox Stewarts. But she feared the English and
their intentions even more. So she embarked on a clever course
of action. She would undermine the newly appointed regent,
who appeared to her to be a willing tool of Henry VIII, by
casting doubts on his motivation and the true extent of his
support for an English alliance. Sadler, allowed to see the infant
Mary in the flesh and admire her for the bonny child she was,
fell for Mary of Guise's wiles.

   The situation required all of the queen dowager's talent for
pretty dissembling. The new governor of Scotland, and officially
tutor to her daughter, was James Hamilton, second earl of Arran,
a great-grandson of James II, whose authority to rule Scotland
during the minority was first declared just over a week after the
death of James V and recognized by parliament in March 1543.
Arran was also declared second person of the realm and was
therefore likely to be Mary Queen of Scots' heir presumptive for
a very long time. Given the high infant mortality rate in the
mid-sixteenth century, it was not unrealistic for the twenty-four-
year-old earl to take his closeness to the Scottish throne very
seriously, even though there were questions about the legality of
his father's second marriage, of which he was the product.
Needless to say, this sense of entitlement, allied to doubts about
his legitimacy, did not endear him to many of the other Scottish
nobles and the existing blood feud between the Hamiltons and
their Lennox Stewart rivals, simmering angrily below the surface
of Scottish politics, was given added spice. Matthew Stewart,
fourth earl of Lennox, then a liegeman in the service of Francis
I in France, was so incensed by the rise to power of the earl of
Arran that he persuaded the French king to let him return to
Scotland as Francis's representative in April 1543, with momentous consequences for both Scotland and England.

   Yet even before Lennox set foot again on Scottish soil, Arran
had run into difficulties. His first quarrel was with the devious,
ambitious cardinal David Beaton, who announced himself to be
the possessor of a last will and testament that James V had
signed on his deathbed. This, it was claimed, had nominated a

regency council, to consist of the leading earls, Moray, Argyll, Arran and Huntly, joined by Beaton. One report even had the cardinal as 'governor of the princess and chief ruler of the council', but this may just have been the assiduous George Douglas wanting to stir things up from England.[3] Arran, however, was not inclined to share the power he believed to be rightfully his. He accused Beaton of lying, saying that he had caused James V to put his signature to a blank sheet of paper when the king was so ill that he did not know what he was doing. Whatever the truth – and it is possible that David Beaton did have some private communication with the dying monarch, though whether this amounted to coherent instructions is another matter – Arran was not going to back down. At the end of December he threatened to draw his sword on the cardinal in an angry meeting, calling him, with Shakespearian drama, a 'false churl'. The two men had to be physically separated. But by 10 January, Arran had overcome his dislike of the cardinal (his mother's cousin, and a man nearly a quarter of a century older than he) enough to grant him the office of chancellor.

Arran's motives for this change of heart could have been purely pragmatic but they may also indicate that the cardinal's assertion of Arran's exclusion from the regency council was correct and that he did have some form of documentation to prove it.[4] James V, even in the extremity of his illness, might well have had reservations about someone who had so close a claim to the throne being put in charge of his heir. Beaton's triumph was, though, to prove short-lived. Within days of his appointment, Arran welcomed the Douglas brothers back from their long exile. The 'assured lords', on parole to Henry VIII, soon followed them. The political and religious landscape was changing fast again in Scotland and the pro-French Beaton could not, at that point, survive. He was arrested in council at the end of January and deprived of the chancellorship he had held for little more than two weeks, accused of plotting to increase French influence in Scotland. Imprisoned in the grim fortress of Blackness Castle on the Firth of Forth, Beaton's ascendancy looked as if it was over. Arran had apparently rid himself of a powerful enemy and forged an unlikely alliance between the Hamiltons and the Douglases that would underpin his regency and deliver to Henry VIII everything he wanted. But in the swirling of events of the year 1543 nothing could be certain. Jacques de la Brosse, newly arrived as French ambassador, had the sense of a country on the brink of violence: 'for all the friends of one faction mistrust all those of the other faction. So much so that not merely is the nobility in arms, but churchmen, friars and the country people only travel through the countryside in large companies all armed with pikes, swords and bucklers and a half pike in their hands, which in this country is called a lance.'[5] The impression of Scotland as being close to civil unrest was one that the new governor, anxious to stamp his authority on government and justice, would have found very troubling.

Until recently, historians have tended to be critical of Arran. The standard depiction is of a vacillating, vain and greedy man, out of his depth in European politics, a great talker but to little purpose, lacking any qualities of real leadership or longer-term vision. But recent writing and a dissertation on the office of regency in sixteenth-century Scotland have presented a more complex and positive picture of the earl and particularly of two key areas for which he has long been criticized: his apparently convenient conversion to religious change in 1543 and his financial record.[6]

Arran's sudden announcement that he had adopted reforming religious ideas caused something of a sensation and was certainly music to the ears of Henry VIII. The governor wasted little time in apprising the English of his intentions, writing to Lord Lisle as early as 18 January 1543: 'we minded, with the grace and help of God, to put some reformation in the state of the kirk in this realm to the high honour of God, setting forth of his true words, and profit to the common weal.' Peace between England and Scotland, was, as Arran pointed out, a prerequisite of success in this lofty aim: 'and if your sovereign and master be of mind that

God's word grow and prosper in this realm, as we trust he is, we doubt not that his majesty will put away the cause and occasion that is obstacle or impediment thereto.'[7] And this was only the beginning. Two lapsed friars, men admired by John Knox, became his court chaplains and by March 1543 he was telling Sir Ralph Sadler that he had regarded the pope as no more than 'a very evil bishop' for the past five years.[8] Sadler noted, however, that while Arran might be content for Scotland to break with Rome, the governor did not have sufficient support among his ministers to take such a momentous step. Nevertheless, Arran was able to introduce in his first parliament permission for the Bible to be read in the vernacular, though discussion of it in Scots was not allowed, and the heresy laws, at first relaxed somewhat, were later actually strengthened.[9]

Yet Arran's personal beliefs and the form of worship he followed showed that he had by no means abandoned Catholicism, certainly not as far as ritual was concerned. He continued to worship as a Catholic during his governorship, spending considerable sums on his private chapel at Hamilton.[10] Nor, in 1543, did he keep his new chaplains around him for long. This may at first seem like the prevarication of a duplicitous man, but it also demonstrates the fluidity of belief at the time and the disservice done to history by the glib labelling of people as 'Protestant' or 'Catholic'. Henry VIII had imposed the Reformation on England but he would not have described himself as a Protestant and neither would the vast majority of his subjects during his reign. It is easy to label the earl of Arran as a man who latched on to new religious ideas for purely political reasons, but even this was not necessarily an unreasonable thing to do given the state of Scotland in early 1543. The governor had identified the need for peace with England as an absolute priority, both for his own survival and the future of the baby whose throne he was sworn to protect. The English king's response to Arran's 'conversion' was to ply him with religious books and encourage him to suppress the Scottish monasteries. Arran continued to pull the wool over Sadler's eyes but, by early

May, he was already hedging his bets by asking for papal protection and aid against England. At the same time, his carefully briefed negotiators were in London hammering out the details of the proposed marriage between the infant Queen Mary and Prince Edward Tudor.

∝

THE TREATY OF GREENWICH, concluded on 1 July 1543, appeared a triumph for English hopes, promising a future union of the two crowns. Alas, for Henry VIII and for peace in the British Isles, what seemed like a great victory – an imperialist expansion, even, of English power – proved to be a chimera. Henry and Arran had, not surprisingly, very different aims. The Scot realized that he needed to be seen to support the English marriage but he was determined to safeguard Scottish sovereignty and independence while maintaining his own position. The prospect of marrying his own son to Anne Boleyn's daughter, the Lady Elizabeth, was tempting but at the back of his mind was the belief that a match between his heir and the Queen of Scots would be even better. Henry, on the other hand, wanted everything – the title of governor for himself and custody in England of Mary herself. He got neither. Arran had sent commissioners to negotiate who he knew would be acceptable to the king of England, headed by earl of Glencairn (one of the leading Solway Moss prisoners), Sir George Douglas and Henry Balnaves, a man of strong Protestant convictions. But Anglophile as these diplomats may broadly have been, they would not agree to all of Henry's demands. Their most significant success was in ensuring that Mary stayed in Scotland until she was ten years old, though the English king reserved the right to send 'a nobleman or gentleman, with his wife or other lady or ladies and their attendants, not exceeding twenty in all, to reside with her.'[11] And Arran remained as governor of Scotland, his title uncontested for the present. Eleven days later, Henry VIII married Katherine Parr and left the threat of plague in London's summer to spend a prolonged honeymoon with his new bride in the healthier countryside of the south of England. He could be well satisfied with life and turned his attention once again to the more exciting prospect of war with France.

In Scotland, however, all was not so rosy as the summer progressed. Many Scottish nobles were profoundly suspicious of the English and unhappy at the idea of their little queen's marriage effectively making them a satellite of an ancient and hated enemy. For such men, the natural ally was France and the course of action enshrined in the Treaty of Greenwich, which Scotland had yet to ratify, seemed perverse. They balked at the idea of subjugation to Henry VIII. The king of England's old rival, Francis I, who had been slow to react to the potential loss of French influence in Scotland, now woke up to the danger after representations by Antoinette de Bourbon, mother of Mary of Guise. He realized that Cardinal Beaton and the pro-French party needed support. As the momentum of opposition to the English match grew, Arran saw that he was running out of time. He faced difficulties at home on several fronts and when Beaton, released from house arrest back in the spring, felt strong enough, he moved to challenge the governor directly. In late July 1543, supported by four earls, eight lords and several notable church-men, Beaton threatened Arran with military force at Linlithgow. Arran responded by calling up his artillery and his supporters, and was still able to get the Greenwich Treaty ratified the next month at Holyrood, but he knew that the momentum was shifting and that his religious reforms were unacceptable to most Scots.

In early September, at a meeting with Beaton in Stirling, Arran made the second remarkable volte-face of what was, for him, an extremely trying year. At the Franciscan convent in Scotland's former capital, he announced his return to Catholi-cism. It seems highly likely that, in his heart, he had never really left it. But now he needed Beaton more than Henry VIII. Scotland was unquiet, the growing revival of French influence threatened Arran's position and he had always to consider the danger posed to him, not just by the cardinal, but by the earl of

Lennox and the queen dowager. For Mary of Guise, apparently a powerless widow at the beginning of the year, had shown cunning, resolve and grit, fooling Sadler, who was ever a poor judge of Scottish affairs, into thinking that she supported the English marriage of her daughter, and dangling the earl of Lennox on a string while she did nothing to discourage his hopes of making her his own bride. She was a much more formidable opponent than anyone had guessed. In late July, supported by the forces of the lovestruck earl of Lennox, Mary Queen of Scots and her mother finally moved from Linlithgow Palace to Stirling Castle, where they would remain in safety for four years. And on 9 September, the thirtieth anniversary of the battle of Flodden and one of the most emotive days in the Scottish calendar, Mary of Guise achieved her own personal triumph when she saw her daughter crowned as Queen of Scots, at the age of nine months. The future did not yet belong to James V's canny widow, but she could no longer be ignored.

Henry VIII's Scottish plans were beginning to unravel and he did not help matters by failing to ratify the Treaty of Greenwich himself. By October he seemed to sense that his grand plan was going awry, accusing Arran of 'forgetting your duty to that realm [Scotland], your honour and estimation to the world and your private and secret promises unto us.' But Arran had made his decision and was not to be swayed by bullying. He presented himself as a true Scot, working for the interests of his county and his queen, and emphasized that he would govern 'to the honour of this realm against all them that would threaten the same'.[12] Henry VIII's bombastic approach did him no favours and his capacity for railing against the duplicity of the Scots made it hard for his supporters north of the border to maintain the upper hand. In the event, it was the Scottish parliament, meeting shortly before Christmas 1543, that threw the treaty back in his face. The rejection of a Tudor marriage for their queen and the renewal of the French alliance were a triumph for Cardinal Beaton and, indirectly, for Mary of Guise.

It has been said that by the end of the momentous year of

1543 little had changed in Scotland and perhaps, to contemporaries, that would have been their perception. Yet though it was to be another sixteen years before the full impact of the Reformation suddenly burst on the country, there had been a brief interlude when Arran's 'godly fit', as his period of flirtation with religious reform was known, gave hope to burgeoning Protestantism in Scotland and hardened the attitudes of those evangelicals who passionately believed in change. Many of these, unsurprisingly, were at least partially Anglophile in outlook because their ideas were supported by their southern neighbour. Scotland may have seemed slow to adopt religious change but events of the first year of Mary Queen of Scots' reign sowed the seeds of a slow-burning revolution in belief that would split the nobility and have immense repercussions for Mary as an adult ruler. But as 1544 dawned, Scotland faced a more immediate threat. The king of England, humiliated by his rejection, attempted to impose his will on Scotland by force. So followed the first of what have been called the 'rough wooings' of the young Queen of Scots.

AT FIRST it might seem odd that Henry VIII, while preparing for war with France, should spend more money on a campaign against the Scots. Yet while desire for vengeance may have played a considerable part in his thinking, there were other motives. The Borders needed to be secured at times of European war, to avoid the kind of excursion into England that had proved fatal to Mary's grandfather, James IV. And while he had clearly lost the support of a number of key Scottish noblemen, whose patriotism proved hard to shake, promises of money and support for religious reform might yet be powerful inducements. Henry liked stirring up trouble in Scotland – it was really the only constant in his policy – and he had never abandoned his claim to overlordship. Finally, he wanted the Scots to understand that he was utterly serious in his intentions and that he intended death and destruction.

In April 1544, at the start of the campaigning season, the
Privy Council in London issued a thunderous set of instructions
which were almost biblical in their apocalyptic vision of Henry's
wrathful intent:

> Put all to fire and sword, burn Edinburgh town, so razed
> and defaced when you have sacked and gotten what you can
> of it, as there may remain forever a perpetual memory of the
> vengeance of God lightened upon [them] for their falsehood
> and disloyalty ... and as many towns and villages about
> Edinburgh as ye may conveniently, do your best to beat the
> castle, sack Holyrood House and sack Leith and burn and
> subvert it and all the rest, putting man, woman and child to
> fire and sword, without exception where any resistance shall
> be made against you and this done pass over to the Fifeland
> and extend like extremities and destruction to all towns and
> villages whereunto ye may reach conveniently, not forgetting
> among all the rest so to spoil and turn upside down the
> Cardinal's [Beaton's] town of St Andrews, as the upper stone
> may be the nether, and not one stick stand by another,
> sparing no creature alive within the same.[13]

This diatribe may have been as much for internal English
consumption as it was a realistic threat to the Scots. Henry
simply did not have a large enough force to realize his bloodthirsty aims, a fact somewhat overlooked by generations of
indignant Scottish historians. Nevertheless, a substantial English
fleet sailed into Leith Harbour, captured two Scottish warships
and disgorged ten thousand men. The English under Edward
Seymour, earl of Hertford, brother to Henry VIII's third wife,
Jane, inflicted considerable damage on the Scottish capital,
deserted in its hour of need by both Arran and Beaton. But
Hertford's forces could not take Edinburgh Castle and soon
retired to pass back into England and thence to France, where
their presence was more urgently required.

The following autumn Hertford was back in the Borders,
hoping not just to undertake another round of crop-burning and

local devastation but to establish a permanent garrison at Kelso. Military theory might have backed his intentions, but some members of the Privy Council, notably the duke of Norfolk, knew the area well and realized it was inappropriate. Hertford's second incursion was really nothing more than a major border raid and Henry VIII's aims for Mary Queen of Scots remained unfulfilled. Further warfare continued in the Borders for several years and the English tried, also, to stir up trouble in the Highlands and Islands, areas of Scotland still barely under control from Edinburgh. But in respect of the fates of two key figures in Scottish politics, Henry did have success. The first of these men was Matthew Stewart, earl of Lennox, a neglected figure in British history but a man whose ambition led him, as a welcome and high-profile prize, to change sides and pledge himself to Henry VIII.

Matthew Stewart was born in Dumbarton Castle, on the south-west coast of Scotland, in September 1516. As the great-grandson of James II, he had a legitimate claim to the Scottish throne, made stronger by the little queen's vulnerability and doubts about his cousin, Arran's, legitimacy. For, unlike the Hamiltons, there was no taint on the Lennox Stewarts and they had, indeed, another particular advantage – a long-standing connection with the French court through the d'Aubigny branch of their family, going back to the previous century when a significant number of prominent Scots had gone to seek their fortune in France. Matthew's great-uncle, Robert Stewart, had been captain of the Scots Guard to Louis XII and fought in Italy. He was a highly regarded soldier and a great landowner in France, marrying a French heiress and spending freely on La Verrerie, the castle that he had inherited in the Loire, as well as constructing his own Château d'Aubigny. To Matthew Stewart and his younger brother, John, Robert had been a conscientious guardian and protector after the murder of their father by Sir James Hamilton of Finnart in 1526. But it was not until 1532 that Matthew Stewart joined him in France, a boy of sixteen with a famous surname but no clear indication of what his future might hold. The young earl accompanied Francis I on the military expedition to Provence that had initially delayed his own king, James V, from pursuing the match with Princess Madeleine, and was commended for his zeal, though his later command of the French king's lances was to prove less successful. Francis I was sufficiently happy with the performance of this young Scottish nobleman to grant him French citizenship and Matthew seems to have thrived in the life of an adopted French grandee. It was, after all, in his blood. The sudden death of James V, however, transformed his life. The French court undoubtedly had its attractions but an altogether greater prospect beckoned at home in Scotland.

After eleven years, he might have considered returning at some point anyhow, but he could not sit by at Fontainebleau while a Hamilton assumed the reins of power in Edinburgh. And Francis I, who had been tardy in his response to the implications of James V's death, grew alarmed by the direction that the earl of Arran was apparently following. The French king liked neither religious reform nor, more importantly, the spreading tentacles of Henry VIII. An English marriage for Mary Queen of Scots needed to be prevented. It was thus a combination of Matthew Stewart's own desire to play a role in Scotland and the anxiety of Francis I that sent the earl of Lennox home as Francis's own ambassador. He arrived at the beginning of April 1543 with just two ships and a small company of twenty men, having evaded the English warships trying to waylay him in the Irish Sea. It was a low-key beginning to what would be a dramatic fourteen months for an ambitious young man.

Lennox's return altered the balance of power in Scotland, giving Cardinal Beaton a new ally and hope in his struggle to wrest power from Arran. It also provided Mary of Guise with a further weapon in her armoury of deception as she flirted with the handsome earl, alarming Henry VIII, whose decision to send Sadler back as ambassador shortly before Lennox arrived was at least in part prompted by concern that Arran and the 'assured lords' would now waver in their support for the English marriage. These fears were to be fully realized later in the year, but even before four weeks had passed, Lennox's capacity to cause trouble was evident. In the Scottish parliament of late April 1543, Lennox refused to acknowledge Arran as governor and second person of the realm. For this truculence, Arran ordered him to surrender Dumbarton Castle, his ancestral home and the most formidable fortress of western Scotland. Lennox then fled to the Highlands, where he had a significant number of supporters, and opened negotiations with Beaton. By late July he had sufficient forces to face down Arran at Linlithgow and offer protection to Mary of Guise and the infant queen. His success at this point effectively made the Treaty of Greenwich a dead letter, though public rejection of the diplomacy was still some way off.

The earl himself, however, still lacked a clear body of supporters, or, indeed, any coherent policy of his own. He probably spent much of 1543 testing the waters, though this cannot be conclusively proved, entering into secret correspondence with Henry VIII early on. It has been said that he was neither a competent rebel nor effective politician at this time, though in the shifting currents of Scottish politics and with a remorseless if deluded English king still seeking to impose his rule on Scotland, it is hardly surprising that Matthew Stewart did not cover himself with glory. There was no reason why he should have been cleverer than anyone else and he was out of touch with his native land. He did, as has been pointed out, manage for a while not to alienate either the French or English factions in Scotland, something of a feat in itself.[14] In fact, the Douglases and the earl of Glencairn, originally supporters of England, had left open lines of communication to him. And then, in the autumn of 1543, his luck suddenly changed altogether. The French government sent six ships, bearing two new ambassadors and the papal legate, Grimani, together with munitions and money to the tune of £83,600 (more than £37 million today). Lennox was no doubt pleased by the diplomatic support, but he liked the arms and money much more, and duly stored them away in the fastness of Dumbarton Castle, where no one else could get at them.

At last, he could proceed from a position of real strength. But he trusted no one and, increasingly, no one in Scotland or France trusted him as he manoeuvred for political advantage. Mary of Guise and Beaton, always a formidable alliance, implored Francis I to 'recall the earl of Lennox, whom they now found to grow factious, and by appearance a troubler of the state.'[15] He continued in this mode into 1544, when a new agreement, the Treaty of Greenside, was brokered between Lennox and Arran's government in a last-ditch attempt to bring the recalcitrant earl to obey Arran and profess his loyalty to Mary Queen of Scots. Lennox, however, could not be contained. He continued to assault Hamilton strongholds, taking both the Bishop's Palace in Glasgow and the abbey of Paisley, and in March 1544 he had still not given up entirely on the hope of marrying Mary of Guise, a hope which that indefatigable dissembler was unlikely to crush conclusively. But such a union was never to be. By the spring of 1544, Matthew Stewart knew that his future lay elsewhere, for the time being in a different country and with an entirely different wife. The Scottish nobleman who was a naturalized Frenchman would become, instead, an Englishman and loyal subject of Henry VIII.

The prize was Margaret Tudor's only daughter, Lady Margaret Douglas, sole offspring of the unhappy marriage between James IV's widow and the earl of Angus. Lennox knew he was running out of options in Scotland: 'he is now brought to such a straight as I think he must needs condescend to such covenants as your highness will appoint, for he knoweth that the French king cannot trust him and the Governor and he will never agree,' wrote the shrewd earl of Hertford to his monarch on 12 April 1544.[16] Switching his allegiance to Henry VIII was dictated in part by pragmatism but there were notable advantages to the offer of the hand of the niece of the king of England, who had a legitimate claim to its throne. Though Margaret was not mentioned in the

Act of Succession of 1544 and Henry had always been loath to acknowledge his sister's children as possible heirs to his throne, Margaret's proximity to the Crown could not be denied. Unlike Henry's two daughters, Margaret Douglas's descent was unblemished. Henry knew very well her value to him and had kept her unmarried, as he did his elder daughter, Mary. He was never going to give her away lightly, though he does seem to have been rather fond of his niece and surprisingly tolerant of her romantic escapades. Margaret's weakness for men close to the two queens consort that Henry executed did not demonstrate the best of judgement. Anne Boleyn's uncle had been imprisoned in the Tower of London and died there for daring to consider an engagement with Margaret Douglas and in 1541 Margaret became entangled with Charles Howard, one of Queen Katherine Howard's many siblings. Sent off once more to Sion Abbey (though by then without its nuns following the dissolution of the monasteries), Margaret had been reproved by Archbishop Cranmer for 'lightness of behaviour' and warned that a third such escapade would have the gravest of implications.

How much Matthew Stewart knew of his intended bride's racy past is unclear. Perhaps he found it titillating. Certainly, with all the chivalric aplomb of a gentleman of his time, he declared himself in love with Margaret Douglas before they even met. She was an attractive prospect both dynastically and personally, her beauty and popularity at the English court having been remarked upon by the French ambassador in 1543. Though no firmly identified portrait of her from this period survives, a miniature in the Royal Collection, which may be her, suggests that she had the red hair of the Tudors and an intelligent face. And she was also a Douglas, which meant that the earl of Lennox was allying himself with one of the most powerful and durable of Scottish families in marrying her, though Margaret and her father were not on good terms. But at the time she married Lennox, Margaret appeared to be one of the greatest heiresses in Scotland, as well as a serious claimant to the English throne. She was not Mary of Guise, but a highly acceptable alternative. And Lennox realized that he was on the back foot in Scotland.

The wedding of Lady Margaret Douglas and the earl of Lennox was the society event of the year in 1544. It took place on 29 June in the splendid surroundings of St James's Palace (while Henry was deep in preparations for his last tilt at glory in France) and was attended by the king and Queen Katherine Parr, in whose household Margaret served as one of her chief ladies-in-waiting. One week later, Lennox was naturalized as an English subject. Pragmatic as the origins of their marriage may have been, the Lennoxes do seem to have quickly developed a deep and abiding love for each other. Henry VIII had professed himself anxious that his niece should not be married against her will, though one wonders what the outcome might have been if Margaret had rejected Lennox. But though she might have allowed her emotions to run away with her just three years earlier, Margaret was no longer a heady girl. She was a woman of twenty-nine, very old for a first marriage by the standards of the day, and she knew that she was unlikely to be made a better offer. Matthew Stewart connected her with her Scottish heritage and together they might forge a partnership that would enhance their prospects in both Scotland and England. It is unlikely, however, that they foresaw just how crucial a role they might play in British history.

For the present, however, they had to be content with grants of property in London and in the north of England, at Temple Newsam, outside Leeds, which would be both a refuge and a headquarters for them in difficult times to come. Nor did they spend much time in each other's company. Lennox was bound now to Henry VIII and the English king was swift to call in his debts. The earl was to be his spearhead in Scotland, reclaiming Dumbarton Castle if he could tempt other, wavering Scots to serve Henry as he had done. It was also hoped he could raise the Highlands and Islands against the Scottish government, though this idea did not succeed. In cajoling and bribing other Scottish noblemen and generally stirring up trouble, however, Lennox met with considerable success – an aspect of the 'rough wooings' that has tended to be overlooked in favour of more colourful tales of rapine and plunder. Matthew Stewart, with his claim to the Scottish throne still very much alive and his new wife keen to lend him all her support, did not come badly out of the violence and uncertainty of the 1540s. The same could not be said for his one-time ally, Cardinal David Beaton, the other key figure of this period.

✼

OPPOSITION TO THE marriage of Mary Queen of Scots to Prince Edward Tudor had crystallized (as Beaton wished) around the determined, if devious, figure of the Scottish cardinal. Age had not diminished his zeal against heretics or his hatred of the English. David Beaton was not entirely a churchman of the old order since he appears to have appreciated the need for some sort of reform, but, like many younger sons thrust into the Church at the time, he was primarily interested in secular rather than spiritual power. Something of this can be seen in his portrait, which shows him resplendent in his cardinal's robes. Yet Beaton looks slightly ill at ease. It is the image of a man who does not trust readily, wary of the wider world. This was, though, a world he knew well. As a diplomat and negotiator who had spent four years in France, he was a stalwart supporter of the Auld Alliance. But he and Mary of Guise were not always natural or comfortable allies, since both wanted power for themselves. As his attempts to hold the centre ground of Scottish politics fell apart in 1543–4, the queen dowager made her own, ultimately unsuccessful, bid for power. Though he had been a prime mover against the English marriage of his infant monarch, Beaton seems not to have appreciated adequately the fury of Henry VIII's response, or the personal danger to himself that might ensue from his being the architect of rejection. Belatedly, he understood, too, that he could not expect any real help from France, with Francis I fighting against both Charles V and Henry VIII and chastened by his experience with the earl of

Lennox. A French military commander was sent to Scotland but refused to acknowledge Beaton's authority and the two men had to be prevented from physically assaulting one another. Beaton, despite being fifty years old and a cardinal of the Church, was not noted for turning the other cheek. In the end, he hastened his own doom.

By 1546, the cardinal was isolated and unpopular. Henry VIII wanted him dead and there were those in Scotland happy to get rid of him. At the beginning of the year, he made what was to prove a disastrous move, though it was in keeping with his own beliefs and vision of his authority. He pursued the Protestant preacher, George Wishart, a reformer with influential friends who saw him as a beacon of hope. Wishart was, though, a firebrand with little care for the law and an increasing reckless-ness about his own safety. Among those attracted to his uncom-promising stance was a young priest called John Knox, radicalized by the fate of his mentor. For Beaton could not sit by in his archbishopric of St Andrews while Wishart roamed nearby towns and countryside preaching in open defiance of the anti-heresy laws.

Wishart had run into difficulties in the preceding decade in England, where Cranmer found him too extreme, and he had then spent some time on the continent, probably in Switzerland, where his beliefs and vehement style of preaching seem to have been shaped. Some found him inspiring but others were less impressed by the violence of his rhetoric. Beaton simply could not stomach him and when Wishart arrived in Fife, he was sailing too close to the wind. Arrested and brought to trial at the beginning of March 1546, at St Andrews, Wishart was given little chance to defend himself properly against a raft of accu-sations brought against him. Defiant to the last, he was hanged and burned immediately after Beaton pronounced the death sentence on him. Wishart's furious supporters plotted revenge against the man they regarded as his murderer.

The motives of those involved in Beaton's assassination were not simply confined to religious differences. The archbishop had fallen out with a number of lairds in Fife who had known him for years; there were property disputes and growing ill feeling which added to the mix of hostility and resentment. Grudges, dismay at Wishart's fate and an underlying pro-English sentiment among the conspirators all contributed to a determination to be rid of this proud prelate. And even at a time when it was widely accepted that Scotland's leading churchmen were more interested in secular power than spiritual devotion, Beaton's ostentatious lifestyle made him vulnerable. He lived like a lord, had eight children by his mistress, Marion Ogilvy (with whom, it should be made clear, he seems to have had a monogamous relationship over many years that would have been viewed as a marriage if Catholic clergy had been permitted wives), and was a conscientious parent. The marriage of his daughter, Margaret, at Arbroath just a month before he died was apparently an affair befitting a princess.

Beaton returned to St Andrews from a council meeting in Edinburgh on 28 May 1546. Although the garrison at the castle numbered about a hundred men, there appears to have been collusion between the conspirators, who had been planning to dispose of Beaton for some time, and those who were supposed to defend him. There were also workmen in the castle, making it easier for people who actually had no business to be there to slip in and out unremarked. By the time the small band of attackers had penetrated the inner close of the castle, there was no escape for David Beaton. Alone except for a servant, he tried, unsuccessfully, to barricade himself in his chamber and plead for his life, reminding his assassins that he was a priest. For his murderers, this was something he had too long forgotten. One of the assassins, James Melville, told him that he sought his death 'because thou hast been, and remain, an obstinated enemy against Christ Jesus and his holy Evangel'. Stabbed several times, Beaton fell, saying, 'I am a priest, I am a priest. Fye, fye, all is gone.'[17] And so it was, at last, for a man whose life had begun in the previous century, in what was still the medieval kingdom of Scotland, a land for which, despite his worldliness and ambition, he had striven as diplomat and statesman. In his final moments, he tried to take refuge in a religious identity flagrantly disregarded over many years but it would be wrong to think that it had never meant anything to him at all.

The murderers showed him no respect in death. The body was hung over the castle walls for the populace to see and the chronicler Pitscottie, admittedly a source often more colourful than reliable, recounts a final indignity – one of the assassins loosened his breeches and urinated in the corpse's mouth.

Beaton's death removed a major figure from Scottish politics and was a conclusive break with the past. It also had considerable repercussions outside Scotland, for Beaton was a European figure. Officially, the English adopted a low-key response, calling it a lamentable crime and a reflection on the state of Scotland. But Bishop Thirlby, writing to William Paget, Henry VIII's secretary, from Ratisbon in Germany, was much more ebullient, telling of 'my gladness at your tidings of the Cardinal of Scotland. It is half a wonder here', he continued, 'that ye dare be so bold to kill a cardinal.' Philip of Spain's ambassador to France relayed to his master the French conclusion 'that the King of England caused the murder' because Beaton had opposed the English marriage of Mary Queen of Scots.[18]

So Beaton was gone but not forgotten and St Andrews Castle remained in the hands of men regarded as rebels for another year. Arran could neither pursue the murderers nor retake the stronghold without assistance and his own son, the boy he hoped might marry the Queen of Scots now the English match was a dead letter, was being held hostage by the insurgents. For a brief period, as the war between England and France was finally ended by a treaty in 1546 that also brought a halt to hostilities in Scotland, the 'rough wooings' ceased. But in England the reign of Henry VIII was drawing to a close, though, as would soon become apparent, this did not presage an easier relationship between Scotland and its southern neighbour.

❦

THE BEGINNING OF the year 1547 saw two major departures from the European stage. In England, Henry VIII died at Whitehall Palace on 28 January, having spent the last six weeks of his life in detailed preparation for the regime that would support his heir, nine-year-old Edward. The old king had put in place a closed conciliar system that he thought would represent a balance of interests and guard against the rise of any one faction, but the truth was that his will and his plans were all too easily disregarded once his towering presence was gone. Eschewing emotional farewells with his wife and elder daughter, Henry died with none of his family present. Princess Mary and Queen Katherine Parr had spent Christmas 1546 together at Greenwich Palace but though the queen seems to have returned to Whitehall in mid-January 1547, she was kept well away from her husband by the men jockeying for position as he declined. Her expectations of the regency, a position she had filled with grace and competence in 1544 during the French war, were soon dashed when Edward Seymour, earl of Hertford and soon to be duke of Somerset, assumed the role of Protector to the boy king.

In France, the news of Henry's death was received with satisfaction. The imperial ambassador reported that the duchess d'Étampes, long-time mistress to Francis I, ran to Queen Eleanor's bedchamber yelling, 'News! News! We have lost our chief enemy and the king has commanded me to come and tell you of it.'[19] Dismayed by this incursion of her rival, Eleanor, who was a sister of the emperor Charles V, at first thought this was triumphalism of a particularly nasty sort, and assumed that it was her brother who had died. Francis may have derived considerable pleasure from outliving the king of England, but he was not long for this world himself. It has been alleged that Henry VIII sent him a message from his deathbed reminding him that he, too, was mortal. If so, this proved prophetic. Within weeks of Henry's death, Francis himself fell ill. His health had been in decline for some time but though he had lived a life of dissipation and was long thought to have succumbed to syphilis; it is now thought that his death was brought about by a serious infection of the urinary tract that attacked his kidneys and led to major organ failure. He had travelled outside Paris into the nearby countryside on a brief hunting expedition when it became obvious that he was too sick to go any farther. He died at the château of Rambouillet on the last day of March 1547, his son and heir, Henry, at his side, but without Queen Eleanor or his beloved sister, Marguerite. So of the three rulers who had dominated Europe for the first half of the sixteenth century, only Charles V was left. He would live on for another eleven years.

Henry VIII and Francis I were both commanding personalities whose rivalry encompassed Scotland and influenced the course of events there. But however personally they had viewed their relationship, their passing did not change the underlying truth that the French would continue to view Scotland as a natural ally against England, and the English, even without an adult monarch, would not abandon the idea of a marriage between Mary Queen of Scots and Edward VI, nor desist from their campaign to bring Scotland to heel by military might. In fact, over the next year, attitudes hardened as Henry II of France, young, vigorous and ambitious, saw an opportunity to impose himself more completely on Scottish politics than his father had ever done and Protector Somerset tried to smash the Scots into submission. The deaths of the two old kings, far from giving Scotland a remission, heralded a period of even more intense wrangling. Its outcome profoundly affected the northern kingdom of the British Isles and the child who was its queen.

❧

THE FIRST BOUT of the struggle for Scotland went to the French, though its importance has often been overlooked by historians. St Andrews Castle, on Scotland's east coast, had been held by Cardinal Beaton's murderers for more than a year when it was spectacularly recovered by a French naval fleet under the command of the Italian Leone Strozzi in July 1547. The English had given aid to the insurgents and attempted to maintain the castle's fortifications, but they failed to anticipate the keenness of

Henry II to strike an embarrassing blow against them. Governor Arran had tried to raise the siege of St Andrews using Scottish forces, but perhaps concerned about the fate of his hostage son inside, his rather half-hearted attempts to deal with the rebels had come to nothing. The French fleet battered the castle into submission in six hours, a stunning victory made easier by the defection to the French king by the able cartographer and hydrographer Jean Rotz, formerly in the service of Henry VIII but overlooked by Somerset, who was a soldier rather than a sailor. This was the new king of France's first taste of military victory and his confidence grew as a result. Carefully planned and superbly executed, the recapture of St Andrews heralded a new dynamic in Franco–Scottish relations, demonstrating Henry II's determination to gain the upper hand in influence there and to impose his own dynastic ambitions, just as the English were trying to do with theirs. It was certainly a setback for the reformers and one in particular suffered directly. John Knox was captured by the French and consigned to the galleys, though he spent the winter on the Loire before being sent back to Scottish waters to assist in repelling further English incursions. He wrote little of his experience of French captivity subsequently, though he continued to give spiritual advice to the Protestant lords from St Andrews imprisoned in France and his anti-Catholicism became more virulent.

The loss of St Andrews was a setback for the English and Somerset began immediately to formulate an armed response. By the summer of 1547, he was in full control of Edward's Privy Council and ruling the country on behalf of his nephew. Like other men of his background, he was both politician and soldier by training. For many years, he was admired by historians as the 'Good Duke', a man of principle who sought to rule wisely and was eventually undone by power-hungry enemies, most notably his one-time friend and fellow soldier John Dudley, earl of Warwick and later duke of Northumberland. But more recent assessments and analysis of what he actually achieved, and especially his manner of government, have revealed a man of limited ability and vision, increasingly autocratic in his approach, self-important and unresponsive. He certainly espoused religious reform and supported the sweeping changes that were being championed by Archbishop Cranmer and other reformers, but, like many men of his class, he had benefitted from the Reformation in terms of office and lands and the depth of his religious conviction is difficult to determine. There is no doubting, however, that his grab for power after Henry VIII's death was single-minded and successful and his approach to Scotland ruthless in the aftermath of the loss of St Andrews. For this time he planned a full-scale land campaign rather than a series of disjointed raids. The Scots had a remarkable ability to recover from such attacks and had won a victory of their own against the English at Ancrum Moor in 1545. This rankled with Somerset and he was determined it should not be repeated. His ultimate aim, as he had intimated two years earlier, was to establish permanent fortifications north of the border, a 'pale' very like that which still surrounded Calais. What followed was yet another major defeat in a pitched battle for the Scots and the last conflict fought between the two countries before their union.

The battle of Pinkie (also known as Inveresk in the sixteenth century) was fought on Saturday, 10 September at Musselburgh at the crossing of the river Esk, just over six miles from Edinburgh. Sometimes characterized as the first modern battle fought on British soil, detailed accounts survive from a number of sources. The best known is that of the Englishman William Patten, who accompanied Somerset on what he termed 'the Expedicion into Scotlande' and was extravagant in his praise of the duke. Patten's is a curious account, couched in the language of a zealous Protestant and full of biblical and classical allusions, as well as a virulent and contemptuous dislike of the Scots. There are also other reports, from a French Protestant in the service of John Dudley, earl of Warwick, and from the French ambassador in London, Odet de Selve, who obtained his information from the earl of Huntly, a commander of the Scottish army. Finally, there are contemporary maps of the battle arrays and the course of the conflict itself, rediscovered in the Bodleian Library, Oxford, in the last century.

Somerset had ridden north during August 1547 to take command of an army of just under twenty thousand men, made up mostly of northern levies who mustered at Berwick. He was supported by seasoned military commanders such as the earl of Warwick and Lord Grey of Wilton, but a notable absence was his own brother, Thomas, Lord Seymour of Sudeley, the Lord Admiral, who might have been expected to command the fleet. The relationship of the Seymour brothers was already souring and would get worse.

Whatever the reason for the younger Seymour's omission from the Pinkie campaign, Somerset was not diverted from his purpose by family quarrels. His force, as was so often the case at the time, was not entirely English in composition: six hundred foot soldier mercenaries commanded by an Italian and two hundred arquebusiers on horseback under a Spanish captain. But though Somerset's was the main army – and the one intended to engage the Scots – there was also a smaller group of two and a half thousand foot soldiers and horsemen in the western marches, led by Wharton, the architect of victory at Solway Moss, and by the earl of Lennox. It was intended as a feint, which was perhaps just as well as the anticipated support for Lennox from western Scotland did not materialize and many men from the area actually fought for Governor Arran. In fact, there was very little support for Somerset from within Scotland, despite assurances from the earl of Glencairn to the contrary. When it came to major confrontation with England, most Scots still put their country first.

Arran himself knew that the death of Henry VIII did not mean the end of hostilities. Having re-armed and provisioned the major castles of Edinburgh, Dunbar and Stirling during the spring and summer, by 17 August he was ready to send out letters ordering the mustering of the Scottish host. But he was sufficiently concerned by the danger of an invasion on two fronts that he made the wrong choice of mustering place. The Scots were commanded to meet at Fala, fifteen miles south-east of Edinburgh. The English, meanwhile, were advancing up the east coast, supplied by an English fleet waiting offshore, and Arran realized that he could not defend the Scottish capital unless he moved rapidly north to cut off the invaders.

He had a very substantial army. Estimates vary as to precise numbers and, as was often the case, the English tended to claim that the Scots had a far bigger force than they did. The earl of Huntly's figure of about twenty-three thousand men is probably the most reliable, making the Scottish force larger than the English, but not overwhelmingly so. The Scottish artillery was greater in terms of numbers of guns but not in size of the weapons themselves. Neither army consisted of any great number of professional soldiers but there was nothing unusual about this. Both divided their forces into three groups, or 'battles', the English infantry armed with bills (the weapon that had wrought such destruction at Flodden) and pikes, which were now more frequently used. But, unlike the Scottish force, many of the English infantry were equipped with firearms. The Scots again carried pikes and were supported by several thousand archers but the lack of firearms put them at a disadvantage.

The Scots established their camp on the western side of the river Esk, giving them control of the bridge which was a key crossing point on the road to Edinburgh. Protected by marshland to the south and the river itself to the east, the camp lay behind a turf defence to protect it from artillery fire from the English fleet. They were a formidable force, but with a mindset grounded, for better or worse, in a glorious past; 'a chivalric elite armed for battle', as the historian Marcus Merriman described them. As well as the earl of Arran, the army was commanded by the earl of Angus, now fifty-eight years old, and the earl of Huntly, who was resplendent in a shining new suit of armour. All three men, and especially Angus, were experienced but they were put at an immediate disadvantage when the English army, approaching from Prestonpans in the east, sent out a detachment of cavalry to engage the Scottish horsemen holding the vital vantage point of Falside Hill. The pursuit after this skirmish saw eight hundred Scots captured and Lord Hume, in command of Falside, was so severely injured in a fall from his horse that he had to be taken back to Edinburgh.

What followed is the subject of dispute between English and Scottish accounts. It seems probable, however, that Somerset, believing that he had scored a notable early success but equally aware now of the strength of the Scottish position, decided to make one last pitch for the marriage of his nephew with Mary Queen of Scots. He may have promised not merely to withdraw but to pay compensation for damage and plunder. George Buchanan and Pitscottie both concur that Somerset's offer, contained in a letter sent to the Scottish council, was kept from Arran. Whether this is true or not, it seems unlikely that the governor would have agreed, even to more generous terms. He had made his decision four years earlier and stayed true to it. Somerset now prepared for a frontal attack on the Scottish army. But before he could move he learned that Arran was advancing on him. 'The Scots,' wrote Patten, 'hasted with so fast a pace that it was thought of the most part of us they were rather horsemen than footmen.'[20]

Arran was advancing against the advice of both Angus and Huntly. His decision may have been less bravado and more the realization that Somerset would come at the Scottish army with the fully force of his artillery. The governor's aim was to establish himself on Falside Hill, hoping to outflank Somerset and protect the route to Edinburgh, but the ground was difficult, marshy on one side and hilly and furrowed on the other. Of greater significance in the outcome of the battle was the inescapable fact that Arran did not have enough horsemen, especially after the encounter with the English the previous day, and that those that were left to him were demoralized by their recent losses. Nevertheless, the English were still some way short of Falside Hill when the main fighting began in the late morning. Although Angus's division had advanced ahead of the other two, the restrictions of the terrain meant that the Scottish army was becoming too densely packed together (again, reminiscent of Flodden) and the Scots soon found themselves just 'two bow shots asunder' from the English lines, meaning that they were well within the sort of range where artillery could inflict severe damage.

Initially, the Scottish pikemen held off the English advance led by Lord Grey of Wilton but as the English artillery fire began to rake them, the Highlanders under the earl of Argyll misinterpreted a wheeling manoeuvre by Angus as a retreat. Panic spread like wildfire, soon reaching Arran's division. Somerset was far too seasoned a soldier not to notice what was happening to his foes. Angus strove desperately to keep the Scottish force together even after the three original battles had disintegrated. As he tried to regroup with Huntly, the latter's men mistook Angus's force for the English. Huntly stayed with his rearguard until he saw that the Scottish position was hopeless and then withdrew. He was subsequently taken prisoner. How and when Arran left the field is open to doubt, though the tale of his cowardice in calling for his horse and fleeing early on is one put about by his enemies and perhaps understandable given the scale of the defeat of the Scots. Angus, however, showing his powers of survival, hid in a ditch and managed to escape.

Ten thousand other Scots were not so fortunate. The rout of a broken enemy was a long-established rite of medieval warfare and Pinkie, despite its more 'modern' tactics, was no exception to this bloodletting. Fleeing in panic, some towards Dalkeith and others overland or along the shore to Edinburgh, the Scots were pursued and cut down over a period of about five hours. Large numbers of them drowned in the river Esk or simply dropped dead of exhaustion. The variety of miserable ends they met was chillingly described by William Patten:

> Dead corpses lying dispersed abroad. Some with their legs cut off; some but ham-strung and left lying half-dead; others with the arms cut off; divers, their necks half asunder; many, their heads cloven; of sundry, the brains smashed out; some

others again, their heads quite off; with a thousand other
kinds of killing . . . And thus, with blood and slaughter of
the enemy, the chase was continued.[21]

Many prominent Scottish families lost one or more of their sons
and heirs at Pinkie, where a generation of promise and the hope
of continuity vanished almost as completely as at Flodden forty
years before. The studious and rather priggish little boy who was
king of England wrote to congratulate his 'dearest uncle' for the
victory, thanking God for his support and promising to reward
the earl of Warwick and the other English noblemen who had
been instrumental in defeat of the Scots. It seemed as if history
was repeating itself and that Scotland, utterly defenceless and
broken, stood once more at the mercy of the Tudor dynasty.

Astonishingly (at least in retrospect), Somerset did not follow
up his victory. He marched as far as Leith and then left for
England on 18 September, little more than a week after his
stunning defeat of the Scots. Like English soldiers before him in
the sixteenth century, he seems to have accepted that taking
Edinburgh was a move too far. He was also fixated on the idea
of a series of fortified garrisons in southern Scotland that would
give a permanent presence and launch point for future offensives
without the apparently impossible task of occupation. The duke
now embarked on a serious propaganda campaign of tracts and
publications urging union between England and Scotland as
the best way forward for both countries. Aimed primarily at the
Protestant minority and wholly unacceptable to most Scots, it
nevertheless set the tone for a debate and an alternative vision of
their future that would become more urgent and divisive with
the passing years. Initially, Somerset's literary efforts probably
had more effect in England, where they formed an important
element in the thinking of a trusted member of his household,
one William Cecil, who would later play a crucial role in Anglo–
Scottish relations. Cecil was already taking an interest in the
career of John Knox, who became chaplain to Edward VI. But
in Scotland the opposing view, based on an appeal to patriotism,

albeit with large elements of self-interest in the actions of some of the leading Scottish aristocracy, was always very powerful. In the case of the earl of Angus, it ultimately proved stronger than any monetary inducement he had received from the Tudors over the years. In February 1548, the earl defeated an English force led by Wharton and the earl of Lennox in the western Borders, effectively putting paid to Somerset's ambitions in that part of Scotland. He and the duke hated one another.

But his warrior's life and his wanderings, his betrayal of the Stewarts and his distant period of power in the 1520s were now well behind him. Angus spent the last years of his life doggedly pursuing the restitution of his lands, supported by his loyal brother, George. He never forgot that, first and foremost, he was a Douglas and he had little respect for the niceties of court etiquette. Mary of Guise, a woman he could not abide, once rebuked him for turning up at her court clad in armour and was told: 'It is only my old dad Lord Drummond's coat, a very kindly coat to me. I cannot part with it.' Towards the end of his life, he regretted that he had not seen his grandson, Lord Darnley, the child of Margaret Douglas and the earl of Lennox. Yet he was not willing, when he died in 1557, to leave Margaret his lands, entailing them instead on the male Douglas line. Though she had forgiven her second husband on her deathbed, Margaret Tudor would not have been pleased.

The Scottish defeat at Pinkie, remembered in popular folklore as 'Black Saturday', sent waves throughout Europe but was especially significant in France, where Henry II, determined to challenge the English, began to perceive how he could derive the maximum advantage from the renewed reliance of this small northern ally on his support and goodwill. During the year 1547–8 he concentrated his financial inducements, his *largesse*, on the leading Scottish magnates – Arran, Argyll, Huntly (who escaped from his English prison at the end of 1548 and immediately, through Mary of Guise, offered his services to the French king), the earl of Angus and his brother, Sir George Douglas. As has been pointed out, together with the Crown lands and those controlled by the queen dowager, the territories and clan loyalties these nobles held made up the greater part of Scotland.[22] The Scottish author of *The Complaynt of Scotlande*, a rebuff to English propaganda, wrote that realms were not conquered by words but rather by blood. He might have added financial inducement into the mix, for it was undoubtedly powerful, and the English nobility, many receiving generous pensions from the emperor Charles V, were no more immune to it than their Scottish counterparts. But the person who would be most directly affected by the Scots' acceptance that their independence from England could not be achieved without French military and monetary aid was their young queen, now in her fifth year and fast developing into a bonny, self-confident and intelligent child.

⤲

IMMEDIATELY AFTER the rout at Pinkie, Mary Queen of Scots was moved at night to Inchmahome Priory on an island in the Lake of Menteith on the upper reaches of the rivers Forth and Teith, north of Stirling, a city which had been her home since she was nine months old. Mary's reaction to being spirited away in such tense circumstances is not known but she was certainly safer in this remote part of central Scotland than if she had stayed put and perhaps suffered a siege in Stirling Castle. After three weeks, when it became apparent that Somerset intended no attack on Edinburgh or further inroads into the heart of Scotland, Mary was able to leave. She spent the autumn of 1547 and the early part of the winter of 1548 back in Stirling but there was continued concern over her safety and discussions with the French were intensifying following Arran's agreement in principle with Henry II of France in January 1548. Though it would be some months before the detail of these negotiations was finalized and put to the Scottish parliament, Mary was moved on the last day of February in preparation for her journey to France. Accompanied by her guardians, Lords Livingston and Erskine, who had day-to-day responsibility for her education and security, she spent the next five months in Dumbarton Castle on the west coast of Scotland, the former stronghold of Matthew Stewart, earl of Lennox. The irony of this was probably lost on Mary, though we have no idea how much she was told of the state of her realm and that the castle's traditional lord was now in English pay.

Indeed, we know very little of her early education and daily life. She appears to have been an energetic and largely healthy child, though she did contract measles while at Dumbarton and the inevitable rumours of her death, from what was admittedly a serious childhood disease in those days, swirled around. There are no surviving portraits of Mary from this period but those painted in her early teens suggest a pretty girl. She became tall for her age and soon demonstrated the easy charm and affability of both sides of her family. At five years old she would probably, given her status as queen, have commenced lessons in the basics of reading and writing. She spoke Scots and strove to keep it up during her time in France, but no English (which she did not learn to write until she had fled Scotland in 1568) and apparently little, if any, French, which is somewhat odd given her mother's background and ambitions for her. The formal part of Mary's education was, however, to follow in France.

The earl of Arran, despite criticisms of his conduct and his apparent capitulation to the French when offered a duchy in Poitou and the revenues of the estate that went with it, was never going to let his little queen go without getting the best terms and assurances that he could for Scotland. In this, he had the full support of the Scottish parliament and the natural enthusiasm of Mary of Guise to see her daughter become a queen in two countries. The governor's price, Scotland's price, as he justified it, for the French marriage was the arrival of sufficient French troops to defend Scotland against further English depredations, for Henry II to acknowledge Arran's continued role as the head of Scottish government and for the king of France to 'keep and defend the realm, laws and liberties thereof . . . as has been kept in all Kings' times of Scotland bypast and to marry her upon no other person but upon the said Dolphin only.'[23]

The Scottish parliament, meeting in tents outside the walls of the east coast town of Haddington, then held by the English, ratified the treaty on 7 July. The French force, under the Sieur d'Esse, had arrived in mid-June and disembarked at Leith. It duly laid siege to the English fortification at Haddington but was not able to recapture the town. But for Mary of Guise, this was a small setback. The day after the Treaty of Haddington was signed she wrote in triumph to her brothers at the French court: 'I leave tomorrow to send her [Mary] to him [Henry II].' For the Guise family, upstarts or no, the marriage of their Stewart niece into the French royal family promised to make them the most powerful men in France and power brokers in Europe.

The greatest victory, however, was that claimed by Henry II in a letter to the Ottoman Sultan:

> I have [he wrote] pacified the kingdom of Scotland, which I hold and possess with such authority and obedience as I do in France, to which two kingdoms I am joining another, namely England, which by perpetual union, alliance and confederation is now under my control, as if it were my own self: the King, his subjects and his powers; in such a manner that the said three kingdoms together can now be regarded as one and the same monarchy.[24]

Had they known of these claims, Arran and the Scottish nobility might have winced, but would no doubt still have believed that being a client state of France was preferable to union with England. Yet insofar as Henry II's posturing accurately reflected the position of England, it was an empty boast. Neither widespread revolts in the summer of 1549 nor the ensuing fall of Somerset brought England under French control. The regime of the duke's erstwhile friend, John Dudley, now duke of Northumberland, took a more conciliatory and pro-French view, returning Boulogne, the great prize of Henry VIII's 1544 war, for a much needed payment of 400,000 crowns into the English exchequer. The rapprochement even led to talks about a marriage between Edward VI and Henry II's eldest daughter, Élisabeth, though Edward VI died before he could be united with the French princess, whose sizeable dowry he found as attractive as the young lady's person. Even if the marriage had one day gone ahead, this scarcely meant that Tudor England was under French control – merely that Henry II liked to think it might be.

Mary Queen of Scots left Dumbarton for her new life in France on 29 July 1548, kissing her mother goodbye and walking with all the self-possession of royalty on to Henry II's royal galley, one of an escort sent to transport her safely through the dangerous waters of the English Channel, where English ships were expected to try and intercept her. But it was the weather, rather than the English, that held up Mary's departure. Delayed by storms for a week, Mary and her retinue finally arrived in Brittany, at St-Pol-de-Léon, on 18 August 1548. It would be thirteen years before she saw Scotland again.

CHAPTER TWELVE

Daughter of France

'*She is the most perfect child that I have ever seen.*'

Henry II of France to the French constable Montmorency,
describing Mary Queen of Scots in December 1548

MARY'S EXUBERANCE and natural confidence at such an early age have been much remarked upon but she was still only five and a half years old and the voyage from Scotland had been arduous. After landing in Brittany, it was felt advisable that she rest before commencing her journey to the French court. Nothing less than a full royal progress had been planned for the young queen. It took her first to Nantes and then by barge along the Loire, visiting some of this beautiful region's main towns, via Tours and Orléans, where the journey would be concluded overland. Mary was to take up residence with the French royal children at the château of Carrières in St Denis, to the north of Paris. She did not meet Henry II until the second week of November, in his favourite palace of St Germain, just outside the capital. By that time, she had already won the hearts of many French citizens who had warmed to this attractive, confident child.

Her first few days in France were passed in the peaceful surroundings of a Dominican convent at Morlaix. Some time for recuperation was needed by the rest of her substantial entourage, many of whom had suffered more than Mary during the sea crossing. For Mary had a considerable number of companions and servants to support her and ease the pain of parting from the familiarity of Scotland and her mother. Accompanying the queen were three of her illegitimate half-brothers, Lords James, Robert and John Stewart. It is possible that Mary had not been much in contact with these siblings before leaving Scotland. Lord James Stewart was the son of Margaret Erskine, the favourite mistress of James V. At seventeen, he was the oldest of the brothers (the other two each had different mothers) and en route for university in Paris. Though he also spent time at the French court, Lord James never took his sights off political developments in Scotland and was to become a major player in the unfolding drama of Mary Stewart's life.

Four young Scottish noblewomen of the same age and sharing her first name, the Marys Beaton, Seton, Livingston and Fleming, also went to France with the queen, though they were separated from her once she had settled in to the French court. Lords Erskine and Livingston, her official guardians, the nurse who had cared for her since her infancy, Janet Sinclair, and her lady governess, Lady Janet Fleming, née Stewart, an illegitimate daughter of James IV and widow of Lord Fleming, who had died at Pinkie, completed her household staff. Lady Fleming, a sensual and handsome woman who shared her father's weakness for passionate romantic adventure, was a confidante of Mary of Guise. As befitted her role as Queen of Scots, Mary also had her own staff of spiritual advisers.

So Mary was certainly not isolated from her Scottish roots as she sailed along the Loire. The journey was not without incident, as a serious outbreak of dysentery, perhaps caused by drinking water, nearly felled Lords Livingston and Erskine and proved fatal to the young brother of Mary Seton. At the official level, however, all went smoothly. On 21 September 1548, Mary made her entry into Angers, a splendid fortified town in the western Loire. A magnificent display greeted the Queen of Scots. She and her party processed from the gate of St Nicholas to the main church, where speeches were made by the mayor and gifts of sugared almonds, fruits and jams, all demonstrating the bounty of the region, were provided for the visitors. The Scottish queen's governors received presents of red and white wine. Mary's own regal status was underlined when she granted letters of remission to a number of prisoners in the town. The organization of this and Mary's other entries into towns along her route was entrusted to Henry II's valet de chambre, the Sieur de la Cabassoles. The king himself, however, had made it very clear to the inhabitants of Angers two months previously that he expected them to put on their very best for Mary:

> As our very dear and beloved daughter and cousin the Queen of Scotland will shortly be arriving in our kingdom, we wish that by the towns and places where she will pass, that she should be well honoured and well treated as if she were our own daughter. And for this cause, we command and expressly entreat you that when the said Queen passes by our town of Angers you will come before her with the best company of high-ranking men that can be assembled in order to receive and honour her and make gifts of wine, fruits and other offerings . . .[1]

Evidently the good citizens of Angers responded with enthusiasm to these instructions.

At Tours, Mary was met by her maternal grandmother, Antoinette de Bourbon, and the half-brother she had never seen, her mother's son, François de Longueville. Both were delighted with her. Even before she had met Mary, the duchess of Guise sought to reassure her own anxious daughter in Scotland that all would be well now the child was in France. After meeting Mary, Antoinette wrote to her own son, the future cardinal of Lorraine: 'I assure you, she is the prettiest and best for her age that you ever saw. She has auburn hair, with a fine complexion, and I think that when she comes of age she will be a beautiful girl, because her skin is delicate and white.'[2] The sixteenth century prized pale skin as a mark of true beauty and Mary impressed at an early age.

To judge from his comments, the man who was to take responsibility for the direction of Mary's life for the next twelve years was himself instantly charmed by the little girl who now joined his family. Perhaps it was his own dramatic and often unhappy childhood that made Henry II an attentive father, determined to do his best for his children and for the Queen of Scots, who had so providentially come under his protection and would, he hoped, allow him one day to unite the three crowns of France, Scotland and England.

Henry II was twenty-nine years old when Mary arrived in France and the father of four children – Francis, his heir, two girls, Élisabeth and Claude, and Louis, who would die of the measles not long after. Carefully nurtured and educated, they did not have to endure the dislocation that had shaped Henry's early years or the feeling of being second best that his father, Francis I, had so unfortunately inculcated in him. The entire balance of Henry's life had been thrown out of kilter by the humiliating defeat visited on Francis I by the emperor Charles V at the battle of Pavia in northern Italy in 1525. Francis was imprisoned for a year and the price of his release was high, especially for his two eldest boys, the dauphin (also Francis) and Henry, who were to be sent to Spain as hostages. Henry was not quite seven years old and the effect on him of an increasingly hard captivity was profound. Although the boys arrived in Spain in 1526 with a considerable retinue of servants, their lives were made much more difficult when their father double-crossed Charles V in creating the League of Cognac two years later. They were subsequently deprived of their French household and sent to the fortress of Pedrazza in the mountains north of Segovia in central Spain. By now speaking more Spanish than French, existing on a frugal diet and not allowed any visitors, their outlook seemed bleak until Queen Isabella, the Portuguese wife of Charles V, intervened to alleviate their condition. Concerned for their health, the queen provided money and instructions to improve the boys' well-being. Charles V's aunt, Margaret of Austria, also added her voice to pleas for better treatment for the two French princes. But even then, matters proceeded slowly. In 1529 a huge ransom of two million gold ecus (approximately £320 million today) was demanded for their release and a representative of Francis I was not allowed to see the boys until the money had been gathered. He was so appalled by their forlorn condition and ragged clothes that he burst into tears. Finally, on 1 July 1530, accompanying Charles V's sister, Eleanor, who was to marry Francis I, the boys were handed back on a raft in the middle of the river Bidassoa, the Pyrenean boundary between France and Spain. They had been exiles for four years.

Henry never hid his contempt for his Spanish gaolers or his hatred of Charles V. When it came his turn to challenge the man who ruled most of Europe, he was very happy to take up the Valois cause. Not that it seemed, until the summer of 1536, that his destiny would allow him such revenge. The unexpected death of the dauphin that year devastated Francis I, who had adored his outgoing elder son. With the more timid and reserved Henry now his heir, Francis could not hide his disappointment, informing the bewildered seventeen-year-old that he must strive to be more like his dead brother. The king himself, however, did not make much attempt to transfer his affections to Henry, reserving them instead for his third son, Charles.

If all of this made Henry miserable, his marriage in 1533 to Catherine de Medici, the plain fourteen-year-old heiress of one of the wealthiest families in Europe and niece of the pope, was a further contributory factor. It is an often overlooked irony that Henry VIII, godfather to Henry II and for whom he was named, objected to the match on the grounds that the bride was not good enough for the second son of a French king. But though Catherine soon fell deeply in love with her husband, the marriage seemed to be a disaster for almost a decade. Henry II was besotted with his mistress, Diane de Poitiers, duchess of Valentinois, a woman twenty years his senior. His own mother had died when he was five, he did not like his stepmother, Eleanor, despite her attempts to become closer to him, and, without seeming too Freudian, it is hard to escape the view that his relationship with Diane de Poitiers might not at least partly be explained by the absence of a maternal figure in his life. Indeed, it was Diane who kissed little Henry goodbye when he went into exile in Spain and on his return Diane was there to help train him in the courtly manners that he had lost. Small wonder, then, that he came to adore her. She was probably his mistress by 1538, a handsome rather than beautiful woman, with deep-set eyes, a prominent nose and slightly pointed chin. Several nude paintings of her suggest that her main attraction was a fine figure, with lovely breasts. Certainly, Henry II seems to have thought so, as he often fondled them on front of his courtiers. For the rest of his life, she exercised a powerful personal and political influence and though Catherine de Medici understandably resented Diane greatly, she owed the preservation of her marriage to her rival's insistence that Henry should perform his marital duties with the wife who was so obviously less attractive in every way.

For ten years, Catherine was childless, a circumstance explained by both her husband's reluctance and the late onset of puberty. Then in 1543 she finally gave birth to a son, the first of a large family of eleven, not all of whom survived. Mary Queen of Scots would soon get to know this growing brood and her future mother-in-law, who took a keen interest in her education, very well. What she made of Diane de Poitiers is impossible to say, though she must have observed that lady on her visits to court. In one respect, however, Diane had a very direct influence on Mary, when she ousted Lady Fleming, the young Queen of Scots' governess, in 1551. Henry II may have been devoted to Diane but he was not immune to the temptations offered by the daughter of James IV and they began an affair. As Lady Fleming occupied the same suite of accommodation as her charge, Henry's nocturnal visits and surreptitious early morning exits were soon known to Diane de Poitiers, who made a scene and accused Henry of dishonouring the Queen of Scots by such behaviour. After giving birth to a son by the French king, Janet Fleming was sent back to Scotland in disgrace. Diane did not tolerate rivals, except, of course, Queen Catherine herself. But then she hardly regarded Henry's wife as a threat to her own position.

While he may, from time to time, have had trouble with the women in his life, Henry II began his reign with notable successes on the international scene. He was supremely confident about Scotland now that he had its monarch under his wing and there was every reason to believe that Mary of Guise, though not yet regent in Scotland, would continue to influence affairs there in his favour. He had bought (or so he thought) the regent Arran, now enjoying his French title of duke of Châtelherault, and most of the Scottish nobility preferred a French alliance to English domination. There was the possibility of religious divisions working against him but he would commit men and arms to keep this in check and support the queen dowager in every way he could.

❧

So MARY STEWART remained firmly in France and there her education and training, eventually overseen by her Guise uncle, Charles, the cardinal of Lorraine, began in earnest. There was also input from Catherine de Medici, who corrected some of Mary's earliest efforts at Latin, and the ubiquitous Diane de Poitiers. The Queen of Scots was given an education that was very typical of that prescribed for Renaissance ladies of high birth, with the notable difference that, because she was also a queen in her own right, her curriculum more closely matched that of the dauphin. Soon after she arrived in France she was learning French, and her quick mastery of the language was noted. Dancing, that vital accomplishment of aristocratic ladies, also featured firmly as she became familiar with the etiquette of the court. By 1554 there was a much more serious academic emphasis. Mary was learning to compose letters, including formal ones to the dauphin, her intended husband, and to the other royal children; she had also begun to translate from French into Latin, write poetry and learn about ancient Greece and Rome.

Later she would write speeches and even deliver an oration to Henry II, but in this she evidently had to be heavily coached. In addition, she had lessons in history, geography and languages, becoming fluent in Italian as well as French, and learnt some Spanish. She may also have known a little Greek and Hebrew. Nowadays we would regard her curriculum as notably lacking in the development of numeracy skills, though she must have learned basic arithmetic.

A functioning grasp of accounts was necessary for the running of any household, large or small, and Mary's was no exception. Women were not remote from the day-to-day management of their estates and households in the sixteenth century and, indeed, in the frequent absences of their husbands on military campaigns or at court, many aristocratic ladies handled family and estate finances with great success. In England, Mary Tudor, Henry VIII's elder daughter, had been signing off her monthly privy purse expenses since she was in her teens and as a great landowner in her brother's reign kept a close eye on expenditure, even though she had trusted servants to undertake the detail of such work for her. Mary Queen of Scots began to sign her accounts from an even earlier age. But before that there had been difficulties in the payment of servants and a dispute about the significance of her own status.

The problem was partly, if unintentionally, exacerbated by Catherine de Medici. When the dauphin was given a separate establishment of his own, the queen wanted her daughters to stay together at court, and it was at first expected that Mary would remain with them. This arrangement, which appeared to suggest that a queen regnant of Scotland was the equivalent of the daughter of a king of France, did not go down well with the Guise family and was probably troubling to Mary as well, as she had already begun to exhibit a keen awareness of who she was. Feeling that her continued presence in the princesses' establishment undermined his niece's status (and therefore family honour as well), the cardinal of Lorraine pressed Mary of Guise to find the money to fund a separate household for Mary. The justification for this was to be provided by declaring that the young queen had attained her majority at eleven years of age, a year earlier than was the custom in Scotland. By the beginning of 1554 she had her own apartments and presence chamber, where, as Queen of Scots, she could receive official delegations and hold audiences.

It was possible to set up the separate household because Mary of Guise signed over to her daughter the pension of 20,000 livres she received annually from the king of France, an additional 25,000 from her estates in Scotland and some smaller sums from her French estates. Of the total of 58,000 livres, 5,000 went on 'clothes, plate and pocket money'.[3]

So life was not all learning and official functions. The young Scottish queen was the possessor of an elegant and growing wardrobe and a collection of jewellery. And there were pleasurable pastimes. Queen Catherine taught her how to embroider and Mary's skill in this respect provided comfort in the long years of her English exile. Some of her work can still be seen, most notably at Oxburgh Hall in Norfolk. Mary also loved music and was a competent musician, as befitted someone of mixed Tudor and Stewart descent. Her singing voice, though not outstanding, was better than that of her father, James V, and she could play a variety of instruments, including the virginals and lute. Painting and chess were other pastimes and Mary was also an enthusiast for outdoor sports. She loved horse riding, hunting and playing tennis.

Mary's tutors, Claude Millot, Antoine Fouquelin and Jacques Amyot, the last a classicist, also employed to teach the dauphin more advanced Latin, were carefully chosen to give her the best possible education. The training she received was impeccable so far as it went, but what did it fit her for? Despite the fact that she kept up her Scots and some evidence that at least as early as 1552 she was being kept informed about Scottish affairs by her mother, presumably so that she would not be completely cut off from an understanding of the governance of the country she ruled at least in name, it is hard to escape the view that Mary was being brought up as a queen consort of France, not as a queen regnant of Scotland. She might have had her own rooms at court, but her destiny had changed when she crossed the sea. One day she and Francis would be king and queen of Scotland and, as a woman, she would defer to him, even if she was the true hereditary occupant of the throne. Her isolation from Scotland and all things Scottish began early, when her Scottish male attendants, thought by the refined courtiers of France to be lacking social skills and even basic cleanliness, were sent back home. Lady Fleming clung on until her pregnancy became an embarrassment and she, too, returned. The Four Marys were packed off elsewhere to be educated separately, though they still saw the queen from time to time and figured among her servants in her household accounts. This left Mary with a new governess, Françoise d'Estamville, dame de Parois, an elderly lady of unimpeachable virtue but a rigid and unloving woman who did not get on with her high-spirited and proud charge. This lady's subsequent vindictive backbiting demonstrated to Mary early on that the French court was not a carefree place. Trust must be given carefully and spying was rife. It was better, in this atmosphere where superficial politeness and exquisite manners often hid much darker intentions, not to give too much of yourself away.

Mary's relationships with the French royal children were, nevertheless, positive and affectionate. She was fond of the king's daughters and initially shared a bedroom with Princess Élisabeth. The dauphin Francis, a year younger than Mary, had been taught to pay her small attentions as soon as she arrived in France. They were to grow up together, working towards the bond of matrimony that would unite their crowns. Such closeness was unusual for sixteenth-century monarchs, many of whom did not meet their spouses until just before the wedding. But though there seems to have been a genuine warmth and concern for each other as the two children grew, this does not mean that it would have translated into deep love in adulthood. They were two very different people. Mary grew tall, regal and confident. Francis, though intelligent, was a stunted stammerer who was never really well. Their relationship, not surprisingly, seems to have been more like that of brother and sister, even by the time they married. Both were content to do their duty – the course of their young lives had been shaped around this concept – and romantic love, if it ever came, would be a bonus. And though Mary may have looked more robust than her baby-faced intended, her own health was far from certain. Especially from her early teens onwards, she was often ill. There were unexplained fevers, fainting fits and ongoing digestive problems. These latter, in particular, would bedevil Mary throughout her adult life and bring her apparently close to death on more than one occasion. Opinion is still divided as to the causes of Mary's frequent bouts of ill health, but stress undoubtedly played its part in some of these episodes. A gastric ulcer is probably a more likely explanation for her eating disorder than acute intermittent porphyria, a rare hereditary disease affecting the blood, even though this diagnosis is favoured by one of her more recent biographers.[4]

The high point of Mary's early childhood in France, however, came in 1550–51, when she was reunited with her mother, Mary of Guise, during a long and momentous visit by the queen dowager of Scotland. There were several reasons why James V's widow wished to visit France at this time. Of course, the desire to see her daughter again, and also her son, the duke of Longueville, from whom she had parted so sadly eleven years before, weighed heavily on Mary of Guise. But there were political motives beyond these natural desires to spend time with her children again. Her influence in Scotland had ebbed and flowed in the years since the death of James V, but she had maintained and even improved her position. Arran had not succeeded in negating her influence and she was still determined to oust him if she could. The assistance and support of Henry II in achieving this aim was vital. Now that her daughter was safe across the water and successfully established in France, she believed the time was right to make the journey home.

She arrived in September 1550 with an impressive retinue of

Scottish nobility. Always keenly aware of the benefits of distrib-
uting patronage effectively, the dowager queen did not want to
lose this chance of making further allies and tying Scotland ever
more tightly to France. The senior nobles accompanying her
were the earl of Huntly, ready to offer his services to anyone for
a price, and the earl of Cassilis. Mary of Guise was probably
reunited with her daughter on 25 September 1550 at Rouen
and as the child had recently recovered from a bout of illness it
must have been an especially happy occasion. The grandest of
festivities was to follow this personal triumph, for Henry II,
determined to display his successes as protector of Scotland and
recoverer of Boulogne, planned an official entry into the major
city of Normandy that would leave no one in doubt of the
imperial nature of his aims. This very public projection of his
image was intended to challenge that of the Emperor Charles V.
After a series of parades featuring the great and the good of the
town, a series of impressive tableaux entertained and awed the
crowd. But nothing was more inspiring than the representation
of the king himself. A chariot carried a lifelike effigy of the king,
wearing a splendid suit of armour 'surrounded by palm leaves,
his head wreathed like a Roman victor's. Seated at his feet were
his four children, Francis, Elisabeth, Claude and two-year-old
Louis.'5 No opportunity was lost to emphasize the future role of
the dauphin as King of Scots when he married Mary. Scotland
was accorded a significant place in the pageant and the associated
celebrations, but only because its already crowned queen was
going to marry the heir to the French throne. Mary Queen of
Scots and her mother watched the processions from a gilded
pavilion but the Scottish queen was given no formal role in the
festivities. She would be an appendage, not a major actor. It is
hard to believe that the two queens regnant of England, Mary
and Elizabeth, her contemporaries, would have accepted such a
role with equanimity.

Mary of Guise and her daughter took no direct part in these
festivities but the dowager made sure that her long visit would
bear fruit. At some point, perhaps at Blois in February 1551, she

apparently persuaded Henry II that, if he wanted her to return to Scotland, then she would only agree to do so with the full powers of the regency. Arran must go if she was to stay. The Scottish nobility who formed part of her train, even the former 'assured lords' who had promised much and delivered little to Henry VIII, seem to have accepted this outcome. Their acquiescence may, in part, be explained by the generous financial inducements Henry II was offering.

Although Mary of Guise stayed in France for more than a year, her visit did not always go well. In April 1551 a plot to assassinate the Queen of Scots was uncovered. Improbable as it sounds, one of the Scots who had attacked St Andrews Castle and been imprisoned in France had found his way into the king's Scottish Guard and was planning to seek revenge by poisoning the young queen, blackmailing her cook into spiking her favourite dessert, frittered pears. The plot was foiled but left Mary of Guise understandably nervous for her daughter's safety. Worse was to follow for the dowager, however. On her way back to the French coast her son, who was travelling with her, fell mortally ill. He died in her arms, the fourth son she had lost and perhaps the most distressing of all. Even when she finally set foot on Scottish soil again, she still had to wait more than two years before Arran was finally removed from the regency. Her daughter's official coming of age provided the occasion. On 19 February 1554, after eleven years of warfare, plots and recriminations, Arran finally agreed to go. Mary of Guise had been greatly helped in the achievement of this aim by Henry II's lieutenant governor and ambassador in Scotland, Henri Cleutin, Sieur d'Oisel, who had supported her and challenged Arran for a number of years.

Arran did not go easily and he negotiated safeguards for himself and his reputation that show that the man often represented as a ditherer was very difficult to remove. D'Oisel reported back to Henry II: 'with the help of God, this Princess's leadership and also the fact that the said Governor has seen and knows all the Lords of this kingdom, both spiritual and temporal, who accompany us here and remain firm and steadfast, we have finally won the victory to the great regret of the said Governor.' Arran's regret was both personal and patriotic. He must have known, in the two days of fierce bargaining in which he gave up the role he considered as his birthright, that the French would now rule in Scotland. For, dynast and diehard supporter of her daughter as she was, Mary of Guise was also, in reality, an agent of France.

⁂

THE NEW QUEEN REGENT took up her post after a summer of high drama in her southern neighbour, England. Its outcome would have a palpable effect on both Scotland and France. For in the winter of 1553 Edward VI, the fifteen-year-old monarch who had been carefully prepared to assume the full mantle of government by the duke of Northumberland, fell ill. At first, it seemed nothing more than the sort of heavy winter cold that still afflicts many people at that time of the year. Apart from the normal childhood ailments, Edward had been an active boy who enjoyed sports. He was by no means the sickly swot of popular historical fiction. Whether he had an underlying tubercular condition of the sort that seems to have run in the males of the Tudor family we shall never know but there had been nothing that had caused serious alarm. Yet as the spring arrived it was evident that the king was not recovering as he should. A bacterial infection seems to have slowly but remorselessly overwhelmed him. By early June it was obvious even to the boy himself that his illness was mortal. This raised the pressing and difficult question of who should succeed him.

The immediate heir, according to Henry VIII's Act of Succession of 1544, was his much older half-sister, Mary, followed by his father's younger daughter, Elizabeth, the child of Anne Boleyn. But though Edward had been close to Mary during his childhood they had grown apart during his reign. Mary stayed steadfast to the Catholic religion while Edward, educated by religious reformers and encouraged by his bishops and advisers, was, by this time, a convinced, even zealous,

Protestant. The thought of Mary ascending to the throne of England and undoing all the ecclesiastical changes that he had enthusiastically supported distressed the dying youth. It also disturbed Northumberland and the king's councillors, who saw their influence waning rapidly if Mary should become queen. There was, however, another way out of this succession dilemma. Edward had earlier pondered on the question of who might succeed him in a schoolroom exercise. He decided that the best way forward was to remove both his sisters from the succession altogether (on the grounds that they were still declared illegitimate) and substitute his Protestant cousin, Lady Jane Grey, the great-niece of Henry VIII and granddaughter of Princess Mary Tudor, younger sister of Queen Margaret of Scotland. One can only imagine Margaret's fury had she still been alive.

This was a bold move but there were doubts about its legality, as some members of the judiciary in England had the temerity to point out. But Edward refused to listen to their arguments and was supported by Northumberland – unsurprisingly, since Lady Jane Grey had conveniently become his daughter-in-law a matter of weeks earlier. When Edward died on 6 July at Greenwich, Lady Jane was proclaimed queen and brought by river to the Tower of London, at first her palace but later her prison. Mary had fled to East Anglia, a conservative, largely Catholic area where she was a major landowner. Elizabeth, whose reaction to the crisis remains opaque, stayed put at Hatfield House in Hertfordshire, perhaps wondering why her extravagant overtures of devotion to her brother had not borne fruit.

After nearly two weeks of uncertainty and the threat of civil war, Mary Tudor, a woman of thirty-seven who had survived psychological and emotional torment following the divorce of her parents, Henry VIII and Katherine of Aragon, as well as political marginalization for much of her adult life, acquired sufficient support in the east of England and the Thames Valley to drive a wedge through the increasingly divided Privy Council in London. Northumberland had left the capital with a substantial force but it never saw military action. Ever the pragmatist, he knew he had lost. Even a last-minute rediscovery of his Catholic roots could not save his life and he was beheaded at the end of August 1553, one of the few immediate victims of the Succession Crisis, as it has come to be known.

The Scottish reaction to these unfolding events in England has largely escaped attention but there was certainly an impact on Scottish politics and not merely because Mary of Guise was yet to achieve the removal of Arran as regent. Once more the Lennox family entered the frame. Matthew and especially Margaret had been quiet but determined opponents of Edward VI's religious changes; their house at Temple Newsam outside Leeds was a gathering place for northern Catholics and, in a region that had not forgotten the Pilgrimage of Grace against Henry VIII's religious changes in 1536 nor forgiven the dissolution of the monasteries, this gave the Lennoxes considerable influence. They had been careful, however, not to offend or contradict Edward VI as publicly as his sister Mary had done and when their second surviving son, the future Henry, Lord Darnley was born, Margaret felt it prudent to put in an appearance at court with her baby, who had deliberately been given Tudor rather than Scottish names.

Margaret Douglas was a childhood friend of the new queen and in 1553 the Lennox stock rose dramatically in England. They were showered with gifts at Mary's coronation – the best horse from Edward VI's stable and some of the late king's clothes for young Darnley. Apartments were found for them in White-hall Palace and they were generously provided with tapestries, expensive furnishings, clothing and jewels (a gold belt set with diamonds and rubies for Margaret) as well as having their household's expenses in London paid for by the Crown and a grant of 3,000 marks a year from wool trade taxes. And if all of this did not make the Lennoxes think their time might have finally arrived, the queen's increasing coolness towards her half-sister, Elizabeth, was interpreted by the imperial ambassador, at least, as a sign that Margaret would take precedence at court and might even be regarded as Queen Mary's heir. Yet though Mary was clearly delighted to be able to favour her cousin, there is no evidence that she ever contemplated such a move.

With so many reasons to be hopeful and Mary of Guise looking for support, the earl of Lennox found that, once again, he might be considered as a player in Scotland, despite his defection to Henry VIII a decade earlier. Mary of Guise wrote to him (the letter has not survived) asking for his support against Arran. In return, she offered to restore his lands in Scotland. Mary Tudor and her council decided to support the earl, but only on condition that he double-crossed Mary of Guise. Thwarting the French dowager would also strike a blow against France, a policy favoured by the queen of England, who was half-Spanish and a natural ally of the Habsburgs, not the French. So the earl of Lennox was encouraged to 'secretly enter into communication with the Regent [Arran] against the Dowager, with a view not only to driving her from the country, but to making himself King if possible and throwing Scottish affairs into confusion. If he is able to do this, the Queen will help him with money to the best of her ability.'[6]

This scheme, which sounds somewhat fanciful, might well have foundered on the deep-seated animosity between the Hamiltons and the Lennox Stewarts, even if the increasingly desperate Arran could have been induced to see the earl of Lennox as a temporary solution to his own difficulties. It does, though, indicate how importantly Matthew Stewart's claim to the Scottish throne was viewed in England. In fact, nothing came of it but this did not quell the earl of Lennox's ambition. For much of the 1550s he continued to intrigue and plot, hoping to restore his Scottish fortunes. But his time had not yet come.

The French, meanwhile, followed Mary Tudor's accession and pro-Habsburg policy with alarm. Their fears seemed fully realized when, after prolonged and detailed treaty negotiations, she was married to Philip of Spain, son of the Emperor Charles V, in the summer of 1554. Mary was no warmonger but she felt an overwhelming sense of gratitude to her cousin Charles, despite the fact that during the reigns of her father and brother he had done nothing besides giving verbal support and sending a boat to allow her to escape from England if she wanted. Mary, showing true Tudor spirit, had stayed but it was no thanks to Charles V that she triumphed over Lady Jane Grey in 1553, since he never lifted a finger to help her. Nevertheless, she regarded him as a father figure and she fell deeply in love with his son, who may have been a prince of Spain but was a true Burgundian in his features and colouring. If her Habsburg husband and the emperor, her cousin, wanted to involve England in a war with France, Mary would not oppose them. Indeed, her council and the majority of her nobles, eager for gain and glory in France, were in full support. In 1557, when English forces crossed the Channel for France once again, the French suffered their most humiliating defeat of the sixteenth century at the battle of St Quentin. Revenge was not long in coming. In the unpromising dead of winter, a time not normally regarded as suitable for a military campaign, Henry II inflicted a blow on English pride fully commensurate with that he had suffered himself months earlier. Crossing the frozen marshland that surrounded Calais, the French won back this poorly armed and defended fortress, finally ending an English presence in France that had once been a substantial empire.

It was not just Mary's foreign policy that affected Scotland, however. Her determination, one might almost call it a crusade, to restore the Catholic faith and quell religious opposition led to an exodus of Protestants from England. Many went to Switzerland or Germany, where they joined forces with Scottish religious exiles, creating, for the first time, a 'British' Protestant identity. This was, though, a gradual outcome. An English congregation in Frankfurt asked John Knox, increasingly radicalized by contacts with Heinrich Bullinger and John Calvin, to be their minister but he was such a divisive figure that he lasted only a year. His assault on the *Book of Common Prayer* enraged his flock but he had already fallen out with the regime of Edward VI before the young king's death. Cranmer and Northumberland found him too curmudgeonly for their liking but he remained as one of the king's chaplains and even when Mary came to the throne, he bided his time in the north. He did not leave England until the beginning of 1554. Returning to Scotland in 1555, he found a country where religious opposition to the established Catholic faith was growing but was not yet ready to challenge the status quo seriously.

There continued to be tensions along the Anglo–Scottish border and the French tried to stir up trouble amongst Mary Tudor's subjects in Ireland. It seemed that very little in the centuries-old struggle between the two British kingdoms had altered. The only thing that Mary of Guise and Mary Tudor had in common was their first name and the Catholic religion and even here there were important differences in how they approached the spread of heresy. In all other respects, they were natural rivals. Mary of Guise may not have been born a Stewart but she was committed to ensuring that the Stewart dynasty survived and, in her regency, to assuming the powers and persona of a Stewart monarch herself. She believed she owed her daughter no less.

∽

MARY OF GUISE had waited more than eleven years since the death of her husband to assume a regency that she had always believed was rightly hers. But the triumph was very much that of France as well, and lest the Scots who attended Mary's investiture as regent should be in any doubt of where power lay, it was d'Oisel, the French ambassador, who placed the crown of Scotland on her head and gave her the sword of state and sceptre to hold. At this highly symbolic moment, the Scottish nobles who had chosen French influence over capitulation to the English could not have been left in any doubt of the implications of their decision. Franco-Scotland was a reality and Mary of Guise its embodiment. The country's actual monarch, a twelve-year-old girl being brought up as a French queen consort, was irrelevant to these proceedings.

The new regent intended to display her power and keep a court that would underline her prestige. While her household expenses were not exorbitant, being roughly equivalent to those that she had incurred as a queen consort, her public image was important. She left her mark on the Scottish coinage by incorporating the cross of Lorraine, a Guise symbol, on coins that were issued before her daughter's marriage to the dauphin.

Aided by d'Oisel as her newly appointed lieutenant governor, Yves du Rubay as French vice chancellor and Bartholomew de Villemore as her comptroller, with responsibility for financial management, Mary of Guise set about imposing her own French-influenced style of government and justice on Scotland. Though many of the Scottish clerics and lords who served on Arran's Privy Council remained in office, the assumption of key positions, including the possession of the Great Seal of Scotland by du Rubay, was always going to be a possible source of friction with all but the most Francophile of Scottish magnates. And what Mary of Guise overlooked, or perhaps discounted while she could call upon the financial and military support of France, was that resentment could lead to more serious disaffection. The country's foreign policy was already dictated by Henry II but in domestic matters the regent had somewhat more leeway. Though she was aware of the need to tread carefully with the Scottish nobility, she was quite capable of challenging them in pursuit of her aims. One of the major reasons for this was Mary of Guise's view that government and justice in Scotland needed to be more centralized. Undercutting the authority of the Scottish nobility in their local power bases was always going to be a difficult course of action and one where immediate gains might have much more dubious long-term implications. A particular case in point was the regent's attempt to bring to heel the earl of Huntly, her late husband's childhood friend and a man who was not known as the 'Cock o' the North' for nothing.

The earl had been a supporter of the regent at various times in her decade-long struggle with Arran, but he began to abuse his position and the rewards she gave him in a manner that put enhancement of his local position above the authority of the Crown. Determined to gain control of the whole of Moray in north-eastern Scotland, Huntly's high-handed behaviour in dispensing summary justice to local clan leaders and his abject failure to follow this up militarily were too embarrassing to be ignored. The lady who believed that it was her duty as a de facto Stewart monarch to dispense justice herself came in person to Huntly's region and made her point by holding justice assizes in all the major towns in 1556. Initially, Mary of Guise imprisoned Huntly in Edinburgh Castle but having extracted a large fine and sent him packing to the Borders, Mary felt sufficiently confident to restore him slowly to favour. What she privately thought of his magnificent palace at Strathbogie, or the equally splendid castle at Balvenie owned by the earl of Atholl, Huntly's son-in-law, we do not know, but her visits to both these properties must have brought home to her the power and pretensions of Scotland's leading families. She was not cowed, however, for she had earlier set out her commitment to making a difference in the administration of Scottish justice in a letter to her brother, the cardinal of Lorraine: 'my determination [is] to see justice take a straightforward course, and they that find me a little severe, they will not endure it, and say that these are the laws of the French, and that their old laws are good, which for the most part are the greatest injustices in the world, not in themselves, but from the way they are administered.'[7]

Clear in her aims as Mary of Guise undoubtedly was, she could not always achieve them. Money was a particular problem and one that brought her into conflict with parliament. The regent was perfectly willing to work with Scottish institutions but in her efforts to get parliament to approve a new tax regime she was unsuccessful. A tax proposed on goods and wealth rather than valuation of lands seemed to be the precursor of annual tax demands by the Crown. Feeling threatened, the lesser Scottish nobility turned out in force for the parliamentary session of 1556 and voted down the new proposals. Mary of Guise believed the extra money was needed if England invaded yet again as a result of the deteriorating relations between France and Mary Tudor's England. This did not happen, but the regent had lost a major battle.

It was not the only cause of alarm for her regime as the 1550s progressed, for religious opposition was also becoming more pervasive, though the full force of Protestant dissent was yet to be realized. There were attempts at reform in the Scottish Catholic Church, but vested interests remained strong and there was a fundamental belief that laymen should not be included in any considerations of change. This was completely at odds with the beliefs of evangelical reformers, radicalized by their direct involvement in matters of organization and the development of doctrine. A new social class was growing in Scotland, made up of lesser nobility and tenants of Church lands who had prospered from the practice of 'feuing', whereby Church property increasingly ended up in the hands of laymen in return for a yearly rent, or by the direct transfer of Church lands to private ownership. Articulate, comfortably off and frequently attracted to new religious ideas, many of these Scots formed their own small 'privy kirks' where visiting ministers, such as John Knox, administered the sacraments. But Knox would not stay quiet for long and it was from men like him that the steadily increasing band of Scottish Protestants heard preaching that told them that the Mass was idolatrous. Many of his listeners hedged their bets, not yet ready to make a clean public break. Disgusted, Knox went back to Geneva in 1556. But his time, and that of the growing number of Scots who shared his ideas, was growing ever closer.

✌

IN 1557, as warfare broke out between England and France, the relationship between France and Scotland became more strained. Mary of Guise tried to do Henry II's bidding by sending an army to invade England. Undermanned and acutely mindful of past failures under such circumstances, the Scots went reluctantly to the Borders where they eventually argued with their French commanders and chose to return home instead of fighting. The regent had demonstrated her loyalty to the king of France by accompanying the abortive expedition in person and this was her second humiliation at the hands of the Scots in a few months, as parliament had earlier taken her to task for the continued delay in the marriage of Mary Queen of Scots to the dauphin. This had been a recurring theme since one of the young queen's more serious bouts of illness two years previously. At that time Mary of Guise sent her brother Charles a letter which reveals the full extent of her frustrations, as well as her accurate assessment of the problems with which she was confronted. In its heartfelt description of the difficulties faced by any regent, but especially a woman, it is reminiscent of a similar missive written in the 1550s by the regent of the Netherlands, Mary of Hungary, to her own brother, the Emperor Charles V. Scotland's politicians had told her, Mary of Guise reported:

> that it would be putting the cart before the oxen and deceiving myself if I thought of settling anything before the marriage is accomplished . . . Moreover, my daughter's illness has put many things in doubt, and, to keep nothing back from you, men's minds have been so changeable and in such a state of suspense that those from whom I hoped the most I have found more estranged than I have ever seen them, not just since I have ruled them but since I came to Scotland . . . God knows, brother, what a life I lead. It is no small thing to bring a young nation to a state of perfection and to an unwonted subservience to those who wish to see justice reign. Great responsibilities are easily undertaken but not so easily discharged to the satisfaction of God. Happy is he who has least to do with worldly affairs. I can safely say that in twenty years past I have not had one year of rest and I think that if I were to say not one month I should not be far wrong, for a troubled spirit is the greatest trial of all.[8]

By the spring of 1558, however, and despite signs of growing unrest in Scotland, the queen regent's troubled spirit was temporarily lifted when her daughter's marriage to the dauphin

Francis was finally celebrated. In fact, it is hard to see how it could have come about much sooner, since Francis was only fourteen and his bride a year older. The timing of the marriage followed the huge propaganda victory of the French over the English when they retook Calais and was, at least in part, intended to keep the pressure on the regime of Mary Tudor by publicly reinforcing the ambition of Henry II to unite the Crowns of France and Scotland. It was also a recognition of Mary of Guise's loyalty to the French king and a demonstration to wavering supporters of the French alliance in Scotland that Henry would keep his word.

The ceremony took place at the cathedral of Notre Dame in Paris on 24 April 1558. It was a Sunday and the citizens of Paris flocked to see the spectacle, as was intended. Henry II would not have wasted the opportunity to display Valois power and prestige and his mastery of the public event was very much in evidence at the wedding of the Scottish queen destined to be the wife of his eldest son. A covered walkway had been erected to frame the bridal procession as it made its way from the palace of the archbishop of Paris to the main entrance of the cathedral itself, where a raised stage across the west front allowed onlookers a better view of the leading participants in this wedding that was intended to unite two kingdoms forever. No doubt the Scottish lords present would have taken great pride in their queen when she appeared, flanked by her future father-in-law and her cousin, the duke of Lorraine.

Mary was tall for her age and already a fine-looking woman. She had deliberately broken with tradition and chosen a white wedding dress, presumably because she thought it showed off her colouring better and would also attract attention. White was normally the colour of mourning in France and the widows of French kings were supposed to wear it for months after their spouse's demise, so Mary made an emphatic break with tradition when she chose it for her wedding day. Those who saw portents in such choices might have felt a frisson of concern for this confident beauty who flaunted the traditions of French royalty so alluringly but Mary does not seem to have been subject to such doubts. The dress itself was made of white satin and it glittered with diamonds and jewelled embroidery. Over it she wore a mantle of blue velvet embroidered with white silk and pearls, tapering into a long train that was carried by two maids of honour.

The jewels worn by Mary were equally impressive. She had a splendid pendant around her neck, engraved with Henry II's initials. She called it 'Great Harry' and eventually placed it among the Scottish Crown jewels. Her hair hung loose down her back, as was customary with brides in those days, and on her head was a magnificent gold crown studded with gems – rubies, diamonds, sapphires, emeralds and pearls – all gleaming in the bright light of a Parisian spring day.

The marriage ceremony was performed by Charles Bourbon, the cardinal archbishop of Rouen, and the wedding ring was taken by the king of France off his own finger and handed to his son to be placed on Mary's. This could be seen as a gesture of affection or a further indication of his complete ownership of the Scottish queen herself. A nuptial Mass followed as Francis and his wife sat on thrones beneath a canopy of cloth of gold.

Mary had upstaged her husband by making herself the centre of attention, perhaps the first time in the sixteenth century that the bride, rather than the groom, took all the attention at a royal wedding. Back in 1503 Mary's grandmother, Margaret Tudor, could only have wished for such admiration. The dauphin, however, seems to have taken his bride's stealing of the limelight in good part. Perhaps he was getting used to it by then and he was certainly no heroic figure himself. Physically, he and Mary were a totally mismatched pair. Mary's letter to her mother claiming that it was the happiest day of her life shows, if she genuinely meant what she said, that dynasticism was her driving motive in life. She had, no doubt, learnt this from those all around her. In truth, Mary was marrying a sickly runt. The prince looked younger than fourteen and was reported to be sexually immature; it was said that his testicles had not dropped.

Despite this, there were reports that the union had been consummated but there would scarcely have been any publicity if the opposite were, in fact, the case. Francis appears to have been genuinely fond of the glittering girl who looked at least twenty sitting beside him in Notre Dame and he knew his duty. The marriage would give him the crown matrimonial of Scotland and the impressive if clumsy title of King-Dauphin while his wife became Queen-Dauphiness. Presumably he also knew, as the Scottish nobility watching did not, that his father had made sure that Scotland would remain subject to French rule even if Mary were to die childless. His wife could have her moment in the sun but the Valois family would be winners in the end.

The Scottish commissioners sent to negotiate the marriage treaty between Francis and Mary were headed by her half-brother, Lord James Stewart. Recently converted to Protestantism and always mindful of the fact that he could have been king if his mother had been allowed to marry James V, Lord James did not know that he and his colleagues had been deceived. He believed there were sufficient safeguards in the official agreements. Mary had promised to uphold Scottish laws and liberties and stated that, if she died without issue, the throne would go to the Scottish heir presumptive.[9] The eldest son of Francis and Mary would become king of France and Scotland but if there were only daughters, then the eldest would inherit just the Scottish throne, since women could not rule in France.

This all seemed broadly satisfactory from a Scottish perspective, though there must have been some unease among the Scots whose Protestantism made them wary of Henry II's attitude towards heresy in his own country. The Wars of Religion had not yet begun in France but opinions on both sides of the religious divide were polarizing. Nevertheless, agreements were signed and the marriage of Mary and Francis duly proceeded. But on 4 April, less than three weeks before she took Paris and foreign observers by storm on her wedding day, Mary Stewart had signed away her kingdom to France. She endorsed three secret documents: one stating that if she died without heirs

Scotland would revert to Henry II and his descendants; the second guaranteeing the king of France one million crowns from Scottish revenues to pay for defence against England and her own continuing education; and the third nullifying all future demands of the Scottish parliament that might prejudice these concessions.

The French had every reason to be pleased with the virtual acquisition of Scotland and the celebrations of the marriage of the dauphin Francis and Mary Queen of Scots continued with largesse to the Parisian citizenry and much feasting and ostentatious efforts to impress visiting diplomats. Giovanni Michieli, the Venetian ambassador, wrote:

> These nuptials were really considered the most regal and triumphant of any that have been witnessed in this kingdom for many years, whether from the concourse of the chief personages of the realm ... and all the other ambassadors, or from the pomp and richness of the jewels and apparel both of the lords and ladies; or from the grandeur of the banquet and stately service of the table, or from the costly devices of the masquerades and similar revels. In short, nothing whatever that could possibly be desired was wanting for the embellishment of such a spectacle, except jousts and tournaments, which were reserved for a more convenient opportunity.[10]

Mary's capitulation to Henry II in respect of her kingdom has been excused in various ways: her naïve and trusting nature; her lack of experience in dealing with the complex wording of constitutional documents; her upbringing and education in France. It is tempting to ask what more could have been expected of a fifteen-year-old probably more preoccupied by her wedding dress than the fate of a country that she hardly knew, even though she was its monarch. But there are problems here. One of Mary's recent biographers claims that she had been educated in France to think for herself.[11] If that is really so, then her self-image, and the esteem in which she held her own country, were those of complete subservience. Women were inferior, even queens regnant; Scotland was no more than a satellite of France, convenient only for keeping England at bay; and Mary Stewart, covered in jewels and white satin, was just a pretty bauble. She, no doubt, saw her wedding day as an unqualified success. The woman who, seven months later, became queen of England, would have been horrified at such a loss of independence.

MARY TUDOR DIED on 17 November 1558 at St James's Palace in London, surrounded by devoted household servants and by no means as hated by the populace as her detractors over the centuries have claimed. The husband she loved, Philip II, now king of Spain and the Netherlands, was across the North Sea in Brussels, too preoccupied by the demands of government to mourn greatly the wife he had married out of duty. Though she had not been in good health since adolescence, Mary appears to have been a victim of a widespread and deadly virus that caused havoc in northern Europe in 1557–8. It had been so severe in England that members of parliament and even the Church hierarchy were badly hit by it, dying in such numbers that it was, for a while, difficult for the country's major institutions to function properly. The contagion certainly spread across the English Channel, because Sir William Pickering, on a diplomatic mission to France, was stricken with it at Dunkirk shortly before the death of his queen and was so ill that he did not return home for many months. In Paris, however, the royal family escaped unscathed.

Also unaffected was the young woman of twenty-five who now became queen of England. Elizabeth Tudor was nine years older than her 'sister queen' of Scots and her upbringing and experiences could hardly have been more different. For, unlike her distant cousin, Elizabeth's path to the throne was full of danger and uncertainty and it was only when Edward VI died so young that there was any real prospect that she might, one day, become queen. Although Mary Tudor had nominated her sister as her successor ten days before she died, Elizabeth was still officially the bastard daughter of a king, despite having been given a place in the succession in 1544. Anne Boleyn's child was briefly a princess, from the time she was born in September 1533 to her mother's execution for adultery in May 1536. During those scant three years she was Henry VIII's heir but for all the childhood she could remember she was merely the Lady Elizabeth.

Considerable amounts of that childhood were spent sharing accommodation with her much older sister, Mary (who, despite her fearsome historical reputation, was very fond of her little sister and indulged her with presents and clothes), and sometimes with Prince Edward. The belated arrival of a male heir in 1537 relieved Henry VIII of the embarrassment of having divorced one wife and beheaded another only to find himself the parent of two illegitimate females. Though Henry's tally of illegitimate offspring could not come close to the totals amassed by James IV and James V in Scotland, at least the Stewart kings had made a greater success of royal matrimony itself. The security in Elizabeth Tudor's young life came from her household staff and her education. In that respect, her experience was at least as good, and probably better, than that of Mary Queen of Scots. Elizabeth benefitted from the flowering of English classical scholarship in the first half of the sixteenth century, first encouraged by humanism and later by the growth of new religious ideas. Her education, sometimes shared with her brother, certainly fitted her for queenship, even if she lacked the formal training for such a role. She was intelligent, diligent and rather serious as a little girl. But she was seldom at court and saw little of her father while he made his way through four more wives after her mother's disgrace and death. There was no maternal figure in her life before Henry married Katherine Parr in 1543 and the young Elizabeth became very fond of her stepmother, as were Henry's other two children. In observing Katherine Parr as regent and queen consort, Elizabeth learned a good deal about how women could think for themselves and govern. She greatly admired her stepmother's literary output and clearly discussed religious ideas with her when they met, which was not nearly often enough for Elizabeth's liking.

She was not at court, however, when Katherine's marriage ran into difficulties in the summer of 1546, partly because of the queen's enthusiasm for religious change and her success as a published author, both of which riled the ailing Henry VIII. What Elizabeth knew about this episode is hard to say, though she may well have heard about it afterwards. When her own ordeal came, just a few years later, she, too, found it necessary to live on her wits. The difference was that Katherine Parr, for all the immediate danger she might have been in, still had a strong hold on the old king's affections and was not without supporters. Elizabeth was fifteen and friendless when the first great crisis of her life occurred.

Mary Stewart, as a fifteen-year-old, had known nothing but privilege and respect. She had lived a gilded life. Secure in France, she was a crowned and anointed queen in one country and would one day become the French queen consort. Although she had long been viewed as something of an exotic curiosity from a barbarous land, at least by some elements of the French aristocracy, once married to the dauphin no one could cast aspersions on her anymore. She had all the status, the riches and the attention that she could want. What she lacked was any experience of adversity. Her English cousin, however, learned at the same age just how dangerous proximity to the throne could be, even for someone whose prospects of ever ruling seemed remote.

In 1549, Elizabeth was embroiled in the disaster that over-took Queen Katherine Parr's fourth and last husband, Lord Thomas Seymour of Sudeley, brother of Edward VI's Lord Protector, the duke of Somerset, and uncle to the king. Katherine Parr died shortly after giving birth to her only child, a daughter, in September 1548, and her volatile and unwise widower, whose flirtation with Elizabeth when she lived with Katherine had eventually forced the queen dowager to send the girl away,

considered trying for Elizabeth's hand in marriage. As he was also
involved in a number of shady business deals and was attempting
to build a power base to challenge his brother, Elizabeth's association with him brought her into great danger when Seymour
was arrested and accused of high treason for an apparent attempt
to kidnap the king.

Although the accusations were basically far-fetched, Seymour
was the archetypal loose cannon. He had long charmed the ladies
but he now found himself friendless and attainted without trial.
In the scramble to convict him, those who had been close to him
were themselves in peril, and none more so than Elizabeth and
the dithering and gutless members of her household whom she
loved unreservedly but who were more concerned with saving
their own skins than hers. Deprived of her lady governess and
subjected to days of pointed and remorseless interrogation about
her relationship with Seymour and whether she had agreed to
marry him (a treasonable offence where one so close to the
throne was concerned), Elizabeth at times broke down, but
never gave in. Eventually, through sheer strength of character
and an uncanny ability to defend herself, she turned the tables
on her accusers and wrote furious letters about the attacks on her
reputation – the 'shameful slanders', as she called them, which
suggested that she was pregnant by Seymour. He was executed
in March 1549, but Elizabeth survived. It was an experience she
never forgot.

In her sister's reign, when their once affectionate relationship
was shattered by Mary's suspicions of her sister's loyalty (some of
which were not entirely unfounded) and the inescapable reality
that, as 'second person' in the realm, Elizabeth, younger, more
attractive, clever and resourceful, had become the focus for
opposition and discontent. Always protesting her innocence,
never using one word of justification when twenty would do,
Elizabeth's prolix and evasive answers to Mary's accusations
infuriated England's first queen so much that the gulf between
the sisters could not be bridged. Elizabeth spent a couple of
months in the Tower of London as a prisoner, a stay that has

been hugely romanticized by historians over the years but was, in fact, an honourable and comfortable confinement. Much of the rest of Mary's brief five-year reign Elizabeth spent under some form of house arrest, though restrictions were progressively eased, and for the last months of Mary's life her sister kept what was essentially an alternative court at Hatfield Palace in Hertfordshire as she calmly waited for Mary to die. In November 1558, that moment came.

But though the transition was smooth, the situation in which the new queen found herself was daunting. England was bankrupt, the huge cost of the war with France having undone all the improvements that Mary had tried to put in place through better accounting and financial management. Elizabeth Tudor had to be much more frugal with her coronation robes than Mary Stewart was with her wedding dress. When she was crowned in January 1559, the new queen wore her late sister's coronation outfit, altered to fit her and with some embellishments. Her country was afflicted by a serious epidemic that had affected many of its more powerful and experienced churchmen and policy makers. Poor harvests and bad weather in the later 1550s merely added to the hardship. National pride had been severely dented by the loss of Calais, even though its upkeep was expensive and it acted as a magnate for dissidents.

Elizabeth's England in the winter of 1559 was not a joyful place, whatever hopes might have been aroused by the succession of its lively and personable new monarch. This was a country that had seen religious changes follow one another convulsively as the Reformation unleashed by Henry VIII was hurried forward by his son, only to be halted in its tracks by Mary's return to the old faith and to Rome. What the average Englishman thought of all this is a question that has never been satisfactorily answered, but it is a fair bet that many were simply bemused. Elizabeth's religious views were unclear. It was believed that, because she had been educated by reformers, she was likely to favour Protestantism, though she had been a practising, if not enthusiastic, Catholic during her sister's reign. Protestant exiles who had fled England for Europe were eager to return but Elizabeth needed to tread carefully. One thing, however, seemed evident. She would not completely dismantle her sister's Catholic rites until she was sure that she had a majority of support among the bishops and in parliament. But there was no question of remaining under the rule of Rome. Elizabeth fully believed, as her father had done, that she was Head of the Church in England. Eventually, the Act of Uniformity of 1559, which laid out the Elizabethan religious settlement, was passed by the slimmest of margins. It established Protestantism as the state religion and effectively, though perhaps not intentionally, consigned England's Catholic population to centuries of discrimination. For her day, however, when the principled arguments for toleration were seldom heard, Elizabeth was a surprisingly moderate ruler in religious matters in these early years of her reign.

Her accession was viewed with some passing interest by Anglophile and Protestant Scots north of the border and a few tentative links were opened, notably with the ever-flexible Châtelherault, but there was little firm encouragement given that Scotland would abandon the Auld Alliance, or that England could make much of a practical commitment to help. If there was to be change in Scotland, it would need to come from within the country itself. In France, the latest Tudor lady to occupy the English throne was viewed with disdain. She was not Mary but though she lacked a Spanish husband, the French still saw her as a Habsburg client. Elizabeth had made it clear to the astonished and contemptuous count de Feria, Philip II's representative in England, that she did not regard herself as beholden to Spain, but the reality was somewhat different. There would be no friendly overtures from Henry II. His immediate reaction to the advent of this woman with what he saw as a dubious, not to say, spurious claim to the English throne was to quarter the arms of England alongside those of his son and daughter-in-law, the king and Queen of Scots. This calculated insult did not bode well for Anglo–French relations. But it reminded the world that Mary Queen of Scots, of undisputed legitimate descent from

Henry VII, was a serious claimant to the English throne. Elizabeth's father had, after all, expended much effort to unite her with his son for precisely that reason. As far as Henry of France was concerned, Elizabeth's accession strengthened his hand. 1558 had been, for him, an extremely successful year. He had no inkling of what lay ahead.

❧

THE MARRIAGE OF Mary Stewart did not settle the Scottish kingdom for long. Matters came to a head in the troubled summer of 1559, when outright rebellion ended Mary of Guise's regency and undermined all the gains that Henry II had achieved over a decade of domination of the country. And it was all the more remarkable for being largely unforeseen. 'The revolt of May 1559,' says historian Alec Ryrie, 'seemed to come from a clear sky.' Perhaps it did for the regent, apparently unaware of the growth of resistance to her autocratic French style and the depth of resentment at her withholding of patronage from Scottish lords in favour of her French entourage. Even for the English, as Bishop Aylmer of London dismissively remarked: 'The piddling Scots ... are always French for their lives.' It was a long-held view and the weight of history lay behind it. There was genuine gratitude in Scotland towards France as their centuries-old protector against the English, but there was, by the late 1550s, growing unease at having to support French troops and the superior attitude of their ally, which the French were poor at concealing, that 'this little country is useful and necessary to us.' Not hiding their patronizing attitude that Scotland was like some embarrassingly unkempt little brother that one had patiently to raise to respectable adulthood, the French and Mary of Guise conveniently forgot that Scotland had a claim to nationhood going back as far as 330 BC. And by 1559, if the Scots still did not regard themselves as an occupied colony of France, there were undercurrents of alarm, unfocussed and without any real direction, that this might yet be the eventual outcome. Added to the growth of religious dissent and the Catholic authority that

Mary of Guise represented, the elements for rebellion were certainly there. It was simply that no one had foreseen the swiftness with which, in May 1559, they would coalesce.

The origins of the Wars of the Congregation, as the revolt against Mary of Guise came to be known, are obscure. There are very few contemporary sources and most accounts were written much later and have a heavy Protestant bias, as one would expect from the victors. The most detailed explanation is that of John Knox, but he is unreliable, confusing and completely lacking in objectivity. Furthermore, he did not return to Scotland until the revolt broke out in May, so his knowledge of its background is not first-hand. Even the sequence of events by which Knox was initially invited back to Scotland in 1557 by four influential Scottish lords – the long-time Anglophile earl of Glencairn, Lord Erskine, Lord Lorne (soon to become the earl of Argyll) and, perhaps most significantly, Lord James Stewart, the queen's half-brother – is puzzling. Having assured Knox that the realm of Scotland was safe for him, Knox left Geneva, with some reluctance, only to find a letter awaiting him when he arrived on the coast of Normandy effectively rescinding the invitation. Not a man to take such a rebuff meekly, Knox vented the full fury of his wonderfully effective pen on these doubters and vacillators:

> My words shall appear to some sharp and indiscreetly spoken; but as charity ought to interpret all things to the best, so ought wise men to understand that a true friend cannot be a flatterer, especially when the questions of salvation, both of body and soul, are moved; and that not of one nor of two, but as it were of a whole realm and nation. What are the sobs and what is the affliction of my troubled heart, God shall one day declare. But this I will add to my former vigour and severity, to wit, if any persuade you, for fear of dangers that may follow, to faint in your former purpose, be he never esteemed so wise and friendly, let him be judged of you both foolish and your mortal enemy. Foolish, because he understandeth nothing of God's approved wisdom. Enemy unto you because he laboureth to separate you from

The eldest child of a junior branch of the ambitious Guise family from north-eastern France, Mary had only recently been widowed, after a happy marriage to the duke of Longueville, when Francis I informed her she was to become the second wife of James V of Scotland. She was intelligent, attractive and determined to protect the interests of her daughter, Mary Queen of Scots.

Henry II. The second son of Francis I of France was deeply affected by his years as a child captive in Spain. Some of his underlying melancholy can be seen in this portrait but he also nursed imperialist pretensions, hoping to gain control eventually of both Scotland and England through his daughter-in-law, Mary Queen of Scots. His sense of theatre contributed to his untimely death in a joust in 1559.

Linlithgow Palace, to the west of Edinburgh, was the favourite home of Margaret Tudor and Mary of Guise. It was also the birthplace of Margaret's son, James V, and his daughter, Mary Queen of Scots.

A vision in pink, Mary as a young woman in France.

This portrait of Elizabeth I in her coronation robes, originally worn by her sister Mary but altered to fit the new queen, shows a striking but short-sighted young woman of regal bearing, with the Tudor colouring.

Francis II and Mary Queen of Scots. This dual portrait underlines the contrast between the new queen consort of France and her baby-faced husband, the son of Henry II and Catherine de Medici.

Lady Margaret Douglas, the only child of Margaret Tudor and the earl of Angus. Formidably determined and ambitious, she was eventually reconciled with her daughter-in-law, Mary Queen of Scots, becoming a staunch supporter of the claim to the English throne of her grandson, who became James I of England in 1603.

Henry Stewart, Lord Darnley and King of Scots, was the adored elder son of Margaret Douglas and her husband, Matthew Stewart, earl of Lennox. He was tall, good-looking and accomplished in courtly pursuits. Mary Queen of Scots made him her second husband because he strengthened her dynastic claim to the English throne but his immaturity, illness and heavy drinking ruined their marriage. He was murdered in 1567.

David Beaton came from a family of prominent politicians and churchmen in Scotland. He rose to power during the infancy of Mary Queen of Scots but was a divisive figure in Scottish politics. A committed Francophile, Cardinal Beaton's worldliness and wealth made him many enemies, not the least of whom was Henry VIII, who rejoiced in Beaton's assassination in 1546.

William Maitland of Lethington was the talented son of a Scottish courtier. Described by Elizabeth I as 'the flower of the wits of Scotland', Maitland was an able statesman. Firmly committed to the creation of a unified, Protestant Britain, he was allied with the queen's half-brother, the earl of Moray, but fell out with Mary and deserted her when she married Bothwell.

James Hamilton, second earl of Arran and duke of Châtelherault. Descended from the elder daughter of James II of Scotland, Arran was Mary Queen of Scots' heir presumptive until the birth of her son, Prince James, in 1566. He also acted as regent during the first part of her minority. Often viewed as self-serving and changeable, his patriotism has, more recently, been recognized.

James Hepburn, fourth earl of Bothwell, in a miniature painted in 1566 to mark his marriage to Lady Jean Gordon. An opportunist with a violent nature, Bothwell's first marriage was quickly brought to an end when he decided to marry the queen himself after Darnley's murder, in which he was implicated. His abduction and rape of Mary has been romanticized and his loss of support among the Scottish nobility cost the queen her throne.

Hermitage Castle. This grim fortress, in countryside still remote today, was inhabited by Bothwell when he was responsible for keeping order in the Borders. Mary and her advisers briefly visited him there in the autumn of 1566, after he had been wounded in a fight. It is highly unlikely to have been a romantic tryst and the queen fell seriously ill shortly afterwards.

This early seventeenth-century chart shows the Tudor roots of the claims of Mary Queen of Scots and her son to the throne of England.

Left James VI. Mary Queen of Scots' son knew neither of his parents. He was brought up in a strict environment but his intellectual attainments flourished. His minority was difficult, characterized by faction and plots against his life. But he never lost sight of the goal he shared with his mother – the throne of England – and his accession was welcomed in 1603.

Below The Honours of Scotland. The crown, sceptre and sword that form the royal regalia of Scotland, on display in Edinburgh Castle.

God's favour; provoking His vengeance and grievous plagues against you, because he would that ye should prefer your worldly rest to God's praise and glory, and the friendship of the wicked to the salvation of your brethren.[12]

If Knox's words sound intemperate to modern ears, they still echo down the years. The men whose constancy he sought to encourage were all politicians themselves and the pursuit of personal power was never far from their thoughts. But their fast-changing world was still framed by an overarching belief in God, fear of His vengeance and a yearning for salvation, not just for themselves but for the wider commonwealth. Knox was the most compelling speaker and writer of his generation – he could, of course, be much more intemperate when he felt the occasion warranted it – and no one who met him or heard him was untouched by what he had to say. But the question of open rebellion against the Crown was something that even Knox could not yet condone. Both he and his wavering backers hoped for further religious concessions from Mary of Guise and the nobles clearly felt, at this stage, that they could achieve their aims better if Knox stayed well away. For much of 1557 and 1558 it seemed that a compromise allowing Protestant preaching in private and a vernacular liturgy (the Bible was already available in Scots) for matins and evensong, and perhaps also for baptism, would offer the best solution. But, as became apparent in the parliament of 1558, even as a new regime took over in England with a Protestant queen, this set of compromises, vague around the edges and difficult to police, did not go far enough for a group of increasingly vocal and extreme Protestants. When they petitioned Mary of Guise for greater freedoms, the regent was gracious and appeared to be accommodating. But between the end of 1558 and May 1559 her policy changed suddenly and she was, ever after, viewed as a dissembling Catholic bigot by her detractors.

Mary of Guise was caught between the shifting international situation, where Elizabeth's succession had thrust forward her own daughter's claim to the throne and highlighted their religious differences, the determination of Henry II to crack down on heresy in France after the treaty of Cateau-Cambrésis had ended the Habsburg–Valois struggle in April 1559, and the growing threat of radical Protestantism in Scotland. These men did not want to compromise with someone they viewed as the duplicitous mouthpiece of the French. As Mary of Guise cracked down on iconoclasm and issued an urgent appeal for the proper observation of Easter in 1559, it was obvious that serious battle lines were being drawn. Religious disputes, escalating out of hand and threatening the authority of the regent, were the occasion, but there was a rising undercurrent of resentment against French rule.

The two main centres of Protestant strength were in southwest Scotland and the east coast towns. But neither of these 'congregations' had yet come together as one force and they still lacked the support of some key members of the nobility. At this crucial moment, Knox finally returned to join the eastern movement and his intervention sparked rebellion. Perhaps he had not intended this outcome and merely sought to fire up his listeners. But Mary of Guise had banned Protestant preaching in public and he was in defiance of her law. At Perth on 11 May 1559, Knox preached a sermon that so inflamed one of his listeners that a stone was thrown at a passing priest. It apparently missed but hit the tabernacle on the altar. What followed was a wholesale iconoclastic attack on the Church and its ornaments.

Knox's account in his *History of the Reformation in Scotland* makes it sound like an accident with unforeseen consequences but this is disingenuous. It was almost certainly premeditated violence. The regent could not let it pass without a suitable show of force and her reaction emboldened the 'Congregation', as the Protestant lords now styled themselves. When Lord James Stewart and the earl of Argyll finally joined their number, the Wars of the Congregation can be said to have begun. The long-time Protestant and pro-English Kirkcaldy of Grange wrote in triumph to the earl of Northumberland that the queen regent and d'Oisel had taken refuge in the heavily fortified castle of Dunbar. He went on: 'The Congregation came this last of June, by three o'clock in the morning, to Edinburgh, where they will take order for the maintenance of the true religion and resisting the King of France, if he send any force against them. The Duke [Châtelherault] with almost the whole nobility, has declared to the Queen that they are of the same religion as the Congregation, and will take part with them in that behalf.' Those who professed God's word in Scotland bore the queen of England 'an unfeigned love, which they shall prove indeed or it be long.'[13]

It seemed that Mary of Guise had lost. A woman of her mettle, however, was not so easily to be pushed aside and in the febrile climate of the summer of 1559 in Scotland many lords and even the people themselves were not persuaded of the legitimacy of the revolt. The citizens of Edinburgh greeted the Congregation's forces with notable coolness and many men simply preferred to wait and see what would happen. During July, Mary of Guise forced the Congregation to withdraw from Edinburgh and was busily fortifying the port of Leith. More than one thousand French troops arrived to back her up but this was viewed as a sign of an intended conquest rather than an attempt to restore order against rebels. Leading Protestants believed that this would strengthen defections to their cause. Certainly the brutality of the French during the winter of 1559–60, a desperate phase for the Congregation, bore out this view. Attacks on Fife and Glasgow further inflamed sentiment against the French. Even long-term backers of Mary of Guise began to withdraw their support. France now seemed no better than England in its disregard for the Scottish people and their livelihoods. Eventually, the French garrison withdrew in July 1560, effectively marking the end of the Auld Alliance amidst hatred and civil war in Scotland.

In England, Elizabeth's chief adviser, William Cecil, saw the Wars of the Congregation as an opportunity not to be lost. He felt that England had been humiliated by the Treaty of Cateau-Cambrésis, which underlined the loss of Calais and seemed to threaten a sinister closing of ranks in Catholic Europe against his Protestant monarch. Establishment of English influence in Scotland would distract from many of the difficulties Elizabeth faced as well as building a solid bulwark against the claims of the Catholic Mary Queen of Scots to the English throne. But English help was not automatic. Elizabeth needed some persuading that she should interfere at all and she had been greatly offended by the publication of John Knox's diatribe against female rulers, recently published, with exquisitely bad timing from the English perspective, as *The First Blast of the Trumpet Against the Monstrous Regiment of Women*.

Nor was the idea that England might come to their rescue necessarily comfortable for all Scots who opposed Mary of Guise. Mistrust still lingered and there were many Scots suspicious of replacing one 'protector' with another. Nevertheless, the arrival of English ships in January 1560 was received more warmly than the English themselves expected. The army did not follow until April, but was anticipated by Scots who wanted to know when the English 'would deliver them out of their misery and captivity of the French'. Thomas Randolph, the English diplomat in Scotland, called Anglo–Scottish cooperation in the summer of 1560 a miracle. The English had learned much from the mistakes of the 1540s and were keen to avoid all accusations of pillage and high-handed behaviour. For once, they wanted to be seen as good neighbours. And this is unsurprising, for both the Congregation and the English were not proceeding from positions of strength, and yet the outcome was of far-reaching significance.

The Treaty of Edinburgh of July 1560 has been called one of Cecil's greatest triumphs. In the words of his biographer, Stephen Alford, 'it became the touchstone of his career; he would measure everything by it, and judge everything against it, for nearly thirty years.'[14] The French were compelled to recognize Elizabeth's right to rule England but, crucially, French influence in Scotland was brought to an end. A council of twelve Scottish lords would rule, chosen by the Queen of Scots and the Scottish parliament, who would have the right to approve Mary's nominations. Mary's heirs were confirmed as the House of Hamilton, a belated triumph for Châtelherault, though perhaps a hollow one, as he watched his son and heir, talked of as a possible husband for the queen of England, fall into insanity. Finally, if Mary and her husband Francis refused to ratify the treaty, then the English would intervene in Scotland to protect the Protestant Reformation there.

Cecil, however much he may have believed that the British Isles could be united by the word of God, was in 1560 much more concerned to ensure that Scotland could never be the springboard for a wholesale assault on Elizabeth's shaky throne by the French, who would supplant her with Mary Stewart. His determination and absolute clarity of purpose had been greatly aided by one of those pivotal moments in history that could not possibly have been anticipated. In the end, all Mary of Guise's hopes for Scotland, her years of hard work and scheming and sacrifice, had been shattered by the blow of a jousting lance.

∞

ON 30 JUNE 1559, as the Lords of the Congregation were seeking to establish themselves in the Scottish capital, an impressive public spectacle was taking place in Paris. Buoyed by the end of years of conflict with Spain, proud of the marriages arranged for his sister Marguerite with Duke Emmanuel Philibert of Savoy (a husband rejected by Elizabeth of England) and his daughter Élisabeth with King Philip II of Spain, Henry II celebrated in style. As well as these diplomatic successes on the European mainland he was optimistic, too, that his son and daughter-in-law might not have to wait long before joining the English Crown to that of Scotland. These were heady times for the forty-year-old king. In his portraits, his downcast eyes suggest more of the melancholy he had felt as a boy-prisoner in Spain, but his demeanour on that warm afternoon in Paris was joyful and confident. Three days of festivities preceded the tournament being held on the Place Royale outside the Hôtel de Tournelles and the French king was an eager participant at the lists, as his godfather, Henry VIII, had been. But jousting was a young man's sport, though no one would have tried to tell the king that, and it was late in the afternoon when, unheeding the concerns of Catherine de Medici and Diane de Poitiers, whose colours he still wore, Henry challenged Gabriel de Montgomery, the captain of his Scottish Guard, to another bout. As the two men clashed, Montgomery's lance shattered, the splinters flying up to penetrate the king's visor, lodging in his eye and causing damage to his brain.

Intermittently conscious and in great pain Henry lingered until 10 July. Given the extent of his injuries and the state of medical knowledge at the time, it says something for his constitution that he survived so long. In fact, his life was not despaired of initially and Elizabeth's ambassador in Paris, Nicholas Throckmorton, reported that 'by common opinion, he is in no danger of life, but will lose his eye.' Queen Catherine and his family, including, of course, Mary Queen of Scots, kept vigil at his bedside as this proud and ambitious man, who had effectively been ruler of both France and Scotland, faded away. Catherine would not let Diane de Poitiers see him, despite his pleas, and banished her from court after his death. The mistress might have dominated her in Henry II's lifetime but his queen took charge of his death. Mary Queen of Scots, the child he had raised and loved as his own daughter, now became queen consort of France. She had been very unwell before her father-in-law's demise but, even at this moment of both crisis and fulfilment, it is unlikely that the troubles that were convulsing her native land were at the forefront of her thoughts. Her faith in her mother was always strong. Sadly for both of them, Mary of Guise's own health was beginning to falter under the strain of events.

⌖

HENRY II'S DEATH exposed more clearly the developing struggle over religion in France that would shortly lead to thirty years of bitter civil war. Repression against the Huguenots, the French Protestants, continued; indeed, it was the main plank of the policies followed by the Guise family, who now assumed complete control of Francis and Mary, alienating the Constable of France, Montmorency, and the Bourbons, the junior branch of the French royal family who would succeed if the Valois line failed. In 1560 this seemed highly unlikely – Catherine de Medici's belated production of so many sons appeared to secure the future of the Valois for years to come – but the calculated insult of not giving any government post to Henry of Navarre, the head of the Bourbons, was a costly mistake. Unable as yet to assert herself fully, the queen mother watched as the opprobrium for her late husband's policies and the draconian attempts to recover the huge debts of his wars fell on the increasingly unpopular family of her daughter-in-law. She would bide her time. But the developing crisis in France left the Scottish regent, Mary of Guise, isolated. Her brothers could not help her any more and, thanks to English intervention, she was losing her struggle with the Lords of the Congregation at home. All of this took a tremendous toll on her health. Suffering from dropsy (what we would call congestive heart failure today), Mary of Guise swelled up and became lame. Her spirit remained strong despite the setbacks and she continued, as was the habit of this hardworking woman, a politician to her finger tips, to send reports back to her brothers in France. At the end of May 1560 she wrote her last letter, referring to the parliament that the rebels, as she termed them, had called for July and noting, 'my health has been quite good until two days ago, when I had a relapse and for two nights now have had a return of the fever. I do not know what will happen.'[15]

One suspects that, in fact, she did. By 1 June she could not eat or sleep and six days later, propped up in a chair, she sent for the Scottish lords over whom she had ruled for six years and whom she had known for much longer, since she first came to Scotland as a reluctant but dutiful second wife to James V. Châtelherault, with whom she had vied so long for the regency, Lord James Stewart and the earl of Argyll were chief among those who came for their last audience with her. Still pleading with them to uphold the French alliance, she requested their obedience to her daughter and asked their forgiveness for any offence she had given during her time in Scotland. Even for the stern and ambitious men who had opposed her, it was an emotional interview. Eventually, she lost the power of speech but lingered for a few days more, dying with Lord James and Argyll at her side just after midnight on 11 June 1560. Her body lay in a coffin in the Chapel of St Margaret atop Castle Rock in Edinburgh until, in March 1561, it was returned to France, to be buried in the choir of the church of St Pierre-les-Dames in Reims, where her sister was abbess. Her tomb survived until the French Revolution, when, like the fate that befell the last resting place in Perth of her mother-in-law, Margaret Tudor, it was destroyed.

Mary Queen of Scots was not informed of her mother's death for more than two weeks and was overwhelmed by grief, as her French family had feared. In Scotland, the exercise of power passed to that doughty survivor James Hamilton, duke of Châtelherault, and to Mary's half-brother, the increasingly ambitious Lord James Stewart. William Maitland of Lethington, who had been Mary of Guise's secretary, would serve her daughter in the same capacity. Maitland was a man of great ability, descended from an old Anglo–Norman family but not of the Scottish nobility. He completed the trio of those who now governed in the names of Francis and Mary, whether the young pair in France liked it or not. In agreeing to the Treaty of Edinburgh, the Guise family betrayed their own niece for a brief respite of personal survival, hoping that they could increase their influence over young Francis II.

In August 1560, two months after her mother's death, Throckmorton recorded at some length an interview he had with Mary Queen of Scots at the French court which is highly revealing of the young queen's attitude towards her role at the time – or, at least, the impression that she wished to give. It should be remembered that the ambassador, who had long been in and around the English court but was not as important as he liked to believe (a trait he had in common with most diplomats of the time) was primarily concerned with making the right noises on behalf of his own queen. Punctiliously referring to Mary throughout as 'the French Queen', Throckmorton noted that she deferred to Catherine de Medici in the first instance but when the ambassador had said his little piece to her mother-in-law, Mary then conferred with him in Scots.

Throckmorton defended Elizabeth's honour and intentions:

> however much she [Mary] might have been persuaded of his mistress's sinister intentions and unkind dealings towards her, she now saw whereunto it tended . . . he further thought that she would not be so bent to serve the affection of the King [Francis II] as utterly to neglect her country and suffer it to be suppressed by strangers, and under a foreign government.

Mary sidestepped this swipe at her dependence on France and refrained from pointing out that the English, who had effectively toppled her mother, might also be viewed as 'strangers'. Instead, she merely thanked Elizabeth 'and said that the duty she ought to bear to her husband was none otherwise than to have a care for her country, which she could not easily forget . . . She said that she was glad of peace and hoped that Elizabeth would continue it, as she would do.' Later in the month Mary saw Throckmorton again and he once more tried to get her to say something definite about ratifying the Treaty of Edinburgh. Again, she demurred politely, saying 'that what the king, her husband, resolved in that matter, she would conform to herself, for his will is mine and . . . I have as much cause to esteem her amity as any other, for I am the nearest kinswoman she hath, being both of us of one house and stock.'[16]

This clever reminder of her proximity to the English throne was probably not what Throckmorton or, indeed, Elizabeth wanted to hear. It was not precisely true, since Elizabeth's other cousins, the sisters Catherine and Mary Grey, were favoured as Protestant successors to the English queen by a substantial number of parliamentarians, though they were descended from Henry VII's younger daughter, Mary, and not Margaret, the elder, as was Mary Queen of Scots. And there was also one other, overlooked figure who could claim descent. This was the young Henry, Lord Darnley, son of the earl and countess of Lennox. They had certainly not forgotten that he had a claim in both England and Scotland, and had sent him hurriedly to Paris to commiserate with Mary following the death of Henry II. She does not seem, at this stage, to have paid him anything other than polite attention, perhaps because he was only fourteen years old at the time.

Mary's interviews with Throckmorton, her first recorded meetings with an English diplomat, show a young woman of dignity and intelligence, using her husband as a shield when pressed on Scottish matters but cleverly reminding Elizabeth that she could be viewed as her heir. Her apparently submissive attitude was a convenient cover while affairs in Scotland were so fraught, for even as she spoke to Throckmorton, what became known as the Reformation Parliament was making sweeping changes in Scotland. It abolished the Mass, denied the pope's authority and established a new Confession of Faith. Catholic clergy remained in charge of their own benefices but their future was uncertain. The same session also petitioned Elizabeth of England to marry the earl of Arran, Châtelherault's son, thus uniting the realms of England and Scotland if Mary died without heirs.

This must have been an alarming development for the Queen of Scots but worse was to follow. In the space of a year she had lost her father-in-law and mother, two key figures in her life. But she had at least the comfort of a secure place in France, troubled though the country was. There were some signs that Francis II might have adopted a more conciliatory attitude towards the Huguenots if left to make his own decisions, though the religious opponents of the French monarchy were articulate, determined and increasingly militant. In October, amid high security, Francis and Mary established themselves in Orléans for the autumn hunting season. But by mid-November 1560 Francis was seriously ill. He had mastoiditis, an infection of the ear that can affect the brain and lead to seizures. Extremely painful, it was, until the advent of antibiotics, a notable killer of children and young people. The king had never been strong but even someone in better health might well have succumbed. There is evidence that his surgeon, Paré, who had attended on his dying father as well, was unwilling to make the incision that would drain the infection because he was a Protestant and feared that if Francis were to die anyhow, he would be blamed because of his religion. So he did nothing.

With his distraught mother and anxious, confused wife in attendance, the teenaged king of France died on 5 December, having reigned for barely eighteen months. Mary was left with only grief and uncertainty, to pass Christmas in the white mourning garb of a widowed French queen.

CHAPTER THIRTEEN

The Return of the Queen

'To promote a woman to bear rule, superiority, dominion
or empire above any realm, nation or city, is repugnant to
nature, contumely to God, a thing most contrarious to His
revealed will and approved ordinance, and finally it is the
subversion of good order, of all equity and justice.'

John Knox, *The First Blast of the Trumpet Against the
Monstrous Regiment of Women*, 1558

'Yet you like better of yonder long lad.'

Elizabeth I perceives that the young Henry Stewart, Lord Darnley,
may be more acceptable to the Scots as a consort for their queen
than her favourite, the Earl of Leicester

MARY QUEEN OF SCOTS passed her eighteenth birthday three
days after the death of her husband. Widowhood at such an early
age was not unusual in the sixteenth century, when many
noblewomen married men much older than themselves, but in
the case of a younger spouse it was less predictable. Though
Mary knew that Francis was far from robust, his passing was a
great shock. Having sat beside the dead body overnight, Mary
then donned the white robes customary for a widowed queen of
France and began the period of forty days' mourning that
etiquette dictated. She retired into the darkness of a private
chamber lit only by candles, its windows blacked out. For two
weeks she pondered the blow that had befallen her and con-

sidered its implications. During this time she saw her Guise uncles and other family members but refused to receive the condolences of the diplomatic community until she felt more in command of her emotions.

There was plenty to occupy her thoughts. The death of her husband following so closely on that of her mother was a personal tragedy but its immediate effect was even more disquieting. Childless queen dowagers of France, as her great-aunt, Henry VIII's sister, Mary, had found nearly half a century earlier, had no further role to play. They were unwelcome reminders of what might have been and, furthermore, a potential drain on the state's coffers. And while Mary sat in the suffocating isolation of her widow's weeds, events were moving fast around her. She would have realized from the information imparted by her uncles that their day, too, was passing. The impetus came from her mother-in-law, Catherine de Medici.

We do not know how much relations between Mary and Catherine had already cooled but the queen mother of France exhibited little sympathy for the predicament of the Queen of Scots. The meeting of the French Estates General that Francis II had coincidentally called shortly before his death went ahead and now it confirmed Catherine in the official role of regent for her ten-year-old son, the new king, Charles IX. Catherine took her opportunity to end years of Guise domination boldly and its inevitable consequence, regardless of how she felt about her daughter-in-law, was to marginalize Mary. But it appears that their relationship was no longer close, if, indeed, it ever really had been. Catherine cannot have forgotten the unwelcome intrusion of her bitter rival, Diane de Poitiers, in Mary's upbringing and there were rumours that Mary had compounded this by referring to Catherine as 'a merchant's daughter'. It would have suited Mary's uncles if the queen mother had acquiesced in their first idea to salvage their influence and their niece's position. This was the scarcely credible proposal that Mary should retain her role as queen consort by marrying Charles IX, despite the fact that he was half her age and could not be expected to cohabit with her as man and wife for at least five more years. But Catherine now held the whip hand and she was having none of this distasteful proposition. Neither would she support the possibility of a match between Mary and Don Carlos, son of Philip II of Spain, fearing it might undermine the position of her daughter, Élisabeth, Philip's wife. Catherine was not about to give the Guise family an alternative power base in Spain, particularly as it was becoming apparent that France was spiralling closer and closer to religious civil war.

Before Mary even emerged from seclusion to attend a Requiem Mass for Francis II in Orléans, once the period of mourning was passed, it must have been obvious that her options were diminishing. Perhaps there had only ever really been one. She was not wanted in France and had no status there any longer. But she was, as she had always been, Queen of Scots. There she would rule in her own right, not as a consort. It was time to go home.

Mary's decision to return to Scotland appears to have been taken within a month of her husband's death and she did not waver from it once made, despite the depth of her attachment to the country in which she had passed most of her life. France and all things French would always retain the primary place in her memories and affections. Scotland was largely unknown. It was a place of mists and winter darkness, a minor player on the European stage compared to her adopted country. But her father and grandfather had ensured that it was not to be ignored, that its court and palaces were fit for kings, and Mary knew that she had a claim to the throne of England that might, one day, see her as ruler over the whole of Britain. Here was a prize worth having. With the instinctive Stewart confidence that she would soon win the hearts of her Scottish subjects, of all ranks and degrees, Mary began to put in place her plans. She would not be pushed out of France in unseemly haste and there was, in any case, much to be settled before she could take up the reins of government at home. Questions of religion, of political roles and the choice of advisers for the queen all had to be addressed. As these were aired, Mary must have at least glimpsed the complexity of the situation in Scotland and the potential for difficulty. She was not entirely unfamiliar with Scottish politics, having received regular reports from her mother and from members of the Scottish council after the death of Mary of Guise. Still, it was one thing to read these and to absorb their implications and quite another to enter into the fray, as a woman in a man's world, and try to direct government. Mary had been educated for the role of queen consort of France, not queen regnant of Scotland. And advice, as she would find before she left France, could come from different sources and lead to conflicting viewpoints.

The reaction in Scotland was mixed. For nearly twenty years there had been no resident adult monarch in the country and, despite Mary of Guise's best efforts to be a surrogate Stewart, some of the prestige associated with the family name had worn off. James V's many bastards were wealthy and, in at least one case, influential, but the taint of illegitimacy hung over them. The religious upheaval came late and its effects were still unfolding. The country remained much as it had been under James IV: overwhelmingly rural, with prosperity confined mainly to the central Lowlands, the eastern coast between Edinburgh and Aberdeen, and the valley of the river Tweed in the south. In these areas, where the mix of rich agricultural land and busy ports ensured considerable prosperity, trade thrived and urbanization grew, but only very slowly. Edinburgh's population in 1550 was around 15,000, only 5,000 more than it had been at the start of the sixteenth century. The comparison with London, then a city of 120,000 souls, was stark. Family and clan loyalties remained strong in Scotland and could lead to decades (or longer) of simmering hatred, as the Hamilton feud with the Lennox Stewarts illustrated. This was very much a masculine society, though not one in which women were entirely powerless. Some titles could pass in the female line and where management of businesses and property rights were concerned, women could and did take to the courts to resolve disputes and gain what they believed to be rightfully theirs. But a strong, male monarch, who understood the country, was still the leader that the Scots desired. Mary was essentially a charming Frenchwoman who they did not know. Ruling them was never going to be an easy task.

Although the Scottish response to Mary's announcement that she would shortly be governing them in person did not divide cleanly on religious lines (she had many Protestant supporters as well as Catholics), her religion was certainly an issue. Firebrands like John Knox, who despised Mary doubly because she was a woman and a Catholic, would make much of it, thus over-emphasizing its significance for posterity. But while she was still in France, Mary received earnest supplications from two quite different sources that must have brought home to her that, however much she was prepared to compromise personally, there had been a revolution in Scotland that her mother had ultimately failed to contain.

News of the queen's intention to return greatly heartened the Catholic nobility in Scotland and the future bishop of Ross, John Leslie, was sent to see her in the spring of 1561 by the earl of Huntly. He promised that if Mary landed in Aberdeen, 20,000 men would be waiting to help her restore Catholicism. Mary was no longer at the French court at this stage, but when Leslie saw her, at Vitry in Champagne, she listened politely to Huntly's proposal but rejected it. Leslie, however, clearly won a place in her esteem, for she remained close to him thereafter and invited him to join her entourage. Yet another aspect of his advice she rejected at the time of their first meeting, which she would eventually have cause to regret, was his warning against her half-brother, Lord James Stewart. And Lord James was hot on Leslie's heels.

Lord James was the much older sibling who accompanied Mary when she left Scotland in 1548. Then he had been on his way to university in Paris, a predictable development for the illegitimate seventeen-year-old son of a European king. It appears that he did not stay long. On returning to Scotland, he continued his support of Mary of Guise, travelling with her to France in 1550 and attending his sister's wedding in 1558. But as the troubled decade of the 1550s unfolded in Scotland, Lord James began to weigh the favours he had received from France against the price that his country was paying and his allegiance was gradually whittled away from the regent. There were other factors at play, too. He wanted a role in Scottish politics on his own terms and his religious views were turning towards Protestantism. Still, he acted with caution in committing himself wholeheartedly in opposition to the influence of France, and it was not until the last day of May 1559 that he openly declared his support for the Lords of the Congregation. Thereafter, he was firmly committed to amity with England and earned the approbation of Cecil, who admired his military and political skills. These were amply displayed in 1560 when he supported the Hamiltons as the legitimate heirs of Mary Queen of Scots and the young earl of Arran, son of Châtelherault, as a suitor for the hand of Queen Elizabeth of England.

Elizabeth's rejection of Arran cast a pall over Anglo–Scottish relations. But it was the death of Francis II and Mary's projected return to Scotland that brought everything into sharp relief. While she had been queen consort of France, there were clearly opportunities for men like Lord James to exercise real power and influence in the running of Scotland. It was in his own interests, and not merely those of the Protestant lords, to ensure clarification of Mary's intentions and to brief her on what could and could not be done.

Lord James met his sister at St-Dizier, which lay in the Guise heartlands of north-eastern France, on 15 April 1561. It was not an interview she was likely to forget. Her brother was a man who did not mince his words, though he could be persuasively charming when necessary. He expected that she would listen to him. Of stern, even austere countenance, he resembled his father but lacked the good looks of James V. He was also much more self-contained than Mary and his strategy for facilitating her return to Scotland in a way that would be acceptable to her and her subjects was carefully considered. Cecil's respect for his Scottish ally's diplomatic skills was amply justified. For although Lord James was representing the Scottish Protestant lords, he was also a Stewart and concerned that his sister should rule with her personal dignity and beliefs intact.

The five days he spent with her convinced Mary that she should pay him heed. So much so that she considered appointing him regent until her return (a post that Lord James would no doubt have welcomed) until she was subsequently made aware of the fact that her brother had gone straight to Paris after seeing her for discussions with Throckmorton, the English ambassador, and had then briefed Cecil and Elizabeth in London on his way home. Though she now had ample cause to wonder whose side Lord James was really on, Mary still preferred his advice over that of Leslie. She did not wish to return home to immediate hostilities and precipitate civil war. Instead, Lord James offered her a compromise – one that Mary found easier to accept than John Knox. She agreed to recognize Protestantism as the dominant religion in her country (despite the fact that the majority of the population were probably still Catholic in their beliefs) and work with her brother and his close ally, William Maitland of Lethington, her mother's former secretary, as her chief advisers. Their part of the agreement was to ensure that the queen could practise her religion in private without interference. They also undertook to promote something perhaps even dearer to Mary's heart: her claim to the English succession.

Lord James went back to Scotland pleased with his success. He believed his sister was biddable but in this he was deceived. Mary would do precisely what she wanted when it suited her. For the present, however, she heeded the advice he gave her in a letter written the following month, which shows an underlying level of anxiety he probably did not reveal when they had talked at St-Dizier: 'Madame,' he wrote, 'for the love of God, press no matters of religion, not for any man's advice on the earth.' For he assured Mary, in this long and detailed missive, that 'I also promise your grace in presence of my God to adventure my blood and my life in the defence of your highness's realm whenever that or the like occasion shall be offered without exception of any person under God.'[1] In defence of her realm but not, explicitly, of her person. One wonders whether she noticed the distinction.

SCOTTISH POLITICS may have been thrown into confusion by the death of Francis II but 1560 had not been a good year for Elizabeth, either. Her dismissal of the Arran proposal highlighted the fraught question of marriage and appeared to her advisers to emphasize her own vulnerability. Cecil and the council simply could not accept that she would remain unmarried for much longer. Only Robert Dudley, her undisputed favourite, seems to have recognized all along that Elizabeth's determination to remain single was never likely to be swayed. The mysterious death of his own neglected wife, Amy Robsart, in September caused speculation and scandal and had the perverse effect of freeing him while at the same time making marriage with the queen out of the question. Probably Elizabeth never seriously considered it anyway. Her emotional dependence on Dudley was extreme but she was always clear-headed enough to recognize that there were many, including her most trusted advisers, who harboured grave doubts about this son of executed traitor the duke of Northumberland.

William Cecil, who disliked Dudley but accepted that he would have to work with him, became increasingly desperate. Affairs in Scotland, at least while Mary remained in France, seemed to be turning to England's advantage but he could not seem to get his queen to take the business of ruling seriously. She was forever on progresses, hunting or dancing. She would not make decisions or listen to his earnest concerns. Mr Secretary was a prodigious worker, frequently at his desk until midnight, and his health began to suffer under the strain of business and the frustrations of the queen's attitude. He considered resigning but his sense of duty and an underlying belief that Elizabeth's qualities would somehow come to the fore kept him going.

The perils of these early years of Elizabeth's reign still tend to be underestimated, a product of the hagiography of the queen. We forget that it was Elizabeth herself who created the image of Gloriana later in her reign and that successive generations have been taken in by biographies where adulation replaces a more balanced analysis. If anyone had told William Cecil in 1560 that Elizabeth would still be viewed in the early twenty-first century as England's greatest monarch, his jaw would surely have dropped. Economic recovery seemed elusive, there was rebellion in Ireland, the queen was unpopular and her frequent bouts of ill health merely added to the sense of insecurity. In July 1561, just a month before Mary Stewart returned to her kingdom, Cecil wrote to Throckmorton in Paris: 'Well, God send our mistress a husband and by him a son, that we may hope our posterity shall have a masculine succession. This matter is too big for weak folks and too deep for simple. The Queen's Majesty knoweth of it. And so I will end.'[2] In England, no less than in Scotland, the desirability of a masculine ruler was taken for granted.

The problem of Elizabeth's continued evasion on this key issue was compounded when another cousin, Lady Katherine Grey, the sister of Lady Jane who had ruled so briefly in 1553, secretly married the earl of Hertford and became pregnant. Katherine, a Protestant, was the nearest heir to Elizabeth by Henry VIII's will and the favoured candidate of parliament should anything happen to Elizabeth. But the queen apparently disliked the Grey family, perhaps because of this very proximity to her throne and the memory of their grab for power less than a decade before. She may have been willing to overlook the part of the Dudleys in all of this, who were heavily embroiled due to Guildford Dudley's marriage to Lady Jane, but she was less forgiving of the Greys. When Elizabeth found out about Katherine Grey's irregular marriage arrangements and her pregnancy, she was enraged. The unfortunate couple ended up in the Tower and were eventually able, through lax supervision, to produce another son to add to the one they had conceived on their wedding day. For the rest of her short life, Katherine was kept under house arrest. Elizabeth was not merciful to those who crossed her. But what did she make of the return of her 'sister queen' to Scotland?

As with many aspects of Elizabeth's behaviour, the truth is hard to know. She at least affected to be less concerned about the implications of Mary's presence in the same isle than Cecil. Elizabeth respected Mary as an anointed monarch, the crowned head of state and her royal equal, despite the tensions that traditionally bedevilled Anglo–Scottish relations. The religious difference between Mary's observant, if not fervent, Catholicism and her own brand of Protestantism was less significant than the ties of blood that they shared. It is possible that, even at this early stage of her reign, she accepted privately that if she stuck by her decision to remain unwed, then the Stewarts were her rightful successors, regardless of her father's will. But she had a morbid fear of acknowledging any heir apparent publicly, lest they become a focus for opposition. Her manoeuvring to maintain this position has often been depicted as one of her great skills but she was lucky to get away with it, given the state of England in the 1560s and the accepted practices of the time.

Cecil was, at first, relieved that Lord James and the Protestants in Scotland appeared to have worked out a system of government that would contain any threat that Mary's return might pose. He was keeping a very close eye on affairs north of the border from the moment of her return in August 1561. There was, in his view, no cause for alarm: 'She hath no soldiers nor train,' he wrote, 'but a few household; she meaneth to commit herself to the trust of her own.'[3] Elizabeth, on the other hand, was more interested in her cousin's person. She wanted a picture of Mary and there was talk of a meeting between the two queens, something that Mary earnestly encouraged. Cecil, however, was dead set against it and Elizabeth eventually realized that personal feelings should not be allowed to get in the way of political caution. In addition, there was always likely to be an element of rivalry and Elizabeth's vanity may have warned her off discovering that tales of her cousin's beauty, charm and accomplishments were true. Yet, in reality, the mere fact of Mary Stewart's homecoming and assumption of personal rule threatened the short-lived amity with England much more profoundly than Cecil had, at first, hoped. Elizabeth's refusal of the Arran match compromised it severely. When Mary began her personal rule in Scotland the amity was effectively over, though its acknowledged demise was still several years off. When, in the autumn of 1562, Elizabeth contracted smallpox, the fear that she would die was palpable in London. By then, Mary Queen of Scots was establishing her rule in Scotland with apparent success. But Elizabeth recovered, so the question of the English succession and Mary's place in it remained unresolved.

MARY HAD TAKEN a gentle, prolonged leave of France. The preparations for her departure began in June 1561. Elizabeth having refused her a passport (not a sign of sisterly commitment) and then, typically, changed her mind too late, Mary was obliged to make the entire journey by sea, as she had done in 1548. Most of the spring was passed in Champagne, but by June she was back in Paris, installed in the Louvre. Her final days at the French court were spent in July at St Germain, attending a four-day fête in her honour. Afterwards, she left for the Channel ports, accompanied by a large train, but her departure point was deliberately kept vague to confuse English spies. Finally, on 14 August, she boarded her galley at Calais, taking leave of her uncles and the country that had nurtured her. 'The queen,' it was reported, 'broke down in tears and said that she would miss the pomp, the attentions, the magnificence and the superb mounts of France that she had enjoyed for so long, but that she would be patient now that her paradise was to be exchanged for a hell.' If she did actually utter those words, then they were prophetic but it seems unlikely that Mary, despite the fact that she was

undoubtedly regretful to leave France, said anything so undiplo-
matic. There were reasons, on the contrary, to be optimistic. She
could establish her own style and court, get to know her subjects
and still pursue the great goal of England's throne. For, in the
months before she left France, even the experienced Throckmorton could not get the Queen of Scots to ratify the Treaty of
Edinburgh. Her excuse that this would need verification with
the Scottish lords cut no ice with the English ambassador – after
all, they were the people who had negotiated it – but Mary's
reply that things would be different once she returned was
alarming to Cecil, who had calculated on them staying the same.
Yet the men in whom he had placed his confidence, who would
now become Mary's advisers, knew that there would be repercussions in the relationship with England when she returned. It
remained to be seen how these could best be managed.

Mary's unexpectedly fast voyage of just five days from Calais
to Leith caught those waiting to receive her by surprise. The
absence of any official welcoming party was hastily remedied
when her brothers, Lord James and Lord Robert Stewart, rushed
to greet her and to conduct her to Holyrood Palace. It must have
seemed, in those first days of the queen's residence there, an
empty and disquieting place. Work had not even been completed
on making it ready for her when she arrived and it had been
unoccupied, its furniture stored away, since her mother's death.
Mary had never lived at Holyrood, so would not even have had
childhood memories. But it was a fine building, extensively
remodelled on the lines of the Loire château of Chambord by
her father, James V, and with the support of her French staff
and the arrival of her belongings it soon became habitable again.

There was much to be done in the first weeks but in the
crucial area of religion, Lord James and his sister kept their word
to each other. When Mary heard Mass in her private chapel on
Sunday, 24 August, her male half-siblings barred the door from
those trying to disrupt the service and protected the priests
conducting it. The following day, Mary, for her part, issued a
proclamation forbidding religious changes and announcing that

she would call a parliament at a convenient time and take their counsel. But she also required her subjects to keep the peace and to refrain from attacking her French attendants, an indication that she knew very well that she was a target for the vocal and often physically aggressive Calvinist minority. When she made her official entry to Edinburgh on 2 September, it was apparent even during the pageants and speeches that no opportunity would be lost to remind her that Protestantism was the state religion of Scotland and that she was expected to be a 'godly prince'. There were also signs of the restiveness of the population, made unruly by fountains flowing with wine for the occasion. It was rather a strange and contradictory event, certainly a contrast to the superbly orchestrated entries of her late father-in-law, Henry II of France, and must have brought home to the queen her brother's words. Mary's displeasure at the audacity and sheer rudeness of her religious opponents was demonstrated by her order to the Edinburgh council that the provost and bailies involved in the organization of her entry be dismissed. In private, however, she resolved to meet the chief of her Calvinist critics as soon as possible.

Mary had both friends and enemies when she returned to Scotland but, by his own admission (and it should be remembered that he had a flair for over-dramatization that went with his self-image as a latter-day Old Testament prophet), John Knox was the most consistent and relentless of these. The week after Mary heard her first Mass at Holyrood he preached one of his epic fire and brimstone sermons against idolatry. By his own account, he 'showed what terrible plagues God had taken on realms and nations for the same,' and added, 'One Mass is more fearful to me than if ten thousand armed enemies were landed in any part of the realm . . . when we join hands with idolatry God's amicable presence and comfortable defence leaveth us, and what shall then become of us?'[4]

For all his eloquence, Knox was not preaching to the majority and he knew this. In Edinburgh the Mass was still heard frequently and most Scots outside urban areas remained true to

Mary's faith. As in England under Edward VI, it was one thing to legislate sweeping changes and quite another to instil them in the hearts of the population. Mary's Catholic supporters, led by the earl of Huntly, represented in reality the views of most of her subjects. Perhaps it was this realization and a feeling that Knox's challenge to her authority must be contained that caused Mary to decide to confront her stern opponent as soon as possible.

The interview, the first of four that Knox had with the queen, did not go well. She accused him of inciting her subjects to rebellion and undermining the entire basis of her sovereignty. Had he not said that princes could be resisted, the more so if they were mere women like herself? Knox defended his right to hold his own opinion and added, 'If the realm finds no inconvenience from the rule of a woman ... [I] shall be as well content to live under your Grace as St Paul was to live under Nero.' This comparison with one of the great villains of Roman history did not go down well with Mary and Knox's final assertion that if princes exceeded their bounds they could be resisted 'even with power' only made matters worse. After an argument about interpretation of the scriptures, the meeting came to a close when Mary was called to dinner. Knox took his leave of her with the words: 'I pray God, Madam, that ye may be as blessed within the Commonwealth of Scotland, if it be the pleasure of God, as ever Deborah was in the Commonwealth of Israel.' But he later told friends who asked him what he thought of the young queen at this first meeting: 'If there be not in her a proud mind, a crafty wit and an indurate heart against God and his Truth, my judgement faileth me.'[5] He did not know that, shocked and frustrated, Mary had burst into tears once he had gone. Lord James Stewart, present throughout the interview, had nothing whatsoever to say.

Mary's positive reaction, after the tears subsided, was to go on a progress before the winter arrived. She wanted to see more of her country, to revisit the palaces of her childhood, like Linlithgow and Stirling, where there were happy memories of her mother, and to show herself to the people. During the year 1562–3 she travelled 1,200 miles, leaving a legacy of strong personal loyalty among the lords she visited in distant parts of her kingdom, from Inverness in the north to Ayr in the south-west. In this, she exhibited the true spirit of the Stewarts, for whom travel and personal visibility were so important. Accompanying her were Huntly and Lord James, the two men who represented opposing religious views and also different personal interests. The Gordons, Huntly's family, were de facto rulers of northern Scotland, while Lord James was hoping, if he stayed on the right side of his sister, to gain an earldom and more lands; he did not care if these were at Huntly's expense. The tensions between the two men would grow steadily and as Lord James was still hoping not to lose Cecil's support entirely, he was keeping his lines of communication with England open. Mary remained committed to her brother but her return had produced its own strains and she was fast gaining an appreciation of the difficulties that faced her as a young female ruler in a divided country. In Perth during her autumn progress she once again experienced the contradictions of being joyfully received by some of her subjects and baited by Protestants. She felt unwell and had to retreat indoors from public gaze for a while. This kind of physical reaction to stress was not just an emanation of regal disapproval; it was part of a pattern that would be repeated in similar circumstances. Mary, for all her height and bearing, was not a woman who enjoyed good health and her frequent bouts of illness would have an undoubted impact on her ability to govern. Yet in these first months of her rule, she had shown a determination and clear-headedness that appeared to bode well for the future. This was particularly apparent in the balanced choice of advisers for her Privy Council, made as early as 6 September. A number of these men were to play a crucial part in the continuing drama of the rivalry between the Tudors and the Stewarts.

THE QUEEN OF SCOTS' first Privy Council consisted of sixteen men: twelve members of the nobility and four officials. The earls of Athol, Errol, Montrose and Huntly were the only Catholics. The rest were all key players among the Congregation. Most, with the notable exception of the earl of Morton, a man personally disliked by Mary, were politically beholden to Lord James. Châtelherault, always a hard man to categorize but ever present, remained as a councillor. The most important, however, after the representatives of the old families and the coming men of the new Protestant elite, was William Maitland of Lethington, a close ally of the queen's eldest half-brother. He would play a crucial part in the early successes of Mary's reign yet finally desert her at her hour of greatest need.

Maitland's family of Scottish courtiers was on the rise in the mid-sixteenth century. His father, Sir Richard Maitland, was an accomplished poet and he passed his courtly skills on to his son, who used them to excellent effect in Mary's company as well as in his dealings with European politicians. William Maitland had been born some time between 1525 and 1530 and well educated, in Scotland and in Paris, as was so common among prominent Scots at the time. He was highly intelligent, widely read and, uncommonly for the age in which he lived, tolerant of different ideas and religions. Well informed on theological matters, he was not afraid to challenge Knox's emphatic interpretations of scripture and was even denounced by the preacher as an atheist at one stage, though Maitland would have counted himself as a good Protestant. Contemporaries, even those who thoroughly disliked him, testified to his abilities and intellect. Elizabeth I herself called him 'the flower of the wits of Scotland' – no mean compliment. His portrait shows a man soberly but richly dressed, his starched white collar edged with fine lace. It is a compelling face but also one with a hint of good humour around the eyes.

There are gaps in our knowledge of Maitland's early career but towards the end of 1554 his prospects were immensely improved when he was appointed as assistant to the Scottish secretary, David Paniter. As the first ever clerk to the Privy

Council, he gained unparalleled knowledge of its workings and acted as a gatekeeper on financial matters to the queen regent, Mary of Guise, who clearly valued him highly. During this time, he was also gaining diplomatic experience and was sent on a mission to London early in 1558 to try to mediate a peace between England and France. The mission did not succeed (England had just lost Calais and Queen Mary I was not in the mood for compromise) but it did give Maitland useful contacts for the future.

Following his appointment to the secretaryship in 1558 on Paniter's death, Maitland was able to exploit his position to the benefit of the Lords of the Congregation while still seeming to serve Mary of Guise. Opponents criticized this subsequently as devious Machiavellianism. He did not openly defect to the Congregation until the end of 1559, at a time when its future looked inauspicious. His subsequent involvement in the negotiations that led to the Treaty of Berwick greatly enhanced his stock with the English and with Cecil in particular. But it was only after the Treaty of Edinburgh was signed and the opportune death of Mary of Guise that the victory of the Congregation was ensured and Maitland and Lord James could breathe more easily. Maitland had played a double game in the last years of Mary of Guise's rule with consummate skill and did not, at first, welcome the return of her daughter, believing it would be a disaster for Scotland. In a letter to Cecil the downhearted Scottish secretary predicted 'wonderful tragedies'. History would prove him correct, though not in the timing or manner that he dreaded in 1560. He was soon won over by Mary and changed his tune completely, to the bewilderment of his English counterpart, when he wrote: 'The Queen my Mistress behaves herself so gently in every behalf as reasonably as we can require. If any be amiss, the fault is rather in ourselves ... [She] doth declare a wisdom far exceeding her age ... Surely, I see in her a good towardness, and think the Queen your sovereign shall be able to do much with her in religion, if they once enter in a good familiarity.'[6] This was not really what Cecil wanted to hear but he was soon to have it confirmed by the arrival of the man himself in London. Within two weeks of her homecoming, Mary, whose flexibility and maturity had so impressed her highly experienced Secretary, sent William Maitland south to London, ostensibly to announce officially her return to Scotland, but, in reality, to begin the process of establishing her recognized place in the English succession.

Armed with two letters for the Queen of England, a personal one from Mary herself and a much more forthright one from the Scottish nobility, which greatly annoyed Elizabeth, Maitland set about achieving his goal. In the course of three separate meetings with Elizabeth, it was made clear that the Scots desired to continue their friendship with England, but on the clear understanding that their queen would only ratify a modified version of the Treaty of Edinburgh if she was also recognized as Elizabeth's successor. Of course, it is easy to say with hindsight that Maitland never stood a chance of persuading Elizabeth to agree to such a course of action but this is to overlook the fact that Maitland had come up against a woman who could outdo him where deviousness was concerned. It was in her interests and England's to appear, at least, to keep the door open. There were warning signs: 'This desire,' she told him, 'is without an example to set my winding sheet before my eye . . . think you that I could love my own winding sheet?'[7] But then Elizabeth waxed so lyrical about 'her sister' as she referred to Mary, that there still seemed to be some real hope for resolution of these difficult issues, especially the following year when Maitland was back in London to put the case all over again and press for a meeting between the two queens.

Maitland reported the tenor of his meeting with Queen Elizabeth to Mary at the beginning of June 1562. His letter reveals Elizabeth's skill in saying all the right things without making any actual commitment. She told the Scottish secretary:

> My sister hath no greater desire to see me, than I have to see her . . . Lord, how merry shall we be together. I will

marry her, be you sure, I will never have another husband. I would to God we might marry together. I hear of many that we do somewhat resemble, but I take it to be spoken to me for flattery. For if I thought that indeed there were anything in me that were like unto her, I would like myself a great deal the better.

Maitland let Elizabeth's bizarre comments about marrying Mary go by, but there are hints that he had reservations about the queen's overall sincerity, commenting that Mary's good wishes 'were accepted in so good part as I could wish, the visage and countenance always so accompanying the words that it might thereby well appear they did proceed from an inward affection.'[8] Yet for all Elizabeth's gushing, she balked at the idea of an interview taking place within two months, pointing out that her father's abortive meeting with James V at York had been nine months in the planning. This was an unhappy precedent to have raised but there was more to be considered. Elizabeth used the possibility of Guise interference as a further excuse for delay. Being a public person, she said, she could not follow her own inclinations, though she would go on foot to see Mary if she could. So Maitland returned once more to Scotland having failed to make progress.

Yet the commitment to union between England and Scotland that formed the backbone of his political ideology remained unshaken. Before coming to London in the summer of 1562 he had reiterated this to Cecil, despite his frustrations with the suspicions of his English colleague: 'I have,' he wrote, 'in a manner consecrated myself to the commonwealth. The uniting of this isle in friendship hath in my concept been a scope whereof I have long shot and whereunto all my actions have been directed these five or six years.' And he would keep going, despite changes of monarch and shifting developments. 'And as ever as one occasion doth fail me I begin to shuffle the cards off new, always keeping the same ground. I shall not weary so long as any hope remaineth.'[9] The following year, he demonstrated his absolute commitment to this goal and to his queen in a four-month mission to London in which he again demanded recognition by the English parliament of Mary's right to the succession. But he was also looking for ways to bring pressure on Cecil and Elizabeth by advertising Mary's importance in the European marriage market, an area that was bound to cause friction while Elizabeth herself remained without a husband. The English queen's support of the Huguenots in the French Wars of Religion added to the atmosphere of doubt. Maitland was playing for high stakes and he knew it. Meanwhile, his own standing and that of his staunch and, as he acknowledged to Cecil at one point, only true ally, Lord James Stewart, remained high. For while the Queen of Scots rewarded her secretary with the gift of the abbey of Haddington, she had bestowed the title of earl of Moray on her half-brother and provided a lavish ceremony for him early in 1562 when he married Agnes Keith, daughter of Scotland's third earl marischal. Mary appeared to be establishing her rule in Scotland with considerable success, using her own personal skills and following the guidance of the two men to whom she had committed herself in these first years of her reign. But it was impossible to please everyone and allegiances could be lost quickly, as Mary was soon to discover.

MARY HAD NEVER intended to use her return to Scotland merely as a stepping stone to the throne of England. She wanted to be a successful ruler in her own realm. The romantic Hollywood image of a pretty woman who allowed her heart to rule her head does Mary Stewart a great injustice. She worked hard at the business of being queen and is often given insufficient credit for her role in the government of Scotland at this time. An acute listener and observer, she sat in Privy Council meetings working on her embroidery, but while her head was bent over her needle she paid attention to what was going on around her and would take people aside if she wanted subsequent private conversations. This was a tactic she employed after meetings with the English emissary, Thomas Randolph, who felt flattered by such individual attention. Her grandfather, James IV, had enjoyed his needle and silk threads but it seems unlikely that he used them in meetings with his councillors. Nor, so far as we know, did Elizabeth I sew during discussions on weighty matters of state but then she seldom attended council meetings. But Mary had learned this art from Catherine de Medici in France and though it may have reinforced her femininity with men who had their own reservations about being governed by a woman, it meant that she could be at the hub of what was going on without seeming threatening.

The Queen of Scots also took her commitment to rule in conjunction with Scotland's institutions seriously. In the space of six years, five parliaments or conventions were held. The most important of these was the first, held in May 1563, when Mary processed into the parliament house adorned in her royal robes and wearing the crown. The meeting was well attended and its legislative programme steered clear of contentious religious matters, a remarkable testament to the political skills of the queen and her chief advisers. On theological issues, Mary had attempted to contain any difficulties that might ensue from the still strident views of John Knox by having two interviews with him on successive days in the weeks before the parliament met. Knox stuck to his hard line that all who celebrated Mass were lawbreakers and eventually Mary agreed that anyone hearing Mass outside her court itself could be prosecuted. Yet even her confirmation that she would not try to undo the Protestant Reformation in Scotland and her concession to Knox's uncompromising views failed to stop him preaching against the queen and her religion at the end of May 1563. In this sermon he raised the question of the queen's marriage, claiming that if she married a Catholic, the entire Reformation in Scotland would be jeopardized. Mary, like Elizabeth, was extremely sensitive on the issue of her marriage and reacted with tears and anger in a subsequent confrontation with her Protestant tormentor.

Knox's vehement hostility was never going to lessen, but

Mary's life as Queen of Scots was not all weighty affairs of state. She was a cultured young woman who loved the style of the Renaissance court and she was determined to live in the manner that she believed befitted a European court. Mary would have agreed with Sir Richard Maitland's poem that contained the line: 'He rules well that well in court can guide.' Etiquette was carefully observed, nowhere more so than in the elaborate arrangements for dining, where the queen's household sat in hierarchical arrangement. While she enjoyed a varied diet, consuming a variety of meats, seafood and game and drinking good wine, the lower orders, in separate rooms, generally had bread and ale at the main midday meal.

Mary's pastimes ranged from the energetic to the contemplative. Like her English cousin, she loved riding, hunting and walking and she was also fond, when the Scottish summer weather permitted, of going on picnics near Linlithgow Palace. Dining al fresco was another pleasure that she had learned from Catherine de Medici. Mary was a keen tennis player and was competent with a bow and arrow. A love of drama and music was also in her blood; masques were performed in the evenings and Mary's penchant for disguisings (made easier by her height, since she could pass herself off as a man) would have pleased her great-uncle, Henry VIII. On a number of occasions she and her ladies wandered around Edinburgh dressed as ordinary citizens. The queen wrote poetry, though some of the verses later attributed to her are almost certainly forged, and encouraged poets at her court. Alexander Scott was the leading vernacular poet of her personal reign and George Buchanan, who sometimes read Livy with Mary in the evenings, was her Latin court poet. Like a number of the men who partook of the queen's generosity and the vivacity of her person and court, Buchanan, too, would abandon her in 1568 and become one of the most vicious of her critics in the propaganda warfare that followed her deposition. Appointed as tutor to her son during his minority, James VI came to regard his teacher with a mixture of admiration and fear.

Mary's court undoubtedly presented opportunities for poets,

lawyers, philosophers, musicians (including an Italian, David Riccio, who would rise greatly in her favour with disastrous repercussions) and the Scottish nobility. Her household, however, was much more closed. It was, in the words of the distinguished historian Michael Lynch, 'heavily French in both numbers and its cultural leanings, largely Catholic in its sympathies, and on the whole made up of lesser nobles.'[10] Here Mary exercised her own prerogative to organize and appoint as she saw fit, supported by her ladies, including the four Marys, who had all touchingly sworn not to marry before the queen chose a new husband, and by the youngest of her Guise uncles, René, marquis d'Elbeuf.[11] The royal household was an important part of Mary's identity, a piece of France that had returned with her, providing continuity and reassurance. She was reluctant to compromise on its composition. The Protestant culture at her court centred on the figure of her half-brother, Lord James. Paradoxically, it was his wedding in February 1562 that was one of the great set-piece festivities of Mary's reign.

Lord James had been secretly given the earldom of Moray (vacant since the death of its earlier holder, the illegitimate son of Janet Kennedy and James IV) on 30 January 1562. It was his sister's acknowledgement of the role he had played in helping facilitate her return to Scotland and of his support in her claim to the English succession. But while the earldom may have been available, it was highly coveted by the earl of Huntly, whose lands were adjacent and who had been administering it since the previous incumbent's death. The choice of Lady Agnes Keith as Lord James's bride was equally provocative, as the Keiths were also rivals of the Gordons, Huntly's family. This was not, however, a match prompted solely by political ambition and the sizeable dowry that his new wife brought with her. Agnes and Lord James seem to have been genuinely in love. They had known each other for some time – she was then aged twenty-two and he thirty – and became a very happy couple. The countess of Moray, one of a family of eleven children, was a formidably capable woman as well as an attractive one. Nobly born, she appreciated the importance of playing her part, both in the way that she dressed and her frequent appearances at court. A firm favourite with her sister-in-law, the queen, their friendship survived the anguish of Mary's eventual split with her half-brother.

The austere Calvinist marriage ceremony in St Giles Cathedral in Edinburgh was conducted by John Knox. This was appropriate for the avowed Protestantism of both bride and groom but it was followed by a lavish celebration at Holyrood House on the wedding night. It was reported that the whole nobility of the realm was present and that there was much celebration afterwards (to the horror of Knox) with fireworks and feasting. Mary intended to make a point and succeeded in combining spectacle and magnificence with a political message about her own power and intentions. She also knighted a number of Moray's associates. The stock of her half-brother had never stood as high. Huntly, however, was so aggrieved that he rose in rebellion against the queen, attempted to kidnap her when she came to Aberdeen to confront him, and was eventually defeated by Moray in a skirmish at Corrichie. His forces largely deserted him and he died of a stroke while still astride his horse, either during or just after the battle. One of his sons, Sir John Gordon, was hanged in Mary's presence two days later. The queen had won an important victory over one of her most powerful subjects, a man who shared her religion and had been a reluctant rebel, but whom she wanted to be rid of, nevertheless. Mary could be ruthless when she chose. But her faith in Moray was not, ultimately, to be rewarded. It foundered on the twin difficulties of her marriage and the continued refusal of Elizabeth to acknowledge Mary as her successor.

⚛

WHILE IN ENGLAND Queen Elizabeth prevaricated on the question of marriage, Mary was actively searching for a husband for herself. Her uncle, the cardinal of Lorraine, believed that the most suitable Catholic bridegroom was the archduke Charles of

Austria, younger son of the Holy Roman Emperor, Ferdinand. Such a match would, in his view, greatly strengthen Mary's ability to govern Scotland. Archduke Charles was also the first choice of Cecil for Elizabeth's hand. Yet, perhaps sadly for the young man himself, neither queen was really interested and he became something of a footnote to British history. As the ruler responsible for inner Austria, however, he played a more significant role in Europe and his marriage to his own niece, Anna Maria of Bavaria, produced fifteen children.

Though there was continued talk of the possibility of a French marriage, with the younger brother of Charles IX being suggested as a possible candidate, Mary was only using this possibility as a feint. The Queen of Scots was not going to marry a child. Yet her own first choice in the early 1560s was, in reality, even more unsuitable. Mary liked the idea of an alliance with Spain and she seriously considered Philip II's son, Don Carlos, as a prospective husband. This was despite the fact that every court in Europe had heard rumours about the prince's vicious behaviour and his precarious sanity. An obsession with his stepmother, Élisabeth of Valois, added to the embarrassment and misgivings of his father. This was, after all, the heir to the great Spanish empire. Don Carlos was also physically unprepossessing, with a twisted face, misshapen legs and a slight hunchback. Though not unintelligent, he was, in truth, a very disturbed young man and his condition worsened after a fall in 1562 that nearly killed him. Probably saved by trepanning and the advice of a Moorish doctor, his survival was, at the time, credited to his having been made to touch the embalmed body of a local saint. But the incident left him wilder than ever. This was the seventeen-year-old youth Mary believed could be her consort. Luckily for her, his father did not agree and the marriage idea was slowly abandoned, but not before Mary had been seen studying Spanish as an apparent preparation for becoming Don Carlos's wife.[12]

As the negotiations for Mary's marriage continued in different European courts, the queen and her councillors received a new offer that was much closer to home. On the surface, it appears almost as strange as the idea of her marrying a sadistic Spanish prince. For the candidate supported by Elizabeth was none other than her favourite, Robert Dudley.

It is fair to say that there was considerable surprise in Scotland in March 1564, when Elizabeth's proposal was laid before Mary by Thomas Randolph, the English representative in Scotland.[13] The Scottish queen's immediate response was to ask why it stood with her honour to accept him, a reasonable response given the fact that Dudley was a subject of the English queen, known to be so close to her as to suggest, at least to the malicious, that their relationship was improper, and, furthermore, the son of a man executed for treason. Don Carlos might have been unstable but at least he was the heir of Europe's most powerful ruler. Dudley must have seemed to Mary an extraordinary suggestion. But Randolph could offer more than just Dudley's hand; there was also the tantalizing promise that accepting him might finally smooth her path to the Crown of England. Mary was taken aback. The matter, she said, 'came so suddenly upon her' that she needed time to digest it and discuss it with her councillors. The next day, Randolph had his knuckles wrapped by Maitland for revealing Elizabeth's offer to her cousin without first mentioning it to him. He had been operating on the premise that keeping up the appearance of the search for a Catholic husband for Mary would put pressure on England to acknowledge his mistress's place in the succession. Now it became apparent that this effect had, indeed, been achieved but had not brought forth the unequivocal declaration he and Mary were looking for, while at the same time throwing a name into the ring that neither of them had considered.

Was Elizabeth serious? She certainly appeared to be, ennobling Dudley with the title of earl of Leicester to make him more acceptable. It has even been suggested that she anticipated a future in which Mary abandoned Scotland to live at the English court with her new husband and Elizabeth in a sort of royal *ménage à trois*. Elizabeth may have been something of a fantasist but it is hard to believe that she really considered such a possibility. In Scotland, both Moray and Maitland were willing to accept the new earl of Leicester as Mary's husband, but only and always providing that their queen's place in the English succession was guaranteed by parliamentary statute in London. They held on to this hope throughout 1564, despite a very unsatisfactory meeting in Berwick between the two leading Scottish politicians, with the earl of Bedford and Randolph representing England. Here Maitland showed his country's displeasure when he commented: 'It is now two years since this advice was demanded, a year since my Lord Robert was offered and named to us.'[14]

There was to be no further progress. Leicester himself was a reluctant party to being dangled as bait for so long and perhaps embarrassed as well, since his own relationship with Maitland had been good before Elizabeth thrust him into the limelight. In October 1562, as Elizabeth recovered from the smallpox that nearly killed her, he wrote to Maitland: '[I] do wish her majesty [Mary] had two Lethingtons that she might spare one here.'[15] His relationship with Cecil was not necessarily as bad as it has often been depicted – tales of faction and personal enmity at Elizabeth's court have been overplayed – but Leicester might well have desired the Scottish secretary's presence to balance that of his English counterpart. And there was obviously a limit to how long the English could delay, no matter what pretty exchanges had passed between Elizabeth and her cousin in the past. On 5 March 1565, Elizabeth brought a decisive end to the prospect of a marriage with Leicester and, more crucially, to Mary's hopes of her official recognition as Elizabeth's heir. For in this letter Elizabeth stated unequivocally that 'nothing shall be done until her majesty shall be married or shall notify her determination never to marry.' Severe late winter weather delayed the arrival of Elizabeth's missive until 14 March, when an anxious Randolph, who could well appreciate the kind of response it might get, presented it to the Queen of Scots. Mary was furious and tearful, walking out on Randolph to go hunting.

Moray was 'stark mad with rage' and Maitland, though perhaps not surprised, as he had seen the way the wind was setting for some time, was still extremely angry. As well he and the queen's half-brother might have been. There was now no hope for amity between England and Scotland and their own positions and power would be compromised as a result. They were also well aware that Mary now had another husband in prospect. He was young, good looking and possessed his own claim to the thrones of England and Scotland. United with Mary, he offered a prospect that neither Leicester nor any of her foreign suitors could combine in their own persons – the continuation of Catholic monarchy in Scotland, the reinforcement of the Stewart line and a joint claim to the English throne. His name was Henry Stewart, Lord Darnley, and his parents were the ever-ambitious Margaret Douglas and Matthew Stewart, earl of Lennox. They had waited long for their moment and, at last, it had arrived.

☙

In 1565 the Lennoxes had been married for twenty years. They were as devoted to each other as they were to their sense of a destiny that had yet to be fully realized. The couple were confident (sometimes overly so) and did not shy away from taking risks. They were determined to ensure that their potential role, in England and in Scotland, was not something that the rulers of either country could ignore. The countess was more than willing to take on her first cousin, Queen Elizabeth, and to undermine her with the help of European Catholic allies if she could. From her home at Settrington in Yorkshire, far from the prying eyes of the capital, she fostered links with European Catholic allies in Spain and France. As the daughter of Margaret Tudor, the countess never lost sight of her position in the English succession, an inheritance that she was proud to pass on to her two surviving sons, Henry and Charles. She described herself as the second person of the realm of England, a claim that overlooked that of Mary Queen of Scots among the Catholic heirs of Henry VIII. But given the ill health that plagued both

Mary and Elizabeth during the 1560s, the possibility of a dramatic change of fortune could not be discounted and the devoutly Catholic countess believed that God was on her side. Not surprisingly, there was a price to be paid for such bold assertions. Margaret Douglas was viewed by the English Privy Council as a dangerous Catholic intriguer and shortly before Christmas 1561 the earl, the countess, their younger son, Charles, and their entire household were arrested on Elizabeth's orders and imprisoned in London. Henry, Lord Darnley, managed somehow to evade capture and fled to France. The Lennoxes spent more than a year in confinement while the Privy Council tried to find sufficient evidence to proceed further against the countess. No charges were actually brought against Matthew, her husband, but there was real concern about the involvement in the Lennoxes' schemes of the Spanish ambassador, the self-important bishop de Quadra.

Margaret and Matthew were not model prisoners. The countess complained constantly, bombarding Cecil and Elizabeth with letters asking for mercy and a full indication of what charges might be brought. Matthew, in solitary confinement, became unwell and indulged in such violent rages that his gaoler complained of his conduct. In an age remarkable for the public display of private emotions, the Lennoxes were notably unbridled and passionate. In their case, raging and writing helped. By November 1562, Matthew had joined his wife in house arrest at Sheen in Surrey. Not until February the following year, however, were Matthew and Margaret Lennox finally released, unpardoned but free. By the middle of 1563 they were back at court, as was Darnley, and apparently enjoying a burst of royal favour, though one possible interpretation of this Elizabethan change of heart is that the queen thought that she could use them as a counterpoint to the claim of Katherine Grey. Yet using the Lennoxes as a distraction was a course dangerous in itself. It solved nothing in relation to the long-term questions of the English succession and it heightened their sense of entitlement. The earl's proximity to the Scottish throne was a further hand they could play but first he needed to seek rehabilitation of his reputation and restitution of his lands in Scotland. It was his ultimate success in this that would alter the balance of Anglo–Scottish relations.

Matthew Stewart made suit via a trusted servant for his restoration soon after Mary's return to Scotland. Mary did not take immediate action but she made very reassuring noises: 'all she might do for my lord and my lady her aunt, she would do at proper time ... with remembrances to them both.'[16] She did not, however, take any further action. Support for the Lennoxes was not widespread among the Scottish nobility at the time. Mary herself preferred to wait for the next move to come from England. It duly arrived in June 1563, when Elizabeth made a formal request for Lennox's restoration in Scotland. It has been suggested that she well appreciated the ructions this would cause in Scotland (the Lennox–Hamilton feud had certainly not disappeared and Châtelherault could hardly be expected to view his rival's return with anything other than supreme displeasure) but that she wanted, above all, to be rid of the Lennoxes. But since their capacity for intrigue was unlikely to disappear north of the border and the possibilities, not least for their son, Darnley, as a prospective husband for Mary would be greatly enhanced by the earl of Lennox's return to Scotland, this seems unlikely. Perhaps Elizabeth believed that after his long exile in England the earl was more English than Scottish in his sympathies and would prove a useful ally there. If so, she made a serious error of judgement. The Lennox restoration, granted by Mary in April 1564, was supported by both Maitland and Moray, who wished to see the Hamiltons' influence curbed. Elizabeth, perhaps having time to ponder the implications of her support for Lennox, did not let him go until the early autumn.

On 23 September 1564, Matthew Stewart rode into Edinburgh with a glittering retinue of velvet-clad gentlemen. Margaret stayed in England as Elizabeth was unwilling to let her go as well. Margaret is unlikely to have been greatly concerned by this restriction. Like her husband, she had ambitions for her elder son, Henry, and was perfectly confident that Matthew, once ensconced in Scotland, could bring them to fruition. She was even willing to forgo her long-standing claims to her father's lands if this could open the way for her husband and son to be accepted more readily. What the English government, and particularly the English queen, would make of their ambitions was far less important to the Lennoxes than the realization of all their dreams.

∞

THE EARL OF LENNOX speedily set about ingratiating himself with Mary. He made sure he was as close to her as possible, becoming an indispensable part of her social life. At balls and masques, the kind of entertainment she particularly loved, Matthew made sure that he was at Mary's side. And this social proximity gave him an ideal opportunity to influence a young woman who was naturally inclined to admire gallantry and affability. They were blood relations and had the experience of the manners of the French court in common. Keeping up with Mary cost Lennox money, and his restitution, granted in October 1564 and hailed by Maitland in parliament, was, predictably, badly received by Châtelherault, who saw the role of the Hamiltons in Scottish affairs disappearing with the return of his hated rival. Mary, however, was happy to curb Hamilton power, having successfully dealt with Huntly in northern Scotland. Maitland gave a revealing justification of her policy when he declared that she had 'a certain inclination to pity the decay of noble houses, and . . . has a great deal more pleasure to be the instrument of the uphold, maintenance and advancement of the ancient blood, than to have the matter ministered of the decay or overthrow of any good race.'[17] This was music to the ears of the Lennoxes. But what they most wanted to hear were the wedding vows that the Queen of Scots would take when she married their elder son.

Matthew Stewart did not waste time. Two months after his own return to Scotland he made a formal request of Elizabeth that his son be allowed to join him. This was couched as a legal

nicety; Darnley needed to be present so that they could be
restored to their Scottish lands together. By now, the English
were well aware that Darnley's name was in the frame as a suitor
to Mary Queen of Scots. As was her custom, Elizabeth delayed
for a while. Then, in January 1565, she issued a passport allowing
the young lord to travel to Scotland. It had a limited time frame
and she expected him to return. In retrospect, this seems naïve
to the point of foolishness. But Elizabeth was living in a complex
present, not a past for which we seek easy explanations. Her
decision to let Darnley go has been held against her for centuries.
Whether she had carefully, in her own mind, weighed the odds
and convinced herself that Mary would not marry a subject or
whether she calculated that Mary Stewart married to Henry
Darnley was less of a threat to England than her sister queen
married to a member of a powerful European family we shall
never know. Perhaps she was still playing games, hoping to
muddy the waters and prolong the confusion over Mary's marriage and her own. But if this was so, then she had definitely
misjudged Mary's character. Unlike the queen of England, the
Scottish monarch was ready to marry and, if the choice pleased
her personally, then so much the better.

The idea of Darnley as a consort for the Queen of Scots was
raised publicly by Elizabeth herself, after the ceremony in which
Robert Dudley was created earl of Leicester. Elizabeth displayed
an inappropriate affection for Leicester, memorably described by
the Scottish ambassador Sir James Melville who reported that
'she could not refrain from putting her hand in his neck to tickle
him smilingly . . . she asked me how I liked him.' Melville, ever
the diplomat, replied, 'I answered that as he was a worthy subject,
so he was happy who had a princess who could discern and
reward good service.' The Scottish ambassador refrained from
making any observation that Leicester was being elevated to
make him more acceptable to Mary Queen of Scots. It was then
that Elizabeth, indicating Darnley, who had borne the sword of
honour as the nearest prince of the blood, uttered the famous
and prophetic question: 'Yet you like better of yonder long lad?'

Melville demurred, perhaps too fervently: 'My answer was that no woman of spirit would make choice of such a man, that was more like a woman than a man; for he was very lusty, beardless and lady-faced.' (The word 'lusty' in the sixteenth century had several meanings but was often used to denote cheerfulness and good spirits.) The ambassador wanted to make it clear that he felt Darnley was too young to be a serious contender for Mary's hand, though he went on to acknowledge that he had 'a secret charge to deal with his mother, my Lady Lennox, to procure liberty for him to go to Scotland [where his father was already] that he might see the country and convoy the earl, his father, back again to England.'[18] Here Melville was probably being disingenuous. He must have suspected, even before Elizabeth voiced the possibility herself, that the Lennoxes were manoeuvring for something greater than an educational visit for Darnley to the land of his parents' birth. So, actively supported by Leicester, who seems to have viewed the Darnley suit as a way of getting him out of a difficult situation, and unopposed by Cecil, Henry, Lord Darnley, arrived in Edinburgh on 12 February 1565, travelling through some of the most icy conditions in years to get there.[19]

Five days later he presented himself to the Queen of Scots at Wemyss Castle in Fife. Melville's later assertion that Mary was immediately taken with Darnley, saying that he was 'the lustiest and best proportioned long man that she had ever seen; for he was of a high stature, long and small, even and erect, and from his youth well instructed in all honest and homely exercises', was probably written well after their first meeting. Randolph, watching carefully but no doubt bringing his own prejudices to bear (he felt let down by Leicester), reported that Mary did not, initially, show Darnley any particular favour. Things changed, however, with the reception of Elizabeth's letter dashing any remaining hopes of an official recognition for Mary as her heir. For, in truth, there was nothing new about the idea of the Scottish queen marrying Lord Darnley. It had been mentioned several years earlier and made perfectly good dynastic sense.

Mary believed that it would give her freedom to rule Scotland as she saw fit, without being constantly beholden to Elizabeth, while at the same time strengthening her claim to the English throne. Marriage to Darnley would unite two branches of the Stewart family who could, together, work towards the more glorious goal of uniting Britain.

Still, Mary waited before committing to Darnley. At the same time that she was showing him favour by sending him food from her own table while he recovered from a bout of measles in April, Maitland was in London with secret instructions to obtain Elizabeth's permission for the match but also to ascertain, one last time, if there was any possibility remaining of marrying Don Carlos. He got no joy of either and when his report reached Stirling on 3 May, Mary's decision to proceed with the Darnley match appears to have been made irrevocably. It was only now that the English queen and Privy Council suddenly appreciated the problems that such a marriage would mean for them. Elizabeth sent Throckmorton, who knew Mary from her time as queen of France, to try to dissuade her but this probably hardened her attitude. Randolph, an even more helpless witness of events than he had always been, suspected that Throckmorton had earlier made matters worse by encouraging approval of Darnley's return with precisely the outcome of marriage to Mary in mind. 'If,' Randolph threatened Throckmorton, 'you were as innocent as our lord Jesus Christ, if any evil come to me, I will make you partaker.'[20]

The divisions among English politicians on the fraught subject of a husband for the Queen of Scots were more than matched by the opposition it provoked among the Scottish nobility. A watershed in Mary's reign had been reached. She would lose the support of Moray, her half-brother; of Maitland, her clever secretary, who made a dangerous enemy; of the Hamiltons and the influential earls of Argyll and Glencairn. There was still no clear Catholic/Protestant split and the religious views of Lennox and his son were opaque (both had lived as Protestants in England) but the fear of a move towards a more overtly Catholic monarchy grew. None of this deterred Mary. At six in the morning on 29 July 1565, she and Henry Stewart, Lord Darnley, were married in a Catholic service conducted in Mary's private chapel at Holyrood. After the service, Darnley left and Mary heard the nuptial Mass alone. A declaration the previous day had announced that government would be in the joint names of the King and Queen of Scots and silver coins were issued in the names of Henry and Mary. Custom and practice at the time should have meant that Henry would take precedence over his wife but being proclaimed King Henry was not the same thing as the granting of the crown matrimonial and this would speedily become a source of friction between the newlyweds. Mary soon discovered, if she did not know it already, that her nineteen-year-old husband was every bit as immature as Melville had suggested to Elizabeth. Darnley's handsome face could not long conceal his lack of confidence and experience. His was a turbulent and, upon occasion, vicious heart.

CHAPTER FOURTEEN

Downfall

'*Oh Madam! I should neither perform the office of a faithful cousin nor an affectionate friend if I studied more to please your ears than to preserve your honour. Therefore I will not conceal from you that people for the most part are saying that you will look through your fingers at this deed instead of avenging it.*'

Elizabeth I to Mary Queen of Scots, 24 February 1567

'*If you have not pity on me now, I may say with reason that it is all over with my son, my country and myself.*'

Mary Queen of Scots to her uncle, the
cardinal of Lorraine, 21 June 1568

ELIZABETH'S IMMEDIATE REACTION to the marriage of her two distant cousins was to confine the countess of Lennox in the Tower of London. Darnley's brother, Charles, was left in Yorkshire without either of his parents, although supported by loyal servants. His brother's triumph had been dearly bought for this boy of ten. Margaret was not, however, cowed into silence or inaction by her incarceration, the second in a period of four years. From the Tower she maintained contact with the French and Spanish ambassadors and was in regular correspondence with her husband, sending messages to him via the earl of Bedford, who was frequently used by Elizabeth as her senior representative on diplomatic missions to Scotland at this time. If, in retrospect, it seems astonishing that Margaret should have been able to get away with all this, it should be remembered that being held in the Tower, especially if you were a noblewoman, did not mean confinement in some dank dungeon on a diet of bread and water. It certainly entailed loss of liberty but for someone as resourceful and determined as Margaret Lennox it was more of an inconvenience than a disaster. Long accustomed to running her own network of contacts and spies, she would not be stopped so easily.

The English Privy Council, now faced with the full implications of their approval of the queen's ill-judged decision to let Darnley go to Scotland, pondered a more aggressive response. Based on Cecil's mistaken belief that Mary was losing the support of her subjects, they discussed the possibility of removing the Scottish queen from her throne through direct invasion. In September 1565 plans for war were drawn up but they came to nothing.[1] Instead, a wait-and-see policy was followed, perhaps because there was, in truth, no other viable alternative. But this was a period of embarrassment and anxiety for the English queen and her advisers.

So Mary had nothing immediately to fear from London. The response in Scotland, however, proved much more of a problem. Elevating the Lennoxes offended key members of the nobility and led to a split within her own family that became irreparable. For now the earl of Moray, who had left the court in May, refusing to give his consent to the wedding, became the focus of armed opposition to the queen and her new husband. Though it is far too simplistic to say that the Darnley marriage was the cause of Mary's downfall, its impact on her relations with her half-brother is undeniable and the rift with Moray would become permanent, despite an apparent reconciliation the following year. Yet in the early autumn of 1565, as he tried to spearhead a rebellion against his sister, hoping for English support (which did not come) and initially attracting the disgruntled Hamiltons to his cause, not even his acknowledged role as the chief aristocratic defender of Protestantism in Scotland could unite the Protestant nobility to his cause. His attempt at a coordinated uprising was met head on by a determined queen who was able to outmanoeuvre him, both politically and militarily. While the forces of the queen and Moray pursued each other sporadically, without ever actually clashing, Mary was able to depict her brother and his associates as greedy, unpatriotic, power-hungry rebels, men who were attempting to subvert the established order of things with false claims about threats to the Protestant religion: 'For what other is this,' she demanded, reprising her argument with John Knox, 'but to dissolve the whole policy and in a manner to invert the very order of nature to make the prince obey and the subjects to command.'[2]

Moray's rebellion, subsequently labelled the Chaseabout Raid because of its almost farcical nature, did not seem amusing to Mary at the time and there is a sense in her correspondence that her resentment of her brother's role in Scottish politics had been growing. She had heaped honours and money on him and this was how he showed his gratitude. In a letter to Paul de Foix, the French ambassador at Elizabeth's court, she laid out the background to her quarrel with Moray. 'You must understand', she wrote, 'that when the said earl of Moray perceived that I wished to marry the son of the earl of Lennox, he came and told me that, since I had so resolved, he would contrive so well that all the nobility and rest of my subjects should approve of it, provided that he might manage the business himself alone and that my said subjects should know that he was the leader in it.' But this approach (which may well have seemed too controlling to Mary in itself) was to come at a price the queen was not prepared to pay, namely, the necessity of banishing the Roman Catholic religion from Scotland. Mary was willing to reiterate her proclamation made soon after she returned to Scotland, safeguarding Protestantism as the state religion of Scotland and to guarantee liberty of conscience. She even announced that she would listen to Protestant preaching. But she would have her marriage to Darnley on her own terms, not Moray's. 'It appeared to me,' she told de Foix, 'very singular that a subject, upon whom I had bestowed so much honour and wealth, should compel me by his underhand dealing, to undertake nothing except through the medium of him, if I wished to marry.'[3]

Moray then put about rumours that the Lennoxes wished to kill him. He might genuinely have believed this, of course, and it must be the case that both the earl of Lennox and his son would have welcomed Moray's demise, but Moray refused to supply proof and ignored repeated summons from his sister to come to court. In August 1565 Moray was 'put to the horn', a traditional process whereby rebels were publicly proclaimed by three blasts of the instrument. By early October he had sought asylum in London – the most that Elizabeth was prepared to offer – and was given a dressing down by the English queen, more for form's sake than out of genuine conviction. Elizabeth's advisers, and perhaps even the monarch herself, were sorry that he had not succeeded.

Mary had crushed her rebels and shown herself skilful in using patronage as a means of dividing her enemies. She had lost Moray but, for the time being, retained Maitland and Morton, whose support had been secured through a deal that saw the countess of Lennox withdraw her claim to the Douglas lands in Morton's favour. The Scottish queen's marriage to Darnley was dynastically sound, though it had compromised her relationship with England. But that relationship had, in reality, been on the downward path for some years and she was weary of Elizabeth's delays and lies. No doubt she hoped to deal with England and her claim to its throne from a position of strength following her assertion of her own decision-making powers and the reinforcement of her rule in Scotland. Alas, such hopes were fading rapidly. Even as her brother knelt before Elizabeth to be chastised in London, the Darnley marriage was falling apart.

The reasons for this lay in Henry Stewart's character and upbringing. He was a very young nineteen-year-old, immature in outlook and, though well educated, hopelessly indulged by his adoring parents, who put him on a pedestal and encouraged him to think that his birth in itself entitled him to the thrones of the two kingdoms of Britain. Both the Lennoxes, but particularly Margaret, were blind to his failings. They simply could not see that they had raised a vain and shallow youth who had all the outward trappings of regality – the good looks, the height, the carefully acquired manners of the courtier, learned in both England and France – but none of the substance. Darnley was self-absorbed, easily bored and wilful. On top of this, as time was to show, he possessed a decidedly sadistic streak. Some of his behaviour may be attributable to the likelihood that he was already ill with syphilis, a complaint that he had picked up during his time in France.

It has been suggested that Mary was already aware of his failings (but not, presumably, the fact that he was diseased, with its potential dangers for her own often precarious health and any children she and Henry might produce) before the marriage ceremony. Despite this, she decided to go ahead. By July 1565 she was running out of options in the choice of a husband and the dynastic imperative was too strong to be resisted. Nor was Darnley entirely to blame for the disasters that overtook him and his wife. In a more stable environment and with appropriate training and encouragement, he might have grown into a useful and fulfilled consort but circumstances and time were not on his side. He knew nothing of Scotland and failed to appreciate that he could easily be manipulated by resentful or ambitious men who saw his frustration with his role and realized how his wounded pride could be used to their advantage. Darnley's demand that he be given the crown matrimonial and thereby enjoy, in practice, superiority in ruling Scotland over Mary, was firmly resisted by the queen. She would not promote him to power because she did not trust his judgement or his intentions. And in this, as in her handling of Scottish affairs before her marriage, Mary proved her astuteness. It is true that her first husband, Francis II of France, had been given the crown matrimonial but that was in a different time, when Scotland was a client state of France and the real power lay with her father-in-law, Henry II.

It did not take Henry Stewart long to grasp that, for at least the foreseeable future, he was only going to be an appendage, the queen's husband rather than a power-wielding King of Scots. By November 1565 there were reports of rows between the royal pair. Mary was a conscientious queen and took the business of government seriously. This meant that she could not be constantly at her husband's side, as he seemed to expect, and the more he complained and became insolent, the less she was inclined to humour him. Neglected and angry, Darnley took to drink, which only added to the concerns of many that he was entirely unfit to share the Scottish throne. Two further circumstances added to Darnley's woes. During the autumn of 1565 his father, the earl of Lennox, dismayed by the realization that the marriage had run into serious trouble so soon and unable to exert any positive influence over the disgruntled young man, felt it best to leave court. He retired to his estates near Glasgow and the rift between father and son was never fully healed. This increased Darnley's sense of isolation, and his feeling of being utterly irrelevant was further fuelled by the knowledge that Mary was pregnant. Darnley, believing that the birth of an heir would deprive him of the Scottish throne should Mary die, was a most unhappy father-to-be. The queen had conceived in September. By November her marital difficulties were well known and in December she removed from circulation the silver coin with the heads of Darnley and herself on it. And as the king's grievances grew, he believed he knew where to apportion blame; the fault lay in the queen's household and with one individual in particular – Mary's secretary for her French correspondence, the Savoyard, David Riccio.

After the Chaseabout Raid and the flight of Moray and his fellow conspirators to England, Mary had used a policy of conciliation and patronage towards those of the nobility who remained loyal to her. This approach was an essential part of her personal rule in Scotland and generally served her well. It demonstrated a grasp of political and social complexities in her realm that is at odds with the view of an incompetent queen. But she also consulted with members of her household and this led to tensions with the wider Scottish polity that threatened to get out of control if not carefully managed. The nobility as a class believed that the monarch should take counsel from them, not from low-born, upstart foreigners. Riccio was not the sort of man that they respected and he was believed to have the ear of the queen. Certainly she does seem to have enjoyed the company of this erstwhile musician, who had come to Scotland on the strength of his success as a singer at the court of the duke of Savoy. Mary was sufficiently impressed to hire him as a bass to make up a quartet who sang regularly for her. Thereafter, his rise was swift. By early 1562 he was a gentleman of the queen's privy chamber and at the end of 1564 he became her French secretary when she fell out with the previous holder of the post.

Riccio was probably in his early thirties and his general appearance did not match the beauty of his voice. Small of stature and unprepossessing, he made up for his ugliness by wearing very expensive clothes. Now frequently in the queen's company, this proximity seems to have gone to his head as much as it annoyed Darnley and offended courtiers who did not want to go to 'Seigneur Davie' for favours. Upset as Mary undoubtedly was by the behaviour of her husband, she was unwise to allow Riccio as much latitude as she did. His arrogance was a match for her husband's, a conflict that did not bode well for the future.

The relationship between the two men had not always been so acrimonious. Some have even suggested that they were secret lovers when Darnley first came to Mary's court but there is no real evidence that either man was homosexual. It was common for men – and women – to share beds in the sixteenth century. Randolph had once noted with some displeasure that he had been obliged to share a bed with Maitland during one of Mary's progresses in northern Scotland, when accommodation was scarce. Such was not the case, presumably, at Holyrood when

Darnley first arrived from England and Riccio ingratiated himself with the young newcomer. While it is tempting to interpret Darnley's growing hatred of Riccio as the ire of a jilted lover, it seems more likely that the king, like many others, quickly came to despise Riccio's pretensions and the fact that he never seemed to leave the queen's side, staying up late in the night with her playing cards and generally getting under everyone else's skin by ostentatious displays of his newly acquired wealth.

Nevertheless, too much has been made of Riccio's role in the events of March 1566. The little Italian, overly impressed by his own importance, certainly failed to recognize his peril and put too much faith in the queen's power. This left him dangerously exposed. There were few, apart from Mary, ready to defend him. But what happened on the night of 9 March should be seen in a wider context. It has been called an attempted *putsch* and was intended as an assault on the queen and her methods of government. Mary had tried to set her own stamp on the administration of Scotland by choosing conservative Protestants as advisers and increasing the number of Catholics on the council. She also announced that in the parliament called for March 1566, she would introduce legislation to legalize the Mass. This caused great alarm among more extreme Protestants.

Yet there was a good measure of self-interest on the part of the conspirators and, in this respect, the timing was crucial. For the other major piece of legislation to be enacted was the permanent forfeiture of the earl of Moray and his associates in the Chaseabout Raid. This combination of an apparent attempt to restore Catholicism by a newly confident queen, who increasingly ignored her traditional advisers from the upper echelons of the nobility, while at the same time ruining prominent upholders of the Protestant religion, was too much to be borne. Maitland, Lennox and the earl of Morton, to whom Darnley's mother had handed over her claim to the Douglas inheritance in return for his support for her son's marriage to the queen, came together to put an end to Mary's plans. The queen, perhaps distracted by the discomforts of pregnancy and troubled by the collapse of her marriage, failed to read the warning signs. In particular, she totally misjudged the jealousy and viciousness of which her husband was capable. And Darnley's support would be key to the successful outcome of the plot that certainly meant to control the queen and possibly remove her altogether.

So was forged an alliance between the exiled rebels (Moray, the earls of Glencairn, Argyll and Rothes, and Lords Ochiltree and Boyd) and the disgruntled earl of Morton, his illegitimate half-brother, George Douglas, and Lords Ruthven and Lindsay. Also party to the plot were Maitland of Lethington, in theory still part of Mary's administration but a man who now saw his personal influence with the queen seriously diminished, and the earl of Lennox, who despite his difficult relations with his son in the autumn of 1565 still loved him and wished to see Henry granted the crown matrimonial. The conspirators, who began plotting seriously in February 1566, needed to draw the young king into their web. However much they may have disliked him, his many failings meant that he could easily be encouraged to play along and be used as a figurehead, his vanity satisfied by the promises made to him. So Darnley signed a bond with those who sought to challenge his wife, promising to restore them and defend Protestantism in Scotland in return for being granted the crown matrimonial. At the time, the bond must have seemed to hold the promise of a much more glorious future for Henry Stewart. Real power, or so he thought, beckoned and the demons of his marriage, along with his growing conviction (encouraged, of course, by Maitland and the conspirators) that he was being cuckolded by a base-born foreigner, would be exorcized by the dagger he intended to thrust into Riccio's body. It was Darnley himself who suggested that the assassination should be carried out in Mary's presence. He could easily persuade himself that the child Mary was carrying was not his at all. His allies may not have had the visceral hatred of Riccio that characterized Henry's attitude to the plot but they were in agreement that only a dramatic gesture would intimidate the queen and her supporters into submission. Riccio was the obvious sacrifice. It was easier to justify the violent removal of an unhealthy influence on their monarch than it was to admit that they were largely motivated by concern for their own positions and livelihoods. The bill of forfeiture against them was due to be passed on 12 March and the conspirators now needed to move fast.

On the evening of 9 March, Mary was at supper in her private apartments in the James V Tower at the palace of Holyrood, in the company of her half-sister, Lady Jean Stewart, countess of Argyll, and her half-brother, Lord Robert Stewart. Clearly Mary was still close to these two siblings, who had shown her much support since her return. She also had much in common with her feisty and quick-witted sister, whose own marriage had run into insoluble difficulties. A few other close friends, including the master of her horse, Arthur Erskine, and the ubiquitous Riccio were also in attendance. The small supper room adjoining Mary's bedchamber, in which the group was dining, offered an intimate space for a group of friends to chat over a meal but its very restrictiveness also made it a place of deadly peril if ill-intentioned people entered. There could be no escape.

When Darnley suddenly appeared, uninvited, to join the guests at Mary's table, the queen did not, at first, realize what might be about to follow, though she had already been warned of plots against her. But the king had already led Ruthven and a servant through his own apartments and left them to climb the secret stairway into Mary's bedchamber while he went on ahead to distract attention. So when Ruthven, clad in full armour under his nightgown and ghastly of appearance (he was dying of liver and kidney disease and had only two months to live) burst into the queen's presence and demanded that 'yonder man Davie come forth of your presence', Mary, alarmed, was instantly suspicious of her husband but he denied all knowledge of what was happening. Ruthven continued to lecture Mary on her current failings, all of which he attributed to Riccio: 'He hath offended your honour, which I dare not be so bold to speak of. As to the king your husband's honour, he hath hindered him of the crown matrimonial, which your Grace promised him . . . And as to the nobility, he hath caused your majesty to banish a great part of them, and to forfeit them at this present Parliament.'⁴ This succinct rehearsal of the plotters' grievances laid all at the feet of David Riccio but provoked in Mary only the curtly dismissive order that Ruthven should leave her presence under pain of treason. If real cause of offence could be found against her servant, she would ensure that he was dealt with by parliament.

Such a promise was never going to be good enough for the conspirators. As Riccio clung to the queen's skirts in terror and Mary's guests and the servants tried to grab hold of Ruthven, there was a scuffle as Morton and his cronies burst into the little room. Only the presence of mind of the countess of Argyll, who rescued a candelabra knocked over in the fracas, prevented fire taking hold of the tapestries. While a pistol was held to Mary's side, Riccio was dragged from the room and stabbed to death in the outer chamber. By the queen's own account his body had fifty-six stab wounds. He had paid a terrible price for his pretensions, and his failure to appreciate the very real danger that faced him in the weeks preceding his death shows that both he and Mary were out of touch with key developments in Scottish politics.

If Mary had perhaps been overconfident, she was now in fear for her life. Although she did not actually witness the death of her servant, she heard his screams and the terror that these bloodthirsty assassins might turn their daggers on her was very real. She had been restrained by Darnley, who had, when the time came, been too overwrought or too scared to join in the assault on the hapless Riccio. But the conspirators were unwilling to let him remain a mere spectator to the murder of the man they had encouraged him to believe was sleeping with his wife and, grabbing his dagger, they plunged it, as the *coup de grâce*, into Riccio's twitching body and left it there as a public witness of his part in the plot.

Mary was six months pregnant and in mortal terror. Whether

her husband and father-in-law had ever harboured hopes that such a daring and brutal act would cause her to miscarry or even kill her is open to question. They undoubtedly had a claim to the throne in such circumstances but, by law, Mary's heir at the time was Châtelherault, not the Lennox Stewarts. A civil war might have followed with no automatic assurance of success. It seems more likely that the Lennox family's priority was to secure the crown matrimonial and for that they needed Mary alive, not dead. But that such violence should be openly carried out in the queen's presence was an affront even in a troubled kingdom like Scotland. Confined to the palace by Darnley, who answered the concerns of the provost of Edinburgh for the queen's safety by parading his wife in front of a window, Mary had to recover her equilibrium as quickly as she could if she was to safeguard her own position and that of her unborn child.

But though Darnley had at least kept part of the pact with Morton and the others by dissolving the parliament and thus ensuring that Moray and the exiles were not forfeited, he completely underestimated his wife. Mary, perhaps sensing his indecision and noting his refusal to get physically involved in the murder of Riccio, swiftly realized that the most effective way for her to capitalize on her husband's weakness was to remove him from the influence of the plotters. This involved play-acting (she pretended to be having a miscarriage in order to buy time and allow her gentlewomen, who could carry messages to her supporters, access to her that had been severely restricted), making up to Henry and finally spelling out to him that he stood to lose as much by her detention as she did. It also required a reconciliation, at least superficially, with her brother, the earl of Moray, who had been waiting at Newcastle-upon-Tyne in England for word of the plot's success. He arrived back in Edinburgh on the evening of 10 March, barely twenty-four hours after Riccio's murder. Mary pardoned the Chaseabout rebels and promised to pardon the perpetrators of this most recent outrage as well. Then, with promises of support from the earls of Huntly and Bothwell, two key nobles who were opposed to her brother

Moray and to Morton, Mary made a daring night-time escape from Holyrood, despite the restrictions of her pregnancy, and rode with Henry to Dunbar, an impressively fortified castle on the south-east coast of Scotland. From there, she intended to face down this new set of rebels, re-establish her hold on Scotland and prepare for the birth of the child that she believed would secure her position once and for all.

⁓

FROM DUNBAR, as she and her weak-willed, changeable husband waited for her two principal supporters, the earls of Bothwell and Huntly, to sweep her back into power in Edinburgh, Mary wrote to Elizabeth. She did not mince words:

> Did we not know the power of the evil and wrongous report made to you by our rebels, we could not think nor almost bear with the strange devised letter which we have lately received of you ... marvelling greatly how ye can be so inclined rather to believe and credit the false speaking of such unworthy to be called subjects, than us, who are of your own blood, and who also never thought nor made occasion to use such rigour and menacing of us as ye do ... Whereas ye write to us that we in our former letters blamed them that kept not promises, but think one thing and do another, would ye should remember the same ... Last of all, some of our subjects and Council have manifestly shown what men they are – as first have taken our house, slain our most special servant in our own presence, and thereafter held our proper person captive treasonably, whereby we were constrained to escape straightly about midnight out of our palace of Holyroodhouse, to the place where we are for the present, in the greatest danger, fear of our lives and evil estate that ever princes on earth stood in.

She went on to warn Elizabeth against offering succour or aid to the rebels, saying she would look for help elsewhere if the English queen continued in this course, and closed by regretting that she had not written this letter in her own hand, adding 'but of truth we are so tired and evil at ease, through riding twenty miles in five hours of the night, and the frequent sickness and evil disposition, by the occasion of our child, that we could not.'[5]

Elizabeth would not have been pleased by Mary's tone, which was prompted by a criticism in an earlier letter she had sent to the Queen of Scots. But there were other reasons for Elizabeth's displeasure, beyond the very real quandary of what to do with Morton and Ruthven when they fled to England. Her interference in the French religious wars had not endeared her to Catholic Europe and there were signs of a new Catholic League being formed that might favour Mary's claim to the English throne. She was also concerned about the support being given by the Scots to the rebellion of Shane O'Neill, earl of Tyrone, in Ireland. For Elizabeth was not without rebels in her own dominions, though they were not so near to her person as Mary's were in Scotland, nor so numerous. Yet a Catholic revival, spearheaded by Philip II of Spain and encouraged by a revived papacy under Pope Pius V at the Council of Trent, could well give encouragement to Elizabeth's subjects in northern England, where Catholicism remained a significant force and Mary Stewart an attractive alternative as queen of England.

This spat between the two queens was soon glossed over. Elizabeth sent Sir Robert Melville, brother of the Scottish ambassador, to reassure her cousin. This caused Mary to change her tune completely, at least in the correspondence she now addressed to Elizabeth, who, Mary said, had 'shown that the magnanimity and good nature of your predecessors surpass every other passion in you and thus placed me under such an obligation that I do not know how I shall ever repay it, unless it be by placing myself and all my power at your disposal, could these be of service to you.' There is something almost tongue-in-cheek about these sentiments. The 'magnanimity and good nature' of Elizabeth's father, Henry VIII, towards Scotland did not bear much scrutiny and the best service Mary could have done Elizabeth would surely have been to go quiet about her place in the English succession. As was her custom, the English queen wavered about what to do with the earl of Morton. The French had asked her to return him to Scotland but though Elizabeth first issued vague instructions that the earl and his associates should absent themselves from England in some unnamed foreign country, she never, in fact, expelled them and Morton would return to Scotland by the end of 1566. Elizabeth had put on a fine show for Guzman de Silva, the Spanish representative in London, when they discussed Mary's misfortunes and the dastardly murder of Riccio. With a portrait of her Scottish cousin hanging from a gold belt around her waist, she told him that 'she, herself, in her [Mary's] place would have taken her husband's dagger and stabbed him with it, but she did not want your majesty to think she would do this to the archduke if he came.'[6] The long-running discussions about a marriage between the English queen and Philip's nephew were turned to witty effect by Elizabeth in this exchange. Whether she would, indeed, have stabbed Darnley had she been in Mary's shoes on the night of 9 March 1566, is an interesting question.

By early April, Mary was back in Edinburgh and concentrating her thoughts firmly on the immediate future. As she prepared for her lying-in, she instructed Mary Livingston to draw up her will. This sounds morbid to a modern ear but was common practice for well-off expectant mothers in the sixteenth century. Childbirth was a dangerous experience and many who came through the delivery successfully succumbed to puerperal fever in its aftermath. The most notable lady of high degree to suffer this fate was Katherine Parr, the sixth wife of Henry VIII, whose final marriage to Sir Thomas Seymour ended in her death after giving birth to a daughter in 1548. No copy of the will Mary made at this time survives but an inventory of her jewellery, which lists bequests, does. Of the 253 pieces, intended for over sixty recipients, the largest number went to Henry, her husband, and her Guise relatives received as many as the faithful four Marys, though the bequests intended for the Guises were of higher value. To her parents-in-law she left three diamond rings.

None of these gifts was to be made, she stipulated, if the child was living. And in the end, her fears proved unfounded. Both she and her son survived.

Prince James (later King James VI of Scotland and I of England) was born in the secure fortress of Edinburgh Castle at mid-morning on Saturday, 19 June 1566. The labour was long and difficult and throughout Mary was supported entirely by women: her midwife, Margaret Houston, and various aristocratic ladies headed by the countess of Atholl. The earl of Mar, who would become the prince's guardian the following year, fired the castle guns and the citizens lit the customary bonfires of rejoicing. The same day, Henry, the king, wrote 'in great haste' to his wife's uncle, the cardinal of Lorraine, to give him the news. 'The Queen, my wife, has just been delivered of a son, which circumstance, I am sure, will not cause you less joy than ourselves.' Both he and Mary wrote to young Charles IX of France asking him to stand as one of the child's godparents. The child's other godfather was the duke of Savoy. Elizabeth had already agreed to act as godmother. She gave considerable thought to her choice of proxy and eventually settled on the queen's sister, the countess of Argyll. Elizabeth also provided a magnificent christening gift – a gold font worth over £1,000 – though with typical tardiness, it arrived too late for the ceremony itself. The English queen pointed out it could always be used for further offspring. Her oft-quoted reaction to the news of the Scottish heir was that Mary was delivered of a fair son while she, Elizabeth, was 'barren stock'.

Elizabeth sent Sir Henry Killigrew, an experienced diplomat and a man close to both the earl of Leicester and William Cecil (who would later become his brother-in-law), to offer congratulations and, perhaps of even greater importance for her own peace of mind, to see if he could detach the earl of Argyll from his support for Shane O'Neill. Killigrew could not see the Queen of Scots immediately; he was told he 'should have audience as soon as she might have any ease of the pain in her breasts.' Following the custom of the day, Mary did not contemplate feeding the prince herself. Her breasts would have been tightly bound to stop the production of milk and it is no wonder that she was still, on 23 June, in considerable discomfort. Killigrew was invited to supper with the leading nobles – Moray, Argyll, Mar, Huntly and Crawford – but though 'the birth has bred much joy here – the Queen is in a good state for a woman in her case, and the prince is a very goodly child', he also noted ominous signs: 'I find here an uncertain and disquiet sort of men – especially the nobility divided in factions, of which I will write more again. Argyll, Moray, Mar and Atholl ... be linked together and Huntly and Bothwell with their friends on the other side.' Killigrew's astuteness cut to the heart of growing difficulties for Mary. How could she keep above these factions and what impact would they have on her ability to rule effectively?

The queen followed custom and stayed in the lying-in apartments at Edinburgh Castle for nearly six more weeks. Then, having been churched, or cleansed, as was required for all women who had given birth, she departed with Moray and Mar for the latter's castle at Alloa on the Firth of Forth. Darnley joined her and in August they hunted together. For a time, it appeared that they were, indeed, reconciled and the king left at the beginning of September to join his son at Stirling Castle and to make preparations for the child's christening. Mary was determined to make this a memorable spectacle and a celebration of the Stewart dynasty. She borrowed £12,000 from Scottish merchants to fund the celebrations and was clearly anticipating the ceremony with excitement. But by late September 1566, there were clear signs that the rapprochement with Henry had run its course. His time at Stirling had brought home to him how marginalized he had become. The festivities would be all about Mary and Prince James and he would be a mere spectator, not even recognized by Elizabeth as king of Scotland. The only course that seemed open to him was to leave Scotland altogether and he formally requested permission of his wife and the Scottish council to go into exile in France. Horrified, his father intervened, pleading with Mary by letter not to let Darnley go.[7] The king's request could not reasonably be met. It was viewed as dishonourable to his wife and to Scotland if he quit the realm altogether. So having been denied the exit his *amour propre* so desperately craved, Henry set off to join his father in Glasgow. He told Mary she would not see him for a while. Perhaps this was a relief. What neither of them knew was how close she would come to death within a few weeks of his flouncing out of her life at the beginning of October 1566.

∽

MARY DID NOT allow this estrangement to interfere with her duties as queen. A justice ayre was due to take place in Jedburgh in the Scottish Borders and Mary, following time-honoured Stewart precedent, intended to be present at a series of trials for disruptors of the peace in this troubled part of her realm. Disputes with England on Border issues remained high in the list of grievances between the two queens and Mary, like her father and grandfather, was heavily reliant on the local nobility to police and manage her affairs there. But Borderers were notoriously difficult and frequently unreliable, as her predecessors had found when dealing with the Humes. It was better to have them on the side of the monarchy than causing trouble and Mary had reason to be grateful to one particular man with Border connections. This was James Hepburn, fourth earl of Bothwell, a man who had risen in the queen's esteem over the past twelve months. He had supported her mother, been appointed to Mary Queen of Scots' first Privy Council in 1561, approved the Darnley marriage, stayed loyal when Moray rebelled, helped the queen restore her authority after the Riccio murder and tried to keep the Borders under control. As his star had risen, so that of the earl of Lennox waned. Though a Protestant, he was no supporter of England and Elizabeth. He could represent himself as a Scottish patriot and the queen's man. Yet in 1561–2 he had been accused by the earl of Arran, Châtelherault's increasingly deranged son, of suggesting the kidnap of the queen. The state of Arran's sanity made the charge difficult to prove, but it was certainly believed by Randolph at the time. By the autumn of 1566, Mary seems to have put this out of her mind. If so, she was unwise.

The man who was now said by Henry Killigrew to have credit with the queen 'greater than all the rest together' remains one of Scottish history's most colourful figures – and also a conundrum. He was short but muscular, a chancer whose natural response to opposition or threats to his honour (which was dubious, to say the least) was to resort to violence. The one authentic portrait of him, a miniature painted in 1566, when he was about thirty-one, makes him look careworn and shifty. It is the face of a man many would instinctively mistrust. Bothwell had amassed enemies (including the earl of Moray and the Hamiltons) but few friends. He was not a man of subtlety or, so far as is known, wit or grace, and though undoubtedly ambitious, he appears to have been more of an opportunist than a strategist with deep-seated plans. Such an approach to political life could serve him well in the fast-changing world of mid-sixteenth century Scotland. It is easy to dismiss him as a foul-mouthed Lothian lout but he was well educated, in France, at the behest of the great-uncle who brought him up when his parents divorced, and had beautiful italic handwriting. One woman, Anna Throndsen, the daughter of a retired Norwegian admiral, had already fallen madly in love with him after meeting him in Denmark and followed him all over Europe before he returned from exile to Scotland in 1564. The earl of Huntly's sister, Lady Jean Gordon, seems to have been content enough to marry him, clad in a splendid gown of cloth of silver provided by the queen, at the beginning of 1566. Several days of banqueting and jousts followed this match, which linked two prominent Scottish families, the northern Gordons and the Lothian Hepburns. Bothwell's stock remained high as the dramas of 1566 unfolded. Mary needed someone of vigour to depend on as her marriage fell apart and her trusted confidant was murdered so brutally. Bothwell, for all his crudeness, must have seemed a safe pair of hands.

Whether the queen herself had developed a passion for him is quite another matter.

Jedburgh is a handsome border town, its great abbey long in ruins, but its connections with Mary part of its continuing attraction. In October 1566, after administering justice there, the queen decided to visit Bothwell at his fortress home, Hermitage Castle, where he was recovering from serious wounds inflicted in an ambush by one of the Border ruffians he was trying to control, John Elliott, a thief and murderer. Bothwell's physical bravery was considerable, and he had been injured in hand-to-hand combat, eventually killing his adversary. By the middle of the month he had recovered sufficiently to be able to receive a visit from the queen and Moray and other councillors, who wished to discuss Border problems with him.

For historical novelists and even some historians of a romantic disposition, this visit has been seen as proof that Mary was already conducting an illicit affair with Bothwell. Yet it was hardly a private assignation, with her half-brother and several leading councillors accompanying her on the journey, and it took her to what is still one of the remotest parts of the Borders, over difficult terrain and to a castle that is more the stuff of nightmares than fairy tales.[8] Hermitage Castle sits at the heart of Liddesdale, alongside a small river, Hermitage Water, and even today the drive from Jedburgh, along twisting roads, is slow. In Mary's day, the twenty-five miles on horseback presented a considerable challenge. Neither was the building itself the sort one would choose for a romantic tryst. It is a formidable edifice and it had an evil reputation as a prison and place of torture. No doubt Bothwell had made it as comfortable as possible but there is nothing welcoming about the Hermitage or its isolation, though on sunny days there is a grim sort of beauty in the surroundings.

Mary and her entourage did not stay long. Perhaps the castle was simply not able to accommodate all of them appropriately for an overnight stay or maybe they did not want to stay long in this spot. For whatever reason, the decision was made to return the same day to Jedburgh. Within twenty-four hours, Mary fell seriously ill. The story goes that her horse stumbled on the difficult return journey and she was thrown into a bog. She then contracted a fever that nearly killed her. It is more likely, however, that she suffered an attack of the illness that had intermittently plagued her for years, perhaps brought on by the hardships of travelling fifty miles in difficult circumstances in one day. There certainly was fever, but even more alarming were the frequent bouts of vomiting, the loss of sight and consciousness on several occasions and the queen's own conviction that she was not going to survive.

For a week she lay near death in Jedburgh. At one point she summoned her brother and other councillors (Bothwell, hearing of her plight, had arrived on a horse litter from Hermitage Castle, being still too weak himself to ride) and she begged them to work together, protect her son and execute her will. On 25 October there were fears that she had actually died, as she lay for some hours with rigid limbs and closed eyes. Her doctor, Arnault Colommius, refused to give up hope, massaged her limbs, made her imbibe a little wine and administered an enema. Whether despite or because of his efforts, Mary did rally. Darnley arrived on 28 October to visit her but stayed only one day before rejoining his son at Stirling. This may seem heartless but we do not know what passed between him and Mary at Jedburgh and she may have wanted him to stay with her son while her own health was in doubt. Over the weeks that followed, Mary made a slow recovery. By mid-November she was well enough to tour the Borders, again in the company of the earls of Huntly, Moray, Bothwell, Lord Hume and Maitland of Lethington, the latter now restored to royal favour. At the end of the month she went back to Edinburgh and stayed at Craigmillar Castle, just outside the city proper, where she put the finishing touches on arrangements for her son's christening, now two months delayed by family friction and then her own brush with death.

The christening of Prince James, on 17 December 1566, at

the Chapel Royal in Stirling Castle, was the last great public occasion of state in Mary Stewart's personal rule. In the Catholic service (from which the Protestant lords Moray and Bothwell and the English ambassador, the earl of Bedford, absented themselves) the baby was christened Charles James, after his French godfather and his Scottish forebears, though his first name was not subsequently used. Mary's sense of theatre and the importance of her Renaissance court was fully realized in the ceremony and accompanying festivities. The baby was carried into the chapel by the count of Brienne, acting for Charles IX of France, at vespers in the early evening, between rows of candles held by the Catholic lords and gentlemen of Scotland. The countess of Argyll, Elizabeth's proxy, held the baby at the font while he was christened by the archbishop of St Andrews, John Hamilton, and a trumpet fanfare then proclaimed the prince's names and titles. A sumptuous banquet, with the seating carefully arranged by status, followed and the evening closed with dancing and music.

Mary had produced a son and heir and seen him christened amidst the full magnificence of her court. It was an occasion to impress ambassadors, encourage conciliation among her competitive and divided nobility and send a message to the world. Mary also pardoned Morton and his friends, who were allowed to return from England. The Scottish queen may have hoped that this gesture towards the murderers of Riccio, who were being sheltered by Elizabeth, might improve relations with England. She had never lost sight of the goal of being granted official recognition as Elizabeth's successor. But there was one very sour note. Her husband refused to attend the christening and his father was also absent. Just a few days before Christmas, Mary was said to be weeping and depressed. Probably she had not fully recovered her health from the severe illness of the autumn. Yet her sadness was compounded by the petulance of her husband and the growing desperation that some way must be found to be rid of him. This eventuality had already been raised with her by several of her advisers while she was at Craigmillar. It did not bode well for Henry Stewart.

✂

THE CATALYST for drastic action was the return of Morton, who harboured a great hatred for the callow youth, whom he felt had betrayed him over the assassination of David Riccio. This, in Morton's eyes, was more than just a slight; it went to the heart of the accepted forms of behaviour in Scotland at the time. Darnley had tried to wriggle out of the responsibilities that went with the bond he had signed. Morton was a Douglas and the family had a long history of opposition to the Crown of Scotland. Like many Scottish nobles, his primary loyalty was to his family and himself and he could not forget the dishonour that he believed Darnley had done him when, as Mary herself reported to Archbishop James Beaton, her ambassador to France, he had assured the lords of the Privy Council of his innocence 'in this last conspiracy, how he never counselled, commanded, consented, assisted nor approved the same.'[9] Morton was now languishing in exile as the result of these barefaced lies but not everyone had deserted him. He had friends in Scotland who could plead his cause.

In a deposition made two years after the event, Huntly and Argyll recalled the discussions at Craigmillar in December 1566 and the connection then made between ensuring Morton's return and ending Mary's marriage. Maitland of Lethington, they claimed, had suggested that 'the nearest and best way to obtain the said earl of Morton's pardon was to promise to the Queen's Majesty to find a way to make divorcement betwixt her Grace and the King her husband, who had offended her Highness so highly in many ways.' Argyll had responded that he did not know how this could be done, to which Lethington responded: 'My lord, care you not thereof, we shall find the means well enough to make her quit of him, so that you and my lord Huntly will only behold the matter and not be offended thereat.' When the same point was put to Huntly, he did not disagree. The earl of Moray was also party to this conversation and the four men then went to discuss with Bothwell to seek his view. He gave no opposition to their arguments.

It was thus with a united front that the earls and Maitland of Lethington went to present their arguments to the queen herself. Maitland rehearsed the various wrongs and insults offered by the king, 'a great number of grievous and intolerable offences . . . continuing every day from evil unto worse', and proposed that if she would pardon Morton and his companions, 'they should find the means with the rest of the nobility to make divorcement betwixt her Highness and the King her husband' but without the direct involvement of the queen herself. It is interesting that Maitland, who had fallen in and out of favour over the past year, was the spokesman for the group of earls, who all exceeded him in rank. Perhaps none of them wished to be so directly associated with originating the idea. Mary, however, was not offended. She was concerned above all with safeguarding that the divorce be lawful and not prejudice her son's right to the Crown of Scotland. Her doubts about the validity of all divorce would never leave her and surfaced again, in an even more desperate context, the following year. So it is ironic that the person who reassured her on this matter was Bothwell, citing his own experience that the break-up of his parents' marriage had not prejudiced his own rights of inheritance. The discussion closed with the consideration of ideas of where Darnley could reside after the divorce, with the possibilities of his living in a different part of Scotland or even overseas (Mary herself suggested France) being mooted.[10]

This account of the so-called Craigmillar Conference was written well after the event and is undoubtedly partial, though that does not mean that it is entirely inaccurate. Moray subsequently sought to exonerate himself of all involvement in any bond to murder Darnley. It was, he said, 'the custom of my old adversaries rather to calumniate and backbite me in my absence than before my face; and it may happen then, when I am departed forth of this realm slanderously and untruly to report untruths of me.'[11] Moray had a way with words when it came to defending himself and his absence from Scotland in the first half of 1567 meant that he took no part in the chain of events that culminated in his sister's downfall. But he was almost certainly protesting too much. If there was ultimately no love lost between him and the other three earls (and he had become progressively more uneasy about Bothwell), it is hard to believe that he was not, at least, aware of plans to remove Darnley by violence.

At the beginning of 1567 the indefatigable Maitland sought, yet again, to re-establish amity with England. Mary's confidence was returning after the Christmas period and she believed that she was in a stronger position than ever now she had an heir. Prince James's birth seemed, to Mary and her supporters, to confirm and safeguard the future of the British Isles. They would be united under one crown and the Stewarts, not the Tudors, would be the family that ruled. What other eventuality could there be, unless the English parliament (in only the second session of Elizabeth's reign) could persuade their queen to opt for a public acceptance of Katherine Grey and her sons as her successors? There is a strong argument that it was the desire to improve relations with England, but on her own terms, not Elizabeth's, that drove Mary Stewart in January 1567.[12]

Despite these wider political aims, personal problems remained. The question of when and how to remove Darnley could not be ignored. Mary's marital difficulties caused her a great deal of personal stress and threatened her effectiveness in Scotland. They needed to be resolved. Rumours of plots against the king were already circulating early in the New Year. Ambassador Guzman wrote to Philip II:

> The displeasure of the Queen of Scotland is carried so far, that she was approached by some who wanted to induce her to allow a plot to be formed against him, which she refused, but she nevertheless shows him no affection. They tell me even that she has tried to take away some of his servitors, and

for some time past finds him no money for his ordinary expenditure. This is very unfortunate for both of them, although
it cannot be denied that the King has given grounds for it by
what he has done. They ought to come to terms, as if they
do not look out for themselves, they are in a bad way.[13]

As, indeed, they were. The conclusion of this crisis came quickly.
While Darnley may have signed his own death warrant when he
double-crossed Morton, Lindsay and Ruthven, it was eventually
his ill-health that provided the occasion for which his enemies
had been looking. He had fallen ill around Christmas 1566 with
what was probably an attack of syphilis. Sores had broken out all
over his body and though this was politely ascribed to smallpox
(in itself a disease that could be deadly), the greater likelihood is
that it was something even more serious, though not an afflic-
tion that could be publicly acknowledged in the husband of the
Queen of Scots. The treatment that Darnley received, of large
doses of mercury and sulphur baths, was the standard one given
for secondary syphilis, not smallpox. Darnley's constitution was
also weakened by heavy drinking.

Henry was at Glasgow when Mary arrived on 20 January
(just two days after Guzman's letter to Spain) and announced
that she would take him back with her to Edinburgh in the
horse-litter that she had brought with her. He would be housed,
until his recovery was complete, at the old Provost's lodging in
the grounds of the collegiate church of St Mary in the Fields, or
Kirk o' Field, as it is better known. This two-storey house, close
to the old city walls of Edinburgh, near Cowgate, was not the
remote and run-down dwelling that has often been supposed,
but a comfortable place thought to have better air than the city
centre. It was also not far from Holyrood House, where the
queen and her son were in residence. Leaving aside the delicate
question of how much Mary knew, or suspected, of the real
cause of her husband's illness, Kirk o' Field was not an inappropriate dwelling for a convalescent and Darnley does not seem to
have objected to it, whereas he had opposed the idea of going to

Craigmillar, her first choice for him. The queen had installed a fine new bed with black velvet hangings for her husband and he himself credited his fast-improving health to his wife's restored affection for him. In fact, he was greatly cheered by her attentions, writing to his father: 'I assure you [she] hath all this while and yet doth use herself like a natural and loving wife.' But in this he was deceived. Mary wanted him back in Edinburgh to keep a close watch on him. She feared his ill intentions sufficiently to believe that he planned to kidnap their son and depose her, aiming to rule in the baby prince's name. It is not clear how she proposed to deal with him in the long run, since she was still not comfortable with the idea of divorce. But one thing is certain. He would not leave Kirk o' Field alive.

⚬⚬⚬

ON THE NIGHT of 9–10 February 1567, at about two in the morning, a huge explosion awoke the citizens of Edinburgh. Mary wrote to Archbishop Beaton the next day:

> The house wherein the King was lodged was, in one instant, blown into the air, he lying sleeping in his bed, with such a vehemency that of the whole lodging, walls and other, there is nothing remaining, no, not a stone above another, but all either carried far away or dashed in dross to the very stone. It must be done by the force of powder and appears to have been a mine. By whom it has been done, or in what manner, it appears not yet.

The Council, she went on to say, was already looking for the perpetrators of this deed:

> and the same being discovered, which we wot God will never suffer to lie hid, we hope to punish the same with such rigour as shall serve for example of this cruelty for all ages to come. Always whoever has taken this wicked enterprise in hand, we assure ourselves it was designed as well for ourself as the King, for we lay the most part of all the last

week in that same lodging (and was there accompanied with most of the Lords that are in this town) and that same night, at midnight, and of very chance tarried not all night, by reason of some mask at the Abbey [Holyrood House]; but we believe it was not chance but God that put it in our head.[14]

The Scottish Privy Council, writing the same day to Catherine de Medici in France, gave a very similar account and identical interpretation, that the intended target had been the queen herself, and many of her nobility. They also gave an assurance of a speedy enquiry that would lead to the apprehension of the assassins and told the French queen mother that 'having once discovered them, your majesty and everyone shall see that the country of Scotland will not willingly endure a disgrace on her shoulders such as would be heavy enough to make her odious to the whole of Christendom, if these guilty persons remain hidden or unpunished.'[15]

Yet despite this united front of queen and council in assuring the French that Darnley's murder would not go unpunished, there was much that was left unsaid in these missives. The king had not died as a result of the explosion; his body and that of the servant who slept in the same room as him were found under a tree in the garden next to the Provost's lodging, with a strange array of articles, including a chair, a cloak, a dagger and a coat nearby. This suggests that they had heard suspicious noises from below in the house and escaped from a window (the chair may have been used to lower the ailing Darnley), and climbed a wall, only to be apprehended and despatched in the grounds. There were no obvious marks on the bodies, leading to the supposition that they died from suffocation. As enquiries were made of neighbours, there were reports that a man had been heard crying out, 'O my brothers have pity on me for the love of him who had mercy on all the world.' If so, then Darnley had recognized his murderers. And though great emphasis had been placed, by both Mary and her councillors, on the narrow escape that she herself had had, it was natural for sceptics to question whether it was just too convenient for her to have left Kirk o' Field so late on a cold winter's night to attend the festivities of the marriage between Bastian Pagez, one of her favourite French gentlemen valets, and Christian Hogg, a lady-in-waiting.

Mary ordered the court into mourning and had her husband buried in James V's vault at Holyrood. The Privy Council offered a reward of £2,000 to anyone identifying the murderers. Overwhelmed by the enormity of what had happened and by now aware that rumours of a threat to her own life were circulating in Spain and the Netherlands, Mary suffered a further collapse. Henry Killigrew reported to London that she was heavily veiled and scarcely able to speak when he went to offer his condolences on 9 March. Meanwhile, the identity of those who had planned and participated in the murder of Henry Stewart remained the source of speculation, some of it very public. As early as 16 February a placard was placed on the door of the Tolbooth in Edinburgh blaming, amongst others, the earl of Bothwell and Sir James Balfour, whose brother owned the house at Kirk o' Field. Others believed that Mary's household servants, including Pagez himself and the brother of David Riccio, were the prime movers and organizers of Henry's death. Nor was the queen herself spared humiliation. Her complicity was speedily assumed. One of the anonymous placards depicting a mermaid with a crown on her head and a hare with the Bothwell family crest went further in its allusion to an adulterous relationship between the queen and the earl.

To this day, it is not possible to say definitively what happened or who, if anyone, took the lead. Later depositions were obtained under the threat of torture and so should be viewed with caution, colourful and detailed though they are. There is, however, a broad consensus that the earls of Morton and Bothwell, with Sir James Balfour, were actively involved in a conspiracy that resulted in the king's death. If there was a chief organizer, it was probably Balfour, who had composed a bond for Darnley's death and stored the gunpowder at his own houses in Edinburgh. Bothwell's men delivered and fired the gunpowder (in a rather amateurish way) and Morton's Douglas allies patrolled the area to make sure that Henry did, indeed, die. This probably explains the last, desperate plea of the young king to his own kith and kin not to harm him. Historians remain divided about the extent, if any, of Mary's involvement. Over the centuries, opinion has swung between the absolute conviction of her guilt, based on the so-called 'casket letters' proffered later by Moray as evidence and now known to be forgeries, and the equally strong protestations of her complete innocence which have largely characterized recent interpretations. We shall never be able to say with certainty how much Mary knew but she was certainly aware of the fact that her husband was universally detested and would not be mourned except by his parents. She had brought him back to Edinburgh because she was afraid of his unpredictability and his intentions towards their son and she knew full well that her advisers were pressing to be rid of him. The manner of his death may have been a genuine shock to her but only a very naïve woman would have been surprised by it.

The Lennoxes were devastated by the death of their son. All their hopes had been pinned on him and his murder brought despair. In London, where Cecil learned of Darnley's murder four or five days after it took place but was still no clearer as to the identity of the murderers in early March, someone had to break the news to the countess of Lennox. Elizabeth, who wrote so forthrightly to her cousin about the need to bring to justice those responsible, sent Lady Mildred Cecil, her secretary's wife, and Lady Howard to carry the terrible tidings to Margaret Douglas in the Tower. They mistakenly informed her that her husband had been killed as well. Overcome with anguish, Margaret became hysterical and the royal physician and the dean of Westminster were summoned by the alarmed ladies to give help. Cecil reported that Margaret 'could not be by any means kept from such passions of mind as the horribleness of the fact did require.'[16] Ill at the time himself, and overworked as ever, Cecil felt pity for the countess of Lennox and hoped that Elizabeth would show her 'some favourable compassion'. Shortly afterwards Elizabeth agreed that Margaret could be moved from the Tower to the royal residence at Sheen. The countess soon learned that her husband, at least, was alive, but this did not lessen her heartbreak over the fate that had befallen her elder son and the growing suspicion that Mary Queen of Scots herself had connived in his death.

The earl of Lennox heard of his son's murder at Linlithgow and, fearing for his own life, returned to his estates in Glasgow. Yet his fear was mingled with a grim determination that he would have justice for Henry and he began a correspondence with Mary in which he urged action against the murderers. Although he had initially requested that a special session of the Scottish nobility be convened to try his son's murderers, he was not happy when Mary appeared to refer the matter to parliament. It occurred to Lennox, once he thought more clearly, that murder trials were not a normal part of the Scottish parliament's remit. Instead, he asked that those named on the placards be brought to trial. The problem here was that there was a large choice of candidates, as Mary pointed out. In belaboured correspondence with her father-in-law, she asked him to be more specific. Lennox believed that the queen now intended to protect the one man of whose guilt he was already convinced and whose intentions he feared above all others. That man was the earl of Bothwell. And he would now, for a brief and terrible period, take centre stage in Mary's life.

THE UNFOLDING STORY of Mary Stewart's downfall is well known but, like the Darnley murder, there are two entirely opposing versions of her part in it. Looking back into the past, it is all too easy to see a straight line that gives a plausible explanation for historical events. Yet there was nothing inevitable about what happened in Scotland in the spring and summer of 1567. It may seem, in retrospect, that the murder of Darnley led inexorably to his wife's overthrow but this would not have been an outcome automatically assumed by contemporaries. Some may have wished it and the queen's personal reputation was certainly compromised but she had already survived several grave crises, dealing with adversity in a skilful and resourceful manner and emerging stronger than before. She would not, however, do so this time.

The disaster that overtook Mary has become the stuff of romantic legends, dewy-eyed films and numerous historical novels. In these versions of the past, the beautiful queen is in thrall to a handsome swashbuckler who risks all for her, a stirring tale of doomed love amid the Scottish mists. On the other hand are Mary's contemporary enemies and detractors themselves, seeking to rewrite history as soon as they could, but in a less flattering mode. They labelled her an adulteress and murderess, a weak woman whose head was completely turned by an all-consuming love affair. So an inappropriate passion, only to be expected in a female, forms the basis of both these interpretations.

Yet the truth, known to more than a few at the time, could not have been more different. This is not the stuff of one of history's great romances but a sordid episode of kidnap and rape, of the desperation of a queen regnant trying to keep her throne and the last vestiges of her honour. Opportunism, violence, indignity and betrayal are its key features. Mary realized that she was becoming a victim of events that were spiralling out of her control. She was physically and mentally isolated, at the mercy of a loathsome man whom she had once trusted but who, in reality, cared not a jot for her.

It is true, however, that Mary did not handle the aftermath of Darnley's murder with any resolution. Bothwell was eventually brought to trial, the only one among those who were involved, but he was acquitted on 12 April 1567. The earl of Lennox, who had planned to attend the trial with three thousand armed followers, was told he could bring only six men into Edinburgh. He was already convinced that this was a show trial, being conducted for form's sake, and so he stayed away. Within days of the trial, he left for England where he would eventually renew his pleas for Elizabeth's help. The English queen was sympathetic – Darnley was her relative, too – but her government could not offer Lennox much practical support. Elizabeth and Cecil took no joy in the growing instability in Scotland which was likely to lead to further problems in the Borders. The English queen had come through a rough period with her parliament in early 1567, refusing with what seemed like absolute finality to nominate a successor but saying that she would marry 'as soon as I can conveniently'. She had no such intention in reality, but the stand-off between queen and parliament and the continued friction with her ministers could not be allowed to continue. Elizabeth decided that she would cut her demands for financial support if parliament would back off about the succession. It was a clever, if necessary, ploy. But it brought further restrictions and heartache to poor Katherine Grey, shunted about from one place of house arrest to the next and closely guarded. Stress led to despair and ill health. Parted from her husband and elder son, Katherine lost the will to live and died at the beginning of 1568. There was a lesson to be learned from Elizabeth's treatment of a cousin with a claim to the throne but Mary did not heed it. Her own travails were just about to begin in earnest.

Bothwell's acquittal had two immediate effects. The first was the departure of the earl of Moray. His Hepburn rival seems to have been one of the few men that Mary's half-brother feared. They had long had their differences and were never genuinely reconciled, despite Mary's efforts. Moray was perhaps Scotland's shrewdest politician. He knew Bothwell would be cock-a-hoop and he did not want to stay at a court where this undoubtedly ambitious rival held sway. If there was going to be trouble, he would rather bide his time elsewhere. Suddenly discovering a yearning for foreign travel, Moray took his leave of his sister, who acknowledged that she would miss his counsel, and departed for France and the Low Countries, nominating Mary as his daughter's guardian. By the time he returned in August, his sister had lost her throne.

The second effect was on the growing confidence of Bothwell

himself. Never a man to underrate himself or miss an opportunity, he would not have regretted Moray's departure. It
removed probably the biggest obstacle to a plan now forming in
his mind. Why should he not marry Mary himself? As her
husband, he could enjoy power and wealth, control the future
of her son and effectively rule Scotland. The queen had shown
him favour and he had served her well, policing the Borders
with diligence, even at the threat of his own life. She was still
vulnerable following Darnley's death, emotional and in dubious
health. It would be a great coup and he had the daring to bring
it off. True, there were matters that would need to be dealt with
quickly, not the least of which was to secure a divorce from the
wife he had married only just over a year before. But that could
be handled. He had already been unfaithful to Jean Gordon and
he doubted that she would oppose him. Then there was the
question of how to gain the agreement of the lords and prelates
whose support he would certainly need. But he had a plan for
that, too.

Just two days after his trial, Bothwell ensured that he played
a prominent part in the opening of what was to be Mary's last
parliament, carrying the sceptre and surrounding the queen with
a guard of his own men, a departure from protocol that was
noted at the time (the role was traditionally held by the bailies
of Edinburgh). This physical isolation of Mary was a sinister
prophecy of what was to come. And in parliament, Bothwell
made sure that his Protestant credentials were underpinned by
supporting an act that formally placed the Protestant Kirk under
Mary's protection. He also ensured that his fellow conspirators
in Darnley's murder were bought off when Morton, Argyll and
Huntly had the rights to their ancestral lands confirmed. In
addition, Maitland and Lord Robert Stewart also received grants,
while Bothwell decided to keep Dunbar Castle for himself. He
was also confirmed in his hereditary position of lord admiral of
Scotland. His hand was mightily strengthened but supreme
power was not yet his. He needed the support of at least a
majority of the country's leading nobles and churchmen to

legitimate his ambition. On the evening of 19 April 1567, the day after the parliamentary session ended, Bothwell made his most daring move yet. He invited a number of the most influential lords to a supper where wine flowed and his geniality, which most if not all of those present knew was superficial, was on full display. This studied hospitality is often said to have taken place at Ainslie's Tavern on the Canongate but no such location is given in the sources and it seems more probable that Bothwell used his own lodgings, either in Edinburgh or in Holyrood itself.[17] As the evening wore on, Bothwell produced the draft of a bond he wanted his fellow lords to sign. It was to confirm his innocence of Darnley's murder and to undertake to defend him from further scurrilous lies. But the real blow was in the third aspect of the bond. He sought support for becoming Mary's husband, should she 'happen' to choose him. This implies that the queen could make such a decision of her own free will. But in reality, Bothwell never intended to give Mary a choice.

Nevertheless, there are aspects of the so-called Ainslie's Tavern Bond that have never been adequately explained. Why did all but one of the twenty-five men present agree to sign the bond? It is easy to claim that Bothwell got them all drunk, or that they were so amazed by his effrontery that their judgement deserted them and they signed anyhow. It is true that not everyone regarded such bonds as a permanent obligation and subsequently many of the men who had caroused with Bothwell on that spring night renounced what they had done and signed further bonds to free Mary from Bothwell's control, though by then they were too late. Perhaps they would have stuck by Bothwell had Mary agreed willingly to marry him. When she did not, the signatories would have felt that Bothwell could no longer be supported. At the time, nine of eighteen Scottish earls signed, a remarkable display of unity. Only two of those present at the parliament, Moray's father-in-law, the earl marischal, and the earl of Eglinton, a Catholic lord whose loyalty to Mary was unswerving, did not sign.

The bond was in the form of a petition to Mary, appealing to her to marry as a means of ensuring calm and good government in the realm of Scotland and suggesting that a Scot, not a foreigner, would be an appropriate choice, and who better than the earl of Bothwell himself:

> . . . weighing and considering the time present and how our sovereign the Queen's Majesty is now destitute of a husband, in the which solitary state the commonwealth of this realm may not permit her highness to continue and endure, but at some time her highness in appearance may be inclined to yield unto a marriage . . . [it] may move her Majesty so far to humble herself, as preferring one of her native born subjects unto all foreign princes to take to husband the said Earl.[18]

Eight bishops endorsed the bond, as did the earls of Morton, Huntly, Caithness, Argyll, Cassilis, Sutherland, Crawford, Errol and Rothes and the Lords Boyd, Herries, Ogilvy and Sempill. It is an impressive roll call. Bothwell, for whatever reason, had pretty much got what he wanted. Perhaps realizing that the consensus he had achieved might not last for long, Bothwell wasted no time in taking the petition to the queen. She may have valued his strength and support, though she had already witnessed his capacity for random acts of extreme brutality when, in her presence, he fatally injured an elderly servant of Darnley's who had requested help from Mary while she walked with Bothwell in the garden of Seton Palace, to the east of Edinburgh, at the beginning of April. But it was not just his violent nature that influenced her decision. He was a subject, and though always loyal to the Scottish Crown and vehemently anti-English (not necessarily an advantage if she was to continue to pursue her claim to the English throne), he was also a Protestant. And there was one other, crucial factor – she was not in love with him. So she refused his suit. If she thought that would be the end of it, she was entirely wrong.

For Mary now played, quite literally, into Bothwell's hands.

Had she stayed in Edinburgh, things might have been different. It would not have been easy to coerce her in the capital, where she could muster men and political allies. Instead, Mary made a crucial, if perfectly comprehensible, mistake. Worn out with political wrangling, still suffering from intermittent bouts of serious ill health and anxious to see her son, Mary left Edinburgh on 21 April to fetch Prince James, who was in the care of the earl of Mar, from Stirling Castle. But Mar refused to give up his charge. Mary was not used to being defied but, although she considered his response treasonable, she could not prevail. She left Stirling on 23 April, kissing her son goodbye for the last time, though she did not, of course, know this then. After spending the night at Linlithgow, where she had been born, she made to return to Edinburgh. But she never reached her capital. At the bridge over the river Almond, outside the city, she and her small party were surrounded by Bothwell and eight hundred armed retainers and forced, against her will, to go to Dunbar Castle. She was now Bothwell's prisoner and he was determined that she would become his wife, whether she liked it or not. And so he raped her.

&

BOTHWELL HAD SPUN her the yarn that it was not safe to return to Edinburgh. Holding the bridle of her horse tightly as they rode, and ensuring that she was separated from her servants, he gave her no other option than to return with him to Dunbar, the heavily fortified coastal castle that he had so recently pur-loined. Proponents of the idea that this abduction was all staged and pre-arranged have pointed to Mary's passivity during this journey. She was Bothwell's monarch. If she was truly being kidnapped against her will, why did she not cry out or demand assistance as they passed through the various small towns and villages on route? There are several answers to this, the most obvious of which is that surrounded by a press of eight hundred horsemen it is unlikely that she could ever have been heard. But more persuasive even is the culture of the time: it would have been improper for a gentlewoman to try to fight her way out of the situation physically and, besides, Mary had no means of so doing even if she had been minded to try and escape. She does appear to have sent her messenger, James Borthwick, to Edinburgh to seek help from the citizens there, but all they could manage was two salvoes of cannon as the riders went past them at speed. Mary was now completely at Bothwell's mercy. When they arrived at Dunbar he dismissed all her ladies-in-waiting and replaced them with his sister, Jane Hepburn, the widow of Lord John Stewart, Mary's favourite half-brother. Lord John had died four years earlier and the presence of his wife may have been insufficient to reassure or protect Mary from what happened.

The evidence that Bothwell raped Mary is compelling and what is all the more remarkable, given the many saccharine accounts of their relationship, is that it was widely known at the time. Sir James Melville, who was with the queen when she was abducted, recalled: 'Then the earl of Bothwell boasted he would marry the queen, who would or who would not; yea, whether she would herself or not.' He went on to add that when the court returned to Edinburgh, Bothwell again keeping Mary close, 'a number of noblemen were drawn together in a chamber within the palace, where they all subscribed that the marriage between the queen and the earl of Bothwell was very meet, he having many friends in Lothian and upon the Borders, to cause good order to be kept. And then the queen could not but marry him, seeing he had ravished her and lain with her against her will.'[19] Mary herself never, so far as we know, told anyone outright that she had been raped. It would have been too great a shame for her to admit and the horror of it needed to be shaped in her own mind in as positive a way as possible. She came as close as she could when she remarked: 'Albeit we found his doings rude, yet were his answer and words both gentle.' Bothwell, the captor of a queen, mingled physical force with soothing words to the conclusion he sought. Exhausted, assaulted and without support, Mary gave in and agreed to the marriage. 'As it is succeeded,' she agreed wearily, 'we must take the best of it.' This is not the expression of a woman wildly in love.

Bothwell had committed an act that, even by the standards of the times in which he lived, was remarkable for its violation, not just of Mary as a woman, but of Mary as his ruler and God's anointed representative on earth. Although he claimed to be a good Protestant, there was no religious sentiment in James Hepburn and the fact that Mary was a woman made her extremely vulnerable. Probably Bothwell's views on female rulers were, like those of some of his fellow nobles, much closer in private to the bigoted public utterances of John Knox. Bothwell's rape of Mary proved her weakness and her agreement to marry him, as many Scottish and northern English heiresses who had been similarly kidnapped and raped could attest, was inevitable. No sixteenth-century lady, and especially a queen, could fight back against something that polluted them so completely in their society's eyes. Marriage to the rapist was always the easiest option and Mary's resignation that she must 'take the best of it' was, both psychologically and politically, the only way forward she could see. Her conviction grew even stronger when she realized that she was pregnant, something that she seems to have suspected very early.

Yet there were those who hated Bothwell and, outraged at what they learned of their queen's suffering, wanted to help. On 27 April a petition from Aberdeen made clear how widespread was the knowledge of what had happened to Mary Queen of Scots:

> Please your Majesty, it is bruited and spoken in the country that your Majesty should be ravished by the earl of Bothwell against your will. When we, your Majesty's nobility and subjects, think ourselves most highly offended if such be, and therefore desire to know your Highness' pleasure and will, what we shall do towards the reparation of that matter and in what manner we shall use ourselves, which, being known, there shall be nothing left undone that becomes

faithful and loving subjects to do it, to the advancement and honour of their prince's honour and affairs.[20]

This offer of help, however heartfelt, came too late. Mary could not, in her own mind, deviate from the decision she had made to go ahead and marry Bothwell. On 12 May 1567, she appeared before the lords of the session and declared that she formally forgave Bothwell for the violence which he had used towards her person and assured them that he had entirely restored her to liberty. Two days later she signed her marriage contract. Yet neither of these actions supports the fanciful and demeaning interpretations of her willing involvement in the kidnap and her infatuation with Bothwell that diehard opponents, notably Sir William Kirkcaldy of Grange, were already putting about. The day after the signing of Bothwell's bond, and, incidentally, the same day that Mary first refused to marry her determined suitor, Kirkcaldy claimed that Mary had said 'she shall go with him [Bothwell] to the world's end in a white petticoat before she would leave him.' This statement has so often been taken at face value by Mary's detractors and romantic writers who use it as proof of Mary's devotion that they have overlooked the fact that Kirkcaldy had not accompanied the queen to Stirling and could not have known what she had said since leaving Edinburgh earlier in the month.

Mary was still fearful for her son's future just five days before her marriage. Walking in the gardens of Holyrood, she was reported as saying 'she doth greatly fear, less that Bothwell having the upper hand that he will reign again with the French and either make away with the Prince or send him into France, which deliberation her Majesty would gladly should be stayed, but it is very uncertain how it may be brought to pass.' The queen spoke 'vehemently' against Kirkcaldy of Grange and his blackening of her reputation and warned against him.[21] But whatever her underlying misgivings, Mary was set on following what she saw as an unavoidable course. Bothwell had hurriedly divorced Jean Gordon – she had entered adultery as the grounds and he had argued consanguinity in a separate proceeding, meaning that they were too closely related. His marriage to Mary took place according to Protestant rites in a muted and brief ceremony in Holyrood House, conducted by the bishop of Orkney on 15 May. Mary wore mourning, as was appropriate for a widow, but she was not a joyful bride. Visiting her later the same day, the French ambassador, du Croc, noted her deep depression.

The couple had barely a month of married life together and, by various accounts, it was not a happy one. Mary's depression did not lift; there were reports that she and her husband quarrelled frequently. He had been given the title of duke of Orkney before their wedding but the queen made no attempt to name him king, so his status was below that of Darnley. It was reported that as one quarrel reached fever pitch, Mary threatened to stab herself. Her misery was compounded, as the weeks passed, by the knowledge that she was, indeed, pregnant. But by then, time was running out for James Hepburn and, with it, for Mary's rule in Scotland.

❧

BOTHWELL WAS NOT the sort of politician who held on to allies for long and already his fellow conspirators in Darnley's death were tired of his naked ambition. They may have expected that, by supporting him, they would be part of the new regime but this was wishful thinking. It should have been apparent to gentlemen who so directly followed their own interest that James Hepburn was not the type to share power. But the need to bring him down brought with it a wider opportunity for men like Morton, who had seen their fortunes veer wildly under Mary Queen of Scots and were still not convinced of her goodwill, or her capacity to rule. They felt she had lost her hold on Scotland and began to plan for a future which included neither the upstart Bothwell nor his browbeaten, physically assaulted wife. Removing him opened up the possibility of being rid of her as well. Scotland had survived long minorities before, under the direction of male regents, and could well do so again.

At the beginning of May a growing group of confederate lords gathered at Stirling, where Prince James was still being cared for by the earl of Mar. Chief among them were Morton, Argyll, Mar himself and Atholl. Yet another bond was signed, this time vowing to free Mary and protect her son. Thus battle lines were effectively drawn between Bothwell and his opponents even before his marriage to Mary. As we know, he persisted in his plan but by the end of the month he was sufficiently alarmed by the numbers and influence of those ranged against him, and by very negative reaction to his marriage from England and France, to summon his own liegemen from East Lothian, where most of his lands lay, and prepare for a fight. On 6 June he moved Mary out of Edinburgh to Borthwick Castle, some twelve miles to the south. Hearing that Morton and his allies were advancing on the capital, where another Darnley plotter, Sir James Balfour, made ready to hand over Edinburgh Castle to them, Bothwell slipped away to Dunbar. His wife, disguised in men's clothing, joined him there and they prepared to face the confederate lords.

Why did Mary not use this opportunity to escape from her new husband's clutches? If she hated him enough to consider suicide, surely the protestations of Morton, Atholl and Mar offered her a way out. Yet Mary had good reason to distrust both Morton and Mar, even after they issued a proclamation on 12 June which accused Bothwell of ravishing the queen and forcing her to marry him. They promised freedom for their monarch and justice for the late king. Mary was not convinced. It must have seemed rich to her that Morton, one of the men most closely implicated in Darnley's murder should now be publicly proclaiming his zeal for bringing Bothwell to justice. But such were the twists and turns of family loyalty, personal honour and the basic desire for survival in Scotland during this period that there cannot have been much that surprised her. Her primary consideration, as she later told Sir Nicholas Throckmorton, Elizabeth's envoy, was to ensure the legitimate birth of the child she was carrying. It exercised her mind above all. She may also have weighed up the advantages and disadvantages of deserting Bothwell and reverting to the mercies of the confederate lords. They were offering her fair words but their past actions suggested these were not worth the paper of the bond they had signed. Either way, her future looked dark and dangerous.

The forces of Mary and Bothwell confronted those of the confederate lords at Carberry Hill in Midlothian on 15 June 1567. Bothwell was his normal blustering self, offering to settle matters in single combat, but when his bluff was called by Lord Lindsay, he slipped away from the field, leaving his wife to face their enemies alone, his men drifting away, unwilling to engage their fellow Scots. Bothwell was no James IV. He did not intend to fight to the death. Queen Mary, meanwhile, was compelled to surrender to Kirkcaldy of Grange, a sufficient humiliation in itself, but worse was to come. Still brave in the face of defeat and the desertion of the husband who had ruined her hopes and ravaged her body, Mary believed that she had negotiated honourable terms for her surrender and a promise that she would be treated as befitted her rank. But there was little honour left in Scotland at the time and much to be gained by further blackening of her reputation. The soldiers in the confederate lords' camp shouted that she was a whore and murderess who should be burned. This vile outcry was the last straw for a woman in poor health and the early stages of pregnancy, overwhelmed by the enormity of what had happened to her in the past two months. Mary was led back into Edinburgh, to further public humiliation, and lodged at the Provost's house, in a state of collapse. She was now a carefully guarded prisoner of the very men who had justified taking up arms as a means of freeing her from Bothwell. Later the next day she was moved to Lochleven Castle, a fortress on an island in the middle of a lake, near Kinross. William Douglas, the castle's keeper, was a half-brother of the earl of Moray. Their mother was Lady Margaret Erskine, the lady James V, Mary's father, had hoped to marry but ultimately given up when the necessary papal dispensation for her divorce was not forthcoming. The passing years seem to have increased Margaret

Erskine's sense of bitterness that she could not become queen of Scotland herself, and her son James its heir. She was not a welcoming hostess to the shattered woman now a prisoner in her home.

The confederate lords needed to move swiftly to ensure Mary's incarceration. Isolated she may have been, but she was not without supporters. The Hamiltons, her nearest blood relatives in the Stewart line, were already moving to liberate her and Huntly and Argyll now took up her cause. Huntly wrote to the archbishop of Glasgow, in France, the day after Mary was taken to Lochleven: 'As this taking of our sovereign is against all law and order, we will with the rest of her true and faithful subjects assemble for her relief. And desire you to advertise the king of France hereof, for the same is not only our sovereign's cause, but concerns as well his highness and all other princes.'[22] Mary's husband looked, as he always did, to himself. Having made a half-hearted attempt to raise another army, he took ship for Orkney, his recently acquired dukedom, and from there, reverting to the piracy that was an essential part of his nature, he departed for Scandinavia. But he was stopped off the Norwegian coast and taken to Bergen. Here his past came back to haunt him, for Anna Throndsen was very much alive and determined on financial restitution, believing that Bothwell had broken his promise to marry her. He bought her off and sailed on to Denmark, still claiming that he was supreme ruler of Scotland despite the discovery of documents accusing him of treason. His welcome in Copenhagen was not, however, what he expected and Frederick II decided to imprison him. Bothwell's opportunistic ambition had resulted in disaster for both himself and the woman he had forced to marry him. In Denmark, he was largely forgotten but his wife, in her island confinement, was not. Imprisonment in an apparently impregnable fortress gave further opportunity for Mary's opponents to blacken the queen's name and they worked on this assiduously during her time at Lochleven.

IN ENGLAND, meanwhile, there had been consternation at events in Scotland. Elizabeth would have taken Huntly's comments very much to heart. She was personally affronted by what had befallen Mary; an anointed monarch and near relative basely imprisoned by rebels (even ones Elizabeth had helped) caused her great discomfort. This was not how the established order of things, in which she implicitly believed, should be. Nor was it a happy precedent to have another queen subjected to such treatment almost on one's doorstep.[23] She immediately sent Throckmorton north to argue for Mary's release. Cecil was probably less concerned about Mary's personal difficulties than he was about the implications of a destabilized government in Scotland. The threat of further lawlessness in the Borders was troubling and the one Scot who had made any headway in keeping the peace was the now disgraced Bothwell himself.

Neither Throckmorton nor de Villeroy, the emissary sent by Catherine de Medici, was allowed to see Mary at Lochleven during the crucial five-week period during which the Scottish lords considered what was to be done about their queen. Throckmorton's instructions were to fight for Mary's restoration but he never seems to have regarded this as a realistic or even desirable prospect. The most likely outcome of the discussions between the queen's supporters and opponents was abdication in favour of her baby son, but whether this would also involve exile or long imprisonment, as well as trial for murder over Darnley's death and even possible execution, was not clear. Throckmorton, who knew Mary well from her time as queen of France, felt that the queen's best hope lay in agreeing to divorce Bothwell. But this she absolutely refused to do. On 19 July, in a letter to Elizabeth, Throckmorton explained why:

> I have also persuaded [advised] her to conform herself to renounce Bothwell for her husband and to be contented to suffer a divorce to pass between them; and she has sent me word that she will in no ways consent . . . but rather die; grounding herself upon this reason, taking herself to be

seven weeks gone with child, by renouncing Bothwell she should acknowledge herself to be with child of a bastard and to have forfeited her honour which she will not do to die for it. I have persuaded her, to save her own life and her child, to choose the least hard condition.[24]

She was probably more than seven weeks pregnant but did not want to give the impression that conception had taken place before the marriage. She would still not acknowledge that she had been raped. Only a week later, her concern for her honour had a sad dénouement. She miscarried, reportedly of twins, and in her extremity of grief, depression and illness was apparently visited by her sister-in-law, the countess of Moray, in what was the only humane gesture made towards her at this time.

Mary was now forced to accept that abdication was the only course open to her. It would save her life and safeguard the succession of her son, her rightful heir. She had been bullied into submission and on 24 July 1567, she signed the abdication document, having been told by Lords Lindsay and Ruthven that she would be killed if she did not agree. Her dilemma in some respects recalls that of Princess Mary Tudor in 1536, compelled, under similar threats, to agree that she was a bastard and that her mother, Katherine of Aragon, was never legally married to her father. Like her namesake, Mary Queen of Scots was advised (in this case by Throckmorton) that a deed signed under duress was invalid. There might, perhaps, be a way back.

But, for the time being, Mary's cause seemed lost. James VI of Scotland was crowned king on 29 July. Moray returned from France via England and on 11 August rode into Edinburgh to assume the regency. He had waited long for it. Visiting his sister at Lochleven, he lectured her on her failures during what must have been a harrowing interview. He then departed, promising neither freedom nor any hope of restitution. Mary was left alone.

SHE HAD NOT, however, given up. As the winter of 1567–8
wore on and spring returned to Scotland, she continued to send
secret messages to supporters. Though her health recovered
somewhat she was still far from robust when, on 2 May 1568,
having charmed the brother and cousin of her jailer, she effected
a daring escape by boat from Lochleven. Horses were waiting for
her on the shore and she crossed the Forth at Queensferry, riding
on to Lord Seton's castle at Niddry in West Lothian. Some
members of the Hamilton family and the earl of Argyll rallied
to her cause and she joined them at Hamilton House, near
Glasgow.[25] Two days after her escape she repudiated her abdication, offering Moray a settlement which he refused. The earl
preferred to try and maintain power on his own terms rather
than face an uncertain future on conditions dictated by his sister.
But his treatment of her had disturbed many men of both
Protestant and Catholic persuasions and the queen was able to
put together a substantial force, commanded by Argyll, even as
Moray scrambled to put his own supporters in the field. Though
taken by surprise, he had the advantage of being in the Glasgow
area himself, attending a justice ayre.

The Marian army, now numbering about six thousand men,
planned to move the queen to the great fortress of Dumbarton
Castle but their attempt was foiled when, on 13 May 1568,
Moray's smaller force of about four thousand confronted them at
Langside, then a village just outside Glasgow. Overconfident
because of their superior numbers, the queen's supporters
believed that Moray would not fight them. They were wrong.
After an unsuccessful cavalry charge the two sides fought hand-
to-hand and for a while the outcome appeared in doubt. It was
decided by the oddest of occurrences. Argyll fainted – he may
have had a mild stroke or heart attack – and could not, at a
crucial moment, reinforce his advance guard. Although the
numbers of those killed on the queen's side was small (about
three hundred), the sudden loss of leadership caused confusion
among the queen's supporters, many of whom broke and fled.

Watching the battle from the hillside, Mary believed that her cause was now utterly lost. Having so recently regained her freedom, she could not cope with the idea of surrendering it again. The prospect of even closer confinement, perhaps of death at her brother's hands, was unbearable. Fearful and desperate, Mary now made what was perhaps her greatest mistake, far more significant than the half-hearted attempts to bring Darnley's killers to justice or even the decision to marry Bothwell, unavoidable as that had been in her own mind. She would flee Scotland and seek the support of her cousin Elizabeth in England. Her supporters were appalled. They reminded her of the unhappy precedent of James I of Scotland, who had been a prisoner in England for eighteen years at the start of the fifteenth century. The outcome of Langside, as they realized, was by no means a decisive defeat for Mary. She was urged to stay, to rally her supporters and encourage them to regroup. Guided by Lord Herries, she and her small party travelled south and west at night, until she reached the relative safety of Herries's home near Dumfries. But Mary was worn out by the tribulations of the last two years; she was weary of trying to remain above the factions, of the duplicity and desertion of men she had trusted, like Maitland, who abandoned her after the Bothwell marriage. Above all, she could no longer face the sheer effort of being a woman ruler in Scotland. Though only twenty-four years old, she felt unequal, for the present, to the challenge of fighting any longer.

It was a desperate time. 'God tries me severely,' she wrote, a few weeks later, 'for I have endured injuries, calumnies, imprisonment, famine, cold, heat, flight . . . and then I have had to sleep upon the ground and drink sour milk and eat oatmeal without bread and have been three nights like the owls.'[26] Yet she could not be persuaded to turn back. She spent her last night in Scotland at Dundrennan Abbey near Kirkcudbright, having written to the deputy governor of the town of Carlisle, just across the border in England, saying she was being forced into exile and requesting permission to enter Elizabeth's kingdom. She included in her letter a ring that Elizabeth had given her, as a token of her affection for the English queen and a plea for help.

Mary did not intend to wait for a reply. On 16 May she crossed the Solway Firth in a fishing boat, landing four hours later near what is now Workington in Cumbria. She hoped Elizabeth, a fellow monarch and one of her own kindred, would help her to regain her throne. That this was a disastrous misjudgement soon became apparent. Only six weeks later, the implications of her precipitate flight were already apparent. Writing to her uncle in France, a country itself blighted by civil war, she lamented that she was 'little else than a prisoner'. And so, through nineteen long years of increasingly dismal confinement, a prisoner she would remain.

Epilogue

London, 7 May 1603

King James VI of Scotland and I of England rode into London on a Saturday, to be greeted by the Lord Mayor and City aldermen, resplendent in scarlet and gold, and large crowds of onlookers who pushed and shoved to get a glimpse of the Scot who had become England's king after fifty years of female rule. They saw a man aged thirty-seven, of medium height and with the colouring of his Stewart ancestors. He was a good horseman (that also ran in the family) and generally fit, though he had never walked properly since childhood. Bearded but with short hair, his was an intelligent face with a resemblance to both his parents. Though his gait may have been awkward and his manner of eating messy, James was supremely confident about his intellectual abilities and his capacity to rule in two kingdoms. 'My right,' he said, 'is united in my person . . . my marches are united by land and not by sea, so there is no difference betwixt them . . . but my course must be betwixt both.'[1]

He had been in no hurry to come south after Elizabeth I died on 24 March, pointing out to the astonished and concerned ministers of the late queen that he could not suddenly drop everything in Scotland, the country which he had ruled, as he was wont to remind people, from his cradle. Failing to understand the obsession of the English government with form and precedent, he felt that surely the country could survive without him for a few weeks while he put things in order north of the border. When he did set off in April he moved south at a leisurely pace, indulging his passion for hunting whenever he could and awarding knighthoods with almost unseemly generosity.

James arrived in London without his feisty, blonde wife, Anna of Denmark. She was four months pregnant and until arrangements for their joint coronation in Westminster Abbey were well underway, he preferred her to avoid the rigours of a royal progress and the dangers of a particularly virulent outbreak of the plague that had already hit the English capital. It would kill one quarter of London's population before it burned itself out later in 1603. Anna eventually arrived at Windsor on the last day of June, where all the ladies of the English nobility were waiting to greet her. On 25 July, James and Anna were crowned in Westminster Abbey and a new era dawned.

His mother had died on the scaffold at Fotheringhay in Northamptonshire in 1587, bludgeoned to death with an axe by an incompetent executioner. It was the end of a long journey of despair. For the first few years of her detention in England, she did not lose sight of her long-term goal: to regain the Crown of Scotland and ensure official recognition for herself as Elizabeth's heir. Yet it soon became apparent that her very presence made her a figurehead for Elizabeth's opponents and that she would be increasingly seen not so much as the heir but as a very real alternative to Elizabeth herself. Initially, it also seemed that Mary's cause might not be lost in Scotland. The country was plunged into civil war and the loyalty of Scottish politicians remained as changeable as ever, with William Maitland of Lethington and even Kirkcaldy of Grange rediscovering their support for the exiled queen. In England, meanwhile, one of the leading noblemen, the duke of Norfolk, harboured thoughts of marrying the Queen of Scots himself and was actually encouraged by the earl of Leicester but not by Cecil, who was horrified at the thought of a successful Mary, married to Norfolk and challenging Elizabeth for the English throne. Norfolk lost his nerve but others did not. Continued support for Catholicism and Mary's claim in the north of England came to a head in 1569 when the earls of Northumberland and Westmorland rose in rebellion against Elizabeth. This revolt, a disurbing reminder of the Pilgrimage of Grace thirty years earlier, was ruthlessly suppressed and around eight hundred of those involved were hanged. Northumberland fled to Scotland but was handed over by the regent Morton to Elizabeth in 1572 and executed at York. Westmorland escaped to Flanders, where he died in penury.

The passage of time, which must have sat so slowly on Mary's hands, turned a queen who had pleaded for help, and who only thought to be in England for a short while, into a plotter against her cousin's life. There was not, eventually, any other way out. If Elizabeth would not, or could not, restore her in Scotland, then she would aim to displace her cousin in England. Support came from the papacy when Elizabeth was excommunicated (very belatedly, some might have said) in 1570 but nothing was to be expected any longer from France or from Spain. Eventually, the Scottish queen was manipulated into treason by Elizabeth's redoubtable spymaster, Francis Walsingham. Mary's last letter, written on the evening before her execution, was to Henry III of France, who had been a little boy in the far-off days when she had left France for Scotland. In death, she represented herself as a Catholic martyr. 'I am to be executed like a criminal at eight o-clock in the morning', she wrote, '. . . the Catholic faith and the defence of my God-given right to the English throne are the two reasons for which I am condemned and yet they will not allow me to say that it is for the Catholic faith that I die.'[2] As the red of her petticoats was stained with her blood on the floor of Fotheringay, there was also born the legend of the doomed, romantic Mary Queen of Scots, the only woman ever to occupy the throne of Scotland.

The men who had variously supported and betrayed her, who longed for power but also, in some cases, to bring good government to Scotland, did not in general prosper for long. Moray was assassinated in 1570 and Matthew Stewart, earl of Lennox, who became regent after him, died fighting an insurrection in support of Mary the following year. As the civil war continued, John Erskine, earl of Mar, who had been James VI's keeper and defied Mary at Stirling, also died, after supping with the earl of Morton in 1572. Mary's old opponent then became regent himself, lasting until 1581, when his own enemies, of whom there were many, finally put him on trial for the murder of Lord Darnley. Morton, who had for so long evaded the consequences of his past, was executed in Edinburgh. William Maitland of Lethington had died in mysterious circumstances in prison in 1573, perhaps by his own hand, though possibly of natural causes as he was not in good health. Mary requested the pope issue an annulment of her marriage to Bothwell in 1576 but though it appears to have been granted, no actual documentation has ever been found. When Mary's cause in Scotland seemed incontrovertibly lost, King Frederick of Denmark had no further use for her husband. Bothwell was moved to the castle of Dragsholm on the island of Zealand and kept in solitary confinement. He died insane in 1578. It is ironic that all these men predeceased Mary herself.

Her son, James VI, grew up in a strict and loveless environment, having never known either of his parents. His tutor, George Buchanan, tried to poison the reputation of Mary Queen of Scots but the boy's own attitude towards his mother remains something of a mystery. He learned early on the advantages of independence and self-reliance. But one person, at least, who had been implacably opposed to Mary changed her tune. This was Margaret Douglas, countess of Lennox, who was reconciled to the Scottish queen shortly after Matthew Stewart's death. She had lost much but was now committed to protecting the future of her grandson, the little boy whom she believed, with increasing confidence, would one day become king of England as well as Scotland. Margaret died in 1578, having outlived her second son, Charles.

When Mary Queen of Scots was at last executed on the orders of her cousin, the triumph of the Tudors over the Stewarts must have seemed complete. William Cecil could at last breathe freely. Yet the triumph, at least from the dynastic perspective, was hollow. Those who hated Mary most in England knew that the days of the Tudors were numbered. While she would never rule in England, it was only a matter of time before her son would gain the throne. As Elizabeth's reign ended amid rebellion, economic uncertainty and divisions within Protestantism, a bored aristocracy eyed James VI with increasing anticipation. His succession was unopposed. When he entered London for the first time on that spring morning in 1603, he was fulfilling the hopes of the marriage of James IV to Margaret Tudor a century before that the two crowns might, one day, be united.

Dramatis Personae

✂

THE SCOTS

THE STEWARTS

JAMES III, KING OF SCOTS, 1452–88. The eldest son of James II and Mary of Gueldres, James became king in 1460 aged eight. An austere, remote and unpopular ruler, his regime was shaken by serious rebellion in 1482. Further revolt in 1488 involving his eldest son led to his overthrow and death at the battle of Sauchieburn.

ALEXANDER, DUKE OF ALBANY, 1454–85. The younger brother of James III. Their deteriorating relationship made Albany flee to France. In 1482, allied with England, he invaded Scotland but could not hold on to power. Imprisoned in 1485, he escaped back to France, where he was killed in a joust a few months later.

JOHN STEWART, DUKE OF ALBANY, *c.*1482–1536. Alexander, duke of Albany's son was born in France and brought up at the French court. He was called to Scotland to act as regent in 1515, the first of three separate terms he spent there. Hard-working and genuinely committed, he was frustrated by the complexity of Scottish politics and English opposition to his rule.

MARGARET OF DENMARK, QUEEN OF SCOTS, 1456/7?–86. The wife of James III was a Danish princess. She produced three sons – James, duke of Rothesay (the future James IV), James, duke of Ross and John, earl of Mar. The crisis of 1482 permanently damaged the royal couple's marriage; James stayed in Edinburgh and Margaret resided at Stirling.

JAMES IV, KING OF SCOTS, 1473–1513. The first son of James III and Margaret of Denmark was brought up at Stirling by his mother. He came to the throne, in revolt against his father, in 1488. James married Margaret Tudor in 1503. International success and domestic stability made him the last great king of medieval Scotland. He died at the battle of Flodden in 1513.

JAMES STEWART, DUKE OF ROSS, 1476–1504. The second son of James III and Margaret of Denmark, James was brought up with his brothers at Stirling. James IV secured his appointment as archbishop of St Andrews but he died without being consecrated.

ALEXANDER STEWART, ARCHBISHOP-DESIGNATE OF ST ANDREWS, c.1493–1513. The eldest illegitimate son of James IV by his mistress, Marion Boyd, Alexander was destined for the church. A pupil of Erasmus, much admired by his tutor, he was gifted and charming. He died beside his father at Flodden.

JAMES V, KING OF SCOTS, 1512–42. The son of James IV and Margaret Tudor was aged seventeen months on his accession. His minority was characterized by factional struggles within Scotland. In 1528 he began his personal rule. A capable monarch with a splendid court, James married twice, first to Madeleine of Valois and then to Mary of Guise.

JAMES STEWART, FIRST EARL OF MORAY, 1531/2–70. The son of James V and his mistress, Margaret Erskine. His relationship with his half-sister, Queen Mary, was uneasy and he opposed the Darnley marriage. He was abroad when Mary married Bothwell and he defeated her forces in 1568, precipitating her flight to England. He served briefly as regent before his assassination.

JAMES HAMILTON, SECOND EARL OF ARRAN AND DUKE OF CHÂTELHERAULT, c.1519–75. The second earl of Arran was the great-grandson of James II. He became regent after James V's death. An unsuccessful military leader, his defeat at the battle of

Pinkie in 1547 was the low-point of his career. Arran was a survivor but his pragmatism has been viewed as vacillation. Recent studies suggest that his goal was to defend Scotland and that his patriotism, while not excluding self-interest, was genuine.

MATTHEW STEWART, FOURTH EARL OF LENNOX, 1516–71. Educated in France, the fourth earl of Lennox returned to Scotland in 1543 to pursue his own interest – he was also a great-grandson of James II. In 1544 he changed tack and pledged himself to Henry VIII, marrying the king's niece, Lady Margaret Douglas. Lennox was elated by the marriage of his son, Lord Darnley, to Queen Mary and devastated by Darnley's assassination. He became regent in 1570 and was fatally wounded by opponents in 1571.

ALEXANDER STEWART, DUKE OF ROSS, 1514–15. James IV's posthumous son was born to Margaret Tudor in April 1514. With his brother, James V, he was removed from his mother's care by the duke of Albany in the summer of 1515. He died in December of that year, after his mother had fled to England.

LADY JANET STEWART, 1502–62. The illegitimate daughter of James IV by Lady Isabel Stewart, Lady Janet Stewart married Lord Malcolm Fleming, who died at the battle of Pinkie. A confidante of Mary of Guise, Lady Fleming accompanied her niece, the young queen, to France as governess but her affair with Henry II and subsequent pregnancy caused her to be sent home in disgrace.

MARY QUEEN OF SCOTS, 1542–87. Mary became queen at only six days old. Sent to France in 1548, she returned to Scotland in 1561, after the death of Francis II, her first husband. Her second marriage, to Lord Darnley, was a disaster. Suspected of involvement in his murder in 1567, her third marriage, to the earl of Bothwell, led to rebellion, abdication and imprisonment. Escaping in 1568, she fled into England. Drawn into plots against Elizabeth, Mary was executed in 1587.

HENRY STEWART, LORD DARNLEY, 1545–67. The son of Matthew Stewart and Margaret Douglas, Darnley married Mary Queen of Scots in 1565. Despite the birth of a son, Prince James, the marriage collapsed as Darnley's immaturity became apparent. Implicated in the murder of his wife's favourite, David Riccio, in 1566, he was himself assassinated in Edinburgh the following year.

THE SCOTTISH NOBILITY

The Douglases

ARCHIBALD DOUGLAS, FIFTH EARL OF ANGUS, *c.*1449–1513. A member of one of the leading Scottish families, the fifth earl of Angus was disloyal to both James III and James IV. Briefly chancellor in the 1490s, tensions between Angus and James IV were probably heightened by the transfer of the affections of Janet Kennedy, the earl's young mistress, to the king himself.

ARCHIBALD DOUGLAS, SIXTH EARL OF ANGUS, *c.*1489–1557. The sixth earl of Angus married Margaret Tudor in 1514 and until 1528 he dominated Scotland. In exile in England for thirteen years, he returned in 1543 and discovered his Scottish patriotism. Success against the English at Ancrum Moor in 1545 underlined his prowess as a soldier. Disliking Mary of Guise, he retired from politics and was never reconciled to his daughter, Lady Margaret.

JANET DOUGLAS, LADY GLAMIS, *c.*1504–37. The sister of the sixth earl, Lady Glamis was accused in 1537 of assisting Angus and of plotting to poison James V. The latter charge was almost certainly false but she was sentenced to death and burned immediately on Edinburgh's castle hill, a victim of the king's hatred of the Douglases.

LADY MARGARET DOUGLAS, COUNTESS OF LENNOX, 1515–78. The only child of Margaret Tudor and the sixth earl of Angus, Lady Margaret Douglas was brought up by her uncle, Henry VIII, after her parents' marriage disintegrated. In 1544 she married Matthew Stewart, earl of Lennox. The devoted couple's dynastic ambitions upset Elizabeth I and their Scottish rivals. Shattered by the deaths of her son, Darnley, and her husband, she was eventually reconciled with Mary Queen of Scots.

JAMES DOUGLAS, EARL OF MORTON, *c.*1516–81. Mary's chancellor, who was involved in the murder of Riccio, earning him the queen's hatred. His role in Darnley's assassination remains unclear. Initial support for the Bothwell marriage evaporated quickly and he supported Moray when Mary escaped. Regent between 1572 and 1580, he fell from power and was executed in 1581.

The Hepburns

PATRICK HEPBURN, FIRST EARL OF BOTHWELL, *c.*1455–1508. Patrick supported James IV and the rebels against James III at Sauchieburn and played a major role in government in the early part of James IV's reign. He represented the king at the proxy wedding to Margaret Tudor in London in 1502.

JAMES HEPBURN, FOURTH EARL OF BOTHWELL AND DUKE OF ORKNEY, 1534/5–78. Mary Queen of Scots' last husband was a Protestant but also a diehard opponent of English influence in Scotland. Violent and opportunistic, he arranged Darnley's assassination and then decided to marry the queen himself, abducting and raping her in 1567. Mary's third marriage brought about her downfall and Bothwell fled Scotland, dying in captivity in Denmark.

The Gordons

GEORGE GORDON, FOURTH EARL OF HUNTLY, 1513–62. Close to James V, the fourth earl of Huntly ruled the roost in northern Scotland. Being both pro-French and a staunch Catholic did not protect him from Queen Mary's wrath when he fell out with her over the award of the earldom of Moray to her half-brother, Lord James Stewart. Huntly's forces were defeated outside Aberdeen and he died of a stroke.

GEORGE GORDON, FIFTH EARL OF HUNTLY, d.1576. Imprisoned by Queen Mary after his father's revolt, but released in 1565, the fifth earl of Huntly converted to Protestantism and became a Marian loyalist, supporting her marriage to Bothwell even though the queen's third husband had hastily divorced from his sister.

THE SCOTTISH CLERGY

JAMES BEATON, ARCHBISHOP OF ST ANDREWS, *c.*1473–1539. The chancellor of Scotland, who played a leading role in government after Flodden. Determined to maintain Scotland's independence, he was a supporter of the regent Albany but also believed in peace with England. On uneasy terms with James V, he supported the career of his nephew, David.

DAVID BEATON, CARDINAL OF SCOTLAND, ARCHBISHOP OF ST ANDREWS, *c.*1494–1546. Beaton was an accomplished diplomat, pro-French and opposed to the Anglophile Douglases. Powerful, wealthy and ambitious, he came into conflict with Arran following the death of James V but recouped his position. Created cardinal in 1538, he was a religious conservative. The English government condoned his murder.

JOHN KNOX, RELIGIOUS REFORMER, *c.*1516–72. John Knox was the towering figure of the Scottish Reformation. Imprisoned in the French galleys in 1547, he lived in England after his release and was chaplain to Edward VI. During the 1550s his time in Germany and Switzerland hardened his virulent anti-Catholicism. An unsparing opponent of Mary Queen of Scots, his firebrand preaching helped establish the Scottish kirk.

QUEEN MARY'S SECRETARIES

DAVID RICCIO, *c.*1533–66. Born in Turin, Riccio came to Mary's court as a musician. Appointed French secretary in 1564, he was resented by Darnley, who was manipulated by Morton and others who were fearful that parliament would forfeit them for rebellion. Riccio's brutal murder in the queen's private apartments was intended as a warning to the pregnant queen to desist.

WILLIAM MAITLAND OF LETHINGTON, *c.*1528–73. A tolerant man of great intellect and diplomatic skill, William supported union with England. As Moray's ally, he was Queen Mary's secretary between 1561 and 1565. Involvement in the murders of Riccio and Darnley compromised him, though he married Mary Fleming, one of the 'Four Marys' – an unlikely love-match. Maitland deserted the queen in 1567, but later resumed his allegiance. He died in prison.

THE MISTRESSES OF JAMES IV
(with dates of their liaisons)

MARION BOYD, 1492–5. The mother of Alexander Stewart and Lady Katherine Stewart.

MARGARET DRUMMOND, 1495?–7. The mother of Lady Margaret Stewart. She died in 1502.

JANET KENNEDY, *c.*1500–3. The mother of James Stewart, earl of Moray and two unnamed daughters, one of whom died young.

LADY ISABEL STEWART OF BUCHAN, early 1500s. The illegitimate daughter of the earl of Buchan and distant cousin to James IV. Also the mother of Lady Janet Stewart (b.1502), Lady Fleming, governess to Mary Queen of Scots during her first years in France.

THE MISTRESSES OF JAMES V
(dates of liaisons unclear)

ELIZABETH SHAW. The mother of James I Stewart (1529–57).

ELIZABETH BEATON. The mother of Jean Stewart, countess of Argyll (1530–88).

MARGARET ERSKINE (James V's favourite mistress). The mother of James (II) Stewart, earl of Moray (1531–71).

CHRISTIAN BARCLAY. The mother of James (III) Stewart (*fl.*1533), who died in infancy.

KATHERINE CARMICHAEL. The mother of John Stewart (*c.*1531–63).

EUPHEMIA ELPHINSTONE. The mother of Robert (I) Stewart (1533–93).

ELIZABETH STEWART. The mother of Adam Stewart (d.1575).

TWO UNKNOWN LADIES. The mothers of Margaret Stewart and Robert (II) Stewart (d.1580).

THE 'FOUR MARYS'
(attendants to Mary Queen of Scots)

MARY BEATON, MARY SETON, MARY LIVINGSTON AND MARY FLEMING (the daughter of Lady Janet Stewart) all accompanied Mary Queen of Scots to France, returned with her in 1561, and were much favoured by the queen.

THE ENGLISH

THE TUDORS

EDMUND TUDOR, EARL OF RICHMOND, *c.*1430–56. The elder son of Queen Katherine of Valois by her second husband, Owen Tudor. Edmund and his brother, Jasper, were favoured by Henry VI, their half-brother. He married Margaret Beaufort but died of plague at Carmarthen shortly after his release from imprisonment by besieging Yorkist forces in the early years of the Wars of the Roses.

LADY MARGARET BEAUFORT, COUNTESS OF RICHMOND AND DERBY, 1443–1509. Margaret was the great-great granddaughter of Edward III. Aged twelve, she married Edmund Tudor, was soon widowed and gave birth to a son, Henry. The two were kept apart by the confused politics of the Wars of the Roses. Astute and adaptive, Margaret never lost sight of her son's interest, supported him in 1485 and remained close thereafter.

HENRY VII, KING OF ENGLAND, 1457–1509. The first Tudor had spent half his life in exile before a second attempt at the English crown resulted in a surprising victory at Bosworth in 1485. Clever and resourceful, Henry's policy of financially crippling opponents, rather than executing them, filled his coffers. He married the Yorkist heiress, Elizabeth, to secure his throne. Fond of his family, Henry was also a successful dynast.

JASPER TUDOR, EARL OF BEDFORD, *c.*1431–95. Brother-in-law and protector of Margaret Beaufort when she gave birth to Henry VII in his stronghold of Pembroke Castle aged thirteen. A diehard opponent of the Yorkists, Jasper shared his nephew's long exile in Brittany and France, fought with him at Bosworth and was given prominent office in the new Tudor regime.

MARGARET TUDOR, QUEEN OF SCOTS, 1489–1541. The eldest daughter of Henry VII. In 1503, aged thirteen, she married James IV of Scotland. Only one of their six children, the future James V, survived. Her husband's death at Flodden was a bitter blow and the queen's two subsequent marriages were unhappy. Twice regent for her son, Margaret clashed with her brother, Henry VIII, but was unable to establish herself successfully in Scottish politics.

HENRY VIII, KING OF ENGLAND, 1491–1547. The second son of Henry VII ascended the throne at the age of seventeen in 1509 and married his elder brother's widow, Katherine of Aragon. Henry is best known for his six wives, the witness of his obsessive search for an heir, and for his break with Rome in the 1530s. A dominant presence in sixteenth-century England, his yearning to be a major European player is often overlooked, and can hardly be counted a success. Neither can his persistent interference in Scottish politics, despite three major military victories.

EDWARD VI, KING OF ENGLAND, 1537–53. The son of Henry VIII and his third wife, Jane Seymour. Edward came to the throne aged nine in 1547. His government was directed first by his uncle, Edward Seymour, duke of Somerset and then by John Dudley, duke of Northumberland. Henry VIII wanted his son to marry Mary Queen of Scots, thereby uniting the two kingdoms, but most Scots opposed the match.

MARY I, QUEEN OF ENGLAND, 1516–58. The elder daughter of Henry VIII was England's first queen regnant. She fought for her throne when her half-brother, Edward VI, cut both her and her sister, Elizabeth, out of the succession in 1553. A staunch Catholic, Mary married the future Philip II of Spain. Her persecution of Protestants has overshadowed her domestic achievements. Relations with Scotland were uneasy during her reign.

ELIZABETH I, QUEEN OF ENGLAND, 1533–1603. Declared illegitimate when her mother, Anne Boleyn, was executed, she survived the upheavals of her siblings' reigns to become queen in 1558. Elizabeth consistently refused to marry, declining also to name a successor. She kept Mary Queen of Scots captive after her flight into England in 1568, eventually sanctioning her execution in 1587. Her reign is still viewed as a Golden Age, though it was far from tranquil.

THE YORKISTS

RICHARD III, KING OF ENGLAND, 1452–85. The youngest child of Richard, duke of York, claimant to the English throne, grew up amidst the turbulence of civil war. His elder brother, Edward, became king in 1461 when Henry VI was overthrown. An experienced soldier with strong family loyalties, Richard's grab for the throne in 1483 was unacceptable to many, though he claimed Edward's marriage was invalid and his heirs illegitimate. He died at Bosworth in 1485.

MARGARET OF YORK, DUCHESS OF BURGUNDY, 1446–1503. Sister of the Yorkist kings, Margaret married Charles the Bold, duke of Burgundy, in 1468. Intelligent, well-educated and good-looking, she presided over a rich and cultured court, remaining in Burgundy after Charles the Bold's death in battle in 1477. An implacable opponent of Henry VII, she supported Yorkist plots and claimed that the impostor, Perkin Warbeck, was her nephew, Richard, duke of York.

ELIZABETH WOODVILLE, QUEEN CONSORT OF EDWARD IV, *c.*1437–92. The attractive widow of a Lancastrian knight, Elizabeth was a member of a large and ambitious family. Her secret marriage to Edward IV stunned his politicians. Her brother-in-law, Richard, displaced her elder son as king in 1483 and both her sons – the Princes in the Tower – disappeared, presumed murdered. She supported the marriage of her daughter, Elizabeth, to Henry VII but retired from court in 1487.

ELIZABETH OF YORK, QUEEN CONSORT OF HENRY VII, 1466–1503. Elizabeth's gilded childhood as the eldest of Edward IV's bevy of beautiful daughters was swiftly extinguished by his sudden death and Richard III's usurpation. She married Henry VII in 1486, uniting the houses of Lancaster and York. Only three of their eight children survived. Henry VII was greatly grieved by her death in childbirth, on her thirty-seventh birthday.

ROYAL MINISTERS AND DIPLOMATS

THOMAS WOLSEY, CARDINAL AND ARCHBISHOP OF YORK, 1470/1–1530. Henry VIII's chief adviser, until caught up in the quagmire of the divorce from Katherine of Aragon, Wolsey was of humble East Anglian origin. Educated at Oxford, he rose rapidly to become the king's almoner in 1509 and his principal minister six years later. Ambitious and acquisitive, he lived like a member of royalty, enjoyed the exercise of power and was a major player in European diplomacy over many years.

THOMAS CROMWELL, EARL OF ESSEX, b. (in or before) 1485–1540. Wolsey's servant, royal councillor and secretary from 1534 to 1536. Cromwell orchestrated the downfall of Anne Boleyn, oversaw the dissolution of the monasteries and the introduction of the Great Bible in English. Embarrassed by the failure of the Anne of Cleves marriage and concerned that Cromwell was determined on greater religious reforms, Henry VIII had him executed in 1540.

WILLIAM CECIL, FIRST BARON BURGHLEY, 1520/21–98. From the Lincolnshire gentry, Cecil was educated at Cambridge. Servant of Protector Somerset, he stayed in England during Mary's reign, despite his Protestant faith. Elizabeth admired him, appointing him Secretary of State on her accession. He served her faithfully, though her indecision frustrated him. His over-arching aim was to protect her and the English crown, believing both vulnerable to Catholic Europe.

THOMAS DACRE, SECOND BARON DACRE OF GILSLAND, 1467–1525. One of the great magnates of northern England, he spent much of his life keeping the Scots at bay. Originally a supporter of Richard III, Dacre quickly switched allegiance to the Tudors. Knew James IV well, but it was Dacre's cavalry who helped the English to victory at Flodden. Adviser (sometimes overbearingly so) to Margaret Tudor and her protector when she fled Scotland in 1515.

THOMAS RANDOLPH, DIPLOMATIC REPRESENTATIVE IN SCOTLAND, 1525/6–90. Elizabeth I's representative in Scotland during Mary Queen of Scots' personal rule. He was flattered by Mary's treatment of him but frustrated by Elizabeth's refusal to commit to anything. He pursued the Leicester match enthusiastically but relations with the Scottish court deteriorated and he was expelled in 1566.

THE ENGLISH NOBILITY

THOMAS HOWARD, EARL OF SURREY AND SECOND DUKE OF NORFOLK, 1443–1524. The Yorkist Howards rose to prominence under Richard III. Injured at Bosworth and subsequently imprisoned, Surrey made his peace with Henry VII and served loyally in the north of England. Accompanied Margaret Tudor north to her Scottish marriage and formed a bond with James IV. Outgeneralled the Scottish king at Flodden.

THOMAS HOWARD, THIRD DUKE OF NORFOLK, 1473–1554. Soldier, lord high admiral, diplomat and uncle of Anne Boleyn, Thomas played a major part in the English victory at Flodden and was thereafter consistently involved in politics and court intrigue. An outward affability hid a sometimes violent nature. Imprisoned on treason charges in 1546, Norfolk was saved from execution by Henry VIII's death.

EDWARD SEYMOUR, EARL OF HERTFORD AND DUKE OF SOMERSET, *c.*1500–52. The son of a Wiltshire knight, Edward's prospects were transformed when his sister, Jane, married Henry VIII and gave birth to a son. His stock increased in the 1540s and he became Protector to his nephew, Edward VI, on Henry VIII's death. He defeated the Scots at Pinkie in 1547 but could not follow up the victory. His autocratic style led to his overthrow in 1549 and eventual execution.

JOHN DUDLEY, VISCOUNT LISLE AND DUKE OF NORTHUMBER-LAND, 1504–53. Dudley's father was executed in 1510 but he was able to follow the common trajectory of well-born young men, becoming a courtier and soldier. He was close to Edward Seymour, but led the coup against him in 1549. As chief minister to Edward VI, he encouraged the king's alteration of the succession in favour of his own daughter-in-law, Lady Jane Grey, but misjudged support for Mary I and was executed for treason.

ROBERT DUDLEY, EARL OF LEICESTER, 1532/3–88. The son of John Dudley, Robert claimed to have known Elizabeth I since childhood. Swiftly established as favourite after her accession, the mysterious death of his wife in 1560 compromised him but did not permanently affect his close relationship with the queen. Elizabeth's proposal that he should marry Mary Queen of Scots met with a lukewarm response, from Dudley and from the Scottish queen herself.

THE FRENCH

CHARLES VIII, KING OF FRANCE, 1470–98. Charles succeeded his father, Louis XI, in 1483. His elder sister, Anne of Beaujeu, ruled as regent until 1491. Charles enhanced his power by marrying Anne of Brittany and invaded Italy in pursuit of his claim to the Kingdom of Naples. Dying as the result of a bizarre accident in 1498, he left no immediate heir as his children all pre-deceased him. He was succeeded by his cousin, Louis XII.

LOUIS XII, KING OF FRANCE, 1462–1515. Louis proved an energetic ruler. He divorced his first wife in order to secure Brittany by marrying Charles VIII's widow, Anne. He supported James IV and expected Scottish assistance when Henry VIII went to war against the French in 1512. His third wife was Princess Mary Tudor, sister of Henry VIII. Two daughters but no sons survived him.

FRANCIS I, KING OF FRANCE, 1494–1547. Francis was Louis XII's cousin. His rivalry with Henry VIII was less important than that with the Habsburg Emperor Charles V. Defeated in Italy, he was imprisoned by Charles in 1525 and compelled to leave his sons as hostages. He married Louis XII's daughter, Claude, and Eleanor, sister of Charles V. His daughter, Madeleine, was the first wife of James V of Scotland.

MARY OF GUISE, QUEEN OF SCOTS AND REGENT OF SCOT-LAND, 1515–60. From a prominent family in north-eastern France, Mary was a widow with two small sons when Francis I informed her she was to marry James V of Scotland. Unenthusiastic at first, she did her duty, marrying James in 1538. Mary Queen of Scots was their only surviving child. She was pro-French regent from 1554 to her death.

HENRY II, KING OF FRANCE, 1519–59. Three years' captivity in Spain gave Henry an abiding hatred of the Habsburgs. He married Catherine de Medici in 1533, becoming heir to Francis I following the death of his elder brother in 1536. Dominated by his mistress, Diane de Poitiers, Henry harboured an ambition to rule in both Scotland and England via Mary Queen of Scots, who married his son, Francis, in 1558. Henry himself died in a jousting accident.

FRANCIS II, KING OF FRANCE, 1544–60. The eldest son of Henry II, brought up with Mary Queen of Scots, his intended bride. Intelligent but sickly, he inherited the religious problems that had been growing during his father's reign and was dominated by the Guise family, his wife's relatives. He died unexpectedly of a severe ear infection.

CATHERINE DE MEDICI, QUEEN OF FRANCE, 1519–89. Mary Queen of Scots' mother-in-law was the daughter of Lorenzo II de

Medici. She married Henry II aged fourteen and was childless for many years and without influence, though she helped supervise Mary's education. Her position was transformed by Francis II's death, when she became regent, but her relationship with Mary had soured.

THE HABSBURGS

MAXIMILIAN I, HOLY ROMAN EMPEROR, 1459–1519. A cunning ruler and dynast, Maximilian expanded his lands through marriage and diplomacy. He fought against the French in Italy and was a difficult ally to Henry VII and Henry VIII. He was succeeded as Holy Roman Emperor by his grandson, Charles V.

CHARLES V, HOLY ROMAN EMPEROR, 1500–58. The great rival of Francis I was an unreliable ally to Henry VIII, whom he consistently outmanoeuvred. He arranged the marriage of his son, Philip of Spain, to Mary I in 1554. Ruled much of Europe but the rise of Protestantism challenged his authority. Exhausted and ill, he abdicated in 1556 and retreated to a Spanish monastery.

PHILIP II, KING OF SPAIN, 1527–98. Viewing himself as defender of Catholicism in Europe, relations between Philip and the Protestant Elizabeth eventually broke down. Often depicted as cold-blooded and fanatical, Philip's reputation has been savaged by English-speaking historians but he was a hard-working ruler and the prime force in the western world after 1560.

Notes

❧

Abbreviations

APS	*Acts of the Parliaments of Scotland*, ed. T. Thomson and C. Innes (Edinburgh, 1814–75)
BL	British Library
BN	Bibliothèque Nationale, Paris
Cal SP Spanish	*Calendar of Letters, Despatches and State Papers relating to the negotiations between England and Spain*, ed. G. Bergenroth and others (London, 1862–1954)
CSP Scotland	*Calendar of State Papers relating to Scotland and Mary Queen of Scots, 1547–1603*, ed. J. Bain and others (Edinburgh, 1898–1969)
L&P Henry VIII	*Letters and Papers, Foreign and Domestic, of the reign of Henry VIII*, ed. J. S. Brewer and others (London,1862–1932)
NAS	National Archives of Scotland
NLS	National Library of Scotland
ODNB	*Oxford Dictionary of National Biography*
SHR	*Scottish Historical Review*
TA	*Treasurer's Accounts: Accounts of the Lord High Treasurer of Scotland, 1473–1513*, ed. T. Dickson and J.B. Paul (Edinburgh, 1877–1902)

Prologue – Leith Harbour, Scotland, 19 August 1561

1 John Knox, *The History of the Reformation in Scotland* ed. W. C. Dickinson (1949), p. 267.

One – 'This pretty lad'

1 Francis Bacon, *The History of the Reign of King Henry VII*, 1622 (2007 edition), p. 168.
2 Quoted in Ralph A. Griffiths and Roger S. Thomas, *The Making of the Tudor Dynasty* (2005), p. 63.
3 Sean Cunningham, *Henry VII* (2007), p. 14.
4 Ibid., pp. 16–18.
5 Edward Hall, *The Union of the Two Noble and Illustrious Families of Lancaster and York* (London, 1548), p. 397.
6 Henry Parker, Lord Morley, cited in Michael K. Jones and Malcolm G. Underwood, *The King's Mother* (Cambridge University Press, 1992), p. 65.
7 'The Archives of Lilles, Lettres et Missions', vol. 3, f. 52, quoted in James Gairdner, *Letters and Papers Illustrative of the Reigns of Richard III and Henry VII* (1861), vol. 1.
8 Sean Cunningham, *Richard III: A Royal Enigma* (2003), p. 66.
9 J. O. Halliwell-Philipps, ed., *Letters of the Kings of England* (1846), vol. 1, pp. 161–2.
10 Quoted in Griffiths and Thomas, *The Making of the Tudor Dynasty*, p. 155.
11 Ibid., p. 168.
12 Denys Hay, ed., *The Anglia Historia of Polydore Vergil*, Camden Series (1950), vol. LXXIV, f. 35.

Two – The Field of Stirling

1 *TA*, vol. 1, pp. cciii, 30, 34, 35–6, 39–42, 56–7, 104, cited in Rosalind K. Marshall, *Scottish Queens, 1034–1714* (2007), pp. 77–8.
2 S. B. Chandler, 'An Italian Life of Margaret, Queen of James III', *SHR*, xxxii (1953), pp. 53–7.
3 Blind Harry's *Wallace*, introduced by Elspeth King (1998), p. 150.
4 Chandler, 'An Italian Life', *SHR*, xxxii, p. 56.

5 Ibid., p. 55.

6 Ibid., p. 57.

7 Norman Macdougall, *James III, a Political Study* (1982), p. 245.

8 *APS*, ii, 210. Cited in Macdougall, *James III*, pp. 248–9.

9 It has been speculated that Prince James was with the group who confronted his father at Blackness. If so, it was surely an awkward meeting. Norman Macdougall, *James IV* (1997), p. 34.

10 *APS*, ii, 210. The original is in the National Archives of Scotland (NAS), PA 2/5, f. 98v–98r.

11 Robert Lindsay of Pitscottie, *The Historie and Chronicles of Scotland* (Edinburgh 1899), pp. 214–21.

12 Angus Graham, 'The Battle of Sauchieburn', *SHR*, xxxix, October 1960, pp. 89–97.

Three – Uneasy Crowns

1 Alexander Bruce of Earshall commanded the Scots who fought for Henry in 1485, joined Henry's household in 1485 and became a valet of the royal chamber. See Griffiths and Thomas, *The Making of the Tudor Dynasty*, p. 198.

2 *A Relation, or Rather a True Account of the Island of England about the Year 1500*, by Andrea Trevisan, translated from the Italian by Charlotte Augusta Sneyd, Camden Society, 37 (1847), p. 20.

3 Ibid., p. 21.

4 See paper by UC Berkeley economist J. Bradford de Long, 'Princes and Merchants: European city growth before the Industrial Revolution' (1992), p. 8, at www.j-bradford-delong.net.

5 A. F. Pollard, ed., *The Reign of Henry VIII from Contemporary Sources* (2009), p. 51.

6 A. H. Thomas and I. D. Thornley, eds, *The Great Chronicle of London* (1983), suggests that Henry actually entered the city and went to St Paul's on 27 August 1485 but other sources (Steven Gunn in the *ODNB* entry for Henry VII and BL Harleian MS 541 f. 217) give the date as 3 September.

7 Quoted in Sydney Anglo, 'The foundation of the Tudor dynasty: the coronation and marriage of Henry VII', *The Guildhall Miscellany* (1960–68), vol. 2, p. 6.

8 Ibid., p. 7.

9 For a fuller description, see P. R. Cavill, *The English Parliaments of Henry VII, 1485–1504* (2009), pp. 21–33.

10 Unlike today, there was no specific building set aside for the English

parliament to conduct its business, and meetings could be held in other English towns, such as York and Oxford.

11 See Arlene Naylor Okerlund, *Elizabeth of York* (2009), pp. 35–9.

12 The assertion that Elizabeth was at Sheriff Hutton cannot be proved. Several chroniclers claim that she was there with the earl of Warwick, both having been consigned to this Yorkshire 'exile' by an anxious Richard III. Henry VII was definitely keen to get hold of Warwick very soon after Bosworth, but the assumption that Elizabeth was there too, and that she was brought back south at the same time may be a telescoping of events with hindsight. Henry VII spent September and part of October 1485 with his mother in Surrey, at her Woking residence. See Jones and Underwood, *The King's Mother*, pp. 66–7. It is not clear where Elizabeth was residing and I am grateful for the insights of Rosemary Horrox on this point.

13 Roderick J. Lyall, 'The Medieval Scottish Coronation Service; Some Seventeenth-Century Evidence', *The Innes Review*, xxviii (1), (1977), pp. 3–21.

14 Robert Lindsay of Pitscottie, *The Chronicles of Scotland*, ed. John Graham Dalzell (1814), vol. 1, pp. xix–xxiv.

15 *A Relation, or True Account of England*, p. 15.

16 This may be an overstatement but he was, at least, showing a better grasp of history than the Foreign Office researcher who phoned the distinguished Scottish historian Norman Macdougall, in 1994, asking for further information on the Auld Alliance. She had clearly thought that this was something akin to the Entente Cordiale of 1904 but, on being told that the alliance was an offensive and defensive Franco–Scottish union directed against England, she refused to believe it. 'The concept of civilised life on the planet before the existence of a unitary British state quite defeated her,' wrote Macdougall drily.

17 Macdougall, *James IV*, p. 73.

18 Cited in Ishbel C. M. Barnes, *Janet Kennedy, Royal Mistress* (2007), p. 48.

19 James IV was the last king of Scotland who could speak the Gaelic tongue.

Four – The Impostor

1 Even allowing for minor linguistic variations, Perkin's reference to his parents does not appear to have been entirely accurate. It is now accepted that they were Jehan de Werbecque and Nicaise Farou. (See Steven Gunn, *ODNB* entry for Perkin Warbeck.)

2 Quoted in Ian Arthurson, *The Perkin Warbeck Conspiracy* (1994), p. 49.

3 In the fifteenth and sixteenth centuries Burgundy had a far wider geographical connotation than it does today, encompassing parts of northern France, the Netherlands and Belgium, and was not just restricted to the region of central France it covers now. The Flemish name for Malines is Mechelen.

4 For a fuller description of Margaret and her aims in Burgundy, see Christine Weightman, *Margaret of York* (2009), ch. 4. Weightman notes that Margaret also received income from estates in England and that this source of money dried up when Henry VII became king, perhaps also fuelling her resentment against the new monarch.

5 BN Fonds Espagnol 318, f. 83, cited in Ann Wroe, *Perkin, a Story of Deception* (2003), pp. 116–17.

6 Ferdinand and Isabella to Dr De Puebla, 20 July 1495, *Cal SP Spanish*, ed. G. A. Bergenroth (1862), vol. 1, p. 99.

7 Perth and Kinross District Archive, MS 78/9, cited in David Dunlop, 'The Masked Comedian: Perkin Warbeck's Adventures in Scotland and England from 1495 to 1497', *SHR*, lxx, 2, no. 190 (October 1991), pp. 97–128.

8 The marriage of Perkin Warbeck to Katherine Gordon took place so quickly after the pretender's arrival in Scotland that it is likely to have been arranged in advance with Perkin's advisers, while he was still on the run in Ireland. If so, it was a bold demand and demonstrates that they still believed his cause could succeed.

9 BL MS Cotton Caligula D vi, f. 28, cited in FW Madden, 'Documents relating to Perkin Warbeck with remarks on his history', *Archeologia*, vol. 27 (1838), pp. 153–210.

10 Cited in Ian Arthurson, *The Perkin Warbeck Conspiracy* (Stroud, 1994), pp. 146–7.

11 During the summer of 1496, probably in August, Ramsay had been to see the duke of Ross in St Andrews. Henry VII had sent the duke a crossbow as a gift. The young duke had replied that 'he intends to do your grace service and will not, for anything the king can do, come to his host against your grace.' James IV seems to have been aware of his brother's lack of enthusiasm for war with England, because he gave orders for him to be carefully watched while he was on campaign. Lord Bothwell (John Ramsay) to Henry VII, August(?) 1496, in H. Ellis, ed., *Original Letters Illustrative of English History* (1824), vol. 1, p. 23.

12 *Cal SP Spanish*, vol. 1, no. 210.

13 Quoted in Arthurson, *The Perkin Warbeck Conspiracy*, pp. 166–7.

14 *Cal SP Spanish*, vol. 1, no. 210.

15 *The Great Chronicle of London*, p. 277.

Five – A Summer Wedding

1 Edmund de la Pole went on to become an aspirant to the English throne (he was a nephew of Richard III) and an annoyance to Henry VII throughout the period of the final negotiations for Margaret's marriage.

2 Ayala to Ferdinand and Isabella, 25 July 1498, *Cal SP Spanish*, vol. 1, no. 210.

3 Barnes, *Janet Kennedy, Royal Mistress*, p. 30.

4 *Cal SP Spanish*, vol. 1, no. 210.

5 The treaties are printed in Latin in T. Rymer, *Foedera* (1816–69), vol. 12, pp. 707–803.

6 For more detail on the Borders and the working of justice in this disputed area, see Cynthia J. Neville, *Violence, Custom and Law: The Anglo–Scottish Border Lands in the Later Middle Ages* (1998), ch. 7.

7 Quoted in Macdougall, *James IV*, p. 250.

8 John Leland, *Collectanea* (1774), vol. 4, p. 262.

9 H. Ellis, ed., *Original Letters Illustrative of English History* (1824), vol. 1, p. 46.

10 Leland, *Collectanea*, vol. 5, pp. 373–4.

11 Cited in Okerlund, *Elizabeth of York*, p. 203.

12 For the accounts of Robert Lytton, keeper of Queen Margaret's wardrobe, see Joseph Bain, ed., *Calendar of Documents Relating to Scotland*, vol. 4 (1888), appendix no. 36 and nos 1698–1700, 1705, 1715, 1716, 1720, 1721 and 1725–7.

13 The book survives at Chatsworth House. See also BL Harleian MS 6986, ff. 3–6, which has copies of the inscriptions made by Henry VII in his daughter's prayer book.

14 Leland, *Collectanea*, p. 271.

15 Ibid., p. 274.

16 Ibid., p. 279.

17 The king's second brother, John, earl of Mar, had died in March 1503, so that James, like his bride, had experienced family loss shortly before his marriage.

18 Leland, *Collectanea*, p. 283.

19 Ibid.

20 R. L. Mackie, *King James IV of Scotland* (1958), p. 119.

21 Leland, *Collectanea*, pp. 287–90.

22 See Leslie Macfarlane, 'The Book of Hours of James IV and Margaret Tudor', *Innes Review*, vol. 11 (1960), pp. 3–21.

23 There is a very good facsimile copy in the Manuscripts Department of the British Library, MS Facs 581/85.

24 Mackie, *King James IV of Scotland*, p. 110.
25 Leland, *Collectanea*, pp. 292–6.
26 BL MS Cotton Vespasian F XIII, f. 61b.

Six – Brothers in Arms

1 Queen Margaret's master of the wardrobe was Piers Mannering. *TA*, vol. 2.
2 Barnes, *Janet Kennedy*, pp. 42–3, which also has the original version. I have left a few words from the Scots as I think they are perfectly comprehensible today.
3 The description of Sir James Balfour Paul, editor of the Treasurer's Accounts, in 1901. *TA*, iii, xlviii–xlix.
4 Thomas Penn, *Winter King: The Dawn of Tudor England* (2011).
5 For a compelling view of the less savoury side of Elizabethan government, see John Cooper, *The Queen's Agent: Francis Walsingham at the Court of Queen Elizabeth* (2011).
6 *Cal SP Spanish*, vol. 1, no. 436.
7 D. Starkey, *Henry: Virtuous Prince* (2009), pp. 169–70.
8 Starkey, *Henry*, ch. 11 and Penn, *Winter King*, ch. 7.
9 The description of Dr Ranald Nicholson, in *Scotland: The Later Middle Ages* (1974), p. 575, quoted in Macdougall, *James IV*, p. 257.
10 BL MS Cotton Caligula B VI, f. 74, also printed in Ellis, *Original Letters Illustrative of English History*, vol. 1, pp. 64–5, where the Scots word 'fremdly' (strangely, or unkindly) is wrongly printed as the English 'friendly'.
11 Julius II died shortly after pronouncing the excommunication but it was not immediately rescinded by his successor, Leo X, and was still in force when James IV declared war on England.
12 Quoted in Peter Reese, *Flodden: A Scottish Tragedy* (2003), p. 65.
13 *L & P Henry VIII*, vol. 1, no. 2157.
14 The post of Lord Admiral had originally been held by another Howard, Surrey's daring middle son, Edward, but he had died during an ill-advised attempt to storm the French admiral's flagship off the Brittany coast in the summer of 1513.
15 *Hall's Chronicle*, p. 557.
16 Reese, *Flodden*, p. 122.
17 Ibid., p. 138.

Seven – Queen and Country

1 *L&P Henry VIII*, vol. 1, no. 2268.
2 *Flodden Papers: Diplomatic Correspondence between the Courts of France and Scotland, 1507–1517*, ed. Marguerite Wood (1933), p. 87.
3 R. K. Hannay, ed., 'Acts of the Lords of the Council in Public Affairs, 1501–54: Selections from the Acta Dominorum Concilii' (1932), vol. 1, cited in Andrea Thomas, 'Coronation Ritual and Regalia', in *Sixteenth-Century Scotland: Essays in Honour of Michael Lynch*, ed. Julian Goodare and Alasdair A. MacDonald (2008), pp. 43–67.
4 Amy Blakeway, *Regency in Sixteenth-Century Scotland*, unpublished PhD thesis, University of Cambridge (2010), pp. 65–6.
5 Flodden Papers, no. 22, quoted in W. K. Emond, *The Minority of King James V, 1513–1528*, unpublished PhD thesis, University of St Andrews (1988), p. 6.
6 See Patricia Hill Buchanan, *Margaret Tudor, Queen of Scots* (1985), p. 84.
7 Emond, *The Minority of King James V*, p. 19.
8 'Acts of the Lords of the Council in Public Affairs', ed. R. K. Hannay (1932), p. 22, cited in Emond, *The Minority of King James V*, p. 28.
9 *Letters of Royal and Illustrious Ladies*, ed. Mary A. E. Wood (1846), vol. 1, pp. 166–9.
10 *L&P Henry VIII*, vol. 2, no. 779.
11 The portcullis episode has been described by a succession of writers as taking place at Edinburgh Castle but only Stirling is mentioned in Dacre's report of this incident and Margaret's subsequent surrender.
12 Margaret's younger sister, Mary, still using, as was her right, the title of Queen of France, wrote personally to Albany expressing her worries about the future of her Scottish nephews. The duke tried to assuage her anxiety, adding, in his own hand, 'As to the Queen of Scots her sister, I swear I have done and will do her all the service I can.' BL Cotton MS Caligula BII, f. 367, *L&P Henry VIII*, vol. 2, no. 1025.
13 *L&P Henry VIII*, vol. 2, no. 1350.
14 Ibid.

Eight – The Young King

1 Lady Margaret Stewart, daughter of James IV and Margaret Drummond, had married John Gordon, the Master (or heir) of the third earl of Huntly. The Master of Huntly died in 1517 and Alexander Gordon succeeded his grandfather in 1524. His wardship had been

given to Queen Margaret but passed to the earl of Moray on Margaret's estrangement from her second husband. In practice, the boy remained under the control of the earl of Angus and their mutual dislike of Angus was probably a further bond, aside from that of blood, between James V and Huntly. The earl would go on to play a prominent part in the history of sixteenth-century Scotland.

2 D. Hamer, ed., *The works of Sir David Lindsay*, four volumes (1931–6), vol. 1, pp. 4–5.
3 *State Papers of Henry VIII*, eleven volumes (1830–52), vol. 4, no. 368.
4 Ibid., no. 243.
5 Cited in Maria Perry, *Sisters to the King* (1998), p. 146.
6 BL Cotton MS Caligula, BVI, f. 270.
7 Princess Mary Tudor, Henry's younger sister, married Charles Brandon, one of her brother's companions, in secret soon after she was widowed in France. The king's displeasure was short-lived and he made Brandon duke of Suffolk. The Suffolks' son, Henry, earl of Lincoln, who was, with his cousin, James V, Henry VIII's closest male heir for many years, died in 1534.
8 *State Papers of Henry VIII*, vol. 1, part 1, no. 1. Cited in Lucy Wooding, *Henry VIII* (2009), p. 93.
9 See Kevin Sharpe, *Selling the Tudor Monarchy* (2009), pp. 163–4.
10 *L&P Henry VIII*, vol. 3, no. 873. See also Linda Porter, *Mary Tudor, the First Queen* (2007), p. 21.
11 Cited in Robert J. Knecht, 'The Field of Cloth of Gold', in Charles Giry-Deloison, ed., *Francois 1er et Henri VIII, deux princes de la Renaissance* (1994), pp. 37–51.
12 Ibid., pp. 45–6.
13 BL Cotton MS Caligula B.1, f. 166 (*L&P Henry VIII*, vol. 3, no. 2038).
14 *L&P Henry VIII*, vol. 3, no. 2039.
15 Ibid., vol. 4, no. 835.

Nine – Uncle and Nephew

1 Both were great-grandsons of King James II through his elder daughter, Mary.
2 Emond, *Minority of King James V*, pp. 504–13.
3 George Buchanan, *The History of Scotland*, translated by J. Aikman (1827–9), vol. ii, p. 234.
4 Peter D. Anderson in the *ODNB* entry on the mistresses and children of James V (2004).

5 An undated note from Queen Margaret from around this time refers to her handing over of Stirling and also states that 'the King of Scots rode privily from Edinburgh to Stirling, with five or six horse.' *L&P Henry VIII*, vol. 4, no. 4532.

6 *L&P Henry VIII*, vol. 4, no. 4505.

7 Joseph Bain, ed., *The Hamilton Papers: Letters and Papers Illustrating the Political Relations of England and Scotland in the Sixteenth Century* (1890), vol. 1, nos 34 and 35.

8 See below, chapter 11.

9 *L&P Henry VIII*, vol. 4, no. 4535.

10 Sir Walter Scott immortalized 'Johnie Armstrang' in his ballad of the same name in *Minstrelsy of the Scottish Border* (1802) but the reality of Armstrong's decade of terror in south-west Scotland was not romantic for the many who suffered his raids and destruction of their homes and livelihoods.

11 C. P. Hotle, *Thorns and Thistles: Diplomacy between Henry VIII and James V, 1528–1542* (1996), p. 73.

12 R. B. Merriman, *Life and Letters of Thomas Cromwell* (1902), p. 43. It is not known if the speech was ever actually delivered in the House of Commons.

13 *L&P Henry VIII*, vol. 7, no. 51.

14 *The Complaynt of Scotlande*, Early English Tract Society, extra series 17 (1872).

15 James V had two illegitimate sons christened James. Margaret Erskine's was the younger of the two and went on to become earl of Moray in 1562. James V's half-brother, Janet Kennedy's son, held the title of earl of Moray until his death in 1544.

16 Albany died in June 1536. The last years of his life in France had been devoted to the interests of his niece by marriage. Catherine de Medici and Francis I, ever shrewd in such matters, made sure that Catherine, his daughter-in-law, would inherit most of Albany's lands and that, through her, the extensive estates owned by Albany in the Auvergne would pass to the French Crown. This seems a poor recompense for his life of service and must have disadvantaged his own natural daughter, the countess of Choisy, born from a liaison with a Scottish gentlewoman.

17 *L&P Henry VIII*, vol. 11, p. 916.

18 Edmoud Bapst, *Les Mariages de Jacques V* (1889), pp. 307–8.

19 *L&P Henry VIII*, vol. 12, pt 1, no. 53.

20 Cited in Caroline Bingham, *James V, King of Scots* (1971), p. 145.

Ten – Solway Moss

1 Quoted in Andrea Thomas, *Princely Majestie: the Court of James V of Scotland, 1528–1542* (2005), p. 69.
2 The thistle also formed part of the badge of the Guise family, so was doubly relevant from the time of James V's second marriage.
3 Thomas, *Princelie Majestie*, p. 96. The comment was made twenty years after the death of James V and it seems unlikely that such a criticism of his singing would have been made during his lifetime.
4 Ibid., p. 134.
5 NAS, E33/1.
6 Simon Thurley, *The Royal Palaces of Tudor England* (1993), p. 39.
7 Quoted in Robert J. Knecht, *The French Renaissance Court* (2008), p. 77.
8 David Loades, *The Tudor Court* (1992), p. 110.
9 For further information on Henry VIII's literary pursuits, see James P. Carley, *The Books of Henry VIII and his Wives* (2004).
10 Jamie Cameron, *James V: The Personal Rule* (1998), ch. 9.
11 A. Clifford, ed., *The State Papers and Letters of Sir Ralph Sadler, Knight-Banneret* (Edinburgh, 1809) pp. 38–9.
12 Tim Thornton, 'Henry VIII's progress through Yorkshire in 1541 and its implications for northern identities', *Northern History*, XLVI, 2 (September 2009), pp. 231–44.
13 Hall, *Chronicle*, ii, p. 313, quoted in Wooding, *Henry VIII*, p. 247.
14 'The Tragedie of the Cardinall' by Sir David Lindsay, in *The Complaynt of Scotland*, Early English Text Society (EETS), Extra Series, no. 17 (1872).
15 Sadler, *State Papers*, p. 37.
16 *Hamilton Papers*, p. 99.
17 *L&P Henry VIII*, vol. 17, no. 1033.
18 *Hamilton Papers*, p. 312.

Eleven – 'Rough Wooings' and Reformation

1 *Hamilton Papers*, vol. 1, no. 261.
2 John Leslie, *The History of Scotland* (1830), p. 157, quoted in Thomas, *Princelie Majestie*, p. 212.
3 Margaret H. B. Sanderson, *Cardinal of Scotland, David Beaton, c. 1494–1546* (1986), p. 154.
4 Ibid., pp. 156–7.
5 G. Dickinson, ed., *Two Missions of Jacques de la Brosse* (Scottish

Historical Society, 3rd series, XXXVI (1942), pp. 9–10, quoted in Jane E. A. Dawson, *Scotland Re-Formed, 1488–1587* (2007), p. 158.

6 Alec Ryrie, *The Origins of the Scottish Reformation* (2006), ch. 3 and Blakeway, *Regency in Sixteenth-Century Scotland*, passim.

7 *Hamilton Papers*, vol. 1, no. 282.

8 *L&P Henry VIII*, vol. 18, pt 1, no. 324.

9 Ryrie, *Origins of the Scottish Reformation*, p. 58.

10 Blakeway, *Regency in Sixteenth-Century Scotland*, pp. 141–2.

11 *L&P Henry VIII*, 18, pt 1, no. 804.

12 Quoted in Marcus Merriman, *The Rough Wooings, Mary Queen of Scots, 1542–1551* (East Linton, 2000), pp. 135–6.

13 *Hamilton Papers*, vol. 2, p. 326.

14 Sarah Macauley, *Matthew Stewart, Fourth Earl of Lennox and the Politics of Britain, c.1543–1571.* unpublished PhD dissertation, University of Cambridge, 2005, p. 42.

15 Ibid., p. 49.

16 BL Additional MS 32, 654, f. 88v.

17 Quoted in Sanderson, *Cardinal of Scotland*, p. 227.

18 Ibid., p. 229.

19 R. J. Knecht, *Renaissance Warrior and Patron, the Reign of Francis I* (1994), p. 541.

20 William Patten, *The Expedicion into Scotlande of the Most Worthily Fortunate Prince Edward, Duke of Somerset*, reprinted in *Tudor Tracts, 1532–1558* (1903), pp. 110–11.

21 Quoted in Merriman, *The Rough Wooings*, p. 234.

22 See Elizabeth Bonner, 'The Earl of Huntly and the King of France, 1548: Man for Rent', in *English Historical Review*, cxx, 485 (Feb 2005), pp. 80–103.

23 *APS*, ii, 481–2.

24 Quoted in Merriman, *Rough Wooings*, p. 37.

Twelve – Daughter of France

1 Quoted in Alexander Wilkinson, *Mary Queen of Scots and French Public Opinion, 1542–1600* (2004), p. 14.

2 Quoted in John Guy, *My Heart Is My Own: The Life of Mary Queen of Scots* (2004), p. 45.

3 Marguerite Wood, ed., *Foreign Correspondence with Marie de Lorraine, Queen of Scotland, from the Originals in the Balcarres Papers, 1547–1557* (1925), pp. li–liii

4 Retha M. Warnicke, *Mary Queen of Scots* (2006), pp. 129–30. For an

interesting angle on porphyria and the health of Mary's son, James VI and I, see T. Peters, P. Garrard, V. Ganesan and J. Stephenson, 'The nature of King James VI/I's medical conditions: new approaches to the diagnosis', *History of Pyschiatry* 23 (3), 2012, pp. 277–90.

5 Merriman, *Rough Wooings*, p. 30.

6 *Archives des Affaires Etrangères*, Paris, Correspondance Politique Angleterre, XII, p. 204, quoted in Pamela E. Ritchie, *Mary of Guise in Scotland, 1548–60* (2002), p. 101.

7 J. H. Pollen, ed., *Papal Negotiations with Mary Queen of Scots* (Scottish History Society), 1st series, 37, 1901) pp. 427–30, quoted in Dawson, *Scotland Re-Formed*, pp. 189–90.

8 Quoted (without footnote giving source) in Rosalind K. Marshall, *Mary of Guise* (2001), p. 82.

9 At this time, still James Hamilton, duke of Châtelherault.

10 *Calendar of State Papers Venetian*, vol. 6, no. 1216.

11 Guy, *My Heart is My Own*, p. 84.

12 Knox, *The History of the Reformation in Scotland*, p. 132.

13 *Calendar of State Papers Foreign: Elizabeth*, (*CSP Foreign Elizabeth*), vol. 1, p. 907.

14 Stephen Alford, *Burghley: William Cecil at the Court of Elizabeth I* (2011), p. 111.

15 Marshall, *Mary of Guise*, p. 96.

16 *CSP Foreign: Elizabeth*, vol. 3, nos 411 and 446.

Thirteen – The Return of the Queen

1 Letter from Lord James Stewart to Mary Queen of Scots, BL Add MSS 32091, f. 189, printed in D. Murray Rose, 'Mary Queen of Scots and Her Brother', *SHR*, vol. 2, no. 6 (Jan 1905), pp. 150–62.

2 BL Add MSS 35830, ff. 158r–159v.

3 BL Cotton MSS Titus B13, f. 54, quoted in Alford, *Burghley*, p. 116.

4 Knox, *The History of the Reformation in Scotland*, pp. 269–70.

5 Ibid., pp. 282–3.

6 Quoted in Guy, *My Heart Is My Own*, p. 148.

7 Quoted in Mark Loughlin, *The Career of Maitland of Lethington, c.1526–1573*, unpublished PhD thesis, University of Edinburgh (1991), p. 123.

8 NLS MS 3657, f. 3.

9 *CSP Scotland* 1, no. 1084.

10 Michael Lynch, 'The Reassertion of Princely Power in Scotland', in *Princes and Princely Culture, 1450–1650*, vol. 1 (2003), p. 217.

11 Mary Livingston did, in fact, marry before the queen and was given a generous dowry.
12 Don Carlos became ever more estranged from his father and, after plotting against him and attempting to flee the country, he was placed in solitary confinement by Philip II in 1568. He died six months later, probably from natural causes though, at the time, tales circulated that Philip had decreed his death.
13 Randolph had undertaken a number of diplomatic missions but never served as an official ambassador and was never formally accredited to Mary's court.
14 Loughlin, *The Career of Maitland of Lethington*, p. 193.
15 Simon Adams, *Leicester and the Court* (2002), p. 138.
16 Macauley, *Matthew Stewart*, p. 112.
17 Ibid., p. 145.
18 *The Memoirs of Sir James Melville of Halhill*, ed. Gordon Donaldson (1969), pp. 35–6.
19 Cecil's letter to Randolph explaining his reasoning for releasing Darnley is missing.
20 Loughlin, *Maitland of Lethington*, p. 199.

Fourteen – Downfall

1 Alford, *Burghley*, p. 131.
2 J. H. Burton and D. Masson, eds, *Register of the Privy Council of Scotland*, vol. 1, pp. 369–71.
3 *Letters of Mary Stuart, Queen of Scotland*, translated by William Turnbull (1845), pp. 150–54.
4 Quoted in Guy, *My Heart Is My Own*, p. 249.
5 Printed in F. A. Mumby, *The Fall of Mary Stuart: A Narrative in Contemporary Letters* (1921), pp. 56–8.
6 Martin A. S. Hume, ed., *Calendar of State Papers Spain (Simancas)* (1892), vol. 1, no. 349.
7 There is evidence that Darnley's mother disagreed with her husband on this issue and that she was attempting to facilitate his escape to Flanders. Margaret was unaware, however, that messengers she had previously trusted were now also in the pay of William Cecil. See Macauley, *Matthew Stewart*, pp. 160–61.
8 It is unfortunate that Historic Scotland's information about Hermitage Castle on its website still perpetuates the myth of a romantic assignation.
9 Copy of Mary's letter in NLS Advocates MS 22.2.18, ff. 187–94.

10 NLS Advocates MS 31.2.19, ff. 222–4v.

11 Ibid., ff. 224–5.

12 Loughlin, *Maitland of Lethington*, pp. 239–44.

13 *CSP Spain, Simancas*, vol. 1, 402.

14 Printed in Mumby, *The Fall of Mary Stuart*, pp. 187–8.

15 Ibid., p. 189.

16 Alford, *Burghley*, p. 136.

17 I am grateful to Dr Julian Goodare for sharing his research on this point with me.

18 Printed in Guy, *My Heart Is My Own*, p. 326.

19 *Memoirs of Sir James Melville*, p. 64.

20 W. S. Fitch, ed., *Maitland's Narration of the Principal Acts of the Regency During the Minority and Other Papers Relating to the History of Mary Queen of Scotland* (1833).

21 NLS MS 3657, f. 34, also in *Maitland's Narration* (no page numbers). The identity of the person who received these confidences from Mary remains unclear. The NLS MS attributes it as a letter from Thomas Randolph to the earl of Leicester but Randolph had been ejected from Scotland the previous year and was back in England. Bedford was also away at the time. Mary's discussion may have been with Throckmorton.

22 *CSP Scotland*, vol. 2, p. 523.

23 As late as 23 June, Elizabeth was still writing to Mary upbraiding her for her marriage to Bothwell and her inability to prosecute Darnley's murderers. L. J. Marcus, M. B. Mueller and Rose, eds, *Elizabeth I, Collected Works* (2002), pp. 117–19.

24 Turnbull, *Letters of Mary Stuart*, p. 32.

25 The elderly Châtelherault himself was then still living on his French estates and did not return to Scotland until early 1569, after Mary's flight to England, though he was always a staunch supporter of her restoration to the Scottish throne.

26 Turnbull, *Letters of Mary Stuart*, pp. 163–4.

Epilogue – London, 7 May 1603

1 Quoted in Leanda de Lisle, *After Elizabeth* (2004), p. 151.

2 From a letter to Henry III of France. Quoted in Guy, *My Heart Is My Own*, p. 501.

Bibilography

Manuscript Sources

BRITISH LIBRARY

Additional MS 21505, 24965, 29506, 32646, 72472
Cotton Caligula BVI
Cotton Vespasian FXIII
Egerton 2603
MS Facs 581/85
Sloane 3199

NATIONAL ARCHIVES (LONDON)

Chancery, C82/164
Exchequer, E39, E405/79
State Papers, SP1,9/141, SP14/1, SP49, 1–2, SP53, SP58/1

NATIONAL ARCHIVES OF SCOTLAND (EDINBURGH)

GD1/371, GD149/264–5, GD249/2
SP1, SP2, SP6, SP13, E31/1–8, E33/1–2

NATIONAL LIBRARY OF SCOTLAND (EDINBURGH)

Advocates MS 22.2.18
Advocates MS 31.2.19
MS 3567

Primary Sources

(Place of publication for all printed works is London, unless otherwise
stated)

Acts of the Lords of Council in Public Affairs, 1501–1554, ed. R. K. Hannay,
    Edinburgh, 1931

Acts of the Parliaments of Scotland, ed. T. Thomson and C. Innes,
    Edinburgh, 1814–75, vol. ii (1424–67)

Bacon, Francis, T*he History of the Reign of King Henry VII*, 2007

Balfour, Sir James, *The Historical Works*, vol. 1, Edinburgh, 1824

Blind Harry's Wallace, trans. William Hamilton of Gilbertfield, Edinburgh,
    1998

Boece, Hector, *The History and Chronicles of Scotland*, trans. John Bellenden,
    Edinburgh, 1821

Brantôme, Pierre de Bourdeilles, abbé et seigneur de, *Oeuvres Completes*, 13
    vols, Paris, 1890

Brossse, Jacques de la, *Two Missions: An Account of the Affairs of Scotland in
    the Year 1543 and the Journal of the Siege of Leith, 1560*, ed. G
    Dickinson, Scottish Historical Society, 1942

Buchanan, George, *The History of Scotland*, trans. J. Aikman, Edinburgh,
    1827–9

Calendar of Documents Relating to Scotland, vol. 4, 1357–1509, ed. J. Bain,
    Edinburgh, 1888

*Calendar of Letters and Papers Relating to the Affairs of the Borders of England
    and Scotland*, 2 vols, ed. J. Bain, Edinburgh (1894–6)

*Calendar of Letters, Despatches and State Papers Relating to the Negotiations
    between England and Spain*, 13 vols, ed. R. Tyler et al. (1862–1954)

Calendar of State Papers, Foreign: Elizabeth (1863–1950), 23 vols

Calendar of State Papers Foreign: Mary, ed. W. B. Turnbull (1861)

*Calendar of State Papers Relating to Scotland and Mary Queen of Scots,
    1547–1603*, 13 vols, ed. J. Bain et al., Edinburgh (1898–1969)

*Correspondence Politique de Odet de Selve: Ambassadeur de France en Angleterre,
    1546–1549*, Paris, 1888

*A Diurnal of Remarkable Occurents that Have Passed within the Country of
    Scotland since the Death of King James IV till the Year 1575*, Bannatyne
    Club, Edinburgh, 1833

Drummond, William, of Hawthornden, *History of Scotland from the Year
    1423 until the Year 1542* (1861)

Early Travellers in Scotland, ed. P. Hume Brown, Edinburgh, 1891

Elizabeth I: Collected Works, ed. L. Marcus, J. Mueller and M. B. Rose, Chicago, 2000

Flodden Papers, 1507–17, ed. M. Wood, Scottish Historical Society, Edinburgh, 1933

Flodden: 'A contemporary account of the battle of Flodden' ('Trewe Encountre'), *Proceedings of the Society of Antiquaries of Scotland*, vol. 7 (1866–7), pp. 141–52

Foedera, Conventiones, Litterae et Cuiuscunque Generis Acta Publica, ed. T. Rymer, (1816–69)

Foreign Correspondence with Marie de Lorraine, Queen of Scotland, 1548–1557, from the originals in the Balcarres Papers, ed. Marguerite Wood (Edinburgh, 1925), Publications of the Scottish Historical Society, Third Series, vol. 7

Fraser, William, *The Douglas Book*, Edinburgh, 1885

―――― *The Lennox*, Edinburgh, 1874

Frescoln, K.P., 'A letter from Thomas Randolph to the earl of Leicester', *Huntington Library Quarterly*, 37, pp. 83–8

Hall, Edward, *The Union of the Two Noble and Illustrious Families of Lancaster and York, Hall's Chronicle*, 1809

Halliwell-Philipps, J. O., ed., *Letters of the Kings of England*, vol. 1, 1846

The Hamilton Papers, ed. J. Bain, 2 vols, Edinburgh, 1890–92

Hay, Denis, ed., *The Anglia Historia of Polydore Vergil*, Camden Series, vol. LXXIV, 1950

Keith, R., *History of the Affairs of Church and State in Scotland from the Beginning of the Reformation to the Year 1568*, ed. J.P. Lawson, 3 vols, Edinburgh, Spottiswoode Society, 1844–50

Knox, John, *History of the Reformation in Scotland*, 2 vols, ed. W. C. Dickinson, 1949

―――― *The First Blast of the Trumpet against the Monstrous Regiment of Women*,1558, ed. E. Arber, 1895

Labanoff, A., *Lettres, Instructions et Mémoires de Marie Stuart, Reine d'Écosse*, 7 vols, Paris, 1844

Leland, John, *De Rebus Britannicis Collectanea*, vol. 4, 1770

Leslie, John, *The History of Scotland from the Death of King James I in the Year 1436 to the Year 1561*, Edinburgh, Bannatyne Club, 1830

Letters and Papers, Foreign and Domestic, of the Reign of Henry VIII, ed. J. S. Brewer and others, 21 vols, 1862–1932

Letters and Papers Illustrative of the Reigns of Richard III and Henry VII, ed. James Gairdner, 1861–3

Letters and State Papers Relating to English Affairs Preserved Principally in the Archives of Simancas, 4 vols, 1892–9

Lindsay, Sir David, *The Poetical Works of Sir David Lindsay of the Mount*, ed. D. Laing, Edinburgh, 1879

Melville, Sir James, *The Memoirs of Sir James Melville of Halhill*, ed. G. Donaldson, 1969

Nau, C. J., *The History of Mary Stuart from the Murder of Riccio until her Flight into England*, ed. J. Stevenson, Edinburgh, 1883

Papal Negotiations with Mary Queen of Scots, 1561–67, ed. J. H. Pollen, Scottish Historical Society, Edinburgh, 1922

Papiers d'État Relatifs a l'Histoire de l'Écosse au 16e Siècle, ed. A. Teulet, Bannatyne Club, Edinburgh, 1852–60

Patten, William, *The Expedicion into Scotlande*, 1548, reprinted in A. Pollard, ed., Tudor Tracts, 1903, pp. 54–154

Registrum Magni Sigilli Regum Scotorum, ed. J. M. Thomson and others, Edinburgh, 1882–1914

Registrum Secreti Sigilli Regum Scotorum, ed. M. Livingstone and others, Edinburgh, 1908

Robert Lindesay of Pitscottie, *The Historie and Cronicles of Scotland*, Scottish Text Society, Edinburgh, 1899–1911

State Papers and Letters of Sir Ralph Sadler, ed. Arthur Clifford, 2 vols (1809)

State Papers during the Reign of Henry VIII, 11 vols, 1830–52

Stewart, A., ed., *The Complaynte of Scotland*, orig. published Paris, 1549[?], Aberdeen, 1983

Teulet, A., *Lettres de Marie Stuart*, Paris, 1859

The Exchequer Rolls of Scotland, ed. J. Stuart and others, Edinburgh, 1878–1908

The Letters of James IV, 1505–13, ed. R. L. Mackie, Edinburgh 1953

The Letters of James V, ed. R. K. Hannay and D. Hay, Edinburgh, 1954

The Reign of Henry VII from Contemporary Sources, 3 vols, ed. A. F. Pollard, 1913–14

The Scottish Correspondence of Mary of Lorraine, ed. A. I. Cameron, Scottish Historical Society, Edinburgh, 1927

Treasurer's Accounts: Accounts of the Lord High Treasurer of Scotland, vols. 1–4, 1473–1513, ed. T. Dickson and J. B. Paul, Edinburgh, 1877–1902

The True History of the Church of Scotland from the Beginning of the Reformation unto the End of the Reign of King James VI, 8 vols, Edinburgh,1842–9

Turnbull, W., *Letters of Mary Stuart, Queen of Scotland*, 1845

Secondary Works

Adams, Simon, *Leicester and the Court*, Manchester, 2002

—— 'The release of Lord Darnley and the failure of the amity', *Innes Review*, 38, Edinburgh,1987, pp. 123–53

Alford, Stephen, *Burghley: William Cecil at the Court of Queen Elizabeth I*, 2008

Anglo, Sydney, *Spectacle, Pageantry and Early Tudor Policy*, Oxford, 1997

Arthurson, Ian, *The Perkin Warbeck Conspiracy*, Stroud, 1994

B. Bradshaw and J. Morrill, eds, *The British Problem, c.1534–1707*, 1996

Bapst, Edmond, *Les Mariages de Jacques V*, Paris, 1889

Barnes, Ishbel C. M., *Janet Kennedy, Royal Mistress*, Edinburgh, 2007

Bingham, Caroline, *Darnley*, 1995

—— *James V, King of Scots*, 1971

Bonner, Elizabeth, 'Scotland's "Auld Alliance" with France', 1295–1560, *History*, 84, 1999, pp. 5–30

—— 'The Earl of Huntly and the King of France, 1548: Man for Rent', *English Historical Review*, cxx 485, Feb. 2005, pp. 80–103

—— 'The Politique of Henri II. De Facto French rule in Scotland, 1550–1554', *Journal of the Sydney Society for Scottish History*, 7, 1999, pp. 1–107

—— 'The Recovery of St Andrews Castle in 1547: French naval policy and diplomacy in the British Isles', *English Historical Review*, 111, 1996, pp. 578–98

Buchanan, Patricia, *Margaret Tudor, Queen of Scots*, Edinburgh, 1985

Bute, John, third Marquess of, *Scottish Coronations*, Paisley, 1902

Cameron, Jamie, *James V: The Personal Rule*, East Linton, 1998

Carroll, Stuart, *Martyrs and Murderers: The Guise Family and the Making of Europe*, Oxford, 2009

Cavill, P., *The English Parliaments of Henry VII*, Oxford, 2009

Chandler, S. B., 'An Italian life of Margaret, Queen of James III', *Scottish Historical Review*, xxxii, 1952, pp. 52–7

Cheruel, Pierre A., *Marie Stuart et Catherine de Medicis*, Paris, 1858

Clark, Peter, ed., *The Cambridge Urban History of Britain*, vol. 11, Cambridge, 2000

Cloulas, Ivan, *Henri II*, Paris, 1985

Crawford, Barbara E., 'Scotland's Foreign Relations: Scandinavia' in J. M. Brown, ed., *Scottish Society in the Fifteenth Century*, pp. 85–100

Cunningham, Sean, *Richard III: A Royal Enigma*, 2003

—— *Henry VII*, 2007

Dawson, Jane E.A., *Scotland Re-Formed, 1488–1587*, Edinburgh, 2007

——— 'Mary Queen of Scots, Lord Darnley and Anglo-Scottish Relations in 1565', *International History Review*, vol. 8, no.1 (February 1986), pp. 1–24

de Lisle, Leanda, *After Elizabeth*, 2005

Donaldson, Gordon, *All the Queen's Men: Power and Politics in Mary Stewart's Scotland*, 1983

Doran, Susan and Richardson, Glenn, eds, *Tudor England and its Neighbours*, (2005)

Drummond, H., *The Queen's Man, James Hepburn, Earl of Bothwell and Duke of Orkney, 1536–1578*, 1975

Dunbar, John G., *Scottish Royal Palaces*, East Linton, 1999

Duncan, T. D., 'The relations of the earl of Murray with Mary Stuart', *The Scottish Historical Review*, vol. 6, no. 21, October 1908, pp. 49–57

Dunn, Jane, *Elizabeth and Mary: Cousins, Rivals, Queens*, 2003

Ellis, Steven G., *Ireland in the Age of the Tudors, 1447–1603*, 1998

Erdington, Carol, *Court and Culture in Renaissance Scotland*, Amherst, 1994

Fraser, Antonia, *Mary Queen of Scots*, 1968

Goodare, J. and Macdonald, A., eds, *Sixteenth-Century Scotland: Essays in Honour of Michael Lynch*, Leiden, 2008

Goodare, Julian, 'Queen Mary's Catholic Interlude', *Innes Review*, 38, pp. 154–70

——— *The Government of Scotland, 1560–1625*, Oxford, 2004

Gosman, M., Macdonald, A. and Vanderjagt, A., eds, *Princes and Princely Culture, 1450–1650*, vol. 1, Brill, 2003

Graham, Angus, 'The battle of Sauchieburn', *Scottish Historical Review*, xxxix, 1960

Graham, Roderick, *An Accidental Tragedy: The Life of Mary, Queen of Scots*, Edinburgh, 2009

Griffiths, Ralph A. and Thomas, Roger S., *The Making of the Tudor Dynasty*, 2005

Gristwood, Sarah, *Blood Sisters: The Hidden Lives of the Women Behind the Wars of the Roses*, 2012

Gunn, S. J., *Early Tudor Government, 1485–1558*, 1995

Guy, John, *My Heart is My Own: The Life of Mary Queen of Scots*, 2004

Hay Fleming, D., *Mary Queen of Scots from Her Birth to Her Flight into England*, 1897

Hosack, John, *Mary Queen of Scots and Her Accusers*, 1869

Hotle, C. Patrick, *Thorns and Thistles: Diplomacy Between Henry VIII and James V, 1528–1542*, Maryland and London, 1996

Jones, M. K. and Underwood, M. G., *The King's Mother*, 1992

Knecht, Robert J., *Renaissance Warrior and Patron: The Reign of Francis I*, Cambridge, 1994

——— *The French Renaissance Court, 1483–1589*, 2008

Lang, Andrew, *The Mystery of Mary Stuart*, 1901

Le Fur, Didier, *Charles VIII*, Paris, 2006

——— *Louis XII; Un Autre César*, Paris, 2001

Loades, D., *The Tudor Court*, Bangor, 1992

Lyall, R. J., 'The Medieval Scottish Coronation Service: some seventeenth century evidence', *Innes Review*, xviii (1), 1977, pp. 3–21

Lynch, M., 'Queen Mary's Triumph: the Baptismal Celebrations at Stirling in December, 1566', *Scottish Historical Review*, 69, pp. 1–21

Macdougall, Norman, *An Antidote to the English: The Auld Alliance, 1250–1542*, East Linton, 2001

——— *James III: A Political Study*, Edinburgh, 1982

——— *James IV*, Edinburgh, 1989

——— *Scotland and War: AD 79–1918*, Edinburgh, 1991

Macfarlane, Leslie J. 'The Book of Hours of James IV and Margaret Tudor', *Innes Review*, xi (1960), pp. 111–29

Mackenzie, W. Mackay, *The Secret of Flodden*, Edinburgh, 1931

Mackie R. L., *King James IV of Scotland*, Edinburgh, 1958

Mapstone, Sally and Wood, Juliette, eds, *The Rose and the Thistle: Essays on the Culture of Late Medieval and Renaissance Scotland*, East Linton, 1998

Marshall, Rosalind K., *Scottish Queens, 1034–1714*, Edinburgh, 2007

——— *Mary of Guise: Queen of Scots*, Edinburgh, 2001

Mason, R. A., ed., *John Knox and the British Reformations*, Aldershot, 1998

Massie, Alan, *The Thistle and the Rose*, 2005

Merriman, Marcus, *The Rough Wooings: Mary Queen of Scots, 1542–1551*, East Linton, 2000

Merriman, R. B., *Life and Letters of Thomas Cromwell*, Oxford, 1902

Murray, Rose D., 'Mary Queen of Scots and her Brother', *Scottish Historical Review*, vol. 2, no. 6, Jan. 1905, pp. 150–62

Neville, Cynthia, *Violence, Custom and Law: The Anglo-Scottish Border Lands in the Later Middle Ages*, Edinburgh, 1998

Okerlund, Arlene Naylor, *Elizabeth of York*, Basingstoke, 2009

Penn, Thomas, *Winter King: The Dawn of the Tudor Era*, 2011

Perry, Maria, *Sisters to the King*, 1998

Porter, Linda, *Mary Tudor: The First Queen*, 2007

Reese, Peter, *Flodden: A Scottish Tragedy*, Edinburgh, 2003

Ritchie, Pamela, E., *Mary of Guise in Scotland, 1548–60*, East Linton, 2002

Ryrie, Alec, *The Origins of the Scottish Reformation*, Manchester, 2006

Sanderson, Margaret H. B., *Cardinal of Scotland: David Beaton, c.1494–1546*, Edinburgh, 1986

——— *Mary Stewart's People*, Edinburgh, 1987

Scott, Sir Walter, *Marmion: A Tale of Flodden*, 1808

———— *From Gileskirk to Greyfriars: Mary Queen of Scots, John Knox and the Heroes of Scotland's Reformation*, Nashville, 2001

Skidmore, Chris, *Death and the Virgin: Elizabeth, Dudley and the Mysterious Fate of Amy Robsart*, 2010

Starkey, D., *Henry: Virtuous Prince*, 2009

Thomas, Andrea, *Princelie Majestie: The Court of James V of Scotland, 1529–1542*, Edinburgh, 2005

Thurley, Simon, *The Royal Palaces of Tudor England*, 1993

Warnicke, Retha M., *Mary Queen of Scots*, 2006

Weightman, Christine, *Margaret of York: The Diabolical Duchess*, 2009

Weir, Alison, *Mary Queen of Scots and the Murder of Lord Darnley*, 2003

Wilkinson, Alexander, *Mary Queen of Scots and French Public Opinion, 1542–1600*, Basingstoke, 2004

Wolffe, Bertram, *Henry VI*, 1981

Wooding Lucy, *Henry VIII*, 2009

Wormald, Jenny, ed, *Scotland Revisited*, 1991

———— *Mary Queen of Scots: A Study in Failure*, 1988

———— *Court, Kirk and Community: Scotland, 1470–1625*, 1981

Wroe, Ann, *Perkin: A Story of Deception*, 2003

UNPUBLISHED DISSERTATIONS

Blakeway, Amy, *Regency in Sixteenth-Century Scotland*, PhD dissertation, University of Cambridge, 2009

Dunlop, David, *Aspects of Anglo-Scottish Relations from 1471 to 1513*, PhD dissertation, University of Liverpool, 1988

Emond, William K., *The Minority of King James V, 1513–1528*, PhD thesis, University of Saint Andrews, 1988

Loughlin, Mark, *The Career of Maitland of Lethington, c. 1526–1573*, PhD thesis, University of Edinburgh, 1991

Macauley, Sarah, *Matthew Stewart, Fourth Earl of Lennox and the Politics of Britain, c. 1543–1571*, DPhil dissertation, University of Oxford, 2005

Picture Acknowledgements

Index

relationship between Henry VIII and
171–2
relationship with father 55–6
and religion 156
search for bride 93
style of government 159
support of French in war against England
168–72
and travelling 87
upbringing and education 53–4, 87
uprisings against regime of 90–1
and Warbeck conspiracy 103, 110–15
wedding day 147–8
will 172–3, 196
James V, King of England and Scotland 2,
152, 195, 206, 470
achievements 290
architectural programme and renovations
of palaces 267–9, 277
attributes 216
birth 153
bond with Earl of Lennox 235–6
breaks free from Angus and declares
himself king 238–40, 241–2
childhood and upbringing 213–17
control of by Earl of Angus 233, 235–6,
237
coronation (1513) 195–6
cultural interests 269–71
death and funeral 289–90, 296—7
and death of first wife (Madeleine) 260
and death of infant sons 279
education 215–17
enhancement of international standing
271
hatred of Douglas family 236, 276–7
historical views of 290
marriage to Madeleine 254, 256–60
marriage to Mary of Guise 262–4
mistresses and illegitimate children
237–8, 252, 264
musical abilities 269–70
provisions made for Mary Queen of Scots
289–90
relationship with the Church in Scotland
247
relationship with Henry VIII 234–5,
242, 247—8, 250, 251, 280, 282–3
relationship with Lindsay 215

relationship with mother 213, 242
reprisals and execution of opponents
276–8
strengthening of rule 276
style of kingship 246–8
visits France 253–9
and war with England 285–9
James VI and I, King of Scotland 399, 428,
433—4, 458, 463–4, 466, 467
John of Gaunt 10
Julius II, Pope 166, 169

Katherine of Aragon 126, 161, 165, 166–7,
175–6, 191, 200, 224–5, 242–4, 245,
458
Keith, Lady Agnes *see* Moray, Countess of
Kennedy, Janet 126–9, 151, 152, 158, 475
Killigrew, Sir Henry 428–9
Kirkcaldy, William 368, 452, 455, 464
Knox, John 315, 320, 349–50, 353, 366–7,
368, 370, 382, 390–1, 398, 401, 474

Langside, Battle of 459–60
Leicester, Earl of (Robert Dudley) 385, 403,
403–4, 482
Lennox, Charles (brother of Lord Darnley)
413
Lennox, Countess (Margaret Douglas) 210,
214, 240–1, 279, 311–12, 327, 347,
405–6, 407–8, 472–3
arrest and imprisonment 406
death 466
and death of son 442–3
friendship with Mary I 347–8
imprisonment 413–14
marriage 311–13
reconciliation with Mary Queen of Scots
466
and son 417
Lennox, 3rd Earl of (John Stewart) 235–6
Lennox, 4th Earl of (Matthew Stewart) 236,
299, 305, 308–14, 347, 405–6, 444–5,
471
ambitions and plotting to restore Scottish
fortunes 348
arrest and imprisonment 406
background 308–9
conflict with Arran 310
death 465–6